SOCIAL ENTREPRENEURSHIP

SOCIAL ENTREPRENEURSHIP

A PRACTICE-BASED APPROACH TO SOCIAL INNOVATION

J. HOWARD KUCHER

Associate Professor of Social Innovation, The University of Maryland, Baltimore, USA

STEPHANIE E. RAIBLE

Assistant Professor of Social Innovation and Entrepreneurship, University of Delaware, USA

Edward Elgar
PUBLISHING

Cheltenham, UK • Northampton, MA, USA

© J. Howard Kucher and Stephanie E. Raible
2022

Cover image: Rocco-Herrmann on iStock

Published by
Edward Elgar Publishing Limited
The Lypiatts
15 Lansdown Road
Cheltenham
Glos GL50 2JA
UK

Edward Elgar Publishing, Inc.
William Pratt House
9 Dewey Court
Northampton
Massachusetts 01060
USA

Companion website material can be found at
https://www.e-elgar.com/textbooks/kucher

A catalogue record for this book
is available from the British Library

Library of Congress Control Number:
2021949014

Printed on elemental chlorine free (ECF)
recycled paper containing 30% Post-Consumer Waste

ISBN 978 1 78897 420 2 (cased)
ISBN 978 1 78897 421 9 (eBook)
ISBN 978 1 78897 422 6 (paperback)

Printed and bound in the USA

CONTENTS

SOCIAL ENTREPRENEURSHIP

A PRACTICE-BASED APPROACH TO SOCIAL INNOVATION

J. HOWARD KUCHER

Associate Professor of Social Innovation, The University of Maryland, Baltimore, USA

STEPHANIE E. RAIBLE

Assistant Professor of Social Innovation and Entrepreneurship, University of Delaware, USA

Cheltenham, UK • Northampton, MA, USA

Published by
Edward Elgar Publishing Limited
The Lypiatts
15 Lansdown Road
Cheltenham
Glos GL50 2JA
UK

Edward Elgar Publishing, Inc.
William Pratt House
9 Dewey Court
Northampton
Massachusetts 01060
USA

Companion website material can be found at
https://www.e-elgar.com/textbooks/kucher

A catalogue record for this book
is available from the British Library

Library of Congress Control Number:
2021949014

Printed on elemental chlorine free (ECF)
recycled paper containing 30% Post-Consumer Waste

ISBN 978 1 78897 420 2 (cased)
ISBN 978 1 78897 421 9 (eBook)
ISBN 978 1 78897 422 6 (paperback)

Printed and bound in the USA

CONTENTS

ABOUT THE AUTHORS

Dr. J. Howard "Jim" Kucher is an Associate Professor of Social Innovation in the Graduate School of the University of Maryland, Baltimore, where he directs the groundbreaking Master of Science in Health & Social Innovation. An internationally recognized thought leader in social entrepreneurship, Dr. Kucher previously led the Baltimore Social Enterprise Collaborative – a program that was nationally recognized for its innovative curriculum and helped over 60 area nonprofits develop new models for meeting the needs of their constituents while increasing the sustainability of their organizations. He has successfully secured over $70 million in working capital on behalf of mission-oriented enterprises and assisted over 100 area nonprofits and social enterprises in developing new models for meeting the needs of their constituents while increasing the sustainability of their organizations.

Kucher earned a doctoral degree in Public Administration with a concentration in Social Entrepreneurship from the University of Baltimore, where he also earned an M.B.A. with an Entrepreneurship specialization. He holds a B.A. from Kean University and a Graduate Certificate in Urban Theology from the Ecumenical Institute at St. Mary's Seminary and University, and has also earned certification as a project management professional and a new product development professional. Among his many honors, he has been recognized as a Baltimore Renaissance Seed Scholar, an Unsung Hero of Small Business, and a Fulbright Specialist Scholar in Social Entrepreneurship.

Dr. Stephanie E. Raible is an Assistant Professor and Faculty Director of Social Innovation and Entrepreneurship at the University of Delaware, where she leads its Social Entrepreneurship Initiative, a 2021 National Model Emerging Program Finalist as recognized by the United States Association for Small Business and Entrepreneurship (USASBE). Having worked within academic and social sectors for the past 16 years, Dr. Raible has held positions within universities and nonprofits in the U.S. and Europe, with the past eight years centering on teaching and instructional design roles in the areas of social innovation and entrepreneurship, cultural entrepreneurship, and leadership. In addition, she has held roles as the Co-Founder of the International Network of Innovators in Education (INIE) and Co-Leader of the REALISE IT (Erasmus Mundus Association) and Erasmus+ Student and Alumni Alliance Entrepreneurship Incubator programs, funded through the European Commission.

Dr. Raible holds a doctoral degree in Organizational Leadership from Northeastern University with her dissertation focusing on the professional identity transition of new entrepreneurs. She earned two Master's degrees from the Institute of Education (UCL) and University of Deusto (joint degree) and the University of Pennsylvania, and a Bachelor's degree from the University of Delaware. She has been recognized as a leader within the fields of social entrepreneurship and entrepreneurship education, being selected as a National Board Member of the Social Enterprise Alliance (SEA), a leader within USASBE's Social Entrepreneurship Social Interest Group, a Social Innovation Fellow of the Algernon Sydney Sullivan Foundation, a Robert Bosch Foundation Program Fellow, and an Erasmus Mundus Scholarship Recipient.

FOREWORD

Tom Lumpkin

Social entrepreneurship (SE) has blossomed in the soil of 21st-century sensibilities as a way to solve humanity's most pressing problems. Those sensibilities include a heightened awareness of acute poverty, environmental degradation, social injustice, and other societal ills that need urgent attention; a renewed realization of the role of local communities and civic responsibility in solving such problems; an expectation that business and especially entrepreneurship will harness its material and creative resources in support of positive societal change; and a belief that science and technology will enhance efforts to improve conditions and contribute to the well-being and security of humankind. These forces have intermingled and cross-pollinated in recent years, leading to the flowering of SE, a new species of entrepreneurship.

There was a time in the U.S. when the engagement of business in the social fabric of communities was far more common, even taken for granted. Andrew Carnegie, the great American industrialist, held the view that business profits should be shared: "Surplus wealth is a sacred trust which its possessor is bound to administer in his lifetime for the good of the community."[1] Although there were problems and abuses caused by corporations in Carnegie's era – even to the point, in some cases, of giving entrepreneurs a bad name – it was an era when business was generally recognized as a positive force and an important partner in community building. In too many communities, however, as populations grew and the philosophy that profits are an end unto themselves took hold, businesses became more alienated from their communities and desensitized to their impact on society. The responsibility to strengthen communities as well as care for the needy and lift up the disadvantaged fell more and more on the shoulders of government welfare programs and charitable organizations.

At the dawn of the 21st century, in his article "What's a business for?", Charles Handy wrote that the time had come for businesses to take the equivalent of the Hippocratic "do no harm" oath: "If business is to restore its reputation as the friend, not the enemy, of progress around the world, then … [it] needs to take the lead in areas such as environmental and social sustainability."[2] And indeed, things have turned around. The role of business involvement in social well-being once again seems to be ascendent – the Internet and other democratizing technologies, along with a fresh appreciation for the power of entrepreneurship to catalyze opportunities for human progress and a new sense of personal and social responsibility, have begun to converge. The most recent manifestation of that shift is the announcement of a new perspective by the Business Roundtable, an association of CEOs of major corporations, that businesses exist "for the benefit of all stakeholders—customers, employees, suppliers, communities and shareholders."[3] With that, the pendulum has swung back from the narrow profit-only view of business purpose to something more akin to Carnegie's view of using the wealth generated by business and commerce for the benefit of society.

In this new world, there are arguably few advances more profound than the rise of SE as a force for bringing about positive social change and sustainable solutions. SE taps into the collective will of community members, businesses, and entrepreneurs to improve conditions for all its members. It leverages the power of innovation and commerce to bring forth new ideas that enable people to stand on their own two feet financially. It engages the very people it is trying to help in creating and implementing the solutions that will improve their lives.

A few years ago, on the last day of my undergraduate course in SE, a student who had been rather quiet during the semester made me aware of just how important SE is. She thanked me for the class and said, in essence, that it had helped her make sense of getting a degree in business. She explained that she had had doubts about studying business because, even though it might help her get a job, she did not see how it would help anybody else, and that was important to her. She then said she wished the whole business school curriculum could be built around the idea of using business and entrepreneurship to lift people up and strengthen communities because that is the power of business and what it should really be for. It was more clear-eyed yet passionate than everything else she had said all semester put together, and I was deeply touched. I have thought about her words often over the years and agree with her more and more. Never before have we needed the talents and creativity of businesspeople who are committed to making a positive difference and entrepreneurs willing to envision a better future and take a chance on it than we do today.

This book reflects that view of SE. It informs the reader of what SE consists of and how it is used. It explains the elements of SE initiatives and how they contribute to SE success … or failure. It reveals the role SE can play in bringing about positive change, and illustrates how SE operates with illuminating examples, both heartwarming and heartbreaking. Most importantly, as Chapter 1 states, the world needs help; it needs to change – this book shows you that with SE, that change is possible. Indeed, SE is about using entrepreneurship skills and practices to pursue social missions and goals, thus providing a whole new reason for studying business and entrepreneurship.

Co-authors Jim Kucher and Stephanie Raible are uniquely qualified to share this view. They are experienced scholars with wide-ranging backgrounds and strong records of compassionate service. Professor Kucher has great insights about SE from years of helping nonprofits and mission-oriented social enterprises to thrive and more effectively serve their constituents' needs. He is a leader in developing innovative SE curriculums whose research focuses on the practical demands of implementing SE agendas. Professor Raible is a remarkably dedicated educator with a reputation for designing highly creative instructional methods and world-class entrepreneurship training techniques. She is an entrepreneurship education researcher who is widely recognized for her leadership in SE and social innovation pedagogy.

Social Entrepreneurship: A Practice-Based Approach to Social Innovation provides an engaging and comprehensive tour of the SE landscape. I invite you to enjoy this tour and the new learnings and memories it will produce.

Tom Lumpkin
Michael F. Price Chair and Professor of Entrepreneurship
Price College of Business
University of Oklahoma
Norman, OK, USA

NOTES

1. The best fields for philanthropy. *North American Review*, 1889, 149(347), 684.
2. What's a business for? *Harvard Business Review*, 2002, December, 49–55.
3. Business Roundtable redefines the purpose of a corporation to promote "an economy that serves all Americans". Business Roundtable, 2019, August 19. www.businessroundtable.org/business-roundtable -redefines-the-purpose-of-a-corporation-to-promote-an-economy-that-serves-all-americans.

ACKNOWLEDGEMENTS

With apologies to the many folks who helped along the way but go unmentioned here, I want to give noted appreciation to Robert Egger, who graciously explained many basic concepts to me in the early days of my work in this field, and who was equally gracious in allowing us to explore his story in our case studies. To Tom Lumpkin, for giving me my first shot at academic publishing and for his fantastic foreword to this work. To Alan Lyles, who guided a middle-aged student through to a successful dissertation defense and continues to be a source of wisdom and support. To Deborah Leather, who opened a door that I wasn't expecting to be opened. To Herb Childress, who painstakingly led me into the deep end of the writing pool. To Marty Schwartz, Cindy Truitt, Rodney Foxworth, and so many amazing Baltimoreans who were social entrepreneurs when social entrepreneurship wasn't cool. To Peggy Coady, Natalie Slawinski, and Nicole Helwig for their warmth and hospitality during the initial project that gave birth to this work. To Fiona Briden, who saw the textbook that I didn't see and had the faith to commission the effort. To the team at Edward Elgar for their patience and support in bringing it to life. To Jenny Owens and Flav Lilly for continuing to provide me with a place to stand while I apply my lever. To Stephanie Raible, who saved this work from the abyss of intolerable circumlocution. Above all else, to Her Royal Highness Cynthia Margaret, Queen of Keswick, whose love, support, patience, perseverance, and good humor are the light of my life.
– J. Howard Kucher

I would like to first thank my husband, Francisco, for tolerating my working hours and review requests; his support has fueled both my contributions to this book and my career overall. Second, I want to thank my family and friends for their support throughout navigating an academic path, and my professional family and students for their flexibility and encouragement. A special thanks to Dominick, Marcaela, and Alison for giving us feedback from the student perspective. Lastly, I would especially like to recognize my wonderful co-author, Jim, who reached out with an offer to include my contributions in the book – thank you for supporting and encouraging me along the way.
– Stephanie E. Raible

A NOTE ON "TONE OF VOICE" AND JOINT AUTHORSHIP

This book is intentionally written so that it doesn't read like a typical textbook. One of the ways that's carried out is through extensive use of the first-person voice. And yet, you can clearly see from the cover that there are two authors. So, there's either some sort of Vulcan mind meld going on, or there's a deeper explanation.

Here's the deal. I wrote the narrative sections – those long, often rambling passages that make up the body of the text. Stephanie wrote all of the sidebars and supplements. So, when you read phrases like "I once had" or "I think", that's me talking – which means that you should hold me accountable for anything that annoys you. And if the language veers into the technical (or worse, pedantic), that's my fault too.

Stephanie is far too nice and humble to say this, but this project would be far more incoherent and long-winded without her deft hand bringing things back into focus.

Enjoy!
– J. Howard Kucher

PART I
SOCIAL, COMMERCIAL, OR BOTH?

1
Crazy little thing called love

Learning objectives

After studying this chapter, you should be able to:
1. Understand the conditions that surround, cause, and reinforce societal challenges and social entrepreneurs' ability to tackle these issues.
2. Describe social entrepreneurship and its role in solving social and environmental challenges.
3. Identify the strengths and limitations of capitalism as it connects to balancing financial gain with the best interests of the community and environment.
4. Appreciate the roles and limitations of charity and governmental social programs and social entrepreneurship's unique positioning to help resolve some of their issues.

NOT YOUR TYPICAL INTRODUCTION

This book is different. And this chapter is different, too. The book is different because I use a writing style that is more conversational than you're probably used to. From time to time, I will drop back into a mode that looks and sounds more like a textbook, but I'll do my best to pull away from that as soon as possible. This chapter is also different because it does not do what a lot of introductory chapters do.

Many textbooks use the opening chapter to set out some basic definitions and go over the outline of the rest of the book. And I will do some of that too. But some of the terms that you'll see used in this chapter won't be defined until later in the book. That's on purpose.

What I hope to do in this chapter is to give you a sense of why I think this work is so important. I want to show you how we came to a point in time where a truly new thing is dawning. I want to inspire you to do something that will be very challenging but also very rewarding. I want to show you that the world needs to change, and that you can be part of making that change happen.

THE WORLD NEEDS HELP

On September 17, 2011, a few hundred people gathered in Zuccotti Park in Lower Manhattan to protest perceived imbalances in economic and social equality, the growing influence of corporations on the political process, and the excessive impact of the financial services sector on the life of the individual (Gitlin, 2012). Part of a global movement that had its roots in

Source: iStock.com/Stacey Newman.
Used with permission

Madrid in May of the same year, within weeks this uprising had gained international media attention and sympathetic demonstrations in countless cities around the globe (Gitlin, 2012).

One of the reasons for this wave of protest was the increasing lack of confidence in major global financial systems. In recent years, significant financial crises have occurred in most of the world's major economies, with many other countries significantly affected as well (Shiller, 2013). While global technological advances have vastly improved society's ability to communicate, to produce goods and services, and to create wealth, those at the bottom of the economic pyramid continue to struggle just to obtain their daily bread. Said simply, the rich get richer, while the disadvantaged just can't seem to get a break.

BOX 1.1   THE NOTION OF THE "BOTTOM OF THE PYRAMID"
The "Bottom of the Pyramid" is a socioeconomic term that generally describes those at the lowest levels of the economy. Originally popularized by Dr. C. K. Prahalad in the late 1990s, the term was used to describe those whose annual earnings (at the time) were less than $1,500 (Prahalad and Hart, 1998).

While there is no doubt that the world is generally a better place, humans seem to have made little progress towards solving many of society's most persistent social problems. A few examples:

● Significant strides have been made in the overall reduction of poverty (World Bank, 2014). However, the number of urban poor appears to have increased significantly. One study observes that "Over 1993–2002, the count of the '$1 a day' poor fell by 150 million in rural areas but rose by 50 million in urban areas" (Ravallion, Chen, and Sangraula, 2007).

● After experiencing significant declines over the past dozen years, global hunger is again on the rise, with 52 countries listed as having hunger levels that are "serious," "alarming," or "extremely alarming." Despite generally better access to food supplies, many urban areas have levels of hunger equal to those in more rural areas (FAO et al., 2017).

● Roughly 2 percent of the world's population (over 150 million people) are homeless. Almost 20 percent (about 1.5 billion) lack adequate housing (Chamie, 2017).

● Substance abuse has been proven to have significant negative effects on health, yet over 250 million people around the world suffer from alcohol abuse disorders. Twenty-two percent of the world's population uses tobacco, despite conclusive evidence that it is the primary cause of preventable cancers. Over 29 million people suffer from drug use disorders, and drug-related deaths account for 43 out of every 1 million deaths around the world (Gowing et al., 2015).

- From 2005 to 2014, over 60 percent of the households in the 25 most prosperous countries in the world experienced stagnant or declining incomes (Kessler-Harris and Vaudagna, 2018).

Government systems, which have often been a source of solutions to these problems, are being disrupted like never before. From the recent turmoil over the U.K.'s exit from the European Union to rising populist movements in the U.S., Italy, and Greece (to name just a few), state-supported systems for meeting the needs of the underserved are facing pressures from many fronts (Annan, 2016). While many of the gaps in government services have often been met by various forms of charity, these institutions are also facing a wide array of challenges. Funding is harder than ever to get, there is increasing pressure to prove long-term effectiveness, and fewer and fewer people are involved in the organizations that have led the fight for centuries (Serougi, 2016). While this news is certainly discouraging, it is important to know that the world has not always been this way.

A (Very) Brief History of Human Kindness

Up until the 16th century, people usually cared for each other directly, through family structures and the small communities that were the norm in early societies. As societies began to develop and expand, problems of inequality and care for the less fortunate came to be addressed by either charitable institutions or some sort of governmental support program (Safley, 2003). Unfortunately, both of those sources of support have become more and more difficult to access, and increasingly subject to concerns about efficiency and effectiveness (a point we'll expand on in just a few pages).

Problems persist, society's ability to address them is shrinking, and individual levels of concern are increasing (Montgomery and Ramus, 2003). It seems like we may be headed to a place where, to paraphrase the philosopher and theologian Frederick Buechner, our deep sadness meets the world's deep hunger (Buechner, 1973).

One possible solution is something known as social entrepreneurship – a concept that has experienced rapidly growing interest over the last 30 years. Fueled by generational shifts in the level of concern for those less fortunate as well as increasing anxiety about exploitive economic systems, it has become a celebrated instrument for creating a more inclusive society.

WHAT'S IT ALL ABOUT?

This is a book about social entrepreneurship. In this book, we will focus on the practical. In other words, we'll spend most of our time talking about how to turn these wild dreams of making the world a better place into vibrant entities that

Source: iStock.com/dragana991. Used with permission

can produce lasting change. As you will see, this is no small order. It requires vision, determination, flexibility, and diplomacy. It requires all the skills needed to run a business (marketing, finance, operations management, product and service development and delivery, sales, project management, and more). It also requires all the skills needed to run an effective social service agency (community organizing, constituent services, grant writing, managing volunteers, raising funding, working with the government, and many more). But if it's done right, it can be an extremely effective tool. How to make that tool as effective as possible is the subject of this book.

If you're reading this, you are probably taking a course in Social Entrepreneurship at a college or university. But more importantly, you were probably drawn to this course because you have some sense, some inkling, that the current systems we have established are not working as well as they should.

Many people think that organizations in general (and businesses in particular) exist for one main purpose, namely to make people wealthy (or at least financially better off than they were). Many people also believe that making the world a better place requires financial sacrifice. I'm here to tell you that this is not true. I'm here to tell you that you can make the world a better place, and that you don't have to take a vow of poverty to do so. How do I know this? In part, I know it because I have seen (and worked with) people at hundreds of organizations who are making a big difference in others' lives while at the same time being able to feed their families, pay a mortgage, and even put some money away for retirement. Maybe they're not getting crazy rich, but life is good.

These fine folks are known as social entrepreneurs. They are doing well while they are doing good. They are creating value in economic terms (making money) while also creating value at social and civic levels. And they are the subject of this book. In these pages, I will show you how they work and how they think. More importantly, I'll lay out a path for you that will allow you to explore how you might join the ranks of these amazing individuals. But first, let's spend some time talking about what this movement is about, and get into more detail on how it came to be.

BOX 1.2   SOCIAL ENTREPRENEURS AS "UNREASONABLE PEOPLE"

While social entrepreneurs get a reputation for being people who are very aware of the social challenges, Elkington and Hartigan (2009) also refer to them as "unreasonable people." The concept of the "unreasonable" social entrepreneur refers to the fact that social entrepreneurs do not accept the status quo as the necessary state, and they push for a new equilibrium. As they explain in their book, *The Power of Unreasonable People: How Social Entrepreneurs Create Markets that Change the World*:

> Social and environmental entrepreneurs lead by example. They attack intractable problems, take huge risks, and force the rest of us to look beyond the edge of what seems possible. They seek outlandish goals, such as economic and environmental sustainability and social equity, often aiming to transform the systems whose dysfunctions help create or aggravate major socioeconomic, environmental, or political problems. In so doing, they uncover new ways to disrupt established industries while creating new paths for the future. (2009, p. 2)

While all of this can seem intimidating and frames social entrepreneurs as superhuman, social entrepreneurs are everyday people who just think things can be better and attempt to make it that way:

> You must never doubt your ability to achieve anything, overcome anything, and inspire everything, because the truth is, there are no superheroes. There is just us, and too often we are the ones that we keep waiting for. (Shiza Sahid, Co-Founder of the Malala Fund[1])

BOX 1.3   PORTRAIT OF A SOCIAL ENTREPRENEUR

ELLEN FROST, LOCAL COLOR FLOWERS

On a nondescript side street in a working-class neighborhood in the city of Baltimore sits a low concrete garage with a few small signs indicating that it is the home of Local Color Flowers. Owned and operated by Ellen Frost and her husband Eric, LoCoFlo (as it is known to many) considers itself a "flower studio." While most of LoCoFlo's business is weddings and events, it also does a brisk retail business and offers classes in flower arranging, wreath making, and other decorative arts.

Source: Ellen Frost. Used with permission

When you encounter the creations that Ellen and her team develop, you are immediately struck by two things. First, the flower arrangements are strikingly beautiful. Second, they are unlike anything that you have ever seen before. If you ask Ellen how she can pull off this unique combination of beauty and originality, she will politely explain that all the materials she uses in her studio are grown within 100 miles of the store. And sometimes, that's the end of the conversation.

But if you press a bit harder, Ellen explains a few things about the typical florist that most of us encounter. First, that the vast majority of the flowers consumed in the U.S. market are grown in other countries (the Netherlands, Colombia, Kenya, Ecuador, and Ethiopia, to name a few of the leaders) (Mergent, 2018). So, in order to get those flowers to your sweetheart's door, they need to be shipped (typically by air) to a regional wholesaler, who then puts them on a truck to a local wholesaler, who then puts them on a truck to your local florist, who then puts them in a van for delivery to your loved one. So, those red roses have traveled thousands of miles, burning up a good amount of fossil fuel along the way. Convenient and efficient for you, perhaps, but not as good for the environment as a journey of 100 miles or less. Second, you find out that the workers in those countries are paid wages that would make most of us blush with shame. For example, the average worker on a flower farm in Ethiopia makes less than $40 per month – less than one-third of the amount needed to provide for basic food, clothing, and shelter (a "living wage") (Melese, 2015). On the other hand, LoCoFlo pays its suppliers (who it considers partners) under fair trade agreements that provide a living wage (in U.S. terms) for the workers on the farms (many of which are cooperatively owned).

While Ellen and Eric are far too kind to make this accusation directly, one quickly realizes that the global flower industry is harming the environment and exploiting the poor. But the best part about these good folks (and their amazing products) is that they are competitively priced, delivered on time, and always produce that "wow" factor that is the real reason for sending flowers in the first place.

Last but not least, it's important to know that Ellen and Eric make their living at this studio and support a small team of workers (as well as their partner growers). This is a business – one that pays taxes and wages and rent and produces enough profit for the owners to live reasonably comfortably. And, if you don't ask, the only thing you'll ever know about Eric, Ellen, and LoCoFlo is that they are good, hardworking folks making unique and exquisite floral arrangements at a competitive price.

But now that we know them, we know that they are saving the world, one flower at a time.

HOW DID WE GET HERE?

Most of the folks who spend a lot of time in this arena agree that a man named Bill Drayton first began to use the term "social entrepreneurship" in the late 1980s (Light, 2009). Definitions vary widely, but most believe that the term describes a practice that seeks to bring the tools and techniques of the entrepreneur to bear on larger issues that affect society (Abu-Saifan, 2012). (We'll dive into the specifics of what makes an entrepreneur different in Chapter 2.) As to the distinct aspects of social entrepreneurship, I like the definition developed by Dr. Tom Lumpkin, who describes social entrepreneurship as the effort to produce civic, social, and economic value within a single specific organization or program (Lumpkin and Bacq, 2019).

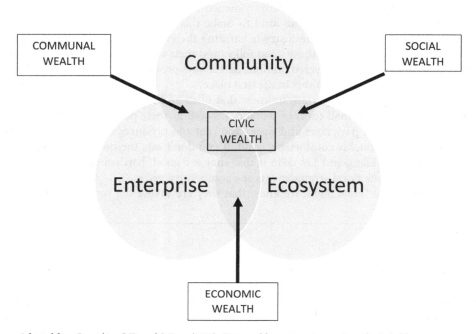

Source: Adapted from Lumpkin, G.T., and S. Bacq (2019). Civic wealth creation: A new view of stakeholder engagement and societal impact. *Academy of Management Perspectives*, 33(4), p. 30. Used with permission.

BOX 1.4   DEFINITION OF SOCIAL ENTREPRENEURSHIP

The area of social entrepreneurship is filled with terms and definitions: "social entrepreneurship," "changemaking," "social innovation," "social enterprise," "impact entrepreneurship," "social business," and many more. There are many debates over the exact meaning of these terms. Rather than attempt to settle that debate, let's look at a few that are particularly helpful.

SOCIAL ENTREPRENEURSHIP

The term "social entrepreneurship" is interchangeable with "impact entrepreneurship," although "impact entrepreneurship" may be considered a bit more expansive. Throughout the book, we favor the term "social entrepreneurship," but this is meant to be understood broadly rather than in its narrowest forms. The following definitions are among the many used for social entrepreneurship:

- Social entrepreneurs play the role of change agents in the social sector by:
    - Adopting a mission to create and sustain social value (not just private value),
    - Recognizing and relentlessly pursuing new opportunities to serve that mission,
    - Engaging in a process of continuous innovation, adaptation, and learning,
    - Acting boldly without being limited by resources currently in hand, and
    - Exhibiting heightened accountability to the constituencies served and for the outcomes created. (Dees, 1998[2001], p. 4).
- "Social entrepreneurship is a process by which citizens build or transform institutions to advance solutions to social problems, such as poverty, illness, illiteracy, environmental destruction, human rights abuses and corruption, in order to make life better for many" (Bornstein and Davis, 2010, p. 1).
- "Innovative, social value creating activity that can occur within or across the non-profit, business, or government sectors" (Austin, Stevenson, and Wei-Skillern, 2006, p. 2).
- "The pursuit of social objectives with innovative methods, through the creation of products, organizations, and practices that yield and sustain social benefits" (Tschirhart and Bielefeld, 2012, p. 36).
- "Social entrepreneurs both take direct action and seek to transform the existing system" (Martin and Osberg, 2015, p. 9).
- Social entrepreneurship is the process of:
    - (1) identifying a stable but inherently unjust equilibrium that causes the exclusion, marginalization, or suffering of a segment of humanity that lacks the financial means or political clout to achieve any transformative benefit on its own;
    - (2) identifying an opportunity in this unjust equilibrium, developing a social value proposition, and bringing to bear inspiration, creativity, direct action, courage, and fortitude, thereby challenging the stable state's hegemony; and
    - (3) forging a new, stable equilibrium that releases trapped potential or alleviates the suffering of the targeted group, and through imitation and the creation of a stable ecosystem around the new equilibrium ensuring a better future for the targeted group and even society at large. (Martin and Osberg, 2007, p. 35)
- Social entrepreneurship is a "market-based, usually sustainable methodology to create social value at the systems-change level" (Ashoka U, n.d., *Working Definitions*). Paired with this definition, Ashoka U defines a social entrepreneur as "a type of changemaker who creates widespread impact by being focused on systems change. Every social entrepreneur is highly skilled at collaboration and is often focused on equipping others to thrive and collaborate in solving social problems (i.e. to be changemakers)" (*Working Definitions*). Within these definitions, social entrepreneurship is understood to be the smaller subset within social innovation and changemaking categories that differentiates itself through an effort to drive change in a financially sustainable, market-informed manner.

CHANGEMAKER/CHANGEMAKING

"Someone who is intentional about solving a social or environmental problem, motivated to act and creative" (Ashoka U, n.d., *Working Definitions*). The notion of being a "change-maker" or engaging in the act of "changemaking" was popularized through Ashoka U and is considered a broad concept that encompasses social innovation and social entrepreneurship as well, but is not limited to those terms.

SOCIAL INNOVATION

- This is:
  - "A novel solution to a social problem that is more effective, efficient, sustainable, or just than existing solutions and for which the value created accrues primarily to society as a whole rather than private individuals. A social innovation can be a product, production process, or technology (much like innovation in general), but it can also be a principle, an idea, a piece of legislation, a social movement, an intervention, or some combination of them." (Phills Jr, Deiglmeier, and Miller, 2008, p. 39)
  - "Methodology to create social value and potentially economic value at the systems-change level, which addresses the root cause of a problem. It includes new strategies, concepts, ideas, and organizations that address social needs of all kinds – from working conditions and education to community development and health" (Ashoka U, n.d., *Working Definitions*). Within this definition, the emphasis of social innovation differs from the broader term of "changemaking" due to its systems-level approach, which means that the innovators are attempting to systematically approach action and efforts to address the root causes of the issue at hand.

Using this framework, it's easy to understand economic value as the financial return received from the sale of a product or service. Social value is the improvement in the well-being of a specific individual, and civic value is the benefit that is returned to society (Lumpkin and Bacq, 2019).

The other term that we will use throughout our time together is "social enterprise." Typically, this term is used to define the specific organization that is working to create these values. In later chapters, we'll dig deeper into how a social enterprise is different from a commercial enterprise, as well as the ways that it differs from a nonprofit or non-governmental organization. For now, let's stick to the basics and say that a social enterprise is an organization that seeks to achieve a particular social objective and derives funding at least in part by means of the sale of products or services (Dart, 2004; Harding, 2004).

BOX 1.5   DEFINITION OF SOCIAL ENTERPRISE

Other definitions of the term "social enterprise" include the following:

- "Organizations that address a basic unmet need or solve a social or environmental problem through a market-driven approach" (Social Enterprise Alliance, www.socialenterprise.us).
- "Social enterprise is simply a more conscious, purposeful way of doing business" and "an alternative to traditional philanthropy models" (Birnbaum, 2018, p. 5).

In contrast, the term "social business" is not synonymous with "social enterprise," as it pertains to a more specific type of social enterprise. The term "social business" was popularized by Muhammad Yunus, Founder of Grameen Bank and the recipient of the 2006 Nobel Peace Prize for his development of the concepts of microcredit and microfinance, which aimed to create a system through which impoverished populations could participate in grassroots economic and social development. As a social entrepreneur and civic leader, Yunus contrasts social business with the traditional notions of charity and business, which were seen as two opposites representing selflessness and selfishness, respectively. He defines a social business as "a nondividend company dedicated to solving human problems" (Yunus, 2017, p. 27) that uses "creativity to solve human problems in a sustainable way" (p. 31). Yunus pushes for the idea that social business is a gateway for creating a more humane, equitable economic system.

All social businesses are social enterprises, but not all social enterprises are social businesses. To this end, while there are similarities between the two terms, we are using the broader notion of social enterprise.

In the next few pages, we're going to spend some time talking about how this exciting new world came to be. We're going to look at how we care for each other, how we look at money, and how both of those things have changed over time. As we journey through this brief history, please keep in mind that economic and social systems are human inventions, not natural laws. Natural laws are things like sunrise and sunset, gravity, and the movement of the tides. Economic and social systems are created by people – sometimes on purpose and sometimes not. So, if people built these systems, then people (hopefully you and me) can change them.

THE GLOBAL ECONOMY

It's no secret that the global economy has been through some rough patches lately. Income inequality is more dramatic than ever, with just 1 percent of the global population controlling half of the world's assets (Credit Suisse Research Institute, 2017). Technology is continuing to replace many traditional jobs that produced solid, long-term incomes. Individual countries are becoming less willing to cooperate and develop economic collaboration and are becoming more interested in protecting their own interests. Increased global migration, driven by increasingly repressive conditions in many countries, is putting pressure on the social support systems of many more established nations (Janse, 2017), and the economic shockwaves of the Covid-19 pandemic will be reverberating for a long time to come. As we saw in the Occupy Wall Street movement, much of the blame for these problems is placed on the unique attributes of American-style capitalism (which certainly has its weaknesses). However, we've also seen that modern capitalism has many strengths.

Modern Capitalism

The benefits of a free-market economy are numerous. Many of the technological advances of modern society have come about due to the incentives provided by a system that rewards innovation and creativity. We could spend all day listing things like robotic surgery, autonomous vehicles, drones, and so on. Suffice it to say that free-market capitalism has made much of the world a far better place in a relatively short period of time (Baumol, 2002). I would submit to you that the ability to create wealth is not the problem. What's currently wrong with the system is how we view our responsibilities about the wealth that is created.

Perhaps the most glaring flaw is that modern capitalism has developed a "win at any cost" mentality. This "everyone for themselves" perspective can be traced back to a seminal moment in global economics. On September 13, 1970, economist Milton Friedman published an article in the *New York Times* in which he stated that "The social responsibility of business is to increase its profits" (Friedman, 1970). Responding in part to the increasing social concerns that arose in the U.S. in the 1960s, Friedman proclaimed what has become one of the most widely held notions of modern capitalism. While this article earned Friedman wide acclaim (and, shortly after, a Nobel Prize), it was not in fact a thought that originated with him.

A few years earlier (1968, to be exact) a man named Garrett Hardin wrote a paper about something called "the tragedy of the commons." Without going into too much detail, what Hardin proposed was that human nature, left to its own devices, would seek to maximize one's own situation, even if it meant that other people's situations were made less in the process (Hardin, 1968).

Spurred in part by the thoughts of these two men, modern capitalism became a winner-takes-all endeavor, where resources, assets, and people are exploited to develop and sustain a competitive advantage, often at all (or any) cost. Happily (I hope) you may find it interesting to note that this is not what the capitalist system was intended to be.

A BRIEF ECONOMIC HISTORY

For a very long time, humankind existed in small groups (15–40 people or so), who hunted and gathered daily just to stay alive. What little they had (likely a few animal skins) and what little they were able to obtain (nuts, berries, and the occasional rabbit or deer) was shared within the group, sometimes referred to as a "kinship" economy (because of its reliance on the immediate family or "kin"; Voutsaki, 2010). Economically speaking, these small groups operated in a fashion that today we would call a commune, and literally lived off the land. Ideas like ownership of property were nonexistent, and these small bands wandered as weather and food sources dictated. As skills in hunting began to progress, these groups became (slightly) larger and developed some areas of specialization (Carson, 1990). If there was any trade at all, it was either between individual members of the group or between members of neighboring groups (Clark, 2016).

Somewhere around 7000 BCE, various forces began to drive these groups to begin planting and managing crops in a more structured fashion. This revolution also led to initial claims of ownership of specific plots of land, as well as the beginnings of more specialized divisions of labor (Carson, 1990), major changes that have had implications on issues of equity and fairness down to this very day.

As social structures began to develop, various forms of government also emerged. Accumulating wealth and prosperity came to be seen as a sign of power and prestige, and trade between nations became commonplace (Clark, 2016). The primary sign of this prosperity was the ownership and management of large agricultural estates along with the equipment needed to work the land. In many cases, ownership also often included the lives of the humans who would perform the work. For example, the population of ancient Rome (from roughly 400 BCE to about 200 CE) was 10 slaves for every one free person. It's also important to note that slavery during that time did not always mean what we understand it to mean today. There were certainly some cases where the slave was literally owned by the master, but there were also many cases where various financial circumstances created a situation where the worker was effectively held captive to the landowner in a category known as serfdom. In either case, the individual worker was not paid a wage for their work and could not independently choose who they would work for. They did receive food and shelter, but often at levels that modern society would not consider sufficient (Carson, 1990).

Over time, these local landowners and the estates they managed evolved into what were essentially independent city-states, known as "manors," under an economic system that became known as feudalism. Each of these manors effectively operated as its own city-state. The landowner (often referred to as Lord, a title for a nobleman) had many people "employed" to support the land and keep it productive. On this land, the primary activity was agriculture (growing crops, raising animals, and the like). To make all of this happen, there were dozens or even hundreds of workers performing manual labor. These folks were not employed like we would think of employment. They didn't have paychecks, or days off, or any sort of job security. They worked (often from sunup to sundown and beyond). They were (usually) given food, a place to sleep, and occasionally something to wear. And that was about it. Survival depended almost entirely on the whims of the lord of the manor. If the lord was happy, then everything was OK. If the lord was unhappy (or worse, lost a battle to another lord), then life was very precarious. Even when the lord was happy, disease was rampant, health care was nonexistent, and the average lifespan was quite short (Seccombe, 1992).

In many ways, what we understand as a plantation is essentially what existed in a feudal manor. There was a lord who owned a large plot of land. Due in part to the wealth (and accompanying leisure time) that many of these landowners accumulated, Europe during these times began to experience an intellectual awakening. Formal exploration of things scientific began to emerge in the late 16th century. In the early to mid-17th century, a larger "enlightenment" began to develop, and the fields of philosophy, art, and music all took great leaps forward – as did something known at the time as "political economy" (what we know now as the field of economics) (Shiller, 2013).

The Moral Origins of Capitalism

This developing field found its first "rock star" in a man by the name of Adam Smith. Born in a small town in Scotland in 1723, Smith was educated at the University of Glasgow and at Oxford University (Campbell and Skinner, 1985). Known as the "founding father of free-market economics," Smith was famous for two works. The first was a book published in 1759 called *The Theory of Moral Sentiments*. The second, and more well known, book was *An Inquiry into the Nature and Causes of the Wealth of Nations* (Conlin, 2016). Distilling the combined wisdom of these two books would (and does) take up several shelves in a library. However, there is a key theme in Smith's work that is critically important to our exploration of social entrepreneurship.

Source: Library of Congress Archives. Used with permission

Smith was adamant that wealth was not a means to an end in and of itself. In fact, Smith felt very strongly that the accumulation of wealth created a moral obligation to care for others, and created a direct path to liberty and equality:

> Commerce and manufactures [*sic*] gradually introduced order and good government, and with them, the liberty and security of individuals, among the inhabitants of the country, who had before lived in a continual state of war with their neighbours and of servile dependency upon their superiors. This, though it has been the least observed, is by far the most important of all of their effects. (Smith, 1796, Book III, Chapter IV, p. 440)

What Smith was trying to do was to create a system where the worker could establish and maintain a level of economic independence that would free them from the physical, social, and economic shackles of the feudal system. Even more importantly, Smith viewed the creation of wealth as something that implicitly included a moral obligation to care for each other – in direct and tangible ways (Satz, 2010).

Smith also proposed that there was a means to significantly improve the efficiency of the production of goods and services through specialization. This process of focusing on a single craft or skill also changed the nature of trade, which increased significantly in both size and scope. As individual workers became more and more specialized, industrialization started to spread throughout the developed world (Cameron, 1993).

So, who's right here? Are Friedman and Hardin correct in saying that "greed is good," or is Smith correct in thinking that wealth has a moral implication? Happily, this debate has recently benefited from some research that seems to point the issue towards a reality that is closer to what some of the earlier models of capitalism had in mind. And it came from a very interesting source.

Elinor Ostrom won the Nobel Prize in Economics in 2009. In addition to the insight she developed, this achievement is notable for two reasons. The first is that Dr. Ostrom was the first woman ever to win the Nobel Prize in Economics. The second is that Dr. Ostrom was not an economist, but rather a political scientist. What Dr. Ostrom demonstrated was that the notions of Hardin and Friedman were not always true, and that humans could work together to create and manage economic systems that benefited the community and the individual in relatively equal measure.

BOX 1.7   ELINOR OSTROM

Elinor Ostrom was born in Los Angeles, California in 1933. She graduated from the University of California, Los Angeles (UCLA) with a degree in Political Science in 1954 and went on to earn her PhD in the same field from UCLA in 1965. She spent much of her career at Indiana University in Bloomington, working alongside her second husband, Vincent, whom she married in 1963. In 2009, Ostrom was awarded the Nobel Prize in Economics. She demonstrated how local resources could be successfully managed by local market participants without regulation by central authorities or privatization. She died in 2012 at the age of 78.

Ostrom's work overturned what had been the conventional wisdom, namely that human nature was such that any natural resource would eventually be exploited for personal gain, even if it meant that the resource was depleted or destroyed in the process. Ostrom conducted studies in the field, observing how local communities managed fisheries, forests, and pastures. She showed that people that share a common resource can and will eventually organize and establish rules of behavior that allow for the resources to be used without being abused (Tarko, 2017).

So, capitalism itself is not a bad thing. In fact, it's neither good nor bad. Much like a hammer (or, for that matter, a gun), it can be used to good purpose, or it can be used to bad purpose. At its best, it can lead to fantastic new technologies, life-changing medical innovations, and vast improvements in the living standards of much of humanity. At its worst, it can decimate natural resources and debase, degrade, and even enslave people. So, it's not making the money that's the problem (if we don't do it in a way that harms or exploits others or the environment), it's what we do with the money that matters.

Can Capitalism Be "Fixed"?

Before we leave this little journey into economics, it's important to note that there have been other attempts to improve economic equality. Perhaps the most noted of these are the various forms of socialism and communism that have risen in the recent past. Much like the early thinking that led to capitalism, each of these economic systems evolved due to concerns over worker exploitation (Clark, 2016). However, the thinkers that developed these alternatives were responding more directly to the abuses that were developing in capitalist systems (Carson, 1990).

BOX 1.8   DEFINITIONS OF SOCIALISM AND COMMUNISM

Socialism is an economic system whereby the means and methods of producing value (the resources and processes used to produce goods and services) are owned and managed centrally (usually by the government). Communism takes this one step further and contends that both the means of production and the products themselves are owned in common, rather than by any one individual (Loucks and Whitney, 1973).

In both socialist and communist economic systems, there is a specific concern that the competitive forces of the free-market system bring out the worst aspects of human nature. In both cases, the decision-making activities of the individual (a core concept of free-market capital-ism) are replaced by some level of state control. The key distinction between these two alterna-tives is that socialism holds on to the ideas of private ownership and wealth creation but gives the government the power to determine how that wealth is distributed, while communism is, well, communal (meaning that everything is owned by the commune, or the government; Clark, 2016). Unfortunately, neither of these alternatives has been able to improve the overall health of the human condition.

Communist systems have tended to develop cultures that had a strong propensity for war, imperialism, and genocide (Clark, 2016). While socialist systems have been able to encourage individual initiative, they have also met with significant challenges due to the lack of individual freedom that a state system of control imposes (Landreth and Colander, 2002). Many Eastern European countries have attempted to implement various forms of socialist economies, without being able to produce long-term success (Clark, 2016).

More recently, an attempt to blend various models has develop a concept known as demo-cratic socialism, which tries to find a balance between market forces and governmental plan-ning, between private ownership and public use, between economic equality and individual incentives. However, no significant economic system has been built using these principles (Clark, 2016).

BOX 1.9 CONSCIOUS CAPITALISM

The notion of "conscious capitalism" has also been gaining momentum since the pub-lication of John Mackey and Rajendra Sisodia's book *Conscious Capitalism: Liberating the Heroic Spirit of Business*. Mackey, Co-CEO of Whole Foods Market, takes the notion that traditional nonprofit models might not allow for innovation and entrepreneurial approaches (for example, co-op food markets) and traditional businesses are missing the mark on their ability to be more human-centered and ethical in their practices. Mackey and Sisodia (2013) position conscious capitalism as consisting of four interconnected, guiding pillars: higher purpose, stakeholder orientation, conscious leadership, and con-scious culture.

In a few pages, I'll offer a few thoughts about what I think is a better way for addressing these problems. But before we do that, we need to talk about some of the other issues that got us to this point. And one of the biggest ones is the means by which we do (or do not) care for those in need.

BOX 1.10 DOUBLE AND TRIPLE BOTTOM LINE

The concepts of double bottom line (DBL or 2BL) and triple bottom line (TBL or 3BL) expand upon the traditional notion upheld within capitalist societies that the purpose of business is to generate financial profit. Connected to the idea that profit should not be the sole aim of business, the term "double bottom line" focuses on profit *and* people, meaning that business can generate both profits and a positive social impact. The TBL takes this one step further to state that business should focus its efforts on profits, people, and the planet, adding the element that business should minimize environmental harm in lieu of sustainable practices. This broader orientation of the economic, social, and environmen-tal value of businesses helps to highlight the ethical practices and their implications.

HELP FOR THE NEEDY

Care for the less fortunate comes primarily from two sources: private charity and public programs. Private charity is delivered through specialized entities known as non-governmental organizations (NGOs; in the U.S., they call them nonprofits). Public programs are run by various government agencies. While many people are better off because of the good work delivered through these efforts, neither system is operating as well as it could be.

Charity

One of the ways that we provide care for the less fortunate is through charity. Charitable organizations have existed in various forms for hundreds of years. Up until the 16th century, people cared for each other directly, through family structures and the small communities that were the norm in early societies, motivated by a sense of obligation that was rooted in religion (Critchlow and Parker, 1998; Safley, 2003). As societies began to develop and expand, problems of inequality and care for the less fortunate came to be addressed by either charitable institutions or some sort of governmental support program (Safley, 2003). Structured charitable entities became a necessary part of our social and economic systems because they provide services that other market or social systems can't or won't produce. For example, many social services are seen as not having any opportunity for profit (a notion we'll take issue with in a later chapter).

BOX 1.11   DEFINITION OF CHARITY

Charities take the form of NGOs and nonprofit organizations (NPOs) in order to raise funds in the support of social and environmental causes and to deliver support, resources, and aid within communities and areas of need. Charities attempt to benefit human welfare and well-being and to better the world through their efforts.

Some services are seen as not being effectively delivered by government structures (mostly because they may be politically unpopular), and some are seen as not being properly served through direct volunteering (Steinberg, 2006). Interestingly, these "failures" can also be the opportunities that lead to innovation (a point we'll explore in depth shortly).

These organizations are typically funded from individual donations and from various forms of grants. Unfortunately, less than one-third of 1 percent (0.3 percent) of global income is returned to charitable efforts (Charities Aid Foundation, 2016). And while it certainly seems like better funding would solve a lot of the issues facing organized charity, it's only one of the problems this industry has.

Over the years, various structural constraints have forced the world of organized charity into a corner. Although there is some hope that things are changing, for many years charitable organizations have been evaluated on their spending habits, and that has imposed some significant restraints (Salamon, 1999).

One of the most significant effects of the concern about spending has been the ability to attract talented individuals to the field. While exorbitant salaries and lush fringe benefits are certainly not appropriate when spending donated money, a fair and competitive wage is a critical tool if we hope to attract the best and the brightest to this work. However, in a misguided effort to control budgets, charitable organizations have a track record of paying less than similar jobs might earn in the commercial sector. If you accept that actions reflect beliefs, this means that society values the work done in the charitable sector as less worthy than a similar job done in pursuit of profit (roughly 30 percent less according to one study[2]). Even though charitable organizations are trying to address society's deepest problems, they are typically unable to hire the best and the brightest due to this staggering gap in pay. It takes a very special (and extremely rare) person to be willing to forgo economic security for their family simply to be able to serve the less fortunate.

However, not everyone who works in this industry has a pure-hearted motive. In some extreme cases, this can lead to a worker that is not motivated by the best intentions, but by a need to be seen as a "good" person, or by a need to invoke some sort of self-sacrificial ritual to atone for perceived sins. If you accept the idea that difficult problems require exceptional talent, then you will see that these concerns about the motivation and compensation of workers in charitable organizations are a significant obstacle to the effective delivery of social change. We also expect charitable organizations to operate on much smaller budgets, to maintain a low profile and not advertise or promote their cause, be conservative with both their funds and their strategies, and avoid profit-making activities at all costs (Pallotta, 2010). It's no wonder that we're not seeing the lasting improvement that we need.

The means and methods used to generate charitable donations are another area that we need to talk about. There is no question that charities need our money. There is also no question that the art and science of professional fundraising is a noble profession. One of the most interesting things that you learn when studying fundraising is that the biggest reason people don't give is because they haven't been asked (Phillips, 2016). Further, one of the reasons that there is such a thing as a professional fundraiser is that the motives behind a specific gift can be quite complex. The reason for that is that charitable donations are a somewhat unequal exchange. When you purchase a product or a service, you get something of equal or greater value in return for your money. When you make a donation, the return on your money is something less tangible (Mixer, 1993). Because this exchange is harder to quantify, the art of fundraising has a structural weakness to it. This weakness is another one of the reasons for the rise of social entrepreneurship.

In some cases, charitable fundraising efforts can play to one of two basic (and somewhat base) human emotions. The first of these is pity. Sometimes, a charity will produce highly emotional appeals that generate deep feelings of compassion. Unfortunately, this compassion is generated at the expense of the dignity of the recipient, who is essentially reduced to a "poster child."

The second human emotion involved that can be manipulated in charitable fundraising is ego. In the case of small donations, there is a funding appeal that speaks to the "warm feeling" you get when you donate. But that "warm feeling" can be your own ego telling you you're a "good" person for doing something to help another (Egger and Yoon, 2004). In the case of large donations, the ego motive becomes even stronger. If you make a big enough donation, the organization may even put your name on the side of the building (in fact, I know of one large donor that requires this as a condition of the donation). In the case of very large donations (usually made through a financial arrangement generally known as a foundation), there are also concerns about how the money was earned in the first place (Bremner, 1993). Two great U.S. examples are Andrew Carnegie and John D. Rockefeller, each of whom built large (and often exploitative) industrial giants and then sought tax relief and social status by directing a portion of their wealth to charitable causes (Egger and Yoon, 2004). In the modern era, industry titans such as Bill Gates and Mark Zuckerberg have come under similar criticisms (Giridharadas, 2019).

How Helping Can Hurt

The most significant problem with charity is the nature of the charitable exchange between the provider of the service and its recipient (Lupton, 2011). While there are certainly situations where we need to care for our fellow humans out of the goodness of our hearts (the chronically disabled and those experiencing catastrophic loss being two good examples), there are also many times where providing a product or service for free can have substantial negative consequences.

These consequences materialize in two distinct ways. The first is that the continued provision of a free good or service can create a form of dependency. Said simply, the less fortunate individual may come to depend on receiving the help (Lupton, 2011). Given the instability of long-term funding for private charity, this can cause significant harm to the individual if the service is suddenly no longer available (Drucker, 1990). The second is that it can also serve to suppress local initiatives (Lupton, 2011). For example, if I provide a community with free shoes, then the local shoemaker loses customers (after all, why buy it when I can get it for free?).

BOX 1.12   CHARITIES: HELPING DRIVE CHANGE OR REINFORCING AN UNEVEN STATUS QUO?

According to the Charities Aid Foundation's *Charitable Giving in the USA 2019* report (2019), 62 percent of Americans gave towards a charitable cause, with an average annual donation of $461, and more than 35 percent engaged in volunteerism in the previous 12 months. The report showed that the majority of the surveyed American public – 73 percent – view the work of charities as either "fairly positive" (44 percent) or "very positive" (29 percent) domestically. However, Americans expressed slightly more reluctance on charities' impact internationally, with only 62 percent reporting that charities have a "fairly positive" (35 percent) and "very positive" (27 percent) impact outside the U.S.

Table 1.1 Global attitudes on charitable activities

	Percent donating to charities in the past 12 months	Percent volunteering in the past 12 months	Reported charities as having a "fairly positive impact" domestically	Reported charities as having a "very positive impact" domestically	Reported charities as having a "fairly positive impact" internationally	Reported charities as having a "very positive impact" internationally
Australia	68%	35%	54%	24%	47%	21%
Brazil	70%	53%	47%	26%	44%	32%
Canada	65%	30%	47%	26%	40%	25%
India	72%	52%	43%	33%	36%	34%
Russia	49%	17%	41%	14%	35%	14%
South Africa	80%	66%	49%	31%	38%	35%
U.K.	57%	16%	48% (report that charities are "trustworthy")			
U.S.	62%	35%	44%	29%	35%	27%

Note: All presented figures in Table 1.1 were compiled from the individual country 2019 reports of the Charities Aid Foundation (CAF). Please note, the CAF UK Giving 2019 report did not ask for the same distinctions as the other country reports and represented the reported trustworthiness of charities in general, as surveyed.

While most of those surveyed from the countries noted in the chart reported a positive perception of charities and their contributions both nationally and internationally, there are notable percentages of these populations that see charities with some level of skepticism. This can also be seen in various other channels, such as the documentary *Poverty Inc.* (2014) and books *Winners Take All: The Elite Charade of Changing the World* (Giridharadas, 2019), *Charity Detox: What Charity Would Look Like If We Cared About Results* (Lupton, 2015), and *Toxic Charity: How Churches and Charities Hurt Those They Help* (Lupton, 2011). These voices represent a questioning of how helpful the traditional forms of charity and aid are, as they have also been criticized for reinforcing a status quo of existing power dynamics and inequities that has not served the communities and individuals in need well in the first place.

Before we leave this thread, there is one other issue we need to talk about. If you really think about it, the true goal of any social change initiative should be to eliminate the social problem that brought about the creation of the organization in the first place. For example, if your concern is hunger, then nothing less than the eradication of hunger should be your goal (granted, that's a huge goal, but you get my point). And when the goal is achieved, then you should go home (or move on to some other pressing concern – of which there are many). While we hope and believe that charitable efforts are initiated with the best of intentions, it does raise concern about any social change organization that has been in operation for decades. You can't help but wonder why 50 or 60 years' worth of work on a specific social problem hasn't produced a substantial reduction in the occurrence of that problem.

Government-Sponsored Social Programs

The other primary source of support for the less fortunate is government-sponsored social programs (often referred to as a "social safety net") (Padró, 2004). These programs are the most recent of the major systems for the support of social concerns, having developed in response to the various fits and starts of the expansion of the modern industrial economy. As we have seen in our discussions of economic systems and charitable organizations, the vast expansion of wealth and prosperity of the 20th and 21st centuries has dramatically improved the lives of many, but has also brought increased awareness of the growing gaps between economic and social classes. In response to these concerns, many believe that government agencies should provide support to those in need (Esping-Andersen, 2006).

According to data from the Organization for Economic Co-operation and Development (OECD), during the years 2013–2016, 21 percent of the total gross domestic product in the 35 member nations was spent on "social protection" programs (OECD, 2018b). To put this into real terms, these 35 spent over $11 trillion caring for the less fortunate in 2016 (OECD, 2018a).

While there are many political and philosophical debates over the size, scale, and scope of government social programs (as well as arguments over the role of government in society) (Padró, 2004), our concern here is about how well these systems may (or may not) be working.

There are two major reasons why governmental social programs are being challenged. The first reason is that changing social structures are producing new demands for social programs that have not existed in the past. The increase in single-parent households, changes in the nature of work, and the increasing acceptance of alternative lifestyles are just a few examples of changing social structures that demand new and different types of social support systems. The second is that the basic financial structures of these systems have become strained as economic fluctuations and an aging population have put pressure on the ability of these programs to meet their commitments (Esping-Andersen, 2006). Said simply, there are more and more demands for social support, and less and less funding available to provide these services.

Government programs are also susceptible to charges of corruption, as well as allegations of inefficient and ineffective operations. One of the leading benchmarks of government corruption suggests that developed countries score an average of 68 on a scale of 100 when measuring public perception about corruption. Said another way, the citizens of most major countries believe that their government is going to be corrupt between 20 and 30 percent of the time (Transparency International, 2018). There are several well documented examinations of government efficiency (Kaufmann, Kraay, and Mastruzzi, 2009; Svensson, 2005). In one study, the researchers mailed letters to fictional businesses – 10 per country to a total of 159 countries. They then measured how long it took for the letters to be returned as undeliverable. They found that only 60 percent of the letters were ever returned at all. Of the letters they did get back, the average return time was over six months (Chong et al., 2014).

A NEW DAWN

Clearly, there are several flaws in our current systems for creating wealth and caring for those who need our help. Just as clearly, there is an amazing movement that is building strength every day. That movement, while still young, has the potential to change the nature of business as well as the way that we help the less fortunate. That movement is the subject of this book.

A 2015 study of 85 countries suggests that between 3 and 10 percent of the new businesses being built are seeking to serve a social purpose, and that maximizing profit is not their primary objective (Bosma et al., 2016). It has become a popular topic for academic research and college courses (Lepoutre et al., 2013), and has spawned numerous support systems (Impact Hub, 2018). Not bad for a phenomenon that didn't even have a name 40 years ago.

Even though Bill Drayton is often credited with coining the term "social entrepreneurship," the notion of using earned income as a part of a larger strategy to fund a mission-oriented enterprise goes back a lot further. Universities (which are usually nonprofit entities) have been charging for tuition for hundreds of years. Hospitals (also often nonprofit) have been charging fees for services for almost as long (Shore, 2001).

But there is clearly something different about this current wave of interest and growth in the notion that a single entity can produce value in multiple ways. One of the best summaries of what's unique about this movement claims three distinctive elements. The first is that the effort seeks to make the world better in some specific way (that's the "social"). The second is that the solution developed is new and different, and seeks to solve a problem (that's the "entrepreneurship"). The third is that there is a recognition that traditional funding sources for social concerns are not enough to support long-term financial stability (Lepoutre et al., 2013).

For me, the most exciting and interesting thing about social entrepreneurship is that it converts the way that social change is funded. It moves the funding stream away from systems where wealth is transferred (such as charity or government funding) and towards systems where the funding stream is self-generated (through the creation of economic value that is then directed towards the social need). There is even a new type of investment capital emerging that recognizes that investors can be repaid not just by the earnings of the firm, but also by the reduction in cost to society. We'll explore this shift in funding streams further at several points in this book, but it's important to state this clearly and directly at the outset.

Most of this book will examine several key issues that I've uncovered in working with dozens of organizations seeking to find a way to build this new model. The biggest thing that I've learned is that there are some things that really matter in building a successful social enterprise. And there are some that don't.

Interestingly, some of the things that seem to get the most attention in other textbooks and articles, as well as in the many debates that still swirl through this space, seem to fall into the second category (stuff that doesn't matter). And there is far too much time spent on definitions, and not nearly enough time spent on practical advice that helps you build an effective social enterprise. So, that's the gap we hope to help fill. And it's exactly where you fit into this journey.

BOX 1.13 ABHORRENCE AND APPRECIATION

It is important for social entrepreneurs to have deep levels of understanding of both why the current state exists and why they want to change it. Martin and Osberg (2015) frame this as balancing abhorrence with appreciation:

> The most successful change agents [...] must manage to both abhor the existing conditions and appreciate the system that produces them, deeply and well. (p. 84)

While appreciation seems antithetical to everything presented about social entrepreneurs throughout the chapter thus far, it raises an important reminder that social entrepreneurs cannot ignore that there will be resistance to what they want to do. Having an appreciation – not a liking but as in a knowledge of why – of the status quo helps social entrepreneurs better understand what resistance they can anticipate, from whom to expect it, and how to use that information to dismantle and rebuild towards the world they want to help create.

How Do We Fix This?

By now, you're probably a bit depressed. Or perhaps you're angry. Maybe you're inspired. Or possibly a bit of each.

Social systems are ever evolving, and each new version does two things. The first is that the world gets a little better, a little more caring, a little more just. The second is that each system, over time, starts to develop flaws and expose its shortcomings. And so, humankind starts to struggle to find a new and better way. It's been this way forever. From the discovery of fire, we get warmth, and cooking, and community. But we also get danger, and a potential weapon. And so it has gone ever since.

I believe that the emergence of social entrepreneurship is not just a cool thing. I believe that it is a better way. Maybe you do too. Or maybe you will by the end of our time together. But it's still a new thing, a thing that is emergent, fuzzy, ill-defined, and very hard to execute. Which also means that there is tremendous opportunity.

This opportunity does not just exist in the chance to build a viable entity that can sustainably produce social change (although that is a wonderful thing in and of itself – and a lot of hard work). But, in building such an organization, there is also real opportunity for each of you to become part of the force that changes the system.

That kind of opportunity doesn't come along very often. And it is now at your doorstep.

BOX 1.14   THE ROLE (AND THE LIMITATIONS) OF THE UNITED NATIONS

When reflecting on the various points within the chapter, you might be asking, "Wait, doesn't the United Nations have a role in social change?" The United Nations (UN) – along with its funds and programs (for example, UNICEF, the World Food Programme, the UN Environment Programme), specialized agencies (for example, the World Health Organization, the World Bank), and other entities, bodies, and related organizations (for example, the World Trade Organization)[3] – do ample work to help address social challenges across the world.

One of the UN's greatest contributions has been to centralize the conversations of social challenges by helping to define them. The Sustainable Development Goals (SDGs) are the UN guidelines on the scope of global challenges that need to be faced in order to create a more healthy, sustainable, and equitable world.

The goals cover the foundations of human needs of health, nourishment, resources, education, work, industry, community, and peace, as well as man's intersections with the planet and environment, including having clean and accessible water and energy, aiming for sustainable and planet conscious action, and the protection of life on land and under water. The 17 SDGs were released and adopted by all of the UN Member States in 2015 as a 15-year blueprint for global and local action, initiative, and partnerships through 2030:[4]

1. No poverty;
2. Zero hunger;
3. Good health and well-being;

4. Quality education;
5. Gender equality;
6. Clean water and sanitation;
7. Affordable and clean energy;
8. Decent work and economic growth;
9. Industry, innovation, and infrastructure;
10. Reduced inequalities;
11. Sustainable cities and communities;
12. Responsible consumption and production;
13. Climate action;
14. Life below water;
15. Life on land;
16. Peace, justice, and strong institutions; and
17. Partnership for the goals.

The 17 SDGs are interconnected and serve to provide enough specificity for focused discussions and intentional action, while remaining broad enough to encompass the expansive breadth of challenges within each goal.

The development of the SDGs followed on the progress and scope established by their predecessor, the Millennium Development Goals (MDGs), which focused on eight areas:

1. Eradicate extreme poverty and hunger;
2. Achieve universal primary education;
3. Promote gender equality and empower women;
4. Reduce child mortality;
5. Improve maternal health;
6. Combat HIV/AIDS, malaria, and other diseases;
7. Ensure environmental sustainability; and
8. Global partnership development.

The UN Development Programme (UNDP) reported that the cross-sectoral, international efforts to approach the MDGs resulted in millions of people being lifted out of poverty, with those living on under $1.25 per day being reduced by half (since 1990); the number of school-aged children not attending school being reduced by half (since 1990); the number of those living with HIV getting appropriate health treatments increasing by nearly 15 times, with the rate of infection dropping by nearly 40 percent since 2000; and incidences of child mortality falling by more than half (since 1990).[5] The 17 SDGs build upon the foundation of both the successes and persisting challenges left from the MDGs, and the SDGs now serve as an active framework for collaboration, partnership, and collective action (SDG 17) between various actors within governments, industry, civil society, and academe.

In addition, the UN has been helping to push for global cooperation to create a better world for the planet and its people. While these two series of global action blueprints have shaped our dialogue and actions in the 21st century, the UN's involvement in the promotion of common standards and human rights has been longer standing. The UN Charter Article 55, drafted in 1945, notes that the UN has the authority to promote the following:

a. Higher standards of living, full employment, and conditions of economic and social progress and development;
b. Solutions of international economic, social, health, and related problems; and international cultural and educational cooperation; and
c. Universal respect for, and observance of, human rights and fundamental freedoms for all without distinction as to race, sex, language, or religion.[6]

Article 56 follows these points, requiring "All Members pledge themselves to take joint and separate action in co-operation with the Organization for the achievement of the purposes set forth in Article 55."[7]

Shortly thereafter, the Universal Declaration of Human Rights (UDHR) served as a landmark document for the establishment of common understandings for human rights, as proclaimed by the UN General Assembly in Paris on December 10, 1948. While the document has withstood the test of time in many of the UN Member States, the Declaration has been criticized for being too Western in its orientation of human rights, which gave rise, in part, to other declarations, such as those of the League of Arab Nations in 1994 (amended 2004) and the 10 member nations of the Association of Southeast Asian Nations (ASEAN) in 2012, which purport to better encompass more cultural representation for their signatories.

While the UN and its broad influence helps to centralize the dialogue and efforts for social and environmental change across the world, it relies on the expertise of its country and community partners, including social entrepreneurs, to help drive change.

CHAPTER SUMMARY

While there have been countless efforts and attempts to solve them, social challenges persist. Actors attempting to tackle these issues range from large national- and multinational-level efforts to those grassroots efforts of independent individuals. While a capitalist economy can foster creativity, innovation, and entrepreneurial approaches, the prioritization of financial gains from those endeavors may counter the interests of the community and environment and jeopardize the anticipated or experienced social or environmental gains. Governmental social programs are experiencing greater pressures from the increasing demands for social support and the decreasing funding available to provide adequate support; likewise, our efforts to "do good" – like through charity – may not be putting enough pressure on the system to change. Social entrepreneurship attempts to balance financial benefits with the prosperity and welfare of the people and our planet by shedding light on the inequalities and challenges of the world, as well as the energy and know-how to ameliorate the situation to create a better present and future.

QUESTIONS FOR DISCUSSION

1. Interview a social entrepreneur of interest in your community, and find out the following information:

   - Who is this person, and what is their background?
   - What is their organization/business/project, and why was it started?
   - What is the social or environmental issue they are trying to approach? With which United Nations Sustainable Development Goal(s) (SDGs) does their work connect (reference the UN SDG website at https://sustainabledevelopment.un.org for more information)?
   - What is the scope of their organization/business/project's impact, and what do they want its future impact to be?
   - What are their thoughts on being a social entrepreneur? What are its benefits and challenges?

2. Social entrepreneurs are in a relentless pursuit of tackling the "root cause" of an issue, which refers to the underlying, originating cause that may be causing other challenges. When digging into many social challenges, there may be a series of interconnected root causes. For example, when looking at a broad span of issues – like housing or food insecurity, poverty, or challenges within the criminal justice system – there are many roots that underpin each of these issues. Take a social or environmental issue of interest, and explore its root causes. After identifying as many of these as possible, ask yourself why the status quo might exist and who could help change it.

3. While their boundaries can be subjective, social enterprises are distinctly different from ethical businesses. According to Social Enterprise UK's website, "a social enterprise's primary purpose is its social and/or environmental mission – it tries to maximize the amount of social good it creates balanced against its financial goals," whereas "an ethical business, on the other hand, tries to minimize its negative impact on society or the environment." Furthermore, as highlighted in the chapter, charities also play important roles in social impact but differ from social enterprises. In order to explore these distinctions for yourself, look up some organizations or businesses you know that might fit each of these categories (Charity, Social Enterprise, and Ethical Business), and classify each organization on a separate sheet of paper. Compare your results with a classmate or within a group. Do you agree with others' classifications? Why, or why not? How did you each make your decisions on distinction?

4. Select a social enterprise and do a "deep dive" into its work and impact. To inform your conclusions, review the organization's website and social impact reports, along with other external media articles of the organization or founder interviews. Ask yourself the following questions:

- In your opinion, is this organization successful in its efforts?
- After reviewing the available materials, what questions or concerns are you left with?
- If you were leading this organization, what might you do differently? What do you think could be improved?

RECOMMENDED RESOURCES

Ashoka (n.d.). www.ashoka.org/.
Ashoka U (n.d.). www.ashokau.org/.
Brooks, A. C. (2008). *Social Entrepreneurship: A Modern Approach to Social Value Creation.* Harlow: Pearson Education.
Lupton, R. D. (2011). *Toxic Charity: How Churches and Charities Hurt Those They Help (And How to Reverse It).* New York, NY: HarperOne.
Martin, R., and Osberg, S. (2015). *Getting Beyond Better: How Social Entrepreneurship Works.* Boston, MA: Harvard Business Review Press.
Social Enterprise UK (n.d.). www.socialenterprise.org.uk.

NOTES

1. Quoted; accessed 28 April 2021 at https://blog.movingworlds.org/quotes-from-social-entrepreneurs-to-inspire-you-to-change-the-world/ (last accessed 28 April 2021).

2. Accessed 28 April 2021 at https://nonprofitquarterly.org/2010/06/21/nonprofit-salaries-achieving-parity-with-the-private-sector/.

3. Accessed 28 April 2021 at www.un.org/en/sections/about-un/funds-programmes-specialized-agencies-and-others/index.html.

4. Accessed 28 April 2021 at www.un.org/sustainabledevelopment/development-agenda/.

5. Accessed 28 April 2021 at www.undp.org/content/undp/en/home/sustainable-development-goals/background.html.

6. Accessed 28 April 2021 at www.un.org/en/sections/un-charter/un-charter-full-text/.

7. Accessed 28 April 2021 at www.un.org/en/sections/un-charter/un-charter-full-text/.

REFERENCES

Abu-Saifan, S. (2012). Social entrepreneurship: definition and boundaries. *Technology Innovation Management Review, 2*(2).
Annan, K. (2016, December 6). Democracy under pressure. *New York Times.*
Austin, J., Stevenson, H., and Wei-Skillern, J. (2006). Social and commercial entrepreneurship: Same, different, or both? *Entrepreneurship Theory and Practice, 30*(1), 1–22. https://doi-org.udel.idm.oclc.org/10.1111/j.1540-6520.2006.00107.x.

Baumol, W. J. (2002). *The Free-Market Innovation Machine: Analyzing the Growth Miracle of Capitalism.* Princeton, NJ: Princeton University Press.

Birnbaum, E. (2018). *In the Business of Change: How Social Entrepreneurs Are Disrupting Business as Usual.* Gabriola Island: New Society Publishers.

Bornstein, D., and Davis, S. (2010). *Social Entrepreneurship: What Everyone Needs to Know.* New York, NY: Oxford University Press.

Bosma, N., Schøtt, T., Terjesen, S. A., and Kew, P. (2016). *Global Entrepreneurship Monitor 2015 to 2016: Special Topic Report on Social Entrepreneurship.* Retrieved from https://ssrn.com/abstract=2786949.

Bremner, R. H. (1993). *Giving: Charity and Philanthropy in History.* New Brunswick, NJ: Transaction.

Buechner, F. (1973). *Wishful Thinking: A Theological ABC.* London: Collins.

Cameron, R. E. (1993). *A Concise Economic History of the World: From Paleolithic Times to the Present.* New York, NY: Oxford University Press.

Campbell, R. H., and Skinner, A. S. (1985). *Adam Smith.* London: Croom Helm.

Carson, R. L. (1990). *Comparative Economic Systems.* Armonk, NY: Sharpe.

Chamie, J. (2017). As cities grow worldwide, so do the numbers of homeless. *Yale Global Online.* Retrieved from https://yaleglobal.yale.edu/content/cities-grow-worldwide-so-do-numbers-homeless.

Charities Aid Foundation (2016). *Gross Domestic Philanthropy: An International Analysis of GDP, Tax and Giving.* Accessed 28 April 2021 at www.cafonline.org/docs/default-source/about-us-policy-and -campaigns/gross-domestic-philanthropy-feb-2016.pdf.

Charities Aid Foundation (2019). *Charitable Giving in the USA 2019: An Overview of Individual Giving in the USA.* Accessed 28 April 2021 at www.cafamerica.org/wp-content/uploads/CAF-USA-Giving -Report-2019-US-Eng-Final16a-1.pdf (last accessed 4/28/21).

Chong, A., La Porta, R., Lopez-de-Silanes, F., and Shleifer, A. (2014). Letter grading government efficiency. *Journal of the European Economic Association, 12*(2), 277–298.

Clark, B. S. (2016). *The Evolution of Economic Systems: Varieties of Capitalism in the Global Economy.* Oxford: Oxford University Press.

Conlin, J. (2016). *Adam Smith.* London: Reaktion Books.

Credit Suisse Research Institute (2017). *Global Wealth Report 2017.* Accessed 28 April 2021 at www .credit-suisse.com/media/assets/corporate/docs/about-us/research/publications/global-wealth-report -2017-en.pdf (last accessed 4/28/21).

Critchlow, D. T., and Parker, C. H. (1998). *With Us Always: A History of Private Charity and Public Welfare.* Lanham, MD: Rowman & Littlefield.

Dart, R. (2004). The legitimacy of social enterprise. *Nonprofit Management & Leadership, 14*(4), 411–424.

Dees, J. G. (1998 [2001]). The meaning of "social entrepreneurship" (draft report for the Kauffman Center for Entrepreneurial Leadership). Stanford University. Accessed 28 April 2021 at https://centers .fuqua.duke.edu/case/wp-content/uploads/sites/7/2015/03/Article_Dees_MeaningofSocialEntrep reneurship_2001.pdf (last accessed 4/28/21).

Drucker, P. F. (1990). *Managing the Non-Profit Organization: Practices and Principles.* New York, NY: HarperCollins.

Egger, R., and Yoon, H. (2004). *Begging for Change: The Dollars and Sense of Making Nonprofits Responsive, Efficient, and Rewarding for All.* New York, NY: HarperBusiness.

Elkington, J., and Hartigan, P. (2009). *The Power of Unreasonable People: How Social Entrepreneurs Create Markets that Change the World.* Boston, MA: Harvard Business Press.

Esping-Andersen, G. (2006). *Welfare States in Transition: National Adaptations in Global Economies.* Los Angeles, CA: SAGE.

FAO, IFAD, UNICEF, WFP, and WHO (2017). *The State of Food Security and Nutrition in the World 2017: Building Resilience for Peace and Food Security.* Accessed 28 April 2021 at www.fao.org/policy -support/tools-and-publications/resources-details/en/c/1107528/ (last accessed 4/28/21).

Friedman, M. (1970, September 13). The social responsibility of business is to increase its profits. *New York Times.*

Giridharadas, A. (2019). *Winners Take All: The Elite Charade of Changing the World.* London: Penguin.

Gitlin, T. (2012). *Occupy Nation: The Roots, the Spirit, and the Promise of Occupy Wall Street.* New York, NY: It Books/HarperCollins.

Gowing, L. R., Ali, R. L., Allsop, S., Marsden, J., Turf, E. E., West, R., and Witton, J. (2015). Global statistics on addictive behaviours: 2014 status report. *Addiction, 110*(6), 904–919.

Hardin, G. (1968). The tragedy of the commons. *Science, 162,* 1243–1248.

Harding, R. (2004). Social enterprise: The new economic engine? *Business Strategy Review*, *15*(4), 39–43.

Impact Hub (2018). *2018 Impact Report*. Accessed 28 April 2021 at https://drive.google.com/file/d/1FGu otp0xLCngiafTuGYeYeZysASBx1rN/view (last accessed 4/28/21).

Janse, K. A. (2017). How to Manage the Top Five Global Economic Challenges. *Knowledge@Wharton*. Accessed 27 April 2021 at http://knowledge.wharton.upenn.edu/article/what-are-the-top-five -challenges-for-international-organizations/.

Kaufmann, D., Kraay, A., and Mastruzzi, M. (2009). Governance matters VIII: Aggregate and individual indicators, 1996–2008. *World Bank Policy Research Paper 4978*.

Kessler-Harris, A., and Vaudagna, M. (2018). *Democracy and the Welfare State: The Two Wests in the Age of Austerity*. New York, NY: Columbia University Press.

Landreth, H., and Colander, D. C. (2002). *History of Economic Thought*. Boston, MA: Houghton Mifflin.

Lepoutre, J., Justo, R., Terjesen, S., and Bosma, N. (2013). Designing a global standardized methodology for measuring social entrepreneurship activity: The Global Entrepreneurship Monitor social entrepreneurship study. *Small Business Economics*, *40*(3), 693–714.

Light, P. C. (2009). Social entrepreneurship revisited. *Stanford Social Innovation Review*, *7*(3), 21–22.

Loucks, W. N., and Whitney, W. G. (1973). *Comparative Economic Systems*. New York, NY: Harper & Row.

Lumpkin, G. T., and Bacq, S. (2019). Civic wealth creation: A new view of stakeholder engagement and social impact. *Academy of Management Perspectives*, *33*(2), 383–404.

Lupton, R. D. (2011). *Toxic Charity: How Churches and Charities Hurt Those They Help*. New York, NY: HarperCollins.

Lupton, R. D. (2015). *Charity Detox: What Charity Would Look Like If We Cared About Results*. New York, NY: HarperOne.

Mackey, J., and Sisodia, R. (2013). *Conscious Capitalism: Liberating the Heroic Spirit of Business*. Boston, MA: Harvard Business Press.

Martin, R. L., and Osberg, S. (2007). Social entrepreneurship: The case for definition. *Stanford Social Innovation Review*, *5*(2), 28–39.

Melese, A. T. (2015). *Living Wage Report: Non-Metropolitan Urban Ethiopia*. Accessed 27 April 2021 at www.isealalliance.org/sites/default/files/resource/2017–12/Ethiopia_Living_Wage_Benchmark _Report.pdf.

Mergent (2018). *First Research Industry Profile: Florist*. Accessed 27 April 2021 at http://mergent .firstresearch-learn.com/industry.aspx?chapter=0&pid=231.

Mixer, J. R. (1993). *Principles of Professional Fundraising: Useful Foundations for Successful Practice*. San Francisco, CA: Jossey-Bass.

Montgomery, D., and Ramus, C. (2003). Corporate social responsibility reputation effects on MBA job choice. *SSRN Electronic Journal*. 10.2139/ssrn.412124.

OECD (2018a). Gross domestic product (GDP). Accessed 27 April 2021 at www.oecd-ilibrary.org/ content/data/dc2f7aec-en.

OECD (2018b). Social spending. Accessed 27 April 2021 at www.oecd-ilibrary.org/content/data/ 7497563b-en.

Padró, F. F. (2004). *Statistical Handbook on the Social Safety Net*. Westport, CT: Greenwood Press.

Pallotta, D. (2010). *Uncharitable: How Restraints on Nonprofits Undermine Their Potential*. Medford, MA, and Lebanon, NH: Tufts University Press and University Press of New England.

Phillips, G. (2016). *The Art of Fundraising: The Appeal, the People, the Strategies*. North Charleston, SC: CreateSpace.

Phills Jr, J. A., Deiglmeier, K., and Miller, D. T. (2008). Rediscovering social innovation. *Stanford Social Innovation Review*, *6*(4), 34–43.

Prahalad, C. K., and Hart, S. L. (1998). The fortune at the bottom of the pyramid. *Strategy+Business*, *26*, 54–67.

Ravallion, M., Chen, S., and Sangraula, P. (2007). New evidence on the urbanization of global poverty. *Population and Development Review*, *33*(4), 667–701.

Safley, T. M. (2003). *The Reformation of Charity: The Secular and the Religious in Early Modern Poor Relief*. Boston, MA: Brill Academic.

Salamon, L. M. (1999). The nonprofit sector at a crossroads: The case of America. *Voluntas: International Journal of Voluntary and Nonprofit Organizations*, *10*, 5–23.

Satz, D. (2010). *Why Some Things Should Not Be for Sale: The Moral Limits of Markets*. New York, NY: Oxford University Press.

Seccombe, W. (1992). *A Millennium of Family Change: Feudalism to Capitalism in Northwestern Europe*. London: Verso.

Serougi, N. (2016). Charity under pressure: Cash, credibility and consumerism. *Discover Society*. Accessed 27 April 2021 at https://discoversociety.org/2016/02/02/charity-under-pressure-cash-credibility-and-consumerism/.

Shiller, R. J. (2013). *Finance and the Good Society*. Princeton, NJ: Princeton University Press.

Shore, W. H. (2001). *The Cathedral Within: Transforming Your Life by Giving Something Back*. New York, NY: Random House.

Smith, A. (1796). *An Enquiry into the Nature and Causes of the Wealth of Nations*. London: Printed for A. Strahan; and T. Cadell, Jr and W. Davies.

Steinberg, R. (2006). Economic theories of nonprofit organizations. In W. W. Powell and R. Sternberg (eds), *The Non-Profit Sector: A Research Handbook* (pp. 117–139). New Haven, CT: Yale University Press.

Svensson, J. (2005). Eight questions about corruption. *Journal of Economic Perspectives*, 19(3), 19–42.

Tarko, V. (2017). *Elinor Ostrom: An Intellectual Biography*. Lanham, MD: Rowman & Littlefield.

Transparency International (2018). Corruption Perceptions Index 2017. Accessed 27 April 2021 at www.transparency.org/news/feature/corruption_perceptions_index_2017.

Tschirhart, M., and Bielefeld, W. (2012). *Managing Nonprofit Organizations*. San Francisco, CA: Jossey-Bass.

Voutsaki, S. (2010). *From the Kinship Economy to the Palatial Economy: The Argolid in the Second Millennium BC*. Paper presented at the Political Economies of the Aegean Bronze Age: Papers from the Langford Conference, Florida State University, Tallahassee, February, 22–24 2007.

World Bank (2014). *World Development Indicators, 2014*. Accessed 27 April 2021 at https://openknowledge.worldbank.org/bitstream/handle/10986/18237/9781464801631.pdf.

Yunus, M. (2017). *A World of Three Zeros: The New Economics of Zero Poverty, Zero Unemployment, and Zero Net Carbon Emissions*. New York, NY: PublicAffairs.

2

The basics of entrepreneurship still matter

Learning objectives

After studying this chapter, you should be able to:
1. Define the term "entrepreneur" and appreciate the diversity of those who are entrepreneurs.
2. Understand the roles of opportunity, need, viability, and innovation within entrepreneurship.
3. Explain the following key concepts of entrepreneurship: beneficiaries, customers, economics of one unit, go/no-go decisions, ideation, iteration, pivot, and sustainability.
4. Identify the basic principles of entrepreneurship that are important to building any venture – social or otherwise – and apply the "Eight Habits of Effective Entrepreneurs."
5. Integrate effective ideation practices into your entrepreneurial process.

WHAT IS AN ENTREPRENEUR?

Quick – think of three words that you associate with the word "entrepreneur" (go ahead, I'll wait). Done? OK, I'll bet some of the words you came up with are: "daring," "visionary," "risk-taker."

And I'll bet that "cautious," "disciplined," "analytical," and "conservative" were probably not on the list.

Thanks in part to the Great American Success Story, we carry around with us a vision of the entrepreneur that owes more to old pirate movies than it does to reality. I call this the *Field of Dreams* myth (and if you haven't seen that movie, you should). If you have, you'll remember that the famous misquote from that movie is "If you build it, they will come."

While the movie is about the power of dreams, it also makes the case that if we just dream hard enough, then we can make a successful reality. Or,

Source: iStock.com/Lynn Bystrom. Used with permission

Source: Julio Andres Rosario Ortiz, Unsplash. Used with permission

like Dorothy in *The Wizard of Oz*, all we need to do is believe (and click our heels together three times) and we'll get our heart's desire.

Now, before you go writing me off as a complete downer (which would be sad, because we've got an entire book to get through together), I want to make sure that you know that I fully support the power of dreams and am a big dreamer myself. But to come alive, dreams need plans, they need goals, and they need to be examined in the light of day to make sure that they are feasible and not just a manifestation of the pepperoni pizza you ate before going to bed last night.

How do I know this? Well, I've got the scars of my own personal failures to show as exhibit A. I've also got the experience of coaching hundreds of aspiring entrepreneurs as exhibits B thru ZZZ. And here's what I know: Good ideas are a dime a dozen. Good ideas that can be developed into viable enterprises are far rarer. And the difference between the two is just plain hard work. It takes a lot of planning and practice.

To get a better handle on this, consider the act of skydiving. On its face, it's kind of crazy. To intentionally throw yourself out of a perfectly good airplane, trusting on some rope and nylon to keep you from crashing into the ground, certainly sounds like something that takes immense courage (and perhaps a bit of lunacy). But if you understand the amount of training that goes into your first jump, it suddenly becomes much more rational.

First, you perform a tandem jump. In other words, you strap yourself to an experienced skydiver, they do all the work, and you're just along for the ride. Next, you take several ground-based classes that orient you to your equipment and teach you how to land, as well as the numerous emergency procedures that can keep you from dying (or getting stuck in a tree!). When you do go back into the air, your next few jumps are also assisted. Finally, if you pass all those hurdles, you get to skydive on your own. So, you do eventually throw yourself out of a perfectly good airplane, but you do it after a lot of practice and testing.

But even when you're certified, you only jump when the conditions are right. Rain, clouds, and high winds are all reasons why a jump might be cancelled. And the more experienced the skydiver is, the more attuned they will be to favorable (and unfavorable) conditions. And, last but not least, when you do jump, you never, ever, ever, ever let someone else pack your parachute. As you make your final preparations, you go back over every line, every shackle, every inch of the harness, and every square foot of the chute (and the emergency backup chute). You double-check the weather, you talk to the pilot, and you even inspect the plane that's going to take you up.

So, the successful entrepreneur is not someone who has a brilliant idea that the world immediately recognizes. It's someone who learns all the ins and outs of recognizing an opportunity and evaluates it to make sure it's real (and not just a fad). It's someone who knows how to build an organization that can develop a viable response to the opportunity in a manner that is financially and operationally sustainable. It's a person who can analyze the current climate to make sure that the conditions for building the venture are favorable (and likely to stay that way for a good bit). And it's a person with the stamina (and patience) to keep moving the venture forward. Finally, it is someone with the courage to start (so yes, you do eventually take that leap). But it's courage drawn from experience, practice, and planning.

Now, picture in your mind someone who wants to make the world a better place. Someone who wants to improve the human condition, to help the weak, to care for the suffering. What sort of person comes to mind? Probably someone with a deep well of compassion and a strong sense of empathy who is kind beyond measure and eternally optimistic. But do you see someone who can manage an organizational budget? Someone who can manage staff (including those dreaded performance reviews, and even terminating a poorly performing employee)? Who can manage payroll, and rent, and insurance, and the numerous interested parties that almost always poke their noses into your business (particularly if you're trying to produce social benefits alongside economic ones)?

The cold hard truth is that passion is not the most important thing in running any successful venture, no matter what the purpose. Now, don't get me wrong – passion is absolutely necessary; it's just that it's far from sufficient (a point we'll spend more time on shortly).

Describing what something (or someone) is not is a useful tool for understanding. But it only gets you part of the way to full understanding. So, let's spend some time defining a few terms more specifically.

BOX 2.1   THE PROBLEM IN DEFINING ENTREPRENEURSHIP WITH STEREOTYPES

The definitions associated with entrepreneurship are broad. Entrepreneurship is a professional role, but it's also a skill, a personality type, and a way of behaving (Casson, 2013) with an ability to stimulate economic growth and job creation, all while pushing forward social change and new innovations (Baumol, Litan, and Schramm, 2007). While the breadth of definitions for entrepreneurship help to cover the broad value of entrepreneurs in our world, there are some challenges with the associated stereotypes.

The notion of a "heroic" entrepreneur underpins many common understandings of entrepreneurship (Ahl, 2002; Ahl and Marlow, 2012; Bridge, 2017; Drakopoulou Dodd and Anderson, 2007; Hytti and Heinonen, 2013; Mitchell, 1996; Nicholson and Anderson, 2005). The heroic entrepreneur is an independent, high-achieving, aggressive, and dominant risk-taker (Ahl, 2002; Mitchell, 1996; Ogbor, 2000). Another problem with these assumptions is that the stereotypes align with masculine qualities (Gupta et al., 2009). This can make entrepreneurship seem to be a path for only the exceptional and those embodying more masculine actions and energy.

Entrepreneurial stereotypes can cause talented and passionate individuals to question whether they can even call themselves (or aspire to call themselves) entrepreneurs. Understanding entrepreneurship in a more inclusive, realistic way can make it seem more feasible and attainable – an especially important issue for social entrepreneurship, where diverse, representative, and grounded perspectives are critical to the success of a social change initiative.

WHAT IS AN ENTREPRENEUR?

The first term we need to talk about is "entrepreneur." We've talked about what an entrepreneur is not, but how, exactly, do you know one when you see them?

To go all the way back to the beginning, you might be interested to know that "entrepreneur" is a term that originated in the French language and is literally translated as "undertaker" (not like the undertaker we know, who buries the dead – but rather as the one who undertakes the initiative) (Long, 1983). The modern definition is more along the line of "a person who starts a business or venture" (Drucker, 1985). Various definitions consider such things as the potential growth of the firm, the level of innovation involved in the venture, and the personal characteristics of the individual. Some define an entrepreneur as "the one who takes the risk" (Carland et al., 2007) (a point that you can see I take a bit of issue with).

One of my favorite definitions of an entrepreneur comes from a man named Howard Stevenson, who teaches at Harvard. He describes an entrepreneur as someone who undertakes "the pursuit of opportunity without regard to resources currently controlled" (Stevenson, 1983). This notion of opportunity (and how you identify, analyze, and prioritize opportunities) is something we'll explore in much greater detail just a few chapters down the road. But for now, it is important to know that opportunity comes in many forms. In the commercial world, opportunity usually looks like a need that's not being met. In the social sector, it more often looks like a problem that hasn't been solved. So, let's break down those terms as well.

The classic definition of a need is the difference between one's current state and one's desired state (Bruner and Pomazal, 1988). At a basic level, you could be hungry and desire to be full. Or you could be homeless and desire to have a roof over your head. At higher levels, you could be driving a Ford and desire to be driving a Rolls-Royce. Recognizing that there is a gap between the current state and the desired state is the first step on the road to entrepreneurship.

The next step is developing a viable solution that fills the gap (and this is where the hard work comes in – an area we will explore in great detail). Depending on your own goals and objectives, as well as the specific population you're seeking to serve, the solution to the problem of hunger could be a hamburger, a fish, or lobster thermidor. Filling the need for a roof over your head could run the gamut from a tent to a 15-bedroom mansion. But regardless of how simple or complex the solution may be, it absolutely must be "viable" (capable of working successfully). Hamburgers may be a great solution for hunger, but if you don't know how to cook (or don't have a grill, or buns, or any of the other many things you need to make hamburgers) then the solution is not viable.

It's at this point that we start to clarify the difference between an entrepreneur and someone who builds or runs a business (and why I like Stevenson's definition so much). You can build a hamburger stand. You can make tents. And even if you have all the things you need, taking on the task is no easy feat. But it's not entrepreneurship.

Peter Drucker (one of the greatest business minds ever to walk the Earth, in my humble opinion), made this distinction quite clear. In Drucker's mind, the entrepreneur also needs to have an element of innovation (doing something new or different) (Drucker, 1985). In other words, an entrepreneur develops a solution to a specific problem or need but does so in a way that also provides a better solution than those that currently exist. In simpler terms, the person who provides the hamburger that is a solution for hunger becomes an entrepreneur when they change the experience in some way. One easy example is the drive-up window (which, although it may be hard to believe, has not existed since the dawn of time). While the hamburger itself did not change, the additional convenience of not having to get out of your car improved the overall process in a fundamental way.

BOX 2.2　PETER DRUCKER

Peter Drucker is one of the most influential management thought leaders of the 20th century. His works, which include 39 books translated into 36 languages, molded theory and practice internationally across sectors, including the business, government, and nonprofit worlds.

In helping to define entrepreneurship, Drucker's definition became a foundational aspect of how we view and define social entrepreneurship. Drucker framed entrepreneurs as change agents, noting that "the entrepreneur always searches for change, responds to it, and exploits it as an opportunity" (Drucker, 1985, p. 28). The sentiment of entrepreneurs being change agents is particularly important for social entrepreneurs who seek to change an unbalanced status quo into a newer, fairer equilibrium through focusing on a systems-level change. Drucker's works also emphasized the need for organizations to have a future-oriented mindset and to build a sense of community, both within the organization and within one's local area (Drucker, 1990). These examples reflect only a handful of Drucker's collective contributions to our modern perspectives of management that continue to distinctly shine through in our best practices of social entrepreneurship.

To continue your learning about Peter Drucker's works, review the Recommended Resources section at the end of this chapter.

So, an entrepreneur identifies a need or a problem, constructs and tests a better way to solve the problem or meet the need, and then goes about gathering the resources needed to build the enterprise that will deliver the solution efficiently, consistently, and sustainably. A relatively simple concept. But, in execution, one quite complex and fraught with pitfalls and problems (a reality that will become quite clear as we walk this path together).

BOX 2.3　CLARIFYING SUSTAINABILITY

The notion of sustainability can differ depending on how it is used. Generally, "sustainability" refers to maintaining a particular state, level, or rate. For example, the sustainability of an organization refers to an organization's financial projections and their ability to predict its continued operations for the foreseeable future.

The term becomes more confusing in the context of social entrepreneurship, where sustainability can also refer to an ability to maintain or grow natural resources in the efforts to stabilize an environment. While "organizational" and "environmental" sustainability have a lot in common – using available resources in a way that maintains or grows their ability to keep a healthy projected state – they refer to different types of resources. Approaches for environmental sustainability include efforts like replenishing crops and reducing carbon footprints. In contrast, the sustainability of an organization depends on resources like stable revenue, access to financial loans and grants, and dependable human capital. While both of these types of sustainability are important, this book will use "sustainability" to refer to organizational sustainability, unless otherwise noted.

When you realize that creating a new venture that solves a problem in a unique way is no easy trick, it often makes you wonder why anyone would even attempt such a thing. It would seem logical that one of the reasons that someone might pursue such an undertaking is that it could present an opportunity for significant profit. In fact, the chance to produce significant wealth is not one of the primary motivators for many entrepreneurs. More often, it is the desire to chart your own course in life and to be your own boss (Shane, Locke, and Collins, 2003). Sometimes (particularly in dire circumstances) it is done out of necessity or a lack of acceptable alternatives (Viswanathan et al., 2014). But the main motivator for entrepreneurs is the desire to make a genuine difference in the world (Carsrud and Brännback, 2011).

Hopefully, you recognize some portion of yourself in this basic description of what an entrepreneur looks like. And hopefully you're starting to see that there is a lot of hard work involved in building a sustainable enterprise. The good news is that the hard work is what reduces the risk and makes it manageable. So, let's spend some time talking about the tools that you can use to help manage the risk of the new venture.

Key Habits of an Entrepreneur

No matter what type of venture you are trying to build, there are a few key practices that set the successful entrepreneurs apart. Each of these practices will help you reduce the risk of the undertaking and increase your confidence that this is a risk worth taking. With apologies to Stephen Covey, I call these the "Eight Habits of Effective Entrepreneurs":

1. Build models
2. Test markets
3. Fail fast
4. Pivot
5. Remember that passion is not enough (the E-Myth)
6. Calculate the economics of one unit
7. Follow an ideation process
8. Develop strict criteria for measuring progress and continued viability (milestones and hurdles).

Let's spend some time talking about each of these habits, how they work, and why they are important.

Build Models

The first tool that comes into play is the one that you probably are using to do the homework for this class (or maybe even using to read this book). Yes, your trusty computer is a fantastic tool for use in building a venture. And of all the tools in the computer, the spreadsheet tool is the one that will become your new best friend, because it is where you will build and test a number of models to help validate the viability of your concept. You will need to build sales models, profit-and-loss models, operating models, and market estimates. Why? Because as dull and unattractive as they may sound, these are the fundamental building blocks of any business (regardless of its objective). But why are all of these models so important? Simply put, it's a lot easier (and cheaper) to see if a business idea works on paper than it is to spend all the time and money to set the thing up only to find that you can't make a profit.

One of my favorite analogies about building models is the aeronautics industry (we do seem to be spending a lot of time talking about airplanes, don't we?). A typical commercial airplane costs over $50 million to build and carries hundreds of people. I know that if I'm one of those people (or perhaps the one who signed the check to pay for the darned thing), I want to have a pretty good idea that it can actually do what it's supposed to do (which is take off, fly, and land again without incident). And when you realize that these things weigh upwards of 75 tons, that is no small trick! It may interest you to know that a large team of engineers spends years on the design of any new aircraft, and that much of the early testing is done in computer-simulated models (yes, you do eventually need to build an airplane, but that comes later).

So, if you are that motivated entrepreneur, which would you rather do? Spend a small amount of money and a good bit of time seeing if your business model works, or spend a lot more money only to see the thing crash on take-off? (An answer that I hope is pretty self-evident.)

Let's talk for a few minutes about some of the specific models you will need, and why they're so important. The first model that you will want to build is a market estimate.

Test Markets

There are a number of tools that can be used to develop a solid market estimate. But before we talk about how, let's spend some time talking about why this is so important, regardless of the type of enterprise. Then we'll talk about the unique need for this kind of analysis in social enterprise.

First, despite how wonderful your product or service might be, not everyone is going to need or want it. For example, you may make the best snow shovel the world has ever seen. But if I live on the Equator, the odds of me ever needing a snow shovel are pretty slim. You may make the best cheese omelet known to humankind, but if I'm lactose-intolerant (or just don't like cheese) I'm not going to be your customer. Second, despite how unique and different your enterprise might be, there are likely many other folks doing things that are quite similar (and if there are truly no other players in your market, then the truth is that there may also not be any customers there). So, not everyone is going to want what you have to offer, and some portion of those who do want what you have are going to get something similar from someone else.

Now, let's suppose that you do enough homework to find that exact person who wants or needs what you have to offer so badly that they can't accept any of the alternatives. That person still needs to be able to access your product or service in some practical manner. So, if I'm hundreds of miles away from you, or don't have the money or time needed to invest in acquiring what you are offering (or any one of a hundred other barriers), then it really doesn't matter how much I want or need what you have.

BOX 2.4   UNDERSTANDING BENEFICIARIES AND CUSTOMERS

When thinking about barriers to entry, it is important to consider one important factor that is unique to social entrepreneurship – your customers may not always be your beneficiaries.

Think about creating the best new pair of headphones. Most likely, when thinking about your customer segments, the ones benefiting from the use of the headphones are the ones buying the headphones, perhaps with the exception of employers buying for their employees or those buying the headphones as a gift. Even in those cases, the buyer is benefiting by having more productive employees or giving their child a birthday present.

When it comes to social entrepreneurship, the connections between customer and beneficiary are not as clear. For example, the purpose-driven business 4ocean sells merchandise that helps to pay for the clean-up of oceans, along with other avenues (for example, advocacy, research, education) that helps it reduce ocean pollution. In this instance, the customer is paying for a product that they receive, but there is an additional value that they are not directly able to see or benefit from (at least when thinking about their individual contribution and impact). The more direct beneficiaries of the social impact are the fishers and residents nearest to their clean-up sites.

Some might argue that the customer is benefiting from being able to wear or display a product that displays and represents a cause they care about, but what about cases where the customer is not a direct beneficiary?

Mothers2mothers (m2m) is an organization that aims to help the health outcomes within sub-Saharan Africa by employing women living with HIV to provide health services to millions of women and their children to reduce the mother-to-child transmission of HIV. They take in money from foundations, corporate partners, and individuals through grants, donations, and fundraising events (for example, bicycle races). The organizations and individuals buying into the mission of m2m are not the ones benefiting from the services they offer.

To create a sustainable idea for a social impact organization, social entrepreneurs need to consider who is helping them to remain financially sustainable, as well as who will be benefiting from the organization's efforts. A good starting point is to look at the status quo and to look closely at the present-day barriers to access for the served population or cause. To use the example of m2m, what are the present issues for expectant mothers in sub-Saharan Africa? Access to HIV testing? Access to maternal health care? Access to counseling and support? Access to medicine? Knowing the breadth of specific barriers that the target population is facing is a necessary starting point for any social entrepreneur wanting to have a meaningful and lasting impact.

From the customer perspective (in the case of m2m, its donors and partner organizations), social entrepreneurs need to think about how to demonstrate the value of their impact to their donors and partners; how to go about this process will be addressed later in the book.

One good way to think about market analysis is to view the market as a swimming pool. It seems obvious that figuring out how much water is in a pool is a smart thing to do before you dive in (although you'd be amazed at how many entrepreneurs don't take that step). But the total size of the pool is not the only information that's needed.

Each dimension of the pool is also important (length, depth, width, and so on). For example, if you find out that the pool is only 2 feet deep, then jumping off a diving board into the pool would not make a lot of sense. To continue with this analogy, you also need to know how many other people are swimming in that pool, and how they are behaving (just bobbing in the water, swimming laps, doing fancy dives, and so on). Armed with this information, you can then determine how much room might be left in the pool for you. And (without even doing much math) if that room is enough for you to be able to successfully and sustainably perform whatever maneuvers you may have in mind.

This issue is important enough that I want to ask you to bear with me for one more example. Imagine your dream is to open a pizza shop. Now, think about where that pizza shop needs to be located. A remote island in the Caribbean or the lower reaches of Antarctica are probably not good places to start. You probably want a busy corner in a relatively densely populated area. But if you look up and down the street when standing on that busy corner, chances are that you will find another pizza shop without having to look too hard. But you know that your pizzas are special in some way (maybe you specialize in extra anchovies). Now, to you, that unique specialization is just the ticket – but it may not be true for many others (like me, for example). So, if you have solid data that says that there is a cluster of anchovy-loving pizza-eaters close to this busy corner, then maybe you should take some additional steps towards developing your dream. But if you find out that the numbers are not sufficient (or, that there is not enough water in the pool), you need to move on (more about that in a minute).

Remember, we said that good ideas are a dime a dozen. And remember that we said that good ideas that work are far rarer. Well, this is the first time that the aspiring entrepreneur meets the cold hard reality of the market. And, no matter how much it may hurt you to walk away from your dream, I promise it hurts less than hitting your head on the bottom of the pool.

Finally, while this concept is important no matter what the purpose of the venture is, it is even more important if you are trying to make the world a better place in some way. The reason is that the level of care (and the consequences of failure) are much higher (Omorede, 2014).

There is no question that the commercial entrepreneur is passionate when talking about their venture. But when you fully understand the depths of human suffering, and then begin to care about those who suffer, your passion is joined by a level of compassion that is truly inspiring. So inspiring, in fact, that it can blind you to the practical realities of the viability of your solution. Said simply (and bringing my analogy full circle), you can easily develop a level of care and concern that is so strong that you go jumping off the diving board without considering if there is water in the pool. And that, my friends, is an outcome that can be painful at best, and truly tragic at worst. And that leads us to our next concept.

Fail Fast

We all want things to be just right. I'm sure you can think of many times where you've worked on a project and felt like it just wasn't ready for other people to see. None of us wants to be embarrassed, or look like we don't know what we're doing, so we often spend a lot of time refining our work before we show it to others. Unfortunately, for the entrepreneur, that tendency can cause you to waste valuable time, energy, and money. You see, feedback from the market (the people who will eventually use your product or service) is vitally important to the success of your venture (Cooper, 2011). If you've ever spent any time in the kitchen, you can quickly understand why this matters.

I love to cook. So does my wife. But the first time trying a new recipe is always an adventure. Why? Because you're not really sure how it's going to taste until you actually make the dish. Once you make it the first time, you make notes about small (or sometimes large) adjustments to the recipe to better suit your tastes and preferences. And sometimes you discard the recipe entirely (and then order carry-out for dinner!). The adventure of building a new venture is a lot like cooking. You need to test and try a number of different things to come up with the right combination. (The experts call this an iterative process.) So, if the process of building a new venture is somewhat experimental, you can quickly see that finding out that a particular "recipe" doesn't do what you need it to do is very valuable, and that the sooner you know that something doesn't work, the sooner you can move on to try other "recipes."

BOX 2.5   DEFINITION: ITERATION

Iteration is a process of repetition with attention to the resulting outcomes. Iteration is associated with the dynamic need of entrepreneurs to try things in the real world – to be able to test their ideas as quickly as possible to determine the best subsequent course of action. Iteration is the underlying concept in many of the field's prevalent and well-known approaches, like Lean Startup and Design Thinking.

This notion of "failing fast" comes from the technology industry, where experiments in specific technical solutions can be quite expensive. But it's vitally important to any entrepreneur, and particularly critical to the social venture as human lives are often at stake. To illustrate, consider that your social concern is hunger, and that you are trying to reduce hunger in a certain place. If your solution doesn't work, then more people go hungry (which can lead to all sorts of health and emotional problems, as well as death itself). So, rather than implementing a huge program that may not work, it makes a lot more sense to build and test some models and pilot programs, learn from what doesn't work, and then build a better model (and test that, and so on – using multiple iterations until you get the "recipe" that's just right).

BOX 2.6   THE NATURE OF SOCIAL CHANGE

Even if you fail in doing something ambitious, you usually succeed in doing something important. (Diamandis and Kotler, 2016, p. 139)

It can be daunting to even start tackling a social challenge at all. However, all efforts have the potential to, at least, "chip away" at the greater challenge at hand. This can be accomplished through raising awareness, inspiring others to push for change, or even by discovering what does not work in order to create something that does the next time around.

Pivot

Now, about that issue of moving on. Perhaps the most important thing to understand about entrepreneurship as an art and as a science is that we are trying to bring innovation to life.

We are trying to bring change into being. That's the goal. And it's the goal that's important, not the path. If you are convinced that there is only one acceptable path to reach a particular goal, you will eventually meet up with two problems. The first is that you will achieve far fewer goals than you had hoped. The second is that the goals you do achieve will be far less significant. Let's spend a few minutes breaking that down.

BOX 2.7　　GOAL ORIENTATION

Remaining centered on the desired impact is a critical component to being successful in delivering on a commitment. There is a reason why the status quo exists, and unfortunately it tends to prefer the most convenient option over the best one. To overcome this, social entrepreneurs need to be focused on what needs to be done to achieve their goal, as there will be many roadblocks within the present system and people who might not see the option to, opportunity for, or value of, change. Thankfully, persistent, goal-focused social entrepreneurs can find partners and resources in unexpected places, and the processes of iterating, failing fast, and remaining goal-centered provide the best opportunity for change.

BOX 2.8　　PIVOT

A pivot might best be initially contrasted with its closest opposite: fixed. A helpful definition of "fixed" as it relates to design and innovation is a "blind adherence to a set of ideas or concepts limiting the output of conceptual design" (Jansson and Smith, 1991, p. 3). In contrast, the act of pivoting – like in basketball – keeps one foot planted in place while the body turns to plant the other foot in a new direction. Eric Ries, in his book *The Lean Startup* (2011), explains that pivoting allows entrepreneurs to "keep one foot rooted in what we've learned so far, while making a fundamental change in strategy in order to seek greater validated learning" (p. 154). Pivoting is an important part of the entrepreneurial process, as it allows for course corrections, new hypothesis testing, and opportunity exploration as new information comes in.

While pivoting happens at a variety of levels, there is a need to balance the fixed with flexibility. Crilly (2018) notes that this balance is based on entrepreneurs' expertise, available information and resources, and orientations towards their ideas and the market. While pivoting enables entrepreneurs to move past any barriers they experience by exploring new directions, ideas, solutions, partners, and resources, the fixed foot of a pivot acknowledges the need for entrepreneurs – and in our case, social entrepreneurs – to always remain centered on and committed to their goal and grounded in their prior experiences and knowledge.

It's Saturday afternoon, and you've decided to go hang out with some friends at a local coffee shop. You get the address, and maybe even take a look at your phone to see how to get there. But five minutes after you leave, there is a major accident on the road you planned to take. What do you do? Easy – you find another route, go around the accident, and continue on towards your destination (and, if you're considerate, you text your friends to let them know you'll be a few minutes late). This little illustration should help you see that there is more than one path to a destination. And that knowledge is critical to success as an entrepreneur. In our world that change is known as a pivot. It's the realization that a specific path (or a specific market) may not prove viable, but that does not mean that the goal is not worth pursuing. It just means that you need to find another way. And that brings us to our next key point – passion.

Passion Is Not Enough (The E-Myth)

One of the things that you hear over and over when talking to folks about entrepreneurship is the concept of passion. You hear people say that you need to be passionate about your business, about your idea, about your customer, and so on. And that is true (although not in the literal sense, which could get you arrested!). The main reason that so many people speak about passion is because the hard work of building an enterprise can grind you down. So, if you don't believe to the depths of your being that what you're doing is right and good, you will likely give up at some point. Therefore, the strength of your commitment is vitally important. However, it is not enough.

In order to be successful in building a new venture, you need to be both wildly passionate and coldly analytical at the same time, and in equal amounts.

One of the best illustrations of how this works on a practical basis is Michael Gerber's *The E-Myth Revisited* (1995). In this great little book, Gerber outlines four key concepts that are the keys for building a venture:

1. Most people go into business because of a love for a particular craft that they already are skilled at, not because they see an opportunity from the outside.
2. A viable enterprise needs to be viewed as a system (or a series of processes) (some people call this the business model, a concept we will dive into later on).
3. The component parts of the system can be developed and improved upon in a continuous fashion.
4. The improvement of the component parts then leads to improvement in the ways that the parts interact, making the entire operation more effective.

While none of these key ideas sound particularly sexy or passionate, the successful venture that results is quite exciting.

Of these four concepts, the first one is the hardest to get past (and even harder if you are trying to create social change). To illustrate, Gerber uses the example of a baker. The baker loves to bake, and makes the most wonderful cakes, pies, and cookies. Everyone tells the baker that she should open her own bakeshop. She dreams of the day that she can be in control of her own business, when she can reap all the profits of her work (and not have to share them with the shop owner she works for). So, she scrimps and saves and goes deep into debt and eventually opens her own bakeshop. Fast-forward to the one-year anniversary of the bakeshop, and the baker is spending all her time on bookkeeping, advertising, and dealing with ovens that don't work and signs that don't light up, and she hasn't baked a cake or pie in over seven months. She's miserable. And the business is not doing well. Dejected, she sells the business and goes back to work as a baker. For a while, she suffers through the depression of being seen as a failure, but eventually the baker realizes that she's much happier (Gerber, 1995).

The moral of the story of the E-Myth is that love for your craft is not enough. You need to also have a love for the process of building a venture (and all of that messy technical stuff like accounting and banking and payroll and maintenance, and so on). And this is where the "passion" people and I part company, because (as Gerber illustrates many times over) passion without pragmatism will lead to disappointment.

In building a social venture, this issue becomes even more important, because now we're not talking about cupcakes but about human lives. Let's take homelessness as an example. It breaks my heart to see someone sleeping on the street. And, because it breaks my heart, I become passionate about finding a way to serve the needs of the homeless. So, I decide to open a homeless shelter. Maybe I even develop a program that helps people get back on their feet so that they are less likely to become homeless in the future. But now I need to find money to pay for staff (and the rent and maintenance on the building). And I need to buy beds and hire a linen service to wash and clean the bedsheets, and so on. All of which requires money. So, I have to raise funds from individual donors, and apply for various grants, and account for all of the money that comes in, and file tax returns and payroll reports. So, just like the baker, I find myself spending my time as an administrator, not working with my clients to help them get better. And then one of the major funding sources dries up (which happens far more often than we wish) and I need to close the shelter. Now, all of my clients are back on the street, and the impact we may have had goes to waste. All of which could have been avoided if we spent more time designing the organization and testing the operating models earlier.

So, regardless of the type of venture, passion is not enough, the E-Myth is just that (a myth), and planning and execution matter. Now, let's talk more about what may be the most important part of planning and managing an enterprise.

Economics of One Unit

One of the great minds in entrepreneurship is a man named Steve Mariotti, who founded something called the Network for Teaching Entrepreneurship (NFTE). Among the many things that Mariotti and NFTE brought to the table was something that they call the "economics of one unit" (Mariotti, 2012). The idea is that you understand the basics of your venture at a core financial level before you go out and try to make your idea work. The way that you do that is by breaking the operation down to a single unit of service, determining exactly what goes into that single unit of service, and knowing what each of those elements costs.

BOX 2.9   STEVE MARIOTTI, FOUNDER OF THE NETWORK FOR TEACHING ENTREPRENEURSHIP

Steve Mariotti began his career in the corporate sector at the Ford Motor Company, followed by him starting his own import–export company. In 1982, he decided to change careers to work as a special education teacher in New York City. Years into his teaching career, Mariotti was inspired to found the nonprofit organization NFTE in 1987.

With offices across the U.S., NFTE works to build an entrepreneurial mindset in youth with both in-person and virtual experiences for students and teachers. NFTE reports a strong emphasis on reaching students from minority groups who might otherwise be underserved with entrepreneurship and business education opportunities.

For more information on NFTE and its current resources and programs, visit its website at www.nfte.com.

To understand this better, let's go back to our pizza shop example from earlier in this chapter. You may decide that your single unit of service is one slice of pizza, but I'm going to use one pie. And, to keep things simple, we'll use a plain cheese pizza.

BOX 2.10   NOTE: THE ECONOMICS OF ONE UNIT

The actual single unit you choose should be based on what your customer typically buys. So, if the majority of your market buys single slices, then you need to understand this at the single-slice level.

To make our pizza, we need dough, sauce, cheese, and some spices. We probably also need a box so the customer can carry the pie, and someone to make the pizza (the accounting folks call these variable costs, but for now we'll just stick to the one unit). So, let's add all this up.

Table 2.1   Economics of one unit

Item	Cost per unit ($)
Dough	0.15
Sauce	0.10
Cheese	0.08
Spice	0.01
Box	0.10
Labor	1.25
Total cost per unit	1.69

Now, let's say that we can sell that pizza for $9. That means we made a gross profit of $7.31 per pizza – not bad! But before you go off and spend that $7, you need to remember that you still have to pay your fixed costs, and taxes, and maybe a few cents for your own pocket. So, let's say that your fixed costs are $700 per week. Some basic math will tell you that you need to sell 100 pizzas per week to pay your fixed expenses (700/7=100). So, we now have something called a break-even point, which pertains to the point at which an organization's revenue can cover its fixed and variable costs. In this example, there are other expenses in running a pizza shop, like the fixed costs of rent, utilities, and equipment (for example, an oven). These will be addressed in a later chapter.

Knowing your break-even point is a key tool for managing any enterprise. But the financial control that it provides is just one of its useful features. Combining the break-even point with the market information you gained in habit #2 will give you another important piece of data. Here's how that works.

Remember in our discussion of habit #2 that we talked about making sure there is enough water in the pool (or enough people in the immediate area that want your unique brand of pizza)? Well, the break-even point gives you the way to measure exactly how much water you need in your particular pool. Using our current example, we know that we need to sell 100 pizzas a week to break even – probably more like 125 if we want to keep some money for ourselves. That means 500 pizzas per month, or 6,000 pizzas per year.

Despite what you may think, not everyone likes pizza. And we've already discussed the idea that not every pizza buyer will like your unique brand of pizza. So, let's say that 5 percent of the population in your market area would consider buying your pizzas. We also know that not everyone is going to buy a pizza every day. Let's say that the average person buys two pizzas per month. That means you need at least 5,000 qualified pizza buyers in your immediate area (and, since most of us tend to make overly optimistic projections, probably more like 6,500). So, if the town we want to open our pizza shop in has 10,000 people in it (which includes children and other non-qualified buyers), we're going to have a hard time keeping this business afloat. Or (to go back to our original analogy), there probably isn't enough water in the pool to make this a safe and successful dive.

So, we can simply give up (an option that is not attractive to most entrepreneurs), or we can move on to another version of our idea. Which opens the door to a discussion of habit #7.

Ideation

Somewhere along the way, you've probably heard about the notion of brainstorming. You may have even heard some of the rules for successful brainstorming (no bad ideas, build on each other, think crazy thoughts, and so on). One of the very best books I've ever seen on creative thinking is called *Thinkertoys* by Michael Michalko (2010). But what we're talking about here is something a bit more purposeful. Many people know "habit" as "ideation." (There are some similar concepts in a field known as Design Thinking, but for now we'll stick with this one.) The concept of ideation is similar to brainstorming, although it's a bit more sophisticated. But before we get into the *how* of ideation, let's make sure we know the *why*.

BOX 2.11   IDEATION

Ideation, or the process of coming up with and reflecting on the potential of ideas, is an important part of the entrepreneurial process. One of the most common challenges within the ideation process is to allow for quantity over quality, meaning that the viability, feasibility, and projected sustainability of an idea should not exclude it from further consideration. This openness to entertaining all possibilities is meant to foster big and innovative ideas, rather than settling for already-existing or overly safe and simplistic solutions.

One of the things that I've seen happen dozens of times is that as soon as someone gets an idea, they immediately dive into the process of figuring out how it would work. But the reality is that many ideas don't work, which leads us back to square one (coming up with a new idea) or even square none (giving up). Wouldn't it be better to have Plan B (and C, D, E, and F) already in hand? Well, that's (part of) what ideation is all about. But it's not just useful in developing ideas for a new venture. It's also very useful as a problem-solving tool as you move along the path to building the enterprise. Remember our conversation about multiple paths to the same destination? Just like the main idea, the tools of a sound ideation process can help you get unstuck when you hit a roadblock.

Here's how it works (with thanks to the Board of Innovation – www.boardofinnovation.com):

1. There are no bad ideas.
    One of the biggest pitfalls in developing ideas is our own inner critic. As soon as an idea pops into our heads, we immediately begin to judge it, and often discard it. We do this for a lot of reasons (low self-confidence, fear of being judged by others, and so on). But the problem is that this immediate judgment also stifles our creative juices and suppresses our ability to think more broadly. There will be plenty of time for evaluating ideas later, but this first stage of idea development is not the time. It might be helpful to think of each idea as one piece of a larger puzzle that you're trying to assemble. And sometimes, it is worth purposely trying to come up with the craziest idea possible, just to see how far you can stretch your brain!

2. Capture everything.
    Every idea, every thought, no matter how big or how small, needs to be recorded in some way. Flip charts, sticky notes, and white boards are all great ways to capture ideas. Another tip here is to not worry too much about a formalized note system while you're trying to develop ideas. You can organize your notes once the session is over, so just be sure that all the great ideas are written down somewhere.

3. Build off each others' ideas.
    Some people refer to this as "hybrid brainstorming." I've also seen this technique described as "Yes and." Simply put, you should allow the ideas of others to serve as a springboard to develop another idea. It's also important here to note that you should not discard the earlier idea (it may turn out that the hybrid idea has some problem that needs to be worked out, and the simpler idea is more feasible – but you can decide that later!).

4. More ideas are better than better ideas
    Another way to think of this is that quantity is more important than quality (and it also echoes the first notion that there are no bad ideas). The goal here is to develop as many ideas as possible. You might even try to set a goal for yourself or your team (no less than 40 ideas, for example). And, once you're done, be sure to congratulate yourselves.

Now, about evaluating those ideas.

Milestones and Hurdles

Last, but far from least, is the concept of milestones and hurdles. If you've been paying attention in this chapter (and I know you have), you have probably begun to realize that the smart entrepreneur does a lot of evaluating before deciding to launch a new venture. You may have also realized that there are certain points in the evaluation process where the wise entrepreneur takes a step back and either rethinks the concept for the enterprise or moves on to another idea. This ability to stop and evaluate before moving forward can prevent a lot of problems from occurring (up to and including losing everything you have in staying with a bad idea for too long).

The wise entrepreneur establishes specific checkpoints along the path to launching and growing a new venture, so that these periodic evaluations are not just random events but planned "pit stops" along the road. And it's from the road that we borrow the concept of milestones.

You may not have ever noticed it, but most major highways have small markers along the side of the road at set intervals (usually every mile or kilometer). These markers help travelers know how far they've gone (or at least they did before we all had GPS in our phones!). They also help emergency personnel to locate the site of a crash or a disabled motorist. Originally, these markers were actual stones placed alongside the road, and despite the many changes in technology, the name has stuck. So, to an entrepreneur, a milestone is a pre-planned time when the fledgling enterprise is evaluated, and a decision to proceed or alter course is made – often referred to as a go/no-go decision.

BOX 2.12   GO/NO-GO DECISIONS

While it is a simple idea, a go/no-go decision helps individuals determine the best course of action at a point in time, with a firm determination of whether to proceed or discontinue with a present activity, plan, or strategy. Go/no-go decisions can help entrepreneurs to decide whether the planned actions and projects are the best use of resources and time with everything considered at a particular moment.

So, what about this "hurdle" concept? Most of you have seen someone competing in a hurdle event in a track and field competition. The hurdle is the thing that the runner jumps over along the way. Taken more broadly, a hurdle is any sort of barrier that needs to be cleared in order to proceed. In entrepreneurship, these hurdles are specific criteria that the venture must satisfy. In the concept-development stage, some of the items we've discussed in this chapter would qualify as hurdles (things like minimum market size and ability to achieve or exceed a break-even point would definitely count). As the venture grows, there might be more sophisticated hurdles, such as a targeted number of customers, a minimum level or amount of gross sales or net profit, and so on.

Source: iStock.com/Robin Skjoldborg.
Used with permission

The point here is that milestones and hurdles should be set out ahead of time, and that the venture should be regularly and methodically evaluated to make sure that it is performing as desired.

WHY THIS MATTERS

No matter what objective you are trying to achieve, a well-formed plan will certainly get you there sooner. The steps outlined here give you a path to pursue a process of enlightened trial and error, which has been proven as the best pathway to entrepreneurial success (Cooper, 2011; Kawasaki, 2015; Kickul and Lyons, 2012). More importantly, these steps are likely to reduce your chances of failure (or maybe even allow you to scrap an unworkable idea before you end up betting the ranch on it). But when you're trying to build a social enterprise and produce value in economic, civic, and social terms, these steps are even more important. There are two reasons why – one practical and one humane.

On a practical level, the social enterprise is a complex entity with many moving parts, and may often need to shift form, format, and organizational structure over time (Battilana and Lee, 2014). There are at least 11 different strategic factors that the fledgling social enterprise must grapple with as it begins to develop its strategic plan (Moizer and Tracey, 2010), resulting in over 120 different possible strategic paths that you might take. So, testing the concepts that seem best before launching the enterprise seems like it would probably save you a lot of headaches and time (or you could just guess – good luck with that!).

The second reason is that the social enterprise hopes to have a positive impact on people's lives. In so doing, we must remember the rule that all helping professions apply, which is that above all else we should seek to do no harm. In far too many cases, well-meaning people bring programs into a community that don't work or don't last, leaving the community worse off than it was before the program arrived (Lupton, 2011). To be blunt, that particular outcome should be criminal. At the very least, it should be openly recognized as bad practice.

These two points (as well as a few others) are the main focus of our next chapter.

BOX 2.13 A VALUABLE LENS FROM HELPING PROFESSIONS

The realm of social entrepreneurship requires a significant level of responsibility to others. Likewise, the practice of medicine is underpinned by the Hippocratic Oath, originally drafted by ancient Greek physician Hippocrates and modernized in the 20th century for medical practice. The Oath acknowledges the responsibility medical professionals have in serving their patients and those in need, and notes the skills and knowledge they have and the sensitive positions they encounter. The Oath centers around the premise that medical professionals must act in the interest of the patient's health and wellness, regardless of obstacles. While commonly associated with the Hippocratic Oath, the quote "first, do no harm" from Hippocrates's *Of the Epidemics* drives home the orientation that those who are helpers have a responsibility, first and foremost, to avoid doing harm to others.

In the areas of counseling and therapy, aspiring helpers are taught to go beyond the Golden Rule of "treat the client as you would like to be treated" and towards the Platinum Rule of "treat clients the way they want to be treated" (Ivey, Ivey, and Zalaquett, 2018, p. 29). The Platinum Rule helps them to respect another person's culture, orientations, and experiences, rather than those of the helper. Especially when helpers are coming from cultures or experiences outside of those of whom they aim to serve, orienting around the Golden Rule might result in a microaggression (Nagayama Hall, 2017). While many microaggressions are not intended to be hurtful or to cause harm, the Platinum Rule helps to orient the helper into the mindset of their client or patient.

These approaches from the healthcare area are great orientations for all helpers, including social entrepreneurs, so do no harm and be sure to treat others in the manner that they want to be treated.

CHAPTER SUMMARY

Chapter 2 defined the term "entrepreneur" and framed entrepreneurship as an ability to recognize a need and to pursue the opportunity to craft a viable and innovative solution to move from the current state to a better, more desirable one. This acknowledges the role of opportunity, need, viability, and innovation within entrepreneurship. In order to accomplish their aims, entrepreneurs need to remain goal-oriented and practice the Eight Habits of Effective Entrepreneurs: (1) build models, (2) test markets, (3) fail fast, (4) pivot, (5) passion is not enough (the E-Myth), (6) economics of one unit, (7) ideation, and (8) milestones and hurdles. The habits help to highlight the distinct roles of customers and beneficiaries and the importance of sustainability in being able to maintain and scale impact. The habits also emphasize the best practices for ideation throughout the entrepreneurial process, outlining that it is important to build a large base of all possible ideas through capturing everything, welcoming all ideas, and building off of them. Especially because social entrepreneurship entails tending to many moving parts, these reputable best practices and helpful orientations form the key habits for effective entrepreneurs, serving as the foundation within their entrepreneurial process.

QUESTIONS FOR DISCUSSION

1. In order to develop your ability to separate real entrepreneurial practice and guidance from unhelpful stereotypes, review a video, article, or podcast featuring a successful entrepreneur or social entrepreneur. Take notes on their attitudes and orientations towards entrepreneurship, as well as their advice for aspiring entrepreneurs (for example, best practices, guidance, lessons learned), and answer the following questions:

    • What aligns with the basics of entrepreneurship highlighted within the chapter? What was different from what you read within the chapter?
    • Did anything within your review reinforce some entrepreneurial stereotypes?
    • What were your overall impressions of the resource that you reviewed?
    • Based on the chapter content, would you recommend the resource to a friend or aspiring entrepreneur? Why, or why not?

2. The ideation process can feel unnatural for many, as oftentimes brainstorming sessions are not as open to wild ideas as they should be. Within a group or independently, try the ideation process to generate ideas for tackling one of the following challenges within your community (or choose your own):

    • Housing insecurity
    • Unemployment of veterans
    • Recidivism rates
    • Environmental pollution
    • Hunger and poor nutrition.

3. After generating a long list of wild and not-so-wild ideas from Question #2, select a few of your favorite ideas from the list. For each selected idea, reflect upon and answer the following questions:

    - Does this idea recognize an opportunity to tackle the selected challenge?
    - Does this idea serve the needs of those who are the most impacted by the selected challenge?
    - Does this idea present a viable solution to approach the selected challenge? If not, what might be adjusted within the idea to make this a more viable solution?
    - Does this idea seem like it would provide a sustainable solution for the selected challenge? If not, how might it be adjusted to be a solution that allows you to better create and scale impact?
    - Does this idea already exist? If so, how successful does this idea seem? Is this possible solution currently in place within your community? If so, how might the idea be adjusted to produce better or more scalable impact? If not, would this idea potentially work within your community, and what might need to be changed to make it fit better?

4. Once you have answered these questions for each of your favorite ideas, select the one or two ideas that seemed to yield the most promising responses. Evaluate the idea further through responding to the following questions:

    - Based on your work within Question #3, what were this idea's weakest points? How might you resolve those points?
    - How does this idea compare to existing solutions for the same challenge? Could this idea be embedded within other existing efforts? How might your idea support, improve, or scale some of the existing efforts?
    - After responding to all of these questions, what are your lasting impressions? Do you think the idea is worth pursuing? Why, or why not?

RECOMMENDED RESOURCES

Cooper, R. G. (2017). *Winning at New Products: Creating Value Through Innovation*. New York, NY: Basic Books. For a reputable guide to building a process of milestones and hurdles that has lasted the test of time, *Winning at New Products* by Robert G. Cooper serves as great start. Originally published in 1986, the book introduces the new product "idea-to-launch" innovation method and model, "Stage-Gate," which has been updated over the decades to reflect the new best practices and knowledge of the area and to reflect the modern, global society that we find ourselves in presently.

Covey, S. (1989). *The 7 Habits of Highly Effective People*. New York, NY: Free Press.

Drucker, P. F. (1985). *Innovation and Entrepreneurship: Practice and Principles*. New York, NY: Harper & Row.

Drucker, P. F. (1990). *Managing the Non-Profit Organization*. New York, NY: HarperCollins.

Michalko, M. (2010). *Thinkertoys: A Handbook of Creative-Thinking Techniques*. Berkeley, CA: Ten Speed Press.

REFERENCES

Ahl, H., and Marlow, S. (2012). Exploring the dynamics of gender, feminism and entrepreneurship: Advancing debate to escape a dead end? *Organization, 19*(5), 543–562.

Ahl, H. J. (2002). *The Making of the Female Entrepreneur*. PhD monograph, Jönköping University.

Battilana, J., and Lee, M. (2014). Advancing research on hybrid organizing: Insights from the study of social enterprises. *Academy of Management Annals, 8*(1), 397–441.

Baumol, W. J., Litan, R. E., and Schramm, C. (2007), *Good Capitalism, Bad Capitalism, and the Economics of Growth and Prosperity*. New Haven, CT: Yale University Press.

Bridge, S. (2017). *The Search for Entrepreneurship: Finding More Questions than Answers*. Abingdon: Routledge.

Bruner, G. C., and Pomazal, R. J. (1988). Problem recognition: The crucial first stage of the consumer decision process. *Journal of Services Marketing, 2*(3), 43–53.

Carland, J. W., Hoy, F., Boulton, W. R., and Carland, J. A. C. (2007). Differentiating entrepreneurs from small business owners: A conceptualization. In Á. Cuervo, D. Ribeiro, and S. Roig (eds), *Entrepreneurship: Concepts, Theory and Perspective* (pp. 73–81). Berlin: Springer.

Carsrud, A., and Brännback, M. (2011). Entrepreneurial motivations: What do we still need to know? *Journal of Small Business Management, 49*(1), 9–26.

Casson, M. (2013). *The Entrepreneur in History: From Medieval Merchant to Modern Business Leader*. Basingstoke: Palgrave Macmillan.

Cooper, R. G. (2011). *Winning at New Products: Creating Value through Innovation*. New York, NY: Basic Books.

Crilly, N. (2018). "Fixation" and "the pivot": Balancing persistence with flexibility in design and entrepreneurship. *International Journal of Design Creativity and Innovation, 6*(1–2), 52–65.

Diamandis, P. H., and Kotler, S. (2016). *Bold: How to Go Big, Create Wealth and Impact the World*. New York, NY: Simon & Schuster.

Drakopoulou Dodd, S., and Anderson, A. R. (2007). Mumpsimus and the mything of the individualistic entrepreneur. *International Small Business Journal, 25*(4), 341–360.

Drucker, P. F. (1985). *Innovation and Entrepreneurship: Practice and Principles*. New York, NY: Harper & Row.

Drucker, P. F. (1990). *Managing the Non-Profit Organization*. New York, NY: HarperCollins.

Field of Dreams (1989). Film. Dir: Phil Alden Robinson. Gordon Company/Universal Pictures.

Gerber, M. E. (1995). *The E-Myth: Why Most Businesses Don't Work and What to Do About It*. New York, NY: Harper Business.

Gupta, V. K., Turban, D. B., Wasti, S. A. and Sikdar, A., (2009). The role of gender stereotypes in perceptions of entrepreneurs and intentions to become an entrepreneur. *Entrepreneurship Theory and Practice, 33*(2), 397–417.

Hytti, U., and Heinonen, J. (2013). Heroic and humane entrepreneurs: Identity work in entrepreneurship education. *Education + Training, 55*(8/9), 886–898.

Ivey, A. E., Ivey, M. B., and Zalaquett, C. P. (2018). *Intentional Interviewing and Counseling: Facilitating Client Development in a Multicultural Society*. Boston, MA: Cengage Learning.

Jansson, D. G., and Smith, S. M. (1991). Design fixation. *Design Studies*, 12, 3–11.

Kawasaki, G. (2015). *The Art of the Start 2.0: The Time-Tested, Battle-Hardened Guide for Anyone Starting Anything*. New York, NY: Portfolio/Penguin.

Kickul, J. R., and Lyons, T. S. (2012). *Understanding Social Entrepreneurship: The Relentless Pursuit of Mission in an Ever Changing World*. New York, NY: Routledge.

Long, W. (1983). The meaning of entrepreneurship. *American Journal of Small Business, 8*(2), 47–59.

Lupton, R. D. (2011). *Toxic Charity: How Churches and Charities Hurt Those They Help*. New York, NY: HarperCollins.

Mariotti, S. (2012). *Entrepreneurship: Starting and Operating a Small Business + MyBizSkillsKit & Business Plan Pro*. Hoboken, NJ: Prentice Hall.

Mitchell, R. K. (1996). Oral history and expert scripts: Demystifying the entrepreneurial experience. *Journal of Management History, 2*(3), 50–67.

Moizer, J., and Tracey, P. (2010). Strategy making in social enterprise: The role of resource allocation and its effects on organizational sustainability. *Systems Research and Behavioral Science, 27*(3), 252–266.

Nagayama Hall, G. C. (2017, February 7). The Platinum Rule: Treat others the way they wish to be treated. *Psychology Today.* Retrieved from www.psychologytoday.com/us/blog/life-in-the-intersection/201702/the-platinum-rule.

Nicholson, L., and Anderson, A. R. (2005). News and nuances of the entrepreneurial myth and metaphor: Linguistic games in entrepreneurial sense-making and sense-giving. *Entrepreneurship Theory and Practice,* 29(2), 153–172.

Ogbor, J. (2000). Mythicizing and reification in entrepreneurial discourse: Ideology-critique of entrepreneurial studies. *Journal of Management Studies,* 37(5), 605–635.

Omorede, A. (2014). Exploration of motivational drivers towards social entrepreneurship. *Social Enterprise Journal,* 10(3), 239–267.

Ries, E. (2011). *The Lean Startup: How Constant Innovation Creates Radically Successful Businesses.* New York, NY: Penguin.

Shane, S., Locke, E. A., and Collins, C. J. (2003). Entrepreneurial motivation. *Human Resource Management Review,* 13(2), 257–279.

Stevenson, H. H. (1983). *A Perspective on Entrepreneurship,* Vol. 13. Cambridge, MA: Harvard Business School.

Viswanathan, M., Echambadi, R., Venugopal, S., and Sridharan, S. (2014). Subsistence entrepreneurship, value creation, and community exchange systems: A social capital explanation. *Journal of Macromarketing,* 34(2), 213–226.

Wizard of Oz, The (1939). Film. Dir: Victor Fleming. Metro-Goldwyn-Meyer/Loew's.

3
Social entrepreneurship is messy

Learning objectives

After studying this chapter, you should be able to:

1. Appreciate the unique and complex nature of social entrepreneurship compared to commercial forms of entrepreneurship.
2. Understand the aim of social entrepreneurship as a producer of a new equilibrium.
3. Explain the value of social entrepreneurship ecosystems.
4. Contrast the notions of stakeholders and shareholders, outcomes and outputs, and identify and apply them to real-life social enterprises.
5. Recognize that, despite all of those operating in the nonprofit sector doing good in our communities and the world, there are some who may feel incentivized to maintain the same social problems they claim to want to eradicate in order to stay employed and relevant.

YES, AND BOTH, AND MORE

In this chapter, we're going to talk about ways that a social enterprise is unique. Yes, it is a business, so there must be some sort of product or service that is being produced and sold at a profit. And, just like the nonprofit or non-governmental organization (NGO) that we know and love, it needs to be working to solve a social problem. So, it's both a business and a charity, at the same time. But, as you will see, it's also more than that. A strong social enterprise is something unique.

One term that's becoming increasingly popular as a way of describing this unique combination is "hybrid organizations," because these firms combine various structures and strategies into a new and different endeavor (Battilana and Lee, 2014; Eldar, 2017). While that's a great

abstract definition, it doesn't really describe how it feels when you're actually working to build a social venture.

One of the ways that I explain this idea in less academic terms is by saying that social enterprise is messy. What I mean by that is not that it's physically messy like an unmade bed (although it can feel that way at times). Rather, it's messy because it's

Source: iStock.com/Motortion. Used with permission

more complicated. The very act of building a social enterprise contains levels of complexity that are not part of the equation when you are building a commercial venture. As if that's not enough, several of these areas of complexity contradict each other, so the aspiring social entrepreneur faces trade-offs that require some tough decisions, and scenarios that require levels of empathy that the commercial entrepreneur does not have to face.

In the next few pages, we're going to walk through several specific areas where these distinctions are evident. By the end of this discussion, I hope that you'll be able to see the "hybridity" for yourself. I hope that you'll have a better handle on the "messiness" of the process. Most importantly, I hope that by understanding these challenges up front, you'll be better prepared to face them when they come.

BOX 3.1   HYBRID ORGANIZATIONS

Hybrid organizations span the middle ground in the spectrum between traditional charitable organizations and grant-dependent nonprofits on one side, and businesses without a social mission on the other. Hybrid organizations hold qualities associated with the nonprofit and business sectors, having a shared orientation towards positive social impact while aiming to achieve financial sustainability.

PEOPLE, NOT PROFITS

A few years back, I was working with a good-sized local nonprofit to help it develop a social enterprise. It had an interesting idea, had done some initial investigation into the market opportunity, and had invited me to help figure out the details. We did some good work together, built a few models, did some testing, and were starting to think about how we might fund the startup.

During a planning meeting, I happily reported that my assessment was that this project had the potential to pay for itself over time. Expecting some approving nods, I was instead met with complete silence. Not knowing what to do, I sat there in silence as well. After a few awkward moments, one of the board members looked at me and asked, "But what about the million dollars?" Dumbfounded, I said, "What million dollars?"

After a good bit of discussion, it turned out that these folks had discovered a similar program in another part of the country that was producing over a million dollars in profit, which this other organization was using to offset some underfunded areas of other programs. It also turned out that the lead fundraiser in the organization I was working with was more than a little burned out and saw this shift into social enterprise as her relief valve. So, these good and well-meaning folks were assuming that a similar effort in a different market would produce similar results and had (mentally and emotionally) already spent the million.

With all the diplomatic skill I could muster, I quietly and calmly stated that "the revenue goal of a social enterprise should be to break even, not to return large profits to a parent organization." Well, that created the second uncomfortable round of silence. Not being one to shy away from a challenge, I explained that a good social enterprise expands a social mission in a manner that is financially self-supporting. Rather than being thought of as a means to earn income, social enterprise needs to be thought of as a tool that can help people, while freeing the folks doing the helping from many of the burdens of traditional fundraising that are tolerated in the nonprofit world.

BOX 3.2   UNDERSTANDING THE FUNDING OF SOCIAL ENTREPRENEURSHIP

According to the Global Entrepreneurship Monitor (GEM) Special Report on Social Entrepreneurship (Bosma et al., 2016), the most frequent source of funding among social entrepreneurs is themselves, ranging globally from its highest representation at 82 percent of social entrepreneurs in sub-Saharan Africa to 64 percent of those within Western Europe. Within the total of all funding, the proportion of the social entrepreneurs' own funds also ranges between its highest representation within South-East Asia (63 percent) and the Middle East and North Africa (62 percent) to the lowest in sub-Saharan Africa (29 percent).

Beyond the social entrepreneurs' own funds, the GEM Special Report notes that the next most utilized funds that social entrepreneurs use globally are from governmental sources (approximately 38 percent of social ventures), as well as banks and family (both representing 24 percent of social ventures). While these are global figures, the representation of different stakeholder funding is greater in certain areas of the world. For example, friends and neighbors play an especially critical role within South-East Asia (47 percent) and sub-Saharan Africa (39 percent), and employers and work colleagues play a proportionally stronger role in Australia and the U.S. (30 percent) and South-East Asia (28 percent).

In a survey of 624 social entrepreneurs and ecosystem builders across 41 American cities, the *Social Enterprise Ecosystems Report, Volume 3* (Halcyon, n.d.) reports that social enterprises are securing their funding through the following means: grants (27 percent); self-financing, friends, and family (19 percent); loans and debt (18 percent); angel investors (11 percent); and venture capital (7 percent). The Report also highlighted the persisting challenges of funding for social impact organizations:

- "Organizations headed by a white person raised almost three times the amount of capital as organizations headed by someone who is Black/African American or Latinx" (p. 17).
- "Among organizations with five or more staff members, organizations headed by men raised over 50 percent more capital than organizations headed by women" (p. 17).

These two reports help to contextualize the commonalities and differences of social venture funding globally and between different demographic groups, highlighting the persisting challenges and areas for growth within financing in the social sector.

Well, we kicked that around the room for a few minutes until one of the board members spoke up and said, "This is a fundamental change in strategy. Can you excuse us while we meet privately to discuss this?" I thanked them for their time, gathered my things, and took my leave. Funny, but I was never invited back.

I tell this story to illustrate one of the most fundamental misunderstandings about social enterprise – namely, that it's about people, not profits. Yes, earned income is a good thing – no, actually, it's a great thing because it frees you from the constraints of the grant-making process and allows you to run your program in the way that you know is best for your folks. But it is a means to an end, not the end itself.

The end can (and must) be that money is a means to develop the human capacity for independence and self-determination. So, while profit does have its purpose, that purpose (at least for us) is subjugated to the higher concern of the social problem we seek to address (Emerson, 2018). But the choices that must be made in order to run an effective enterprise while putting profit second can be quite daunting.

Source: iStock.com/IPGGutenbergUKLtd.
Used with permission

BOX 3.3   VALUE CREATION AND VALUE CAPTURE

The idea of value creation is intuitive: doing or producing something that generates a perceived usefulness or attractiveness greater than the current state. This means that there must be a perceived uniqueness to the product or service, or a unique value proposition (UVP), that gives its creators a competitive advantage.

Value capture focuses on something related but distinctly different. An organization can create ample value within a community without being valuable itself. Value capture helps to emphasize the need for organizations to capture some of the value they are creating in order to be sustainable, a notion popularized by tech entrepreneur and venture capitalist, Peter Thiel.

For social entrepreneurs, focusing on both value creation and value capture is critical. Value creation helps to assess the usefulness and problem-solving capacity of an idea. However, an idea cannot generate sustainable impact without also concentrating on value capture.

PEOPLE, NOT PRODUCTS

Understanding that a social enterprise exists to serve people and not maximize profits leads us to another aspect of the care of our fellow human, namely that people are far from perfect, often difficult to control, and have feelings, opinions, and thoughts of their own. On the other hand, products (the primary focus of a profit-seeking venture) can usually be managed and controlled quite easily.

Consider a simple pottery business, perhaps one that makes coffee cups. Clay is molded into cups that are then fired in a kiln, decorated in some fashion, glazed, fired again, and then finished and prepared for sale. While molding clay can be a bit tricky, you usually don't have to convince the clay to be molded. Nor does the clay express concern over the temperature in the kiln or show dismay at the color of the glaze.

Now take a minute to consider a restaurant that offers job training for citizens returning from incarceration (a great and quite common type of social enterprise). First and foremost, you've got to run a restaurant (which is no small trick in itself). And you've got to do it in a way that produces good food at a fair price, while allowing for the additional expenses needed to train folks. Then add to that the myriad issues that come along with returning from incarceration (Visher and Travis, 2011), each of which can impact the trainee's ability to complete the training. Last but not least, fold in the general issues of the human condition (temperament, world views, personal values, and the like), and you can quickly see that it's a lot "messier" to work to help folks than it is to just make coffee cups.

COMMUNITY, NOT COMMODITY

By definition, social innovation is a community-based process (after all, the word "social" has the same root as the word "society," both derived from the Latin "*sociālis*," which means "partner" or "comrade"). So, when we seek to bring about social change, we need to do it in the context of a community. While the commercial entrepreneur certainly operates within a community (often referred to as a "market" or a "market environment"), the actual product delivered is really a commodity.

Source: iStock.com/Rawpixel. Used with permission

The commercial entrepreneur does need to influence behavior, but only as it relates to persuading a potential customer to change their buying habits in favor of the specific product being offered. The social entrepreneur, if properly focused, is seeking to change human behavior on a far deeper level – and often trying to change the behaviors of a community. And that can make things quite muddled.

Community-based social change is an attempt to alter policies, practices, and traditional behaviors and perspectives (Sen, 2003). It requires both the ability to organize collective action within a specific group and the delicacy to diplomatically manage the various interests within that group (Weiss, 2010). It calls on the entrepreneur to build respect and relationships within the community, and then collaboratively develop plans to bring about the specific change being desired (Alinsky, 1971).

BOX 3.4   THE IMPORTANCE OF COMMUNITY AND PARTNERSHIP

In order to understand the importance of communities, you first have to define them. Communities are social groups that have common interests or qualities that make them discrete from the broader population, meaning that we can identify them relative to the broader society. They can be based on faith, demography, interest, profession, political orientation, geography, or any other distinct characteristic of the collective group. While not homogenous, communities share common interests and challenges, and their "buy-in" is critical to the success of any social impact initiative.

In order to achieve the aim of broad-scale social change, communities and the organizations within them need to work together in partnership with one another. The UN's Sustainable Development Goals include Goal 17, "Partnerships for the goals," for this reason: to acknowledge the need to build a social entrepreneurship ecosystem. The concept of social entrepreneurship ecosystems is addressed later in this chapter.

In order to get a sense of how complicated (or messy) this can be, think back to your childhood. There were probably many times when you gathered with friends to play a game of some sort. Most of the time, those childhood games were loosely organized and did not have a lot of formal structure. Now, recall how much of your time was spent in debate with your friends about a specific aspect of the game – how a particular outcome might not be fair, or how the "rules" (often invented on the spot) might have been violated (and if you don't recall that sort of thing or did not experience it yourself, just go to the nearest playground and you'll see exactly what I'm talking about). In hindsight (or in observation), there can be more time spent in these debates than there is in actual play.

Now, compare that to the creation and delivery of a commercial product. While the software developer needs to be creative, it is not typical for the software to argue about what type of program it wants to become. The pizza does not object to the choice of topping, nor does the fabric comment on the dressmaker's sense of style.

The community, however, can (and should) have a significant amount of input into the specific change to be created, and the means by which it is to be achieved. The community must also have a level of motivation and desire that is sufficient to carry it through the inevitable turbulence that will occur (Alinsky, 1971; Gordon and Perkins, 2013). And the process of building that shared vision and marshaling that motivation can (and will) often look and feel just like that childhood playground.

SHAREHOLDERS VS STAKEHOLDERS

Another area where social enterprise gets messy is understanding whose interests the venture is serving. A commercial enterprise has three primary interest groups – its customers (the folks who buy the product or service), its employees (the people who produce the product), and its shareholders (the people who own the company). Anybody else's interest in the company is fairly irrelevant. Not so in the social space. Because we are dealing with people's lives and the health and welfare of the community, there are a lot more folks who can stake a claim on the work that the enterprise is doing.

The world of nonprofit management and public administration lends a big hand in this matter, in its recognition and understanding of the notion of a stakeholder. Defined as "any person, group or organization that can place a claim on [a venture's] attention, resources, or output or that is affected by that output" (Bryson, 2004, p. 35), the concept of the stakeholder suggests that there is a much broader array of interests and perspectives that can shape any work that seeks to improve a social condition. In a nonprofit context, stakeholders can include funders, constituents (beneficiaries, or the people being served) and their families, taxpayers (particularly if there is public money helping to fund the effort), paid employees, volunteer workers, and the community in which the work is being done, as well as various governmental interests.

Being a "hybrid" venture, the social enterprise needs to understand and navigate both concepts. The business side of the enterprise needs to understand the customer and meet their needs, while the social initiative needs to manage the broader perspectives of a web of stakeholders. Balancing these often-divergent issues can create ethical and operational challenges that can be quite difficult to manage (Smith, Gonin, and Besharov, 2013).

Consider for a moment the issue of a "living wage." From a moral standpoint, it seems clear that paying a decent wage for decent work is the right thing to do. But the basics of business operations tells us that wages are usually the single largest expense of any business. So, raising wages will clearly suppress profits for any venture, social or commercial. Now, since we are clear from our earlier discussion that we are here to serve people, not maximize profits, it would seem like accepting a lower profit margin in order to pay a higher wage would be a reasonable tradeoff for a social entrepreneur. However, the first rule of pricing in any business is that you must cover your costs. So, what happens when the cost of providing a living wage raises your prices to the point where you are no longer competitive in the market? Do you pay your workers less so you can stay in business? Do you charge more and hope that people will pay extra because they know "it's for a good cause"? It's a tough choice either way, and only one example of the many difficult decisions you will face along your journey.

BOX 3.5   LIVING WAGE

"Living wage" refers to the minimum income needed to cover the basic needs of food, housing, clothing, and other essential staples within a particular geographic area. A living wage is not to be confused with a subsistence wage, which only covers the bare necessities to stay alive. It is also not the same as a minimum wage. Within the context of the U.S., there is a federal minimum wage, but some states and cities choose to set higher minimum wage rates. Living wages, which are usually above the set minimum wage, are typically calculated by advocacy groups who are seeking to change minds, practices, and policies to help raise minimum wages to better consider the actual comfort needs of typical individuals and households.

In the U.K., the Living Wage Foundation is a great example of an organization advocating to raise awareness of a living wage and to help more employers move to setting their salaries to a living wage, rather than the minimum wage. It is helping this initiative through designating organizations as "Living Wage Employers" and having an award program to help recognize those who are doing well within this space.

OUTPUTS AND OUTCOMES

A profit-seeking venture only has two concerns – sales and profit. While there are many things that go into making a business successful, the definition of success eventually comes down to these two numbers, both of which are fairly short term in nature. But if you are trying to bring about a change in society, you need to look at things a bit differently.

Traditionally, nonprofits and NGOs have reported how many people they have helped. The academic definition for this is known as an output. But if you really are trying to make the world better, the goal should be to reduce the number of folks who suffer from the specific social inequity that you are trying to address. In technical terms, that's known as an outcome.

BOX 3.6   DEFINING OUTPUT AND OUTCOME

"Outputs" refer to the end-of-process production or delivery amounts. Output measurements can reflect the number of people served, units sold, or programs delivered. While this information presents helpful data to quantify reach, output does not look at the impact or value delivered.

In contrast, outcomes are the manner in which something ends up or comes out, which includes the perceptions of quality, value, impact, and success of the products or services delivered. Because outcomes measure changes in behaviors, attitudes, and opinions, outcomes are critical to knowing if change is actually happening. When social enterprises only report on their outputs, they are neglecting to measure and report on how their efforts are changing or bettering the challenges they aim to tackle.

Measuring an outcome instead of output is easy; instead of just counting people, programs, or units, include surveys of quality, monitor the aftermath, and interview stakeholders to ask them about impact and change. By moving from measuring and reporting on outputs to outcomes, social enterprises can see and improve on their impact rather than reach.

To illustrate, consider a local church that runs a feeding program during the week and provides a hot lunch to those in need. There is no question that this is a good thing. The hungry are fed and live another day. The program proudly reports how many meals are served each day. That's an output. But a deeper and longer-term perspective would try to find ways to help folks reduce their dependency on the daily meal and return to a life of independence. In order to do that, the program would need to understand the factors that brought the folks to the place where they needed the free meal, and to develop programs that helped its constituents to rise up from their circumstances. Such a program might then report on the number of folks who once were recipients but have now returned to more productive and fulfilling lives. That would be an outcome.

While the definitional distinctions between outputs and outcomes are easy to grasp, the technical realities of an outcomes-based program are substantial. An outcomes-oriented program needs to have systems in place to collect data on former constituents and it must be able to analyze that data to revise and refine its programs over time (Scheirer and Newcomer, 2001). It also needs to be able to understand that long-term success in reducing a social inequality means that the program itself should eventually go out of business (after all, if the social issue is addressed, then there is no longer a need for the program). But most important of all, the program needs to clearly be able to tie the long-term change back to the specific interventions the program delivered. That's known as "causality," and it's the next little bit of "messiness" we need to talk about.

Causality

Another area where social enterprise gets messy is around something that the academics call "causality," which is a fancy way of saying "cause and effect." The reason that it's important here is that it is very difficult to prove that a given social program is directly and solely responsible for a specific social outcome (McDavid

Source: iStock.com/SKapl. Used with permission

and Hawthorn, 2006). To explain by example, let's consider a tutoring program in a public elementary school.

In this program, elementary school students who are having trouble learning to read are given extra help so that they can keep up with their studies. The program reports that it worked with 25 students (that's an output). The program also reports that the students it worked with improved their reading scores by 35 percent over the school year (that's an outcome). Now, one of those students goes on to medical school, becomes a doctor, and develops a cure for cancer. Clearly, if the program had not been in place, that student never would have gone on to do the great things that they did. But that's a far stretch from being able to say that the reading program caused the eventual success of the student. There are far too many other factors that could come into play. For one, how much sleep the student got the night before the entrance exam could dramatically impact their chances of admission. On a higher level, what sort of family environment they experienced throughout school could greatly impact long-term success (and I'm sure that you could come up with several more).

To our point about messy social enterprise, let's compare this to a profit-seeking commercial venture. Since the primary concern is producing a profitable product or service, cause and effect is easy. If it sells, sells well, and generates the desired profit, it's a success. And while external market forces do influence the commercial success of a product, navigating those external forces is part of the job for the company that produces the product. So, if the product is a hit (the desired effect), it's pretty clear that it's the company's efforts that made it so (the cause).

BOX 3.7 SYSTEMS THINKING FOR SOCIAL IMPACT
When approaching social issues, social entrepreneurs need to think about all of the relevant stakeholders, consider the underlying factors contributing to the problem, balance the short-term benefits with the longer-term vision, and anticipate the potential unintended consequences (Stroh, 2015). In order to do all of this, social entrepreneurs need to think in terms of systems.
A systems-thinking approach views social problems as complex and interconnected, with the need to bridge together disjointed efforts through cross-sector relationship-building (Kania and Kramer, 2011). For social entrepreneurs, this approach is required for being able to identify root causes and to find the best partnerships, people, and resources to have a sustainable impact over time. Systems thinkers create sustainable impact by motivating and focusing others through collaboration and continuous learning (Stroh, 2015).

THE "NOT FOR PROFIT" MINDSET

I've been involved in this experiment in social entrepreneurship for over a dozen years, both as a teacher and researcher, as well as directly advising over 100 nonprofits and social enterprises as they worked to develop new models for meeting the needs of their constituents while increasing the sustainability of their organizations. During this time, I've noticed a lot of things (many of them the basis for this book). One of the more interesting things I've seen is that there is a direct conflict between the folks researching this new world and the ones that are doing the work.

Most of the research being done on the topic of social entrepreneurship is being done by academics who live inside business schools, while most of the leaders running the ventures being studied come from nonprofit or social work perspectives. So, while most of the "best practices" use language and frameworks familiar to the business world, the people doing the work have some very different perceptions about how the world works. One of the more interesting places where this relates to our concept of the messiness of social entrepreneurship concerns economic value and impact.

Let's start this particular conversation with a staggering set of facts. First, there are over 10 million NGOs worldwide. If these entities were their own country, they would comprise the fifth largest economy in the world (*Global Leadership Bulletin*, 2015). While that number is impressive, I would submit to you that it may even be understated. Happily, the reason is quite simple, and easily explained – nonprofits and NGOs do not usually measure their work in terms of their worth in the economy.

To illustrate, let's look at a job training program that I worked with a few years back. These good and hard-working folks helped individuals returning from incarceration and trained them in the construction industry. When a specific individual graduated the program, the program helped them find a job, using connections to various construction firms it made and maintained. Good work was done, and good results were obtained. But there were two areas where value was being created that was not being claimed. The first was the reduction in the cost to society, since the graduates of the program were less likely to return to jail. The second is much simpler.

When I asked these good folks how they paid for their work, the answer was typical – grants and donations. Then I went to the employers that the program was working with and asked a simple question: "How do you find your other employees (the ones not coming out of the program)?" The answer was that they used an employment service, to whom they paid a fee (and often a substantial one). So, my question to the program was, "If the employer is clearly paying for employees, why are we giving them workers for free?" The answer was startling, and yet not surprising at all. These good folks felt that it was wrong to charge for their services – an attitude that is quite common.

I believe that there are several reasons why many nonprofits and NGOs think this way. The first is that they are not trained to think about revenue opportunities, as that is not part of the curriculum in which they have been schooled. The second is that the notion of profit is somehow considered to be evil (understandable, particularly in our current mode of exploitive capitalism). Third, there is a general sense that folks doing this work should be humble and self-effacing.

Now, consider the same issue (giving away a service that the customer is willing to pay for) from a businessperson's perspective. The simple fact is that any business school student who missed this opportunity would probably fail their course.

THE NATURE OF PRIVATE MONEY

Perhaps the most critical "messy" matter in traditional nonprofit and NGO funding is the very nature of private money, how it is created, and how it gets into the bank account of the folks doing the work.

In one of my stock presentations, I often make the point that "in order to be shared, wealth must first be created." Said more simply, money needs to come from somewhere. And the only place that I know of that creates that wealth (in the true dollars-and-cents definition) is business. And, thanks to the capitalist system, we've gotten quite good at it. But, as we saw in Chapter 1, that wealth often comes at a cost. The term that the economists use is "exploitation." The fundamental economic model of the capitalist system is that resources are exploited in order to gain profit (Barnes, 2018; Novak, 1982). Said plainly, we use wood to make a table that we then sell. The sales price includes both the cost of the materials and compensation for the labor involved, as well as an excess amount that we call profit. That's all well and good (and a basic concept that must be remembered in building a social venture). The problem comes into play when the exploitation becomes excessive or unfair.

Continuing with our wooden table illustration, the capitalist realizes that the cost to replant a new tree to replace the one that was cut down reduces the amount of profit that they can realize from the transaction, so the forest becomes bare over time (and the more popular the table is, and the quicker they can make them, the faster the forest is depleted). Or the carpenter doing the labor of making the table needs to make a certain wage in order to have a decent living, but the owner of the furniture business would need to reduce their profit to pay that living wage. Now, multiply this issue by the thousands of resources that are consumed to build products and services, and the millions of workers employed in making them. Then, take a second look at the pay gaps we mentioned in Chapter 1. When you see that the typical corporate CEO makes over 300 times more than the average worker in the firm that they run,[1] you begin to get the idea that worker exploitation might be an issue.

The reason that this relates to the nature of private money is that the wealth that this CEO makes can be sheltered in a charitable foundation that then proceeds to make grants and gifts to various nonprofits and NGOs (Giridharadas, 2019). In short, the "generous donation" made to the "good cause" is made with money that probably exploited a resource, and probably exploited it to some level of excess.

THE NONPROFIT INDUSTRIAL COMPLEX

I need to start this section with an extremely large disclaimer. So large, in fact, that I need to print it in capital letters. THERE ARE A LOT OF REALLY GOOD PEOPLE DOING REALLY GOOD WORK IN THE NONPROFIT AND NGO SECTORS. So, what follows is not intended to dishonor or disrespect any of those people or the amazing work that they do every day. It is, however, intended to take a clear-eyed look at the systems, structures, processes, and procedures that prevent these good folks from doing work that could be much better. We've already talked about two of these issues in the previous section, namely that even the best of intentions can create situations where co-dependency builds over time, and local efforts to become self-sufficient are unintentionally suppressed. But there are other areas where the "nonprofit industrial complex" stands in the way of truly effective social change (Egger and Yoon, 2004; Mintzberg, 2015).

Empathy Misdirected

As we said earlier, there are over 10 million NGOs worldwide. So, it's clear that we are talking about a major global industry. And just like any other major global industry, there are good things and bad things going on. There are well-intentioned people doing good work. There are also well-intentioned people doing work that is less good. And, because human nature is involved, there are also folks that are not so well intentioned. This creates several areas of dynamic tension that need to be considered.

The first is the means and methods used to raise money for charitable causes. Too often, fundraising efforts play on human emotions – either guilt or ego (Saul, 2011). Consider two common scenarios. In the first, a charitable fundraising campaign uses images of those it hopes to help. The intended recipients of the charitable effort are shown in their "former state" – hungry, homeless, cold, addicted, abused; whatever truly unfortunate circumstances they find themselves in. The funding appeal then makes an impassioned plea for your donation to help those in need. While unquestionably effective, this emotional appeal raises the possibility that the needy may be debased in order to raise money for their aid. So, rather than restoring dignity to those who need it most, we humiliate those we purport to help just so we can raise enough money to help them. Seems like a bit of a vicious cycle to me.

BOX 3.8   SOCIAL SERVICE PROVISION, SOCIAL ADVOCACY, AND SOCIAL ENTREPRENEURSHIP

As we gain a better understanding of social entrepreneurship, it is important to understand the span of social impact work. One of the most helpful visual representations that highlights the various ways in which social impact can be categorized comes from Martin and Osberg (2015, p. 7). The model differentiates the nature of action (direct or indirect) and the type of outcome (maintaining/improving a current system or creating/sustaining a new equilibrium), and there is a need for each one of the categories:

- Social service provision (direct and extant system) helps the here-and-now needs of communities (for example, food banks, soup kitchens, pop-up health clinics). Their work is essential to making sure our world's most immediate needs are being approached.
- Social activism (indirect and new system) works to educate, inform, and change minds. Social activists are trying to convince others that we need a new equilibrium that aligns with the values and causes they support. They are also active fundraisers, helping to both raise awareness and get valuable funds for research, educational, and advocacy purposes.
- Social entrepreneurship (direct and new system), as shared within this book, is trying to push for a new equilibrium through direct action (for example, creating job pipelines for marginalized groups, changing access to financing for the underbanked, improving STEM (Science, Technology, Engineering, and Math) education within impoverished communities). Social entrepreneurs are attempting to tackle the root problems of the status quo.

While we need players in all three categories, we need them to be a united front in wanting both to help the here-and-now *and* to better the future of the cause, with the united aim to eradicate the problem. In fact, many organizations will have efforts and activities spanning these categories in order to have a greater impact.

Connecting back with the chapter, those within the "nonprofit industrial complex" – the bad actors looking for organizational sustainability over eradicating the problem – would likely sit within the social service provision or the social activism space, with an active orientation to limit their partnerships across the areas because they are not interested in directly contributing to an equilibrium shift. As noted in the chapter, while many organizations within social service provision and social activism are doing great, impactful things, it is important to be able to recognize the orientations and behaviors of those looking to sustain themselves over creating real social change.

Ego Misdirected

The other scenario exists in what the fundraisers call "major gifts." These are those large donors (usually six figures or more) who make a truly transformative gift. In so doing, they will often get their name put on a program, or on the side of a building. While this is often done for publicity purposes, and in well-intentioned gratitude on the part of the charity receiving the donation, it's easy to see that there is a good chance that the donor is motivated as much by the recognition and public adulation as they are by the level of need that the donation is intended to address.

Low Pay for Good Work

Another area where the "nonprofit industrial complex" creates issues is in how many organizations treat their employees. In general, nonprofit and NGO salaries are lower than comparable pay in the commercial sector (Pallotta, 2010). While this lower pay rate is driven by genuine concerns about how donated funds are spent, it creates two distinct problems. The first is that the organization is not likely to attract the best and brightest individuals when those talented folks can make a lot more money elsewhere. It takes a truly special individual to voluntarily forgo a substantial increase in pay just so they can work with those who are most in need. In addition, many charities expect their workers to work longer hours, forgo many employee benefits, and even donate large percentages of their pay back to the organization. So, the charitable organization will become less efficient, less effective, less adaptive, and less well managed, simply because its employee base is less well paid. The second issue is related to the first and has to do with the type of person that would accept this tradeoff of a lower salary. While there are certainly many noble folks who truly don't care about the money and truly do care about the cause, there are also some people who find recognition in making sure others know how just how much they are suffering and sacrificing for the cause. In other words, these employees receive psychic compensation in being recognized as "good people" (Lee, 2012). Clearly, that's not a healthy place for either the worker or the organization to be.

BOX 3.9   WORKING AT A SOCIAL ENTERPRISE

Within social enterprises, salaries can vary in ways that we might not expect. In a study of American social enterprises in the arts and cultural industry, salaries depended on what stage of commercialization they were in, with the study finding that the organizations in the transition period to becoming entrepreneurial nonprofits had lower salaries, in part due to the prevalence of part-time employees needed to fill the gaps during the shift to having more commercial activities (Ghosh Moulicka et al., 2020).

While salaries are generally lower than within the commercial sector, working at a social enterprise can be rewarding in other ways. The term "psychic income" refers to all of the benefits of working that are outside the typical, less tangible material and monetary compensation we think of in working (Thurow, 1978). Psychic income can refer to working for a good initiative, towards a passion space, or in a pleasant environment with friendly co-workers. Alternatively, psychic income can also be praise or recognition from your organization or boss. While harder to measure and quantify, the value of psychic income contributes significantly towards job satisfaction, which may be an even stronger need for women (Ross and Mirowsky, 1996).

Power and Philanthropy

While these internal organizational issues are certainly challenging, there are also external forces that serve to restrict the effectiveness of charitable efforts. Perhaps the most difficult to surmount is the power imbalance that exists between grantmakers and the projects they fund. There are several areas where the process and practices of institutional philanthropy can hinder the effective delivery of social change. The first is that most foundation grants are for a relatively short period (one to three years), while effective social change can take 10 or 20 years to truly take root in a community. The second is that foundations often prefer to fund specific projects, while shying away from funding general operations. This makes it difficult for charities to build the needed internal strength to run a more efficient and effective operation (contrast this with the commercial sector, where it is well understood that the "back office" is critical to the successful organization). Most foundations (particularly the larger ones) also have highly educated program officers who are well versed in the best practices of a particular issue area. However, many social programs are context-specific (meaning that there is a unique element of a specific place or population that is key to the effectiveness of the program), which means that the best practices may not apply to (or even conflict with) the local conditions. Consequently, the charity either does not get funded or is forced to perform some sort of sleight of hand to make it look like it is complying with the best practices while still running its operation in the way that it knows works for its folks (Giridharadas, 2019; Pallotta, 2010; Riley, 2009).

BOX 3.10   INSTITUTIONAL PHILANTHROPY

Consisting of the world's largest foundations, endowments, and trusts, institutional philanthropy has shaped the dialogue and practices of social change for decades. Despite institutional philanthropy's declining role within the broader social impact funding options of today, government, business, academe, and civil society still look to institutional philanthropy as a leader within the social impact space (Powell, Seldon, and Sahni, 2019).

Preservation over Progress

But the biggest problem by far is that some charities are more concerned about self-preservation than they are about true change. Consider this basic (and often overlooked) truth. If you are truly trying to help bring about social change, then your goal should be to eradicate the social condition you are seeking to improve. If your work involves hunger, feeding the hungry is certainly a good thing. A better thing would be trying to eliminate the need for the feeding program in the first place. If you are concerned about the homeless, providing a place to sleep is a great start. But the aim of your work should be to reduce or eliminate the conditions that lead to homelessness. Yet we often see charities that are celebrating 20, 30, or 50 years in existence.

Some of this longevity is due to the complexity of the problem. But some of it is due to either fear or ego on the part of the leaders of the charitable effort (Lupton, 2011). The fear comes from a recognition that the reduction or elimination of the social condition means that the jobs of the workers in the program would be eliminated. The ego issue relates to the psychic compensation that is received by workers and leaders in this field, who are often championed for their compassion and concern – recognition that would go away if the need for the charity no longer exists.

So, while the charitable sector does lots of good, and has lots of good people, it also has a number of flaws. The reason that this issue is important in a chapter on the unique issues faced by social enterprises is that the aspiring social entrepreneur needs to understand this landscape, its strengths and its weaknesses, and use that knowledge to build a better process. One where income can be earned, rather than donated or granted. One where the explicit objective is to eliminate a social disparity.

SUPPORT SYSTEMS ARE MESSY

Source: iStock.com/Asnidamarwani. Used with permission

The last issue we need to talk about in this pile of confusing messes is how external support systems are more complicated for the social entrepreneur.

Because new business formation is seen as a critical factor in economic development, organized support for the commercial entrepreneur has become quite common. Financial support is often provided through publicly funded investment programs as well as various tax breaks and research institutions. Legal structures and public policies are often crafted to provide needed support for the new venture. Incubation programs, venture accelerators, and other facilitating services are quite common. Colleges and universities offer courses (including entire degrees as well as minors and concentrations) in entrepreneurship. In law, accounting, banking, marketing, sales, project management, and many other fields, entire divisions of professionals have been set up to support the entrepreneur, and these professionals have been tried and tested on their ability to provide the needed support. These processes and programs have become so complex and sophisticated that they are often referred to as "ecosystems" (Isenberg, 2011).

Because social entrepreneurship is so complex, and blends several different disciplines and structures, an ecosystem for social entrepreneurs does not exist in the same way as it does for the for-profit enterprise. While resources and support organizations do exist, they are not coordinated in the same way, leaving the aspiring social entrepreneur to construct their own networks of support. Having to assemble these networks on your own clearly takes more time, but it also creates an additional level of risk for the organization as the mechanisms for validating the various players also don't exist. So, suffice it to say that it's a mess.

And yet, the field holds much promise – so maybe it's worth dealing with the mess in order to realize the potential for making a better world. And that's where we go next.

CHAPTER SUMMARY

This chapter outlines what makes social entrepreneurship unique relative to commercial entrepreneurship, with its focus on people and our communities rather than profits and products. This orientation entails a lot of complexity, as people and their communities are complex unto themselves. Figuring out how to change their attitudes, orientations, and behaviors is just as challenging. Because community-based social change attempts to advocate for a new equilibrium through crafting new practices, perspectives, habits, and policies, social entrepreneurs must establish credibility, relationships, and partnerships within their communities to be successful. Social change cannot be done alone, and social entrepreneurs need the support of their communities and the social entrepreneurship ecosystem to thrive. The chapter also makes important distinctions between the following terminology pairs: (1) value creation and value capture, (2) stakeholders and shareholders, and (3) outcomes and outputs. Finally, the chapter ends on the problematization of the "nonprofit industrial complex," framing the charitable sector as doing a lot of good, but with some actors having a personal and organizational stake in preserving the root problem rather than striving for transformation and change, which would render their position and organization obsolete.

QUESTIONS FOR DISCUSSION

1. In order to do the social good they seek to accomplish, social enterprises typically need to charge more, with the hope that their customers will pay extra because they know a portion of the profits is going towards "a good cause." While our younger consumers have a reputation for being interested in social responsibility, the Conscious Consumer Spending Index (CCSI) reports declines in the surveyed Americans willing to pay extra for socially responsible products and services within both the 18- to 24-year-old group and the 25- to 34-year-old group (https://goodmustgrow.com). In this exercise, you will get the opportunity to discuss this with others.
   A. Review the most recent CCSI report (available at https://goodmustgrow.com) or another similar source.
   B. Create a survey with questions asking possible customers about their interests, limitations, and thresholds. Ask your survey respondents the following questions and create your own:
      • What products or services do they know – or think – are socially responsible?
      • What socially responsible products or services do they currently buy?

- Which ones are they interested in buying in the future? Why haven't they purchased those products or services already?

C. Through doing this survey activity, what did you learn about customers? How did their responses compare to what you learned in your initial research and reading (of the CCSI report or another source)?

2. Select a social enterprise you are interested in, and do some research on its website to see what the social enterprise does and who the people are, both internal and external to the organization.

A. Using the table below as a model and working with each individual, group, or partner internal or external to the social enterprise, try to identify the following parameters:
   - Are they a shareholder, a stakeholder, or both?
   - Are they a beneficiary, customer (person paying), or both?
   - How did you make these classifications?

Individual/ group/ partner	Shareholder	Stakeholder	Beneficiary	Customer	Notes
Employees		X			Employees at this social enterprise do not own the organization; they do not seem to be paying for the product/service.
ABCDE Foundation	X			X	The Foundation serves a partner and funds several programs for the organization; the Foundation is also represented on the Board.
Those experiencing housing insecurity		X	X		The social enterprise serves this community, and it helps to inform its programming needs.

B. Using that same social enterprise, look to see if there is any public data available that helps to demonstrate its impact.
   - *For organizations that have data available on their website or within an annual or quarterly report*, use the information provided and classify the available data by recreating the table below. In the Notes section, make observations on what is interesting about the data (for example, how the organization collected the information, questions/concerns raised, how the data is/is not demonstrating impact, and so on).
   - *For organizations that do not explicitly provide impact data or reports*, try to find testimonials or partnership information to help give you a bit more

information about the social enterprise's activities. If working with this social enterprise, what could it possibly measure? Mark possible measurement as being an output or outcome, and reflect on how well each item shows impact. Out of your possible measurements, what would you recommend it measure, and why?

Data	Measurement	Output	Outcome	Notes
Ex. "Our yearly participation rate increased by over 30 percent, with 1,000 individuals attending our programming."	Number of people served	X		Shows growth, but does this growth signify that they are doing quality programming?
…				
…				

C.   What have you learned through completing these two tables? Are there any patterns or points of interest that you covered in your analyses?

RECOMMENDED RESOURCES

Living Wage Foundation (n.d.). www.livingwage.org.uk.
Lupton, R. D. (2011). *Toxic Charity: How Churches and Charities Hurt Those They Help (And How to Reverse It)*. New York, NY: HarperOne.
Martin, R. L., and Osberg, S. R. (2015). *Getting Beyond Better: How Social Entrepreneurship Works*. Boston, MA: Harvard Business Review Press.
Stroh, D. P. (2015). *Systems Thinking for Social Change: A Practical Guide to Solving Complex Problems, Avoiding Unintended Consequences, and Achieving Lasting Results*. White River Junction, VT: Chelsea Green Publishing.
Thiel, P., and Masters, B. (2014). *Zero to One: Notes on Startups, or How to Build the Future*. New York, NY: Random House.

NOTE

1.   Accessed 27 April 2021 at www.businessinsider.com/ceo-worker-pay-ratio-gap-grew-in-2020-aflcio-2021 -7#:~:text=The%20average%20CEO%20made%20nearly,new%20AFL%2DCIO%20analysis%20finds&text= The%20average%20CEO%2Dto%2Dworker,%2C%20the%20AFL%2DCIO%20says.

REFERENCES

Alinsky, S. D. (1971). *Rules for Radicals: A Practical Primer for Realistic Radicals*. New York, NY: Vintage.
Barnes, K. J. (2018). *Redeeming Capitalism*. Grand Rapids, MI: William B. Eerdmans Publishing.
Battilana, J., and Lee, M. (2014). Advancing research on hybrid organizing: Insights from the study of social enterprises. *Academy of Management Annals, 8*(1), 397–441.
Bosma, N., Schott, T., Terjesen, S., and Kew, P. (2016). Special topic report: Social entrepreneurship. *Global Entrepreneurship Monitor*. Accessed 27 April 2021 at www.gemconsortium.org/report/gem -2015-report-on-social-entrepreneurship

Bryson, J. M. (2004). *Strategic Planning for Public and Nonprofit Organizations: A Guide to Strengthening and Sustaining Organizational Achievement*. San Francisco, CA: Jossey-Bass.

Egger, R., and Yoon, H. (2004). *Begging for Change: The Dollars and Sense of Making Nonprofits Responsive, Efficient, and Rewarding for All*. New York, NY: HarperBusiness.

Eldar, O. (2017). The role of social enterprise and hybrid organizations. *Columbia Business Law Review*, 92.

Emerson, J. (2018). *The Purpose of Capital: Elements of Impact, Financial Flows, and Natural Being*. San Franciso, CA: Blended Value Group.

Ghosh Moulick, A., Alexiou, K., Dowin Kennedy, E., and Parris, D. L. (2020). A total eclipse of the heart: compensation strategies in entrepreneurial nonprofits. *Journal of Business Venturing*, 35(4). doi: 10.1016/j.jbusvent.2019.105950.

Giridharadas, A. (2019). *Winners Take All: The Elite Charade of Changing the World*. London: Penguin.

Global Leadership Bulletin (2015). Facts and stats about NGOs worldwide. Accessed 27 April 2021 at www.standardizations.org/bulletin/?p=841.

Gordon, W., and Perkins, J. (2013). *Making Neighborhoods Whole: A Handbook for Christian Community Development*. Downers Grove, IL: InterVarsity Press.

Halcyon (n.d.). *A Step Forward: Social Enterprise Ecosystems in the U.S.: Volume 3*. Accessed 27 April 2021 at https://socentcity.org/sites/default/files/seer_2019_brochure_web.pdf.

Isenberg, D. (2011). The entrepreneurship ecosystem strategy as a new paradigm for economy policy: Principles for cultivating entrepreneurship. Babson Entrepreneurship Ecosystem Project, Babson College.

Lee, Y.-J. (2012). Behavioral implications of public service motivation: Volunteering by public and non-profit employees. *American Review of Public Administration*, 42(1), 104–121.

Lupton, R. D. (2011). *Toxic Charity: How Churches and Charities Hurt Those They Help (And How to Reverse It)*. New York, NY: HarperOne.

McDavid, J. C., and Hawthorn, L. R. L. (2006). *Program Evaluation & Performance Measurement: An Introduction to Practice*. Thousand Oaks, CA: SAGE.

Mintzberg, H. (2015). *Rebalancing Society: Radical Renewal Beyond Left, Right, and Center*. Oakland, CA: Berrett-Koehler.

Novak, M. (1982). *The Spirit of Democratic Capitalism*. New York, NY: Simon & Schuster.

Pallotta, D. (2010). *Uncharitable: How Restraints on Nonprofits Undermine Their Potential*. Medford, MA, and Lebanon, NH: Tufts University Press and University Press of New England.

Powell, A., Seldon, W., and Sahni, N. (2019). Reimagining institutional philanthropy. *Stanford Social Innovation Review*, Spring. Accessed 27 April 2021 at https://ssir.org/articles/entry/reimagining _institutional_philanthropy.

Riley, N. S. (2009, March 3). Philanthropy and its enemies. *Wall Street Journal*, p. A.13. Retrieved from www.wsj.com/articles/SB123604548985015461.

Ross, C. E., and Mirowsky, J. (1996). Economic and interpersonal work rewards: subjective utilities of men and women's compensation. *Social Forces*, 75(1), 223–246.

Saul, J. (2011). The end of fundraising: Raise more money by selling your impact. San Francisco, California: Jossey-Bass.

Scheirer, M. A., and Newcomer, K. (2001). Opportunities for program evaluators to facilitate performance-based management. *Evaluation and Program Planning*, 24(1), 63–71.

Sen, R. (2003). *Stir It Up: Lessons in Community Organizing and Advocacy*. San Francisco, CA: Jossey-Bass.

Smith, W. K., Gonin, M., and Besharov, M. L. (2013). Managing social-business tensions: A review and research agenda for social enterprise. *Business Ethics Quarterly*, 23(3), 407–442.

Thurow, L. (1978). Psychic income: Useful or useless? *American Economic Review*, 68(2), 142–145.

Visher, C. A., and Travis, J. (2011). Life on the outside: Returning home after incarceration. *Prison Journal*, 91(3_suppl.), 102S–119S.

Weiss, A. (2010). *Spiritual Activism: A Jewish Guide to Leadership and Repairing the World*. Woodstock, VT: Jewish Lights.

4
The field is extra-disciplinary

Learning objectives

After studying this chapter, you should be able to:
1. Explain the importance of the "social" aspect of social entrepreneurship.
2. Understand how purpose and profit can complement and enhance one another.
3. Distinguish between public and private forms of social welfare.
4. Reflect on assumptions and practices through the use of a Logic model and Theory of Change.
5. Identify the different foundations for why nonprofits exist.
6. Recognize and dissect some of the limiting orientations and practices of the non-profit sector and how bridging "social" and "entrepreneurship" creates a blended value.

A NEW RECIPE

I like to cook. My wife likes to bake. When I cook, I throw in a bit of this and a little of that and stir it up. I love finding out how various flavors combine and complement each other. When my wife bakes, she follows the recipe to the letter, precisely weighing and measuring each ingredient. She does this not because she is a more measured and careful person than I am (although that may be true). She does it because baking is chemistry.

When you cook, you blend ingredients together to combine various elements, but each ingredient still retains its original nature. Pasta does not become a potato just because you add marinara. Salt does not turn into pepper just because you sprinkle it into the soup. But baking takes ingredients and turns them into something completely new. If you mix water, flour, and yeast in the right proportions, you get dough. But if you leave it alone for a bit, the dough rises – which is a chemical reaction that makes a new thing. Bake it for a bit, and you've got a wonderful and nourishing loaf of bread.

At this point, you're probably wondering why I'm rambling on about food (you're probably also getting hungry – so if you need to put the book down for a minute and grab a snack, I'll understand). Well, it's because this notion of making something new out of a pile of ingredients is a critical part of our journey towards a successful social enterprise.

As you may have gathered, there are a number of different fields that come together in our world. In a few minutes, we'll talk about each of those fields and the specific ways that they combine (as well as how a social entrepreneur uses the tools of each area in new and different ways). But before we do that, we need to talk about the larger point of why these very different areas need to combine, and the unique amalgamation that results when they are synthesized.

SOCIAL ENTREPRENEURSHIP IS EXTRA-DISCIPLINARY

There are many folks working and researching in the social entrepreneurship field. And you will hear much conversation about the field of social entrepreneurship being "interdisciplinary" (Acs and Audretsch, 2006). When folks say this, what they mean is that it combines tools, techniques, and concepts from a variety of fields. While this is certainly true, I think it doesn't go far enough in explaining what we do, and the nature of the organizations we build.

I maintain that this world of social entrepreneurship is "extra-disciplinary," meaning that the programs and ventures that are created in this space don't just combine existing worlds, but that they do so in a way that something new and different is created.

Think for a minute about one of the fundamental assumptions of our economic systems. For a long time, the basic perception was that an organization could seek a profit or it could pursue a social purpose. The two were not only seen as mutually exclusive, but often in direct contradiction to each other (Friedman, 1970; Hardin, 1968). But one of the fundamental aims of a social enterprise is that it can (and should) produce both (Emerson, 2003). But that's still only combining ingredients. The outstanding social entrepreneur finds a way that the profit and the purpose actually enhance each other (Lumpkin and Bacq, 2019). That's not only a great recipe, but a tough balancing act that requires a careful combination of elements.

To make a good loaf of bread, you need three main ingredients – flour, water, and yeast. To make a great social enterprise, the two main things that you combine are (no surprise here) the social and the entrepreneurial. In the social, you have three main areas – social work, nonprofit administration and operations, and public administration. So, let's take each of these in turn, starting with the social.

BOX 4.1 THE RELATIONSHIP BETWEEN PURPOSE AND PROFIT

At its essence, social entrepreneurship can feel like it is pulling at two competing oppositions: profit and purpose. There is a familiarity with businesses maximizing their profits and with nonprofits doing good, but it is hard for many to conceptualize how an organization can manage both purpose and profit without sacrificing on either end.

Social entrepreneurship exists across types of organization, so it is best to think of social entrepreneurship as a spectrum. The table below is a synthesis of many existing models that highlight the purpose to the left and profit to the right.

Traditional nonprofit and charitable organizations	Nonprofits with limited profit-generation strategies	Nonprofits with strong profit-generation strategies	Companies with strong social missions	Companies with social good activities (that is, corporate social responsibility)	Traditional for-profit companies
• Strong social mission • No profit-making strategy					• Profit-generation orientation • No social mission

In recent times, there is an increasingly robust middle space, with more businesses wanting to do good and more nonprofits wanting to be financially sustainable. Purpose and profit can strengthen one another because consumers are more informed – and more interested – than ever before on the ethical practices and impact of an organization. In fact, consumers that buy a product or service from a company exhibiting corporate social responsibility (CSR) report being more satisfied with their purchases (Pérez and Rodríguez del Bosque, 2015) and being more loyal to the company (Maignan and Ferrell, 2001).

For more information about consumer consciousness, review the Recommended Resources section at the end of the chapter.

PUTTING THE SOCIAL BACK INTO SOCIAL ENTREPRENEURSHIP

Throughout this book, we've used two words over and over. The second ("entrepreneurship") we've begun to define and shape. But the first one ("social") has been treated more loosely. Well, that's about to change, because the first discipline that the social entrepreneur draws from is social work – and that school of thought is all about society and making it better for all.

Social Work

So, let's start with a basic understanding of what social work is. Formally, social work is concerned with the creation and development of equitable social systems and the administration of specific programs to correct those inequities (Healy, 2008; Shoemaker, 1998). At its most basic, it is an effort to directly change the societal conditions that impact a person, a family, a neighborhood, or a community. More specifically, social work involves a series of planned steps that are designed to help improve the human condition, either at an individual or group level or for society as a whole (Colby and Dziegielewski, 2016). While the roots of organized care for others are as old as human society, the structured and formalized practices of social work have their roots in the establishment of the New York School of Philanthropy in 1904 (Shoemaker, 1998). Since then, social work as a profession has grown significantly, with over 650,000 employed professionals in the U.S. alone, and a projection of continued growth in the coming years.[1]

Source: Gert Stockmans, Unsplash. Used with permission

BOX 4.2   THE "SOCIAL" WITHIN "SOCIAL ENTREPRENEURSHIP"

The roots of the word "social" help to ground why "social entrepreneurship" was termed as such. As mentioned in Chapter 3, the word comes from the Latin "*sociālis*" (adjective) and "*socius*" (noun), which signify alliance, union, or friendship. The "social" within "social entrepreneurship" acknowledges this communal orientation and the activities and engagements that support people acting in respect of others.

The first thing that the social entrepreneur borrows from the field of social work is the notion of "social welfare," which is defined as both "[The] general state of well-being in society" and "society's specific system of programs to help people meet basic health, economic and social needs" (Colby and Dziegielewski, 2016, p. 380). Above all else, improving the social welfare of a specific community or population needs to be the primary goal of any social enterprise. It's also interesting to note that the field of social work makes a distinction between what it defines as "public social welfare" and "private social welfare." Professionals in the field consider the organizations that we've been calling nonprofits to be "private social welfare," in that they are funded and managed independently. On the other hand, what is defined as "public social welfare" are those programs that are funded and operated by national, state, or local governments (Colby and Dziegielewski, 2016). While this is a convenient and useful distinction, it is worth noting that many nonprofits obtain substantial funding from governmental sources (Rose-Ackerman, 1996), effectively serving as a subcontractor in the delivery of social programs (Easley and O'Hara, 1983; Salamon, 1987).

Engaging the Community

One of the most useful tools that the social worker brings to the table is a structured method for providing aid to a community in need that is based on listening first, and then developing and applying evidence-based solutions to the identified problem in a manner that focuses on the issues that the client or community wishes to solve. Further, specific action plans to achieve the desired outcome are developed by the client or community, with the support and assistance of the social worker (Colby and Dziegielewski, 2016).

As early as 1955, the field of social work began to acknowledge that the process of community organizing was necessary to bring about effective and lasting social change (Ross and Lappin, 1967). Ross and Lappin define community organizing as "a process by which a community identifies its needs, ... develops the confidence and will to work at these needs, finds the resources ... to deal with these needs, [and] takes action in respect to them" (1967, p. 40). Social work literature emphasizes that a dialogue with the community that enhances understanding and interpretation must be undertaken before any specific intervention can be brought to bear (Parton, 2000). The role of the social worker as a guide and facilitator that assists in bringing about a desired change (and not a director and producer implementing a pre-ordained solution) is critical not only to the success of the field of social work, but also to the successful development of a social enterprise (a concept that will be developed further in Part II, along with a more technical exploration of some of the topics we're going to cover in the next few pages).

Logic Models

Another useful tool that social work brings to the table is the concept of a Logic model. Also known as a program model, this tool helps to map out the theories as assumptions that support the desired social change. The typical Logic model starts out with a definition of the current situation as well as the specific problem or issue that needs to be changed. It then identifies the desired end state as well as specific interim objectives, the resources needed to achieve the objectives, and the specific activities that will be used to make the change happen. The Logic model will also identify the way in which results will be measured (in short, medium- and long-term timelines) (Alter and Egan, 1997). And that measurement is another crucial tool that comes to us from this field. The experts call it "program evaluation."

Program Evaluation

When it comes to spending our time and money, we all want to have some sense of assurance that it is well spent and put to the use we intended. In making commercial purposes of goods and services, that evaluation is somewhat personal (for example, you may see the value in buying a camping tent, while I may see the value in renting a hotel room). But each of us asks a simple question of ourselves – was it worth it? On a basic level, did it meet or exceed our needs and expectations? In technical terms, did it add value?

Source: iStock.com/Memphisslim. Used with permission

In considering a business proposition or an investment in an entrepreneurial venture, that value is measured on a basic scale of profit and loss. If the investment grows, we get our money back plus some sort of payment for the use of our money over time (commonly known as interest). Theoretically, the amount of interest should reflect the level of risk perceived in the investment (higher risk equals higher interest rate). The only variables are how much time and how much interest. It's all cut and dried (in theory anyway – actual practice is another thing).

But what happens when you are trying to improve a social condition or reduce some sort of inequality? How do you measure return on investment when it comes to tax dollars funding an early childhood program or donated money going to a homelessness support program? Not quite so clear now, is it? Happily, there are some tools that can be used to help meet this challenge – and (like the other areas of this chapter) these tools are being used in new ways to build effective social enterprises. So, welcome to the wonderful world of program evaluation.

At the beginning, you need to know that this is a very active area of discussion and a process that has multiple levels of complexity. It can become quite detailed, and also quite expensive. So, my purpose here is to give you a very broad overview of some key points – enough to raise your consciousness and perhaps pique your interest. We'll dive a little deeper into some areas of this technique in later chapters.

The first thing we need to talk about is the idea of a fundamental purpose or intent. In commercial entrepreneurship, that's pretty clear – we're here to make money (yes, to meet a need, and yes, to make life easier/better; but if it doesn't produce a profit, it belongs in some other category). In a social enterprise, the fundamental purpose is to bring about lasting change in a community or society. Yes, we use entrepreneurship techniques. Yes, we try to produce a product or a service that generates income (and hopefully a profit). But those things are a means to an end, not the end itself.

Theory of Change

Any social program (no matter how it's funded) starts with something called a Theory of Change. Sometimes these theories are well thought out, sometimes they are nothing more than a gut instinct. But even if the folks leading the program don't recognize it, they have a Theory of Change in mind. Paul Brest (former Dean of the Law School at Stanford University), published a great definition of this concept:

> A Theory of Change is the empirical basis underlying any social intervention – for example, the belief that a young person's close relationship with adult role models can reduce [their] susceptibility to violence, or that regular visits by registered nurses to first-time pregnant women can improve parenting skills and children's outcomes. (Brest, 2010, p. 49)

Even if it's not formally developed, every program has some level of a Theory of Change, which is really nothing more than an "If/Then" statement. Some of them are basic: If we provide meals for the hungry, then they won't go starve. If we provide a place to sleep for the homeless, then they won't die outside in the cold. Some of them are more sophisticated, and some are even supported by formal research.

Sue Funnell, in her excellent book on this subject, puts it this way:

> The Theory of Change is about the central processes or drivers by which change comes about for individuals, groups, or communities – for example, psychological processes, physical processes, and economic processes. The Theory of Change could derive from a formal, research-based theory or an unstated, tacit understanding of how things work. (Funnell and Rogers, 2011, p. xix)

So, the Theory of Change becomes the underlying motivation for building a social mission. But theories, without being tested, are just interesting things to talk about. And that leads us to the nitty-gritty details of program evaluation.

Program Evaluation Process

The process of program evaluation begins with our new friend, the Logic model. This is the tool that is used to map out what the program intends to do, the specific activities that it will undertake to achieve its objectives, and the ways in which it will determine if those objectives are met. One of the most critical parts of the Logic model is the distinction between short-term objectives (outputs) and long-term objectives (outcomes).

Let's say that you're running an adult literacy program (helping folks learn to read or read better). It's easy to see that the primary objective would be an increased population of competent readers (although even that could be a matter of debate, in that the definition of "competent" is itself open to interpretation – see what I mean?). So, let's say you get really granular, and decide that the goal is to improve reading scores by an average of 20 percent in one year's time (good work on goal-setting!). Then you define the specific learning activities that will get you there (still OK), and some sort of testing before the learning activities begin as well as after they are done so that you can accurately measure the change (man, you're cooking now!). But isn't the real goal to help folks access the benefits of society that are only available to those with strong reading skills? (Dang!) So, that wonderfully clear objective that you designed is only measuring a short-term result (an output) and not any long-term effect (an outcome). Now, let's say that one of your program graduates goes on to win a Pulitzer Prize for writing a groundbreaking novel. Of course, the chances of that happening when the author can't read are slim. But there are also other factors that may come into play (such as the level of creativity that person can access, or a specific life experience that they use to tell the story that wins the prize). So, up pops our old friend the causality problem. And the simple fact is the farther out you get on the outcomes timeline (the more time passes between completing your program and the result you wish to point to), the harder it is to show that the program was the difference that made the outcome happen.

Now, before you start to nod off completely, let's bring this back to the point of this chapter. Of all the tools available to the social entrepreneur, the Theory of Change and the Logic model are probably the most important. First, without them you really are just guessing as to how you might bring about the change you want to see. Having a proven plan and a way to measure results is the core of any undertaking. Second, any funder worth their salt is going to want to see that you have some idea of how you want to go about doing that thing you do.

The reason why this point is so central to this chapter is that the social entrepreneur uses the Theory of Change and the Logic model not just as a roadmap for change, but also as a means to design and develop the product or service that will generate sustainable revenue for the venture (and that process is so critical that we'll devote an entire chapter to it – so stay tuned!).

Reflecting the conceptual concept of public welfare, one of the places where social workers practice their craft is governmental agencies that deliver care to those less fortunate (in the U.S., entities like the Department of Health and Human Services or the Office of Veterans Affairs are two good examples). In other cases, governmental agencies provide funding to independent organizations that are chartered specifically to provide social services. In the U.S., we generally refer to these organizations as nonprofits. In other parts of the world, they are often referred to as non-governmental organizations (NGOs). As mentioned in an earlier chapter, we'll use these terms interchangeably (mostly because the distinctions are technical, while the general operating principles are similar enough for our purposes). These NGOs are the embodiment of the concept of private welfare and do much good work. So, let's spend some time developing an understanding of why these organizations exist and how they work. We'll also discuss some of the strengths and weaknesses of this field, and then come back to the ways in which the social entrepreneur borrows some of the tools from the nonprofit world and adapts them to do new work.

NONPROFITS AND NGOS

So, why do we have this thing called a nonprofit, and how did it come to be such a large industry? Well, there are lots of theories about that. In the next few paragraphs, we'll briefly review a few.

Governmental and Market Failure

One of the reasons why a government exists is to provide services to the public (although the extent of the depth and breadth of those services is a matter of debate). Despite the common perception, these services are not free – they are paid for by our taxes. And while there are many government programs that are very helpful, there are also times when the government is either unwilling (for political reasons) or unable (for budgetary reasons) to deliver a specific service to a specific group of people (Salamon and Anheier, 1998).

While you may not think of it this way, business and industry also exist to provide services to the public – and in that context, the means in which the services are paid for is much more direct (we buy them). But there are times when the market can't or won't provide a specific service to a specific group (usually because it's not profitable to do so) (Salamon and Anheier, 1998).

Into this gap steps our intrepid friend the NGO, seeking to offer care to those that the systems of government and commerce have either ignored or overlooked. Sometimes, the funding for these organizations comes from a government program, while at other times it comes from private grants or individual donations. Because the provision of these services is often too costly to produce a profit, many countries will offer some sort of tax relief to the enterprises that work in this space, so that the funding received can be put to work more directly in delivering services to those in need (Salamon and Anheier, 1998).

BOX 4.3   WHY NONPROFITS EXIST

While nonprofits are a ubiquitous part of our organizational landscape, it is an interesting reflection to ask, "Why do nonprofits even exist?" Does their existence signal a failure or an opportunity? Are they a natural consequence of development or economic growth? To answer these questions, Salamon and Anheier (1998) compiled six possible theories for why nonprofits exist:

1. Heterogeneity Theory. This theory assumes that the nonprofit sector reflects a failure of the markets or government, representing a gap in support for a diverse population. The theory highlights the possibility of a disconnect between demand and an available and accessible supply provided by the existing private and public sectors.
2. Supply-side Theory. This theory looks at the social entrepreneurs present within systems where there is a higher level of religious competition, or open competition for religious followers. The hypotheses of supply-side theory note that, where there is greater religious competition, there will likely be a larger nonprofit sector, and the reliance on private support will also be greater.

3. Trust Theories. Trust theories relate to consumers' inability to assess the quality of a product or service, and due to the nature that profits are not going to shareholders, nonprofits are trusted more to do what is in the best interest of their stakeholders compared to for-profit companies. The underlying hypothesis behind this indicates that the less the business sector is trusted, the more robust the nonprofit sector will be. In addition, a secondary hypothesis exists that a lower trust in the business sector may also allow nonprofits to be more business-like in their approach to financing, with less dependence on donations and grants and more revenue coming in from fees and service charges.

4. Welfare State Theory. This theory purports that governments are more likely to provide a greater level of social welfare supports with greater economic development. The hypothesis predicts that with a higher income per capita, the nonprofit sector will be smaller.

5. Interdependence Theory. This theory predicts that governments spending greater amounts on social welfare may create larger nonprofit sectors, with larger proportions of their incomes coming from the government. The theory looks at how governmental welfare and nonprofit agendas can benefit from one another through cooperative partnership.

6. Social Origins Theory. This theory positions the relationship between the government and the nonprofit sector as being a bit more complex, depending on both the extent of governmental spending on social welfare and the scale of the nonprofit sector, with each combination resulting in a different environment.

Knowing these theories of why nonprofits exist can help social entrepreneurs to understand the possible conditions, challenges, and opportunities that support nonprofit activity. The theories also tie back to the discussions on entrepreneurial ecosystems from Chapter 3, as they show how the governmental and business sectors may influence the conditions of the nonprofit sector.

There is no doubt that nonprofits serve a needed and useful function in society – so useful that they comprise a major industry (in the U.S., the nonprofit sector contributed roughly $985.4 billion to the American economy in 2015, making up 5.4 percent of U.S. gross domestic product) (McKeever, 2015). In addition to delivering specific social services, NGOs spend a lot of time raising money to fund their work. Unfortunately, the methods that are used to raise these funds are also one of the areas where the nonprofit industry has suffered significant criticism (Egger and Yoon, 2004; Pallotta, 2010).

Flaws in the System

As discussed in the last chapter, emotional appeals made in the interest of effective fundraising can lead to misplaced priorities in both the board of directors and the staff of the organization.

BOX 4.4   INTENTIONS AND CHARITY

Too often, Charity is about the redemption of the giver, not the liberation of the receiver. (Egger, 2015)

If you spend some time in the social entrepreneurship space, you may come across situations where you might wonder about the motivations of donors and social investors. According to Epstein and Yuthas (2014), social investments can happen for a variety of different reasons, including identity, process, financial, and social returns.

To Egger's point, among the identity returns, reputation is one of the motivators. Some social entrepreneurs struggle with this because they want donors and investors that care about what they do and not about what the donor or investor wants other people to think about them. If wanting to work in the social impact space, it might be important for you to reflect upon your values and your personal parameters for what type of funds you are willing to accept and from whom. Some donors or investors with reputation-based motivations may be amazing, but you may come across others who make you think twice. Think about these boundaries early, as feeling the need to accept funds can have you making decisions you may later regret.

Source: iStock.com/Spencer Whalen. Used with permission

From an internal perspective, there are also concerns about the level of planning that goes into the operations of a nonprofit. According to a recent study, the vast majority (90 percent) of U.S. nonprofits engage in some sort of strategic planning. However, less than half of those used the plan to measure performance of either the organization or a specific individual within the organization (Sargeant and Day, 2018). This lack of planning has been a concern of industry leaders for some time, with critics suggesting that many NPOs focus too much on outputs and not enough on outcomes (Hunter, 2013; Morino et al., 2011). As we discussed in the last chapter, concerns about self-preservation can often cloud the strategic planning of even the most well-meaning nonprofit.

BOX 4.5   OVERHEAD SPENDING

The concept of overhead spending is an important element to understand when starting a social enterprise. Overhead is calculated by adding up all administrative costs (including staffing, operations, infrastructure) and fundraising costs, as applicable. An overhead ratio is calculated by taking the total of all administrative and fundraising costs and dividing that number by the total overall expenses. This ratio is an important figure, as these are the costs just to operate and sustain the organization itself and not the funds needed to actually tackle the social or environmental challenge at hand.

While administrative costs and fundraising are critical puzzle pieces in delivering the social impact many social enterprises do, the ratio can signal to others that the organization is being run inefficiently. In fact, with increased financial transparency, potential donors and customers of social enterprises have become savvy about checking if an organization is spending "too much" of its incoming funds on overhead. Some donors even choose to donate with restricted funds, which means that the donated funds can only be applied to specific, specified expenses. In addition, granters have also been known to occasionally limit or prohibit the funds going towards overhead.

So, is overhead a bad thing? Overhead is actually a necessary element of running any organization. However, too much overhead can signal to potential donors and funding bodies that there are inefficiencies or imbalances. A survey from the *NonProfit Times* (Adkins, 2012) reported that there was a difference between what the American public thought nonprofits should spend on overhead and what the average nonprofit reported spending. The surveyed public thought that nonprofits that should not exceed more than 23 percent of their total expenses as overhead, whereas charities reported over one-third of their expenses (36.9 percent) were going towards overhead.

How much overhead is too much? From country to country, there may be regulations, recommendations, or benchmarks for nonprofits to follow. On the Better Business Bureau's Give.org website, its advisory statement suggests no more than 35 percent. Other recommendations are much more conservative, around 10–15 percent.

It is important to note that overhead is a positive thing for providing efficiency as well. Up-to-date technology, a well-trained staff, and healthy wages can help to provide stability and effective practice. To this end, it is important for social enterprises to be upfront and transparent with what is needed and how the organization strives to have the most impact with the resources it has.

Another area of external pressure on nonprofits is the long-standing perception that expenses (including employee compensation) need to be kept low. While reasonable on its face (after all, the money should go to the needy), this concern artificially constrains the organization's growth.

While the charitable sector does lots of good, and has lots of good people, it also has several flaws. The reason that this issue is important in a chapter on the unique issues faced by social enterprises is that the aspiring social entrepreneur needs to understand this landscape, its strengths and its weaknesses, and use that knowledge to build a better process. One where income can be earned, rather than donated or granted. One where the explicit objective is to eliminate a social disparity.

Just to make sure we understand each other, I don't think that the nonprofit sector should be dismissed or discarded. There is much good in this industry, and many good people. And many of the tools translate well into a social enterprise (in fact, organizing as a nonprofit may be the best way to launch a new social enterprise – a notion we'll dive deeper into in a later chapter). And there are lots of really innovative social programs being run in nonprofit organizations that look and feel very entrepreneurial. But before we look at how entrepreneurship adds to our extra-disciplinary concoction, we need to take a quick look at one other field on the "social" side.

BOX 4.6 DAN PALLOTTA'S *UNCHARITABLE*

Dan Pallotta, American entrepreneur and activist, wrote a groundbreaking book, *Uncharitable: How Restraints on Nonprofits Undermine Their Potential* (2008). Pallotta dissected several assumptions and positions that limit the nonprofit sector from generating more capital and having greater impact. His book identified five areas that need further attention, in order to improve the nonprofit sector's outcomes:

1. Compensation. Competitive salaries are critiqued within the nonprofit sector as being contrary to the causes they serve. However, this means the best talent would have to make big sacrifices to commit to a career in the nonprofit sector. With more freedom to offer competitive wages, the nonprofit sector may be able to attract top talent away from going into corporate roles.
2. Advertising and Marketing. Nonprofits are expected to not use their available funds towards marketing, but marketing can also be an important strategic investment to make more money to put towards doing good.
3. Taking Risk on New Revenue Ideas. Nonprofits can feel restricted in their ability to test new ideas and to be innovative in their practices, due to the pressures from those that fund them. This restricts the speed of innovation in the sector, which limits the possibilities for impact within the nonprofit sector.
4. Time. Nonprofits are expected to deliver a return on their funds (that is, measurable social or environmental impact) within the span of a fiscal year or funding cycle. For-profit investors often understand that big returns can take time, but the nonprofit sector is not afforded the same time to show impact.
5. Profit to Attract Risk Capital. The current financial markets do not support the nonprofit sector's ability to attract, sustain, and grow the capital it needs to transform systems and have broader-scale change. For-profits incentivize investments through providing a possible financial return. In contrast, the nonprofit sector is not able to offer its funders and donors financial incentives of any nature.

Pallotta's work has been helping to advance the conversation on how cultural expectations (within his context, the U.S.) limit the growth and impact of the nonprofit sector.

Public Administration

The next field of study that we need to consider is the world of public administration. So, let's start with the question that is certainly at the top of your mind – namely, "What the heck is public administration, and why is this subject included?"

Public Good

To unpack this concept, we need to start with the notion of a "public good." Although we don't usually give it much thought, there are any number of things we encounter each day that are publicly owned and operated. The local park, the highway, the police and sanitation services, and many more. Each of these examples are things that we all need but don't make sense for us to build or operate on our own (imagine the chaos if each of us served as our own security force, or the expense if we each had to build our own highways). So, in one form or another, we band together and agree to have a third party develop and manage resources and programs that benefit us all (and to pay for them with some sort of tax) (Shafritz, 2017).

With that in mind, it's easy to understand that public administration is simply the management of these various public goods – in other words, it's all the things that govern-ment does (Shafritz, 2017). It's also

Source: iStock.com/Sean Pavone. Used with permission

easy to see that the implementation of public policies and programs is chock-full of disagree-ment and contention. Take something as simple as a small public park with a large tree that is showing signs of age. Some might think that the tree is a hazard that needs to be cut down immediately. Others might think that it is a grand feat of nature that needs to be left alone, while others might try to find a middle ground that involves pruning, fertilizing, and nurturing the tree. Each of these possible paths has its own implications – both practical (cost and use of public money) and personal (emotional and spiritual contexts and concerns).

If the tree was on private property (say, your backyard), then the choice of how to proceed would be up to you. But since it's on public property, there are many folks who will feel some level of "ownership" or concern about how to care for the tree. And each of these people will have varying combinations of power and interest in the decision. The local children who reg-ularly climb the tree have a direct interest, but very little ability to influence the decision (high interest, low power). The mayor has a lot of ability to influence the decision but is probably more focused on fighting crime and building the local economy (high power, low interest). The public administration folks call each of these interest areas "stakeholders." There is also a strong body of knowledge in this field about how to analyze each of these stakeholder groups in order to arrive at an appropriate decision and manage the concerns of the various groups (Bryson, 2004) (perhaps the most useful is the Stakeholder Power/Interest Grid).

Having a deeper understanding of the power dynamics in a situation is extremely helpful when one is trying to bring about social change. In addition to their usefulness in managing the interests of the various concerned parties, the social entrepreneur uses stakeholder-analysis tools to help design the products and services to be delivered – a process that will be discussed in Chapter 6.

The field of public administration also has a very strong set of tools for measuring and eval-uating social programs (de Lancer Julnes, 2009; McDavid and Hawthorn, 2006). It makes a lot of sense that the folks who are charged with spending millions of dollars of public funds would want to be able to show that the programs they funded were doing the work they were designed to do. Here too, the social entrepreneur adds an additional perspective to an existing practice.

Public Administration Applied to Social Enterprise

While the public administration folks are concerned about demonstrating that a program is making good use of public dollars, the social entrepreneur uses program-evaluation techniques to help raise additional investor capital as well (a technique we will dive into in Chapter 10). That's one way that the social entrepreneur takes established tools and techniques from the field of public administration and applies them in new ways.

ENTREPRENEURSHIP

So, at long last, we return to the field of entrepreneurship, that powerful and sexy word that drew us all into this space in the first place.

Opportunity

At its most basic, the process of entrepreneurship involves several steps, the first of which is seeing an opportunity. While the exact means and motives of opportunity recognition continue to be debated (Foss and Klein, 2018), just about everyone agrees that it starts with a person or group

of people who gain some sort of sense that there is a problem worth solving, a need that is not being met, or a better way to meet an existing need. Once that moment of awareness occurs, a process of testing and analyzing may (or may not) lead to a determination that the opportunity is big enough and broad enough that it could lead to a viable enterprise. From there, a process of structured planning can lead to the launch and growth of a new business (Barringer and Ireland, 2019).

Source: iStock.com/Johngo Shin. Used with permission

Motive

While the common perception is that the pursuit of profit is what drives the entrepreneur, it is just as often the case that they are motivated by a sense of accomplishment, or an appetite for risk, or even a genuine desire to help people or make the world a better place (Carsrud and Brännback, 2011; Lex, 2017). While profit may not be the motive, it is generally how we tell if the opportunity was genuine – in other words, the venture-creation process is usually measured by some form of revenue or income standard (such as the number of businesses created or expanded, or the amount of wealth created) (Lumpkin and Dess, 1996). So the general rule is that a successful venture produces a profit which thereby creates wealth for the owners and (by inference) value for society (Dees, 1998).

As we talked about in Chapter 2, all the basic tools of entrepreneurship still apply in the world of the social enterprise. But the fundamental distinction is the definition of profit (Mair and Marti, 2006).

Blended Value

For the social entrepreneur, profit and wealth creation are certainly a concern, but they are not the end goal. Rather, they are part of the process of creating an improvement in society. However, this improvement often evades the type of value measurement that is used in business (which, it must be noted, does not make it any less valuable) (Dees, 1998). While there are many great efforts underway to improve the ability for social change to be measured (the work of Jed Emerson being perhaps the leading edge of this endeavor), the fact remains that it is complex and inexact (Dees, 1998) – an idea that was discussed in our last chapter and will be further examined in upcoming chapters.

BOX 4.7   JED EMERSON, THOUGHT LEADER ON BLENDED VALUE AND IMPACT INVESTING
Jed Emerson is an impact investment advisor and thought leader with many publications and talks available related to social entrepreneurship and impact investing. With Antony Bugg-Levine, Emerson co-authored the first published book on impact investing, *Impact Investing: Transforming How We Make Money while Making a Difference* (2011). In this book, Bugg-Levine and Emerson stated that "Impact investing is what we do; Blended Value is what we create" (2011, p. 10).
In fact, one of Emerson's other primary credits is as the originator of the term "blended value," in the year 2000. According to BlendedValue.org, Emerson coined the term following a realization that social entrepreneurs framed "money" and "impact" as "both/and" rather than "either/or." To this end, Emerson argued that the conversation should be on the value created, rather than the dichotomies of for-profit versus nonprofit and "doing good" versus "doing well."

Further, while not discarding the idea that operating profits are a useful tool, the social entrepreneur will tend to reject the profit-maximizing perspective that is generally accepted in the business world (Emerson, 2018). One interesting example of this perspective is the trend in the restaurant industry towards a different type of pricing that pays a fair wage to workers and eliminates the inconsistent practice of paying tips to servers. While the idea of fair wages, employee benefits, and other programs most certainly will force prices up (and are not without their detractors), the notion that the worker is an equal partner with the employer and the customer in the exchange of value is something that the social entrepreneur would most certainly embrace. In the words of Pamela Hartigan (2006, p. 42), "it's about people, not profits."

Exit Strategies

The other area where the social entrepreneur views the world differently regards a concept that investors refer to as "the exit." Said simply, this refers to the specific plans that the entrepreneur has to "cash in" on the growth of the business so that the investors can "cash out" (in other words, get their money back, along with their expected return on their investment). In a commercial business context, the easiest way to think about this is to start with an understanding of a loan from a bank. We all understand that a bank doesn't just give money away – they expect the money to be repaid, with interest. So, if you borrow $50,000 and the terms of the loan are monthly payments at 10 percent interest over five years, you will actually pay the bank just over $63,741 over the life of the loan. In this case, the bank's "exit" strategy is that you make all of your payments on time (and the bank also has other exit strategies if you don't make the payments, like seizing your collateral – but we won't go there). Now, let's turn to the professional investor that is a familiar face to many – the venture capitalist or angel investor.

These folks also want their money back. Just like the bank, they also want a return on their investment (often eight to 10 times what they invested, usually within five to seven years). But unlike the bank, they don't have a payment plan that breaks this up into regular chunks. Further, while a bank loan expects you to have some sort of income that will generate the payments, the professional investor expects you to use the money to grow the business (and grow it fast!). The way that they get paid is through what's known in the business as an "exit." Usually, this involves either the sale or acquisition of the company or some sort of open stock offering (known in the trade as an initial public offering, or IPO – a topic we will dig into in Chapter 10). So, regardless of how the money comes into the organization, it has to go back out at some point, and be worth more than it was when it came in. And that additional amount (the return on the investment) comes from the profit and growth of the business (Sherman, 2005).

But what if the mission of the organization isn't about profit? Well, in traditional nonprofit funding, nobody expects a financial return (after all, that's why they call it a donation). But we're talking about a hybrid venture that seeks both profit and purpose. So, what does the idea of an "exit" look like for the social entrepreneur?

Consider this – if we are really trying to impact a social condition, then the true "exit" is the elimination of the condition. However, for many projects and issues, true elimination of a problem is not realistic (particularly when an issue has many complex factors – like addiction). However, a good program design will also define a specific group or population, and an impact goal (for example, reducing homelessness in the Washington Village neighborhood in Baltimore by 50 percent within 10 years). So, the "exit" would be that this goal is accomplished.

At this point, I'm sure you're asking how this definition of "exit" will satisfy an investor. We'll get into the details of that in Chapter 10, but for now, just know that explaining this outcome in dollars-and-cents terms is one of the most interesting parts of this new world of social entrepreneurship.

So, the first discipline that must be mastered is the process of new venture creation, but with an eye towards a different type of value and a redefined use of the concept of exit. But before we think about that, we need to talk a good bit more about how to build an effective social intervention in the first place. Stay tuned, because that's where we go next.

CHAPTER SUMMARY

This chapter explained the social origins of social entrepreneurship through the field of social work and highlighted theories of why nonprofits exist at all. All social entrepreneurship is underpinned by assumptions about how to enact change, called Theory of Change. In order to assess how programs and activities are accomplishing the change they seek to have, Logic models can help social entrepreneurs to view their process from the inputs and activities to the outputs, outcomes, and impact. Even with measured care for their impact, social entrepreneurs continue to confront issues related to the perceived tension between "doing good" (social) and "doing well" (entrepreneurship), which is evident through several of the nonprofit sector's persisting orientations and practices that limit its impact potential. Social entrepreneurs understand that purpose and profit not only go hand in hand, but the two can actually enhance one another, creating blended value.

QUESTIONS FOR DISCUSSION

1. In order to better understand how purpose and profit can complement one another, you will have the opportunity to select an organization, a Certified B Corporation (B Corp), and to observe how the organization acknowledges its orientation to "do good" and "do well." For reference, according to its website (https://bcorporation. net/about-b-corps), "Certified B Corporations are businesses that meet the highest standards of verified social and environmental performance, public transparency, and legal accountability to balance profit and purpose. B Corps are accelerating a global culture shift to redefine success in business and build a more inclusive and sustainable economy."

    A. Start by visiting the Certified B Corporation's B Corp Directory website at https://bcorporation.net/directory. Use the search parameters to locate an organization that seems interesting to you, and read the information on the website that relates to that organization. What is its rating? Is there a description of the organization or any supporting documents available?

    B. Navigate to your selected organization's website. Search for information about its work and impact, and reflect on the following questions:

        • What is its product or service?
        • What is its impact?
        • Does it showcase its Certified B Corporation status anywhere on its website?
        • Are there any marketing materials available or social media accounts that discuss its impact or certification status?
        • Is there an annual report available that highlights impact and/or profit?

    C. After completing your notes on the selected organization, describe your findings with a classmate or small group, and compare what you found with that of your peer(s).

        • What conclusions do you (or your group) have about that relationship of purpose and profit for your selected organizations?
        • How does this connect or differ from what was stated within the chapter?

2. The following activity will help you to distinguish between public and private forms of social welfare, and their intersections and how they collaborate.
   A. Select a social challenge in your local area that you care about.
   B. Find out what local stakeholders work on this issue.
   C. List those stakeholders, and classify them based on whether they work in public welfare or private welfare.
   - Based on their websites, write down what role or scope each of these institutions or organizations play, as in the table below.

Table 4.1   Sample table for stakeholder analysis

Public welfare institutions + roles	Collaboration space	Private welfare institutions + roles
• Institution #1 • Role, scope • Institution #2 • Role, scope • …	• Public Welfare Institution #2 has worked on programming with Private Institution #1 • …	• Institution #1 • Role, scope • Institution #2 • Role, scope • …

   - Do some digging on how these organizations might work together. In the middle column, jot down your observations. Do they collaborate on programming together? Does one provide funding for another? Does one seem to complement or supplement the services of the other?
   D. After completing this exercise, what conclusions do you have? If you were a consultant and making recommendations to these organizations, based on what you know, how would you recommend they enhance or adjust their actions?

3. Based on your review of the chapter, generate a list of the presented critiques and limiting orientations of the nonprofit sector:
   A. After writing this list, what are your reactions? Have you seen or heard of any of these challenges and issues within your experience?
   B. Discuss with a partner or small group to see what your group agrees upon.
   C. Interview someone who works within the nonprofit sector, and list some of the issues highlighted within the chapter.
   - What are their opinions?
   - What resonates with them and their experiences or the experiences of their colleagues and connections?
   - What do they find challenging within these critiques?
   - According to your interviewee, what challenges within the sector might be missing from the ones mentioned in the chapter?
   - How does their vision of the nonprofit sector align with or differ from what was presented?

RECOMMENDED RESOURCES

Blended Value (n.d.). www.blendedvalue.org.

Bugg-Levine, A., and Emerson, J. (2011). *Impact Investing: Transforming How We Make Money while Making a Difference.* San Francisco, CA: Jossey-Bass.

Funnell, S. C., and Rogers, P. J. (2011). *Purposeful Program Theory: Effective Use of Theories of Change and Logic Models.* San Francisco, CA: John Wiley & Sons.

Good Must Grow Responsible Marketing (n.d.). Conscious Consumer Spending Index. https://goodmustgrow.com/ccsi.

Pallotta, D. (2008). *Uncharitable: How Restraints on Nonprofits Undermine Their Potential.* Medford, MA, and Lebanon, NH: Tufts University Press and University Press of New England.

Pallotta, D. (2013). The way we think about charity is dead wrong. TED Talk. Accessed 29 April 2021 at www.ted.com/talks/dan_pallotta_the_way_we_think_about_charity_is_dead_wrong?language=en.

W. K. Kellogg Foundation (2006). W. K. Kellogg Foundation Logic Model Development Guide. Accessed 29 April 2021 at www.wkkf.org/resource-directory/resource/2006/02/wk-kellogg-foundation-logic-model-development-guide.

NOTE

1.   Accessed 29 April 2021 at www.socialworkers.org/News/Facts.

REFERENCES

Acs, Z. J., and Audretsch, D. B. (2006). *Handbook of Entrepreneurship Research: An Interdisciplinary Survey and Introduction*, Vol. 1. New York, NY: Springer Science & Business Media.

Adkins, E. (2012, August 15). Survey: Charities should spend 23% on overhead. *NonProfit Times*. Retrieved from www.thenonprofittimes.com/npt_articles/survey-charities-should-spend-23-on-overhead/.

Alter, C., and Egan, M. (1997). Logic modeling: A tool for teaching critical thinking in social work practice. *Journal of Social Work Education, 33*(1), 85–102.

Barringer, B. R., and Ireland, R. D. (2019). *Entrepreneurship: Successfully Launching New Ventures.* Harlow: Pearson Education.

Brest, P. (2010). The power of theories of change. *Stanford Social Innovation Review, 8*(2), 47–51.

Bryson, J. M. (2004). What to do when stakeholders matter: Stakeholder identification and analysis techniques. *Public Management Review, 6*(1), 21–54.

Carsrud, A., and Brännback, M. (2011). Entrepreneurial motivations: What do we still need to know? *Journal of Small Business Management, 49*(1), 9–26.

Colby, I. C., and Dziegielewski, S. F. (2016). *Introduction to Social Work: The People's Profession.* New York, NY: Oxford University Press.

De Lancer Julnes, P. (2009). *Performance-Based Management Systems: Effective Implementation and Maintenance.* Boca Raton, FL: CRC Press.

Dees, J. G. (1998). The meaning of social entrepreneurship. Accessed 29 April 2021 at https://centers.fuqua.duke.edu/case/wp-content/uploads/sites/7/2015/03/Article_Dees_MeaningofSocialEntrepreneurship_2001.pdf.

Easley, D., and O'Hara, M. (1983). The economic role of the nonprofit firm. *Bell Journal of Economics, 14*(2), 531–538.

Egger, R. (2015). Robert Egger quotes. Accessed 29 April 2021 at www.robertegger.org/writing/quotes.

Egger, R., and Yoon, H. (2004). *Begging for Change: The Dollars and Sense of Making Nonprofits Responsive, Efficient, and Rewarding for All.* New York, NY: HarperBusiness.

Emerson, J. (2003). The blended value proposition: Integrating social and financial returns. *California Management Review, 45*(4), 35–51.

Emerson, J. (2018). *The Purpose of Capital: Elements of Impact, Financial Flows, and Natural Being.* San Franciso, CA: Blended Value Group.

Epstein, M. J., and Yuthas, K. (2014). *Measuring and Improving Social Impacts: A Guide for Nonprofits, Companies, and Impact Investors.* Oakland, CA: Berrett-Koehler.

Foss, N. J., & Klein, P. G. (2020). *Entrepreneurial opportunities: who needs them?* Academy of Management Perspectives, *34*(3), 366–377.

Friedman, M. (1970, September 13). The social responsibility of business is to increase its profits. *New York Times.*

Funnell, S. C., and Rogers, P. J. (2011). *Purposeful Program Theory: Effective Use of Theories of Change and Logic Models.* San Francisco, CA: Jossey-Bass.

Hardin, G. (1968). The tragedy of the commons. *Science, 162,* 1243–1248.

Hartigan, P. (2006). It's about people, not profits. *Business Strategy Review, 17*(4), 42–45.

Healy, L. M. (2008). Exploring the history of social work as a human rights profession. *International Social Work, 51*(6), 735–748.

Hunter, D. E. K. (2013). *Working Hard & Working Well.* Hamden, CT: Hunter Consulting.

Lex, M. (2017). *It's Time for Change: Toward a Dynamic Perspective on Motivational and Cognitive Processes in Entrepreneurship.* Dissertation, Leuphana Universität Lüneburg.

Lumpkin, G. T., and Bacq, S. (2019) *Civic wealth creation: A new view of stakeholder engagement and societal impact.* Academy of Management Perspectives, 33(4), 383–404.

Lupton, R. D. (2011). *Toxic Charity: How Churches and Charities Hurt Those They Help.* New York, NY: HarperCollins.

Maignan, I., and Ferrell, O. C. (2001). Corporate citizenship as a marketing instrument: Concepts, evidence, and research directions. *European Journal of Marketing, 35*(3/4), 457–484.

Mair, J., and Marti, I. (2006). Social entrepreneurship research: A source of explanation, prediction, and delight. *Journal of World Business, 41*(1), 36–44.

McDavid, J. C., and Hawthorn, L. R. L. (2006). *Program Evaluation & Performance Measurement: An Introduction to Practice.* Thousand Oaks, CA: SAGE.

McKeever, B. S. (2015). *The Nonprofit Sector in Brief 2015.* Accessed 27 April 2021 at www.urban.org/research/publication/nonprofit-sector-brief-2015-public-charities-giving-and-volunteering.

Morino, M., Thompson, C. C., Lowell, W., and Cheryl, C. (2011). *Leap of Reason: Managing to Outcomes in an Era of Scarcity.* Washington, DC: Venture Philanthropy Partners.

Pallotta, D. (2010). *Uncharitable: How Restraints on Nonprofits Undermine Their Potential.* Medford, MA, and Lebanon, NH: Tufts University Press and University Press of New England.

Parton, N. (2000). Some thoughts on the relationship between theory and practice in and for social work. *British Journal of Social Work, 30*(4), 449–463.

Pérez, P., and Rodríguez del Bosque, I. (2015). Corporate social responsibility and customer loyalty: Exploring the role of identification, satisfaction and type of company. *Journal of Services Marketing, 29*(1), 15–25.

Rose-Ackerman, S. (1996). Altruism, nonprofits, and economic theory. *Journal of Economic Literature, 34*(2), 701–728.

Ross, M. G., and Lappin, B. W. (1967). *Community Organization: Theory, Principles, and Practice.* New York, NY: Harper & Row.

Salamon, L. M. (1987). Partners in public service: The scope and theory of government-nonprofit relations. In W. W. Powell (ed.), *The Nonprofit Sector: A Reasearch Handbook* (pp. 99–117). New Haven, CT: Yale University Press.

Salamon, L. M., and Anheier, H. K. (1998). Social origins of civil society: Explaining the nonprofit sector cross-nationally. *Voluntas: International Journal of Voluntary & Nonprofit Organizations, 9*(3), 213–248.

Sargeant, A., and Day, H. (2018). *The Wake Up Call.* Retrieved from Greenville, SC: Accessed 27 April 2021 at https://concordleadershipgroup.com/!WakeUpCall_Report.pdf.

Saul, J. (2011). The end of fundraising: Raise more money by selling your impact. Accessed 29 April 2021 at http://public.eblib.com/choice/publicfullrecord.aspx?p=661493.

Shafritz, J. M. (2017). *Introducing Public Administration*. New York, NY: Routledge.

Sherman, A. J. (2005). *Raising Capital: Get the Money You Need to Grow Your Business*. New York, NY: AMACOM.

Shoemaker, L. M. (1998). Early conflicts in social work education. *Social Service Review, 72*(2), 182–191.

In 1983, Robert Egger's dreams came true. He was the manager of a popular Washington, DC nightclub, booking top name performers and generally making a scene. Recently engaged, he and his fiancé had started attending a local church (more because it would be their wedding venue than because of any particular spiritual calling). One day, having run out of excuses to say no, Robert and Claudia found themselves volunteering for a program run by the church that prepared and delivered meals to homeless individuals in DC. The food that provided the meals was purchased and prepared by the members of the church, and the lines of the needy formed well before the delivery vehicle pulled up to hand out the meals.

Having never really encountered disadvantaged folks up close, Egger was filled with the typical mixed feelings that come when you see poverty first-hand. Part fear, part anger (at both the system and the individual), part frustration (why can't this be fixed?), and part disgust at their situation. But unlike some who have such an experience, this encounter took hold of Robert in a profound way. With nothing more than a vague notion, he began to ask some questions.

The first involved the source of the food. The church parishioners purchased the food from a local grocery store (and not the cheapest one in town, by the way). At the same time, Robert knew first-hand that the hospitality industry (including the nightclub he ran) was notorious for throwing away food (and not just the uneaten portions of individual meals, but larger amounts of both prepared and raw food that may have been perfectly usable but did not meet some particular standard). Somehow, those two things didn't line up – "Why were we buying food when there was an abundant source of free food available right in front of us?"

The second involved the nature of the feeding program. First, it was a very small effort, limited mostly by the number of folks that the church could coerce into participating. Second, it started and ended with the delivery of the meal. There was little or no interaction with the folks being served, and no real effort to try to address the deeper issues that may have caused a person to need the service. Third, there were several churches doing the same thing, each in its own small way. Egger was bothered by the limited scope of these efforts – why couldn't there be a more efficient means of delivering these services, and why didn't the programs try to engage more deeply with those they served?

As these questions rattled around in his head, Egger also realized a few other things. The first was that there was a large population of homeless in Washington, DC, and that most of the programs that worked to help them took the same approach as the feeding program he

was working in – they provided services that kept folks alive, but (for various reasons) stopped short of working to solve the underlying issues (one of which, he realized, was chronic unemployment). The second was that the hospitality industry was always looking for skilled labor.

Source: Courtesy of Robert Egger. Used with permission

Robert used his business experience (as well as the legal help of a friend) and began to research various issues around health codes, nonprofit structures, and the nature of philanthropy. He and Claudia spent over six months building operating plans for the venture and sent them off with grant applications to over a dozen foundations. To their surprise and amazement, one of them got approved (and resulted in more than they had asked for). And so, in January 1989, DC Central Kitchen (DCCK) was born.

At first, DCCK simply re-routed the food, sending it to other organizations in need, using a model like one that had been developed in New York City by an organization called City Harvest. But as DCCK began to grow, it found itself based out of a small rowhouse that actually had a kitchen. And from that kitchen came the second step in the early growth of the venture, repurposing the donated food into meals that could be delivered to individuals and organizations. What started out as a simple delivery service was now a growing nonprofit that required folks with kitchen skills.

After hiring their first chef, Robert and his team came to see that feeding the hungry was not enough – they needed to find a way to reduce the need for their services. And from that epiphany, the culinary training program that would become a central part of the DCCK legend was born – taking some of the folks on the soup line into the kitchen to learn how to do food preparation and then become employable.

QUESTIONS FOR DISCUSSION

1. Did Robert Egger follow the basics of entrepreneurship? Why, or why not? Which of the basics did he apply (and which didn't he use)?
2. Did Egger engage with his stakeholders? In what way(s)?
3. What specific disciplines or skills did Egger use?
4. Do you agree with Egger's approach to launching his venture? How might you have approached this problem?
5. What was Egger's Theory of Change? What tools or techniques did he use to develop his theory?

NOTE

1. In addition to personal interviews with Robert Egger, material for this series of case studies comes from three primary sources: (1) Egger, R. (2010), *Begging for Change: The Dollars and Sense of Making Nonprofits Responsive, Efficient, and Rewarding for All*, New York, NY: HarperCollins; (2) Moore, A. J. (2014), *The Food Fighters: DC Central Kitchen's First Twenty-Five Years on the Front Lines of Hunger and Poverty*, Bloomington, IN: iUniverse; (3) Egger, R. (2019), My nonprofit did so much right, but we still couldn't raise enough money to survive, *Inside Philanthropy*. Accessed 20 November 2021 at www.insidephilanthropy .com/home/2019/6/19/my-nonprofit-did-so-much-right-but-we-still-couldnt-raise-enough-money-to -survive.

PART II
WHO CARES?

5
The basics of product development

Learning objectives

After studying this chapter, you should be able to:

1. Appreciate that successful venture ideas are a result of a greater build-up of other ideas, actions, and efforts.
2. Identify the possible sources of innovation and understand the variety of sources of ideas, as well as how they are contextualized through creative destruction and perceptions of originality.
3. Classify ideas that approach needs versus anti-needs.
4. Create a basic network map and dissect the network's strengths and gaps for engaging in social entrepreneurship.
5. Articulate why the presented basic concepts (idea shifting/sorting, customer discovery, hypotheses, pivots) are considered best practices in entrepreneurship.

Every new venture, every social innovation, starts with an idea. But the gap between ideas and an effective enterprise is wide, and often difficult to span. In this chapter, we will discuss some of the methods that can be employed to help generate actionable ideas for a new venture. We will discuss some traditional methods and sources of ideas, as well as some emerging concepts that may help to increase the likelihood of a venture's success.

Source: iStock.com/JNemchinova. Used with permission

THE BRIGHT IDEA

We all know the story of Sir Isaac Newton and the discovery of gravity. The legend has it that Newton was sitting under an apple tree when an apple fell and hit him on the head. Newton jumped up, hollered out "Aha!", and went off to write the formula that described the pull of gravity.

This "Aha" moment is how many people view the entrepreneur – as a lone genius who experiences a moment of inspiration that leads them almost directly to the development and production of a breakthrough innovation. However, study after study has proven that this is almost never the case (Cooper, 2011). More importantly, the individual that does have this Bright Idea is much more likely to fail than the person who takes a more methodical approach to generating and nurturing new ideas (Cooper, 2011).

BOX 5.1 STEVEN JOHNSON'S "ADJACENT POSSIBLE" AND "SLOW HUNCH"

Steven Johnson wrote a popular book named *Where Good Ideas Come From: The Natural History of Innovation* (2010), in which he argued that the world's greatest innovations were not out-of-place anomalies, but in retrospect could be directly linked with the context of their time. For example, Johnson's notion of the "adjacent possible" refers to the new potential configurations possible from our standard environments, routines, and status quo. Further to the point made at the beginning of this chapter, Johnson also describes the innovation timeline as a "slow hunch," meaning that innovations come from connecting a series of smaller guesses, predictions, or suspicions. To Johnson, these slow hunches formed through the intersection of people over time.

> The Vaseline-daubed lens of hindsight tends to blur slow hunches into eureka moments. Inventors, scientists, entrepreneurs, artists – they all like to tell the stories of their great breakthroughs as epiphanies, in part because there is a kind of narrative thrill that comes from that lightbulb moment of sudden clarity, and in part because the leisurely background evolution of the slow hunch is much harder to convey. But if one examines the intellectual fossil record closely, the slow hunch is the rule, not the exception. (Johnson, 2010, p. 78)

As highlighted in the excerpt, Johnson connects the slow hunch to entrepreneurial story-telling. When we hear stories of entrepreneurship, the best tales reinforce the "Aha" – or "Eureka" – moment ideas; rather, the majority of actual entrepreneurial breakthroughs are a result of many years of build-up and hard work, which is a story that is certainly not as much fun to tell.

Needs and Anti-Needs

If you think back to your basic marketing classes, we can recall that one of the definitions of a need is the difference between one's current state and one's desired state. I once heard of this being described as the need and the anti-need. Imagine for a second that you've been bitten by a poisonous snake, and the venom is now entering your bloodstream. The most important thing to you at that second is finding the antidote – that magic drug that will counteract the effects of the poison and make you healthy again. Similarly, a new product or service, if developed properly, meets the need of the target customer in a manner that fully satisfies the desire. It meets the need so well that it wipes it out. It is, in fact, the anti-need.

But, since we've established that the identification of these needs does not usually fall from a tree, we need to talk about where ideas can be found.

Sources of Innovation

One of the great minds in the study of entrepreneurship, Dr. Peter Drucker, talked about seven sources of ideas for innovation (Drucker, 1985):

1. The unexpected – an event or occurrence that does not happen in the way it was expected to and causes one to wonder why, thereby leading to an insight about a potential opportunity.
2. The incongruity – the observed difference between how things are and how they "ought to be".
3. Inefficient or ineffective process – something that makes you say, "That's not working well," or at least not as well as it could be; that moment when you think, "There has to be a better way".
4. Changes in industry or market structures – times when a major player enters or leaves an industry, a new product shifts how the game is played, or a key resource is developed or depleted.
5. Demographic shifts – changes in population trends such as birth rates, death rates, the number of people getting married or having children, the average size of a household or household incomes, and so on.
6. Changes in perception, mood, or meaning within a culture – such as the recent increase in concern over economic and racial justice.
7. New knowledge – from science, engineering, social science, or any other area of research.

Other Sources of Ideas
Other researchers (Kickul and Lyons, 2012) have suggested that ideas can come from:

1. Personal experience – many things happen to you while at work, home, or school, or during leisure activities. Some of them may not seem fair, right, or correct to you. This can lead to thoughts about how to correct the problem.
2. Hobbies or avocations – often, we want to share the things we enjoy or care about. This is particularly true for hobbies and avocations, which are things that we do because we want to. As we enjoy these activities, we may realize that there are barriers that prevent us from spreading the good news about our interest or passion. Many good ideas can come from thinking about how to break down those barriers.
3. Serendipity or accident – sometimes, an idea does fall from a tree and hit you on the head.
4. Systematic or intentional search – aspiring entrepreneurs can often be found deep in the archives of places like research labs, patent offices, and other areas of academic or scientific inquiry. Many "gold nuggets" of ideas are generated by these sources and can point an entrepreneur towards the beginnings of a path of developing a solution to a specific need or issue. Intentional monitoring of political, economic, social, or technological changes (Bryson, 2004) can also be mined in the same way, and will often lead to thoughts about new opportunities.
5. Awareness aided through external input – those moments where we see something in the news, hear a particularly intriguing speech, or engage in a particularly intriguing conversation with a friend or colleague can often raise our awareness about a particular issue or problem.

It's easy to see that sources of new ideas are all around us. But the entrepreneur needs to be alert to these sources to see the opportunities that may arise from them. Many experts have observed that "alert individuals … apprehend the changing environmental cues and realize that appropriate behavior at that moment requires a reassessment of the situation" (Gaglio and Katz, 2001, p. 98). And from that reassessment comes the beginning of an idea.

Sometimes this process is described as occurring through a series of rational, analytical processes that develop a unique solution to a market need, and sometimes it is seen more like the ability to gather resources that can then be applied to produce a solution that has not yet been fully envisioned (Sarasvathy, 2001).

Picture a moment in your life when you've had an experience that makes you think, "Now, that's just not right." Something in your head has alerted you to an issue, a process, a problem that needs to be fixed. That's alertness. Now picture yourself thinking about how you could make things better. That's the beginning of an idea.

Source: iStock.com/Fizkes. Used with permission

BOX 5.2   CREATIVE DESTRUCTION AND ORIGINALITY

The term "creative destruction" is a process where an innovation replaces another one. It was coined by Joseph Schumpeter, who framed creative destruction as an essential part of capitalism, as free markets encourage growth through the churn of industries and innovations. Examples of this can be seen in communications, with telegrams replaced by telephones and other faster innovations, or transportation moving from horse-drawn carriage to personal automobiles. Contemplating the nature of innovation as a process of creative destruction is important, as understanding the history of what has been, what is, and what can be helps to keep us thinking forward through being informed about the past.

The notion of creative destruction is also the namesake of one of the chapters of Adam Grant's *Originals: How Non-Conformists Move the World* (2016). In the chapter he suggests that achievement happens through both designing and operating within the status quo (conformity) and against it (originality).

> Conformity means following the crowd down conventional paths and maintaining the status quo. Originality is taking the road less traveled, championing a set of novel ideas that go against the grain but ultimately make things better. (Grant, 2016, p. 3)

When thinking about the connections of conformity and originality in social entrepreneurship, both forms exist and both contribute value. While we, as a society, hold originality in high esteem, waiting for a completely original, innovative idea means losing precious time to have a social impact. Most social enterprises will not be original, but a social entrepreneur should always be looking out for obstacles (for example, creative destruction) and opportunities (for example, originality).

Sifting and Sorting

Unfortunately, just having a good idea is not enough. Every idea needs to be tested to see if it can work. Some of these tests are things you may be familiar with from classes in marketing. Some of them may be less familiar to you. There are many methods for evaluating ideas, and no one method is perfect. Some of the differences are matters of taste or preference, and some of them are dictated by the specific idea. More important than the specific process you use is the simpler fact that you develop and utilize some means to sort and prioritize your ideas. Entrepreneurs who employ sound methods for screening and developing ideas into actionable models for innovative ventures have a much higher chance of success than those that do not (Cooper, 2011).

It's also important to know that no single idea is going to be a perfect fit. Every new venture has weaknesses, and part of the process of new venture creation is to consider how to enhance the idea as it grows. The goal at this point is not perfection, but simply a means to consider which idea has the most merits, to decide which one to work on first (Blank, 2013). So, let's spend a few minutes talking about how we can start to decide which of the many ideas we have are worth developing. We'll start with some simple methods and then move to some that are a bit more sophisticated.

Look to Your Heart

The first place you need to look to consider if an idea is worth pursuing is your own heart and mind. You need to be certain that this is an issue that you care about enough that you will be able to withstand the many setbacks and frustrations that are part of the journey of every entrepreneur. This personal dedication (often referred to as "passion") is particularly important for the social entrepreneur because the timeline for creating effective social change is typically much longer than the time it takes to build a successful commercial venture (Austin, Stevenson, and Wei-Skillern, 2006).

You also need to make an initial gut-level assessment about the size and scope of the effort needed to bring your vision to life. Is this an idea that is going to take a lot of time and money? Will you need a large staff or some sort of sophisticated facility to bring this idea to life? If so, it might be better to pursue an idea that is more within your reach.

Assessing your personal skills, strengths, and weaknesses is also important in this early stage. Ask yourself if you are the right person to lead this venture once it comes to life. Will successful execution of this concept require some sort of specialized skill or knowledge that you don't currently possess? If so, you may need to find someone who has those skills (which can be expensive) or go get them yourself (which may take a good bit of time).

Use Your Head

In addition to your own personal motivation, there are other factors that you need to think about that are in your direct control.

The first of these is your own personal network. One of the keys to building a successful new venture is the ability to build relationships. No enterprise (social or commercial) can exist without an extensive network of relationships. Even a simple business like a pizza parlor needs a vast web of suppliers, a strong community of customers, various professional support services (bankers, lawyers, accountants, and so on), and a dedicated staff. A more complicated business (say, a biotechnology firm) is also going to need to build relationships with investors, various regulatory agencies, and partners in manufacturing and distribution, as well as a much wider array of talented employees. Now take this up one more level to a social enterprise, where you are dealing with not just shareholders and business associates but a wide array of stakeholders and constituents as well as a diverse array of funding sources. You can easily see that just managing these relationships could be a full-time job, leaving you with precious little time to serve the community you care about so deeply.

So, in evaluating your idea you need to ask yourself if you have any of these key relationships already in hand. If not, you're going to need to build them. And that takes time. In fact, it takes far more time than you might think. And maintaining the relationships takes just as much effort as building them. Now, this does not mean you should automatically reject the idea if you don't have these key relationships built. It just means that you need to be honest with yourself about how much time it's going to take to turn your vision into reality.

BOX 5.3   NETWORK MAPPING

You have probably heard before that networks are important. In any entrepreneurial adventure, your network can be the difference between your idea getting traction and it being "stuck in the mud." In order to be prepared for when you need this network, it is a helpful exercise to map out who you know and how they might be able to help you.

Some people are worried when reflecting on how their network can support them, as they feel they might be imposing if reaching out. Actually, you would be surprised, because many people want to be helpful; you are just giving them an opportunity to feel that way!

To try this out yourself, see if you can work through the exercise at the end of the chapter.

Fast Feedback

Once you've looked inside yourself and determined that this is an idea worth your time and effort, you can move on to getting some outside opinions. But before you do this, you need to brace yourself, because the outside world is likely to be more critical and objective than you will be. One quick way to get some good feedback is to make a list of people who you trust to give you an honest opinion and ask them to evaluate your idea. This list could include friends, favorite teachers, family members, or other community leaders.

Prepare a short (two- to four-minute) verbal presentation of your idea. Be sure to include things like:

- Who this idea will help
- The specific way in which it will help
- How many people you could (reasonably) reach
- How long you think it might take to deliver the program.

Be sure to listen closely and take note of every comment and question you receive. More importantly, resist the temptation to defend your ideas when concerns or criticisms are raised. The point of this exercise is to get quick constructive feedback that you can use to further evaluate your idea. If you get a lot of good feedback, it's another sign that you should move forward in developing the concept. If the feedback is mostly negative, it may be time to move on to another idea.

Early Market Estimates

Now that you've gotten some good feedback, it's time to take a quick analytical look at your idea (this is not an extensive financial analysis – the time for that will come soon enough). Think in terms of what many call "breadbox" estimating. (Literally, is it bigger than a bread-box? Figuratively, think small, medium, large, extra-large, or gigantic.)

Some of the questions you want to think about are:

- How big is the market? (Or, in social terms, how many lives might you be able to improve?)
- How much money will I need? (Not a detailed cost projection, just a very rough estimate.)
- How much time is it going to take? (If I started tomorrow, how long would it be until I was confident that the venture was successful?)

Taking It to the Next Level

The processes we've just discussed are often referred to as "back of the envelope" calculations or "cocktail napkin" estimates – that's because they can easily be done on any available piece of scrap paper. These quick screening mechanisms can tell you if that big idea you have is really something to explore or just the result of a crazy dream brought on by an anchovy pizza. If the answer to your early analysis is that the opportunity is worth pursuing, then it's time to put in a bit more work to see if you can make this dream into a reality.

CUSTOMER DISCOVERY PROCESS

The most important early step you can take in developing a product or service concept is what's known as "customer discovery." Said simply, it's the process of making sure that the folks you intended to deliver the product or service to actually want it. Believe it or not, many entrepreneurs just assume that other folks will like

Source: iStock.com/Minerva Studio. Used with permission

what they like, and that the intended customer will intuitively appreciate the merits of their wisdom. Oh, if only that were so!

BOX 5.4   HYPOTHESES

The word "hypothesis" (pl. "hypotheses") may sound more appropriate for a STEM (Science, Technology, Engineering, and Math) textbook, but it is perfectly situated here as well. Oxford's Lexico dictionary defines hypothesis as "a supposition or proposed explanation made on the basis of limited evidence as a starting point for further investigation." New ideas, and new ventures for that matter, are guesses based on what information we have and assumptions we hold at any given time. This ties back to Box 5.1's mention of Johnson's "slow hunch," because over time we revisit hypotheses to check for accuracy and adjust them as we learn and experience new things.

What this should also indicate is that getting emotionally attached to an idea or venture, particularly as a social entrepreneur, is a bad idea because even a great idea or a successful venture, with all the information and experiences reinforcing it, is bound to a specific point in time. Box 5.2 expressed how creative destruction churns out less efficient and less useful innovations that used to be pretty useful. This is why the following phrase circulates a lot within social entrepreneurship circles: "Fall in love with the problem, not the solution." This means, if you keep your focus on the problem you are trying to solve, you will not lose sight of what is important. In fact, ideas and ventures can and should pivot as needed over time in order to do the best work they can.

Test Your Hypothesis

When you get down to the root of the matter, a product or service is really a set of hypotheses. It's a series of suppositions about your product or service, the potential users, and the other options that are available.

In regard to the product or service itself, the Product Hypothesis consists of the features and benefits of the product, along with any underlying requirements that must be met (for example, if you are building a software product, you are requiring that the user have a computer capable of running the software). You also need to take a stab at the amount of time you may need to develop the product and make it ready for use, as well as any other contingencies.

The Customer Hypothesis is comprised of a clear statement of the problem and your proposed solution, along with some early research on the size of the market (and any potential competitors). You also need to construct a Demand-Creation Hypothesis that explains how you will get the attention of your potential user and convince them that you have the right answer to their problem. Further, a Market Hypothesis needs to be constructed to determine what type of arena you are entering (is this a new market or an existing one? Is it saturated or relatively open?).

With each of the hypotheses in hand, you then perform a truly radical experiment – you test your hypotheses by asking actual customers.

This simple (but quite scary) step will give you tons of feedback (and more than a few rude awakenings – because none of us is as smart as we think we are). Now, once you get your feedback, you need to take what is probably the hardest step at this point in the journey – you need to listen to the feedback and modify your concept.

THE PIVOT

There is a huge moment of truth that occurs when you first present your ideas to the scrutiny of public opinion. You see, it turns out that none of us are as smart as we think we are. And this brilliant vision you've been carrying around has some significant flaws. And it's at this point that we begin to separate the players from the posers. Because this feedback will cause you to do one of two things. Either you will find ways to convince yourself that the feedback is wrong and you were right (in other words, listen to your ego), or you can take the humbling path of admitting

Source: iStock.com/Mananya Kaewthawee. Used with permission

you missed something and then work to fill the holes in your idea – which may end up looking very different from what you had originally planned. In entrepreneurial circles, this is known as a pivot (a concept we explored in Chapter 2, which may be worth re-reading!).

You'll often hear talk about new ventures making a pivot as they move through the product-development process. But I'd like to suggest that this habit of seeking feedback should begin long before you start to build things. For one, it's a lot cheaper. To build these hypotheses only takes some time, a word processor, and a few sheets of paper. It's also a lot quicker, for the same reasons. Finally, it's a great way to make sure you know what you're doing before you put big money into a project (and if you're not convinced of the value of that, please go back and re-read the story about skydiving in Chapter 2).

A FORMAL PROCESS

Last, but by no means least, the process of product development needs to be seen as just that – a formal process. The absolute guru on this point is Robert G. Cooper, who's *Winning at New Products* (2011) is the definitive guide to structuring the process of developing a new product or service. Cooper spends the first part of this book explaining why new products fail – with the number one reason (by far) being that the firm developing the product was not able to construct a hypothesis that demonstrated superior value to the customer (interestingly, one of the other big failure points is that the firm does not have a formal product-development process).

He then goes on to outline a series of tests or "gates" that should be used to evaluate the product along the way. But perhaps the most valuable thing that Cooper contributes is the idea that each "gate" involves a go/no-go decision. In other words, at each evaluation point a calculated decision is made to either move ahead with the project or set it aside. To be its most effective, this go/no-go decision needs to be made using facts and figures, with the individual egos set aside. Having been there, I can tell you that setting your emotions aside is incredibly hard. But it has to be done.

BOX 5.5   IDEO'S TOM KELLEY ON INNOVATION PERSONAS

When speaking on the topics of idea generation, creativity, and innovation, Tom Kelley has been a prolific thought leader and author. Kelley is an Executive Fellow at the Haas School of Business at the University of California Berkeley and Partner at the design consultancy IDEO.

In one of his earlier books, Kelley, with collaborator Jonathan Littman, wrote *The Ten Faces of Innovation* (2005), which highlights 10 different roles or personas for innovation, classified into three categories: learning personas, organizing personas, and building personas. Learning personas help to make sure the organization is taking in new ideas, perspectives, and information. Organizing personas help to structure and strategically think about time, resources, and effort in order to make sure they are getting used in the best way possible. Building personas help to deliver the value of the organization forward into the real world.

The value of these insights highlights an important lesson for aspiring social entrepreneurs: that there is value in a diversity of skills and orientations for those seeking to innovate. Kelley's books, among other sources, can serve as great reflection tools for aspiring social entrepreneurs to uncover their orientations, skills, and preferences and to identify what elements are missing from their team. This reflection is critical to determine what skills might be important to look out for when building or hiring new team members.

COMBINING FORCES

So, what's the best way to develop new ideas? The honest answer is that no single technique is perfect. If you're the sort of person who has lots of ideas, then the community-participation process might be a way to make sure your ideas are in line with the community you want to serve. If you start with community engagement, then the internal processes discussed can help you confirm that you are the right person to build the program that will meet the needs you've uncovered. Like many things in life, no one approach is right for everyone, and we each need to find our own path.

BOX 5.6   MINI CASE STUDY – BACK ON MY FEET

In the early morning hours of July 3, 2007, 27-year-old Anne Mahlum took off on her daily run through the streets of Philadelphia, PA. Mahlum started running as a teenager as a means of coping with her father's gambling addiction, and knew the power of exercise as a way to recover from personal trauma (Hallett, 2013).

On this morning, Mahlum had some new running partners – nine residents of the Sunday Breakfast Rescue Mission, a homeless shelter in the Callowhill neighborhood. Mahlum had run past the shelter many mornings, waving to the men gathered outside. One day she decided to contact the director of the shelter to see if she could invite some of the residents to come running with her (Berman, 2009).

Born out of this experience, Back on My Feet now annually serves over 1,500 individuals who are currently experiencing homelessness. In partnership with shelters in 11 cities across the United States, Back on My Feet teams shelter residents with local volunteers who commit to running three days a week for 30 days (Sherratt, 2017).

At the end of 30 days, members with 90 percent attendance move into a second-level program that provides job training and placement support as well as access to housing resources and educational support. Over the life of the organization, Back on My Feet has served over 6,000 individuals, and has shown significant positive impact in members' health, mental outlook, employment rates, and housing (Sherratt, 2017).

A highly driven individual, Mahlum grew the organization through sheer force of will (Hallett, 2013). Funded almost entirely by charitable support from individual donors, foundations, and corporations, Back on My Feet now supports a staff of approximately 50 individuals on a budget of roughly $6 million and aims to scale to more cities in the coming years (Sherratt, 2017). Mahlum stepped down in 2013 and was planning a network of health clubs in Washington, DC (Hallett, 2013), which she did in the years to follow.

You can learn more about Back on My Feet at www.backonmyfeet.org.

CHAPTER SUMMARY

Entrepreneurship is the construction of ideation over time, not just a one-off "Aha" moment. Rather, the entrepreneurial process is the sum of its parts, including your ideas, actions, and efforts. Understanding that ideas do not actually come from "out of the air," this chapter highlights the variety of origins of passion, inspiration, and ideas, and frames new ideas as part of a creative destruction of the innovations and ideas that preceded them. The notions of need and anti-need help to shape and categorize your ideas: Is your idea solving the immediate need at hand, or is it eliminating the need altogether? Because of the volatility of ideas over time and the need to be centered on the problem, social entrepreneurs need to be open to constructive criticism and change, whether this means taking a realistic look at their networks (network mapping) or at their idea altogether (considering a pivot).

QUESTIONS FOR DISCUSSION

1.   In this exercise, you will start to see what sort of ideas can be developed to help.

A.   Over the past few chapters, you have probably been reflecting on what social challenges resonate with you. Earlier in the chapter, the sources of innovation were addressed, so hopefully you have had the chance to also reflect on how social entrepreneurs gain their inspiration as well. Now knowing this landscape better, take this opportunity to interview community members who are impacted by the social challenge of interest to you. If possible, ask permission to record the interviews, or bring along a classmate to take careful notes.

B.   Using this information and your own observations, identify specific opportunities where the needs of populations of concern are not being met. Use the table format below to think about each area of expressed concern and attempt to reflect on what opportunities might be embedded within the challenge at hand.

Table 5.1   Identification of social concern and opportunity

Concern	Opportunity

C.   Sometimes, the feedback you collect, observations you make, or ideas you have to solve the challenge can feel at odds, or can feel like they could be paired together. Analyze the table you created and see if you have any items that complement or conflict with each other. Note anything within the table that signals a possible conflict or complementary opportunity.

D.   Earlier in this chapter, need and anti-need were defined. For the final part of the exercise, organize your ideas into categories by the type of need in a table like the one shown here.

Table 5.2   Identification of need and anti-need

Need	Anti-need

E.   After completing this table, what are you noticing? What might this indicate about your ideas? What might it signal about needs and anti-needs?

2.   In the chapter, you were introduced to the concept of network mapping (see Box 5.3). While there are websites that can help you do an electronic version of the exercise, a paper and pencil will also work just fine (a pencil is recommended for its ability to be erased).

A.   Draw a small circle in the center of the page with ample room for writing around it. This circle represents you, and branches outward will represent the people in your life.

B.   Reflect on your top supporters or those closest to you. This can include, if fitting, your immediate family and friendship groups. Draw a circle (or two) close in to your center circle to represent these people. These top supporters will be your cheerleaders and promoters and, possibly, even first funders or customers.

C. Next, think about some of your mentors. These can be bosses, professors, teachers, coaches, and advisors. These are people who might be able to help you in a more professional capacity. Please draw circles for any and all of the mentors who might help you.

D. Think about your communities. Do you do volunteer work? Play a sport? Belong to a club? Think about the different communities you belong to and create circles for each of these groups, placing them as close to your central circle as they are strong.

E. Now, reflect on who is missing from this map of who is in your network, focusing on who is not represented. This could be acquaintances, family friends, co-workers, classmates, neighbors, or anyone who is currently missing from your map. Place their circles as distant from you as those connections might be.

F. With this rough draft of a network map, what does your network say about your own readiness to be a social entrepreneur with aspirations to tackle a social challenge of interest? Do you have connections to the community impacted? Do you have network members who have expertise on this area? Do you know anyone working in this area already? Do you have connections who might be interested and able to help you fund your idea?

G. Write down your observations from doing this network-mapping exercise. How was this helpful for you? How might this be helpful for social entrepreneurs? If applicable, what did your peers observe through this activity?

3. The chapter defined hypotheses and highlighted four different types. Using a website of a social enterprise you find interesting, dissect the following hypotheses you think the organization or business has behind its model, product, or service:

- Product Hypothesis
- Customer Hypothesis
- Demand-Creation Hypothesis
- Market Hypothesis

Once you have finished thinking about each of these hypotheses, reflect on this exercise as a tool for social entrepreneurs. How might this exercise be helpful for aspiring social entrepreneurs?

4. Based on your review of the mini case study described in Box 5.6, answer the following questions:

- What was the source (or sources) of Anne Mahlum's idea for Back on My Feet?
- What process did Mahlum use to evaluate the viability of her idea?
- How did Back on My Feet use the assets of the community to develop or advance its model?

BUILD IT YOURSELF: STEP ONE

Beginning with this chapter, and moving through the balance of the book, each chapter will include a series of prompts for specific steps that you can take to start to design your own social venture.

The first step along the road to building your social venture is to identify areas of concern.

On a separate sheet of paper, identify and describe at least three social concerns that matter to you.

RECOMMENDED RESOURCES

Blank, S. G. (2013). *Four Steps to the Epiphany: Successful Strategies for Products that Win.* Pescadero, CA: K & S Ranch.

Johnson, S. (2010). *Where Good Ideas Come From: The Natural History of Innovation.* New York, NY: Riverhead Books.

Reis, E. (2011). *The Lean Startup: How Today's Entrepreneurs Use Continuous Innovation to Create Radically Successful Businesses.* New York, NY: Random House.

REFERENCES

Austin, J., Stevenson, H., and Wei-Skillern, J. (2006). Social and commercial entrepreneurship: Same, different, or both? *Entrepreneurship Theory and Practice, 30*(1), 1–22.

Berman, J. (2009, July 21). Running program gets homeless residents on track emotionally, physically. *USA Today.*

Blank, S. (2013). *The Four Steps to the Epiphany: Successful Strategies for Products that Win.* Pescadero, CA: K & S Ranch.

Bryson, J. M. (2004). *Strategic Planning for Public and Nonprofit Organizations: A Guide to Strengthening and Sustaining Organizational achievement.* San Francisco, CA: Jossey-Bass.

Cooper, R. G. (2011). *Winning at New Products: Creating Value through Innovation.* New York, NY: Basic Books.

Drucker, P. F. (1985). *Innovation and Entrepreneurship: Practice and Principles.* New York, NY: Harper & Row.

Gaglio, C. M., and Katz, J. A. (2001). The psychological basis of opportunity identification: Entrepreneurial alertness. *Small Business Economics, 16*(2), 95–111.

Grant, A. (2016). *Originals: How Non-Conformists Move the World.* New York, NY: Viking.

Hallett, V. (2013, October 29). Back on My Feet founder Anne Mahlum moves to DC and takes up another cause, Solidcore. *Washington Post.*

Johnson, S. (2010). *Where Good Ideas Come From: The Natural History of Innovation.* New York, NY: Riverhead Books.

Kelley, T., and Littman, J. (2005). *The Ten Faces of Innovation: IDEO's Strategies for Beating the Devil's Advocate and Driving Creativity Throughout Your Organization.* New York, NY: Currency/Doubleday.

Kickul, J. R., and Lyons, T. S. (2012). *Understanding Social Entrepreneurship: The Relentless Pursuit of Mission in an Ever Changing World.* New York, NY: Routledge.

Lexico (n.d.). "Hypothesis." Accessed 28 April 2021 at www.lexico.com/definition/hypothesis.

Sarasvathy, S. D. (2001). Causation and effectuation: Toward a theoretical shift from economic inevitability to entrepreneurial contingency. *Academy of Management Review, 26*(2), 243–263.

Sherratt, K. (2017). Back on My Feet: 2020 Vision. Accessed 28 April 2021 at www.backonmyfeet.org.

6
It springs up from the ground: idea generation and community assets

Learning objectives

After studying this chapter, you should be able to:
1. Appreciate the integral role of the community with its buy-in, participation, and ownership of projects being critical to the success of any social enterprise that involves it.
2. Create and utilize the following tools: participatory asset mapping, ecosystem mapping, stakeholder analysis, and empathy mapping.
3. Recognize different types of capital, including economic capital, political capital, human capital, information capital, and spiritual capital.
4. Contrast the longer-term, systems approach of social entrepreneurship and the short-term, charity mindset, and understand the benefits and limitations of both approaches.

A DIFFERENT WAY

Now that you've gotten a good foothold on some ways to develop new ideas and quickly test them, we need to talk about a unique difference in the pursuit of social change, and how it may impact the places that ideas come from.

You will recall from Chapter 3 that there are several elements of a social enterprise that separate it from a commercial venture. Perhaps the most important of these is the notion of "people, not products." In a commercial venture, the idea is

Source: iStock.com/Orla. Used with permission

to develop and produce an innovative solution that meets a market need and produces an operating profit. In a social enterprise, the "profit" is measured in the extent by which society is improved. So, while the commercial enterprise produces an improved "product," the social enterprise produces an improved person. The second point from Chapter 3 that's worth reviewing is the concept of "community, not commodity."

Any enterprise is also a process. The commercial enterprise takes some sort of input or raw material, performs a process (assembling component parts into a finished automobile, perhaps), and then distributes a finished product or service (such as a completed and filed tax return delivered by your accountant). You will recall that the social enterprise is in business to change lives, not just at the individual level but also at a community level. So, in the case of a social venture, the community is both the "raw material" and the "finished product."

Having refreshed our memories on these concepts, we need to add a new notion to the mix so that we can talk about another way to develop ideas for social ventures. That notion is that people are complex beings, with their own ideas about what's right and wrong, the issues and challenges they face, and the paths they want to take to meet those challenges.

Unlike the clay that an experienced potter can quickly mold into a lovely vase, people often resist being forced

Source: iStock.com/Fizkes. Used with permission

into doing things that they don't want to do. If you doubt this at all, try to convince an over-tired 3-year-old that it's time for bed and you'll quickly see exactly what I'm talking about.

Since we've already established that social entrepreneurship is a relatively new field, it makes sense to see if there are other fields that have been trying to produce effective social change that we can borrow from. Happily, there are several.

BOX 6.1   DEFINING COMMUNITY AND ITS ROLE

"Nothing about us without us." That phrase, in one form or another, is central to the essence of community-based social entrepreneurship. It even pops up as the mantra of many social enterprises who work in communities. But first, what is a community?

A community is a group of individuals who share a common characteristic, which can be centered on geography, interests, profession, orientation, or quality. Now, understanding this broad definition of community, you can assume that no one is just a member of one community. We have multiple communities. We could affiliate as being part of a neighborhood, a city, and racial, ethnic, professional, hobby, political, gender, and sexual-identity groups, all at the same time. So then, when we refer to "involving the community," how do we know which community and who is in it?

For example, if you want to start a community garden in a city neighborhood, geography will inevitably play an important role, but it is also one of the groups easiest to define. Who lives in a certain geographic location? Who might own a business or property within that area? Who works in that location? Who might otherwise have a stake in that geographic area (for example, former residents, governmental officials, schools, and so on). All of these form stakeholder groups with an interest in what you plan to do in that particular geographic area. Do the residents want something like this in their neighborhood? How will your garden involve the people who live there? Will the local schools be invited to join? How will the local businesses benefit? How might the local governmental representatives need to support something like this?

While there are even communities of interest beyond the ones identified geographically (for example, gardeners, sustainability experts, landscape architects), this example sheds some light on how to identify a community and what questions to start with connected to these groups.

With this in mind, it is important to know that these groups are likely to not all see eye-to-eye. If this happens, who do you listen to? Which one is the most important community? While these are difficult questions, it depends. You definitely will not want to do harm or take advantage of a vulnerable or disadvantaged group, but if your interests are in their interest, they might just need some further convincing.

Using the community garden example, if the local community is economically disadvantaged, a garden space might not initially appeal to it as a top priority. However, there are other advantages of community gardens that might be of interest, like the opportunity to lower crime, increase property value, or have an affordable after-school program option or an accessible source of affordable produce. Find out what the community's interests are and do some research and ideation on how a community garden might be able to achieve the desired outcomes it wants to see.

Don't force the issue though – if the research, interests, and model do not align, it may be a time for a pivot (for a reminder of what pivots are, see Box 2.8)

A NEW WAY TO LOOK AT SOURCES OF INNOVATION IN SOCIAL CHANGE ·

Social work, public health, public policy, and public administration are all fields that seek to produce positive change in individuals and communities (Minkler, Wallerstein, and Wilson, 2008; Rothman, 2001). Each of these social science disciplines has come to recognize that community-based processes must be utilized throughout the development and implementation of social change efforts if a specific intervention is to truly meet the needs of the people (Berger and Neuhaus, 1980). While each discipline applies a slightly different label, they all share the same approach, namely that "participatory development" can produce an outcome where the powerless become empowered, share in the fruits of economic development, and attain the tools necessary for long-term self-reliance (Craig and Mayo, 1995).

The field of social work has a long history in developing practices and perspective in what is known in that field as "community intervention" (Rothman, 2001). In the field of public health, the use of community organizing as a tool for effective health education is considered a central principle of effective practice (Minkler, 1990), where it is generally accepted that the proposed intervention must be developed in collaboration with the community if the desired result is to be achieved (Minkler, Wallerstein, and Wilson, 2008). In the field of public policy, the role of the constituent in determining both the need to be addressed and the means by which it should be addressed has become a significant concern (Frohock, 1979). So, it may make sense to look to the community we wish to serve and work with it to develop tools and techniques for improving its members' lives.

Source: Rendy Novantino, Unsplash. Used with permission

Build a Relationship

Before we can convince a person (or a community) that they need to change, we need to build trust – and that means building a relationship (Gecan, 2004). Think about someone (other than a parent) whose advice you trust. You've probably known that person a long time. They have probably demonstrated trustworthiness on multiple occasions. The first time you asked them for advice, it probably was over a relatively small thing. Over time, you learned to rely on them, and they have become a key source of wisdom and guidance for you.

Now picture yourself as a resident of a challenged inner-city neighborhood. One day, a group of folks you've never met (who don't look like you, dress like you, or talk like you) come knocking on your door and tell you that they have the answer to your problems. The first thing that's going to come to your mind is a question: "How can you know what's best for me if you don't even know me?" And, even if it's true that they do have an answer, you're not very likely to listen to them. If you do listen, you will likely make a half-hearted effort to do as they say.

Now, let's say that your circumstances are dire enough that you take whatever charitable contribution these well-meaning folks are offering. While it may be critical to your daily survival, it's not going to help you build self-sufficiency. In fact, it's going to build a dependency, where you're going to start to count on that charitable contribution as a regular occurrence in your life. This sort of co-dependent relationship does not make healthy communities grow (Lupton, 2011). But a relationship that involves spending time with a person (or a community) before developing solutions to specific problems can do wonders in creating sustainable and lasting improvements.[1]

BOX 6.2   STAKEHOLDERS AND EMPATHY MAPPING

In order to frame the value of community as a collective (through tools like those introduced later in this chapter, as well as in Chapter 7), doing an empathy-mapping exercise can help social entrepreneurs first understand who the members of the community are. Within a community, there are likely several categories of people who share similar traits, qualities, orientations, and interests.

For example, if you were doing a social startup that provided educational support in math through an after-school program, you could frame categories as broad as "parents" or, depending on whether their needs or expectations differ too much within that broad category, you could decide to be more specific (for example, "stay-at-home parents," "low-income parents," "working single parents"). What would cause you to be more specific in this case? Well, these groups might each make you think about a distinct need. For stay-at-home parents, they might have more time and interest in volunteering opportunities. Low-income parents might be concerned about costs and interested in scholarship opportunities. Working single parents might be concerned about their child's ability to get consistent and safe transportation to and from the program.

While these are generalizations just to illustrate how narrow you need to go, defining these groups early helps social entrepreneurs to adequately consider the unique needs and expectations of these groups. Each of these groups also represents a distinct stakeholder or customer segment, which will come in handy, as these are used within multiple tools for different purposes (for example, a business model canvas or a Stakeholder Power/ Interest Grid).

As we will see with many tools, there are a variety of variations of the following table for empathy mapping, but the following is a great starting point for understanding the community at either the individual level (informed through one-on-one interviews) or at the group level (compiling perspectives at the stakeholder or customer-segment level).

While some of these boxes may overlap (which is why some models combine them), there is a value in unpacking each of these to really understand your community and its people well.

Say? (Their attitudes, beliefs, values, grievances)	Feel? (Their worries, concerns, hopes, perceptions)
Do? (Their behaviors, actions)	Think? (Their orientations, perspective, issues/non-issues)
Hear? (Their influences, networks, influencers, what they don't hear/don't want to hear)	See? (Their observations of their community, environment, area that you are operating within – for example, education)
Consider to be a pain point? (Their reservations, frustrations, fears, obstacles)	Consider to be a win or gain? (Their wants, needs, aspirations, expectations)

Source: Adapted from Mendelow, A. L. (1981). Environmental scanning: The impact of the stakeholder concept. *ICIS 1981 Proceedings*, Paper 20, p. 142.

Diagnose the Problem Together

Once a relationship is developed, then the aspiring social entrepreneur can work with the community to determine what issues need to be addressed and how best to address them. There are many ways that this can be done, but there are three simple tools that can do the basic work.

Participatory Asset Mapping

This is a process where members of the community specifically identify citizen groups, local institutions, and other assets that can serve as a resource in addressing the issue at hand

(Kretzmann and MacKnight, 1993). Many times, the community is far better equipped than you or it may realize, and a thoughtful and conscientious coordination of existing resources may be all that's needed. If the current resources are not enough to address the problem, a Participatory Asset Map can serve to pinpoint the exact gap and provide a launching point for a new initiative that can fill the void.

BOX 6.3   ASSETS, ABCD, AND ASSET MAPPING

When we talk about communities and their assets, we have to first define what an asset is. An asset is the "status, condition, behavior, knowledge, or skills that a person, group, or entity possesses" (Burns, Paul, and Paz, 2012, p. 6). The identification of assets within the community helps to start the process of capacity-building for community change and development. Asset-based community development (ABCD) entails a process through which "communities map assets, evaluate asset data, mobilize assets for development, and then assess development efforts and the strength of connections" (Lightfoot, Simmelink McCleary, and Lum, 2014, p. 59). The ABCD process helps social entrepreneurs know what advantages and gaps exist within a community.

In order to collect, organize, and display data, social entrepreneurs can look at the assets within a particular geographic area via Google Maps or through a community-walk exercise, where you walk around street by street to look at the local businesses and industries represented. In addition, when discussing the term "mapping," the field of economic geography can also help to provide an interesting visual perspective. Economic geography helps to map physical geography with the economic conditions, activities, and physical resources or assets of the space. Physical assets can be natural resources (for example, a park or lake area), raw materials (for example, coal, wheat fields), or man-made resources (for example, available retail space or benches).

Once a list of assets is generated, items can be coded, and color coding can help you visualize key asset categories at a glance. For an even more engaging and interactive visualization, a Geographic Information System (GIS) can be used to electronically map a specific spatial area (a community, city, region, territory, or country) and pair geography with other data of interest (for example, demographic information, pollution maps, economic development). This type of data visualization can geolocate areas needing attention and action, providing area social entrepreneurs and other decision-makers and stakeholders with the ability to make informed decisions with attention to location.

While GIS visualization can be helpful to show others the rich information you have gathered, this level of technological know-how is not necessary to map community assets. A notebook, pencil, and some colorful writing materials (markers, colored pencils or pens, crayons) will all work just fine. Just remember, involve your fellow community members – they know best the assets that they bring to the collective picture!

Ecosystem Mapping

This is a similar process but approaches the issue from the desired end state rather than the current reality. An ecosystem-mapping process asks the participants to identify all the resources needed for the community to thrive regarding the area of concern. Once this "ideal state" is identified, the process looks back to the present condition and tries to develop pathways to fill in the gaps (Bloom and Dees, 2008). This Gap Analysis (Ansoff, 1965) then serves as a lamp to light the path towards building organizations that can fill in these gaps.

BOX 6.4   ECOSYSTEM MAPPING: RESOURCES FOR EXPLORING ECOSYSTEMS

Ecosystems are central to the establishment, survival, sustainability, and success of all enterprises, but especially social enterprises. While social entrepreneurs in rural, suburban, and small-city settings will likely be mapping their own ecosystems, those living in major world cities or particular countries may find ample resources on their social entrepreneurship ecosystem.

- For those living in U.S. urban areas, the Social Enterprise Ecosystems Report (available at https://socentcity.org) helps to look at the social enterprise ecosystems in cities across the U.S., through considering four areas: funding, human capital, quality of life, and support systems. These measurements help to identify key resources social enterprises need to grow and thrive, like money, good staff members, affordable space, and access to good mentorship and training.
- For those within the European Union, the European Commission supports many reports and studies on entrepreneurship, but one that might be best aligned with this area is *Social Enterprises and Their Ecosystems in Europe* (2020, available at https://europa.eu/!Qq64ny).
- When looking globally, the Global Entrepreneurship Monitor (GEM, available at www.gemconsortium.org) presents reports by country and region.

Beyond using their data, the reports can help social entrepreneurs to think about what kind of ecosystem data they might want to collect for themselves. As noted in the chapter, this is an exercise in figuring out the difference between the current state and the ideal state of the ecosystem. What already exists, and what do you need to find, foster, or create?

Stakeholder Analysis

This can also help to build community involvement and identify specific areas where an intervention might be helpful (Bryson, 2004). Unlike the shareholders of a business, stakeholders can include "any person, group or organization that can place a claim on the organization's attention, resources or output; *or is affected by that output*" (Bryson, 2004, p. 24; emphasis added). It doesn't take long to realize that there are many folks that are affected by the activities of any one organization, so just identifying who all the stakeholders are can be a daunting task. It is also quite likely that a comprehensive inventory of all the concerns of all the stakeholders will produce concerns and needs that are at odds with each other. Happily, this sort of analysis can also help identify the various levels of influence that each stakeholder group holds. At the very least, it will help to "identify who the key stakeholders are and what [solution] would satisfy them. Ideally, the [stakeholder] analysis will help reveal how ways of satisfying those key stakeholders will also … advance the common good" (Bryson, 2004, p. 30). One of the best tools I've come across for stakeholder analysis is the Stakeholder Power/Interest Grid, which helps you plot out the various power dynamics along two axes (Power and Interest). Those with strong power and high interest should be engaged in the project and consulted before making major decisions. Those with high interest but low power should be kept informed to make sure their interest is maintained, but don't necessarily need to be consulted. Parties with high power but low interest should be consulted on major decisions and regularly briefed, but do not need to be involved in the process. Those with low power and low interest (but still legitimate stakeholders) should be kept informed but don't need to be engaged (Bryson, 2004).

BOX 6.5   STAKEHOLDER POWER/INTEREST GRID

Within all social impact work, there are many stakeholders and stakeholder groups involved. Because social entrepreneurs need to prioritize where they put their time and money, the widely used Stakeholder Power/Interest Grid (shown below) helps social entrepreneurs to reflect on the amount and type of energy they need to exert in order to be efficient with their efforts.

The grid helps social entrepreneurs to reflect on two aspects of each stakeholder or stakeholder group. On the x-axis, the grid asks whether the stakeholder is someone with a low or high interest in the impact work being done by the social enterprise. Does this individual, organization, or group have a stake or interest in the issue? Is it an issue they care about? Are they impacted by the work in any way? Are they interested in the same topic? Are they interested in the work due to their location?

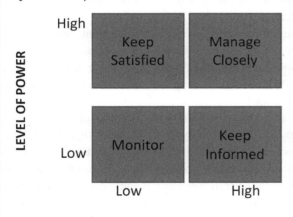

LEVEL OF INTEREST

Source: Adapted from Mendelow, A. L. (1981). Environmental scanning: The impact of the stakeholder concept. *ICIS 1981 Proceedings*, Paper 20.

Stakeholder Power/Interest Grid

The level of the stakeholder's power is on the y-axis. This helps social entrepreneurs to reflect on how much power and influence this individual, organization, or group has on their organization, its operations, and its ability to have an impact. Do they "hold the keys" to be able to do something (for example, permits/certifications)? Are they someone who may be able to use their funds, power, or influence to help or hinder the work?

From the right-side of the grid over (starting with the high-interest stakeholders), the following explains each of the four stakeholder categories:

- High interest, high power: Manage closely. These stakeholders have the greatest ability to move your mission, vision, and impact forward. They need to be closely managed, and social entrepreneurs should consult and work with them. In addition, it is important to keep them actively engaged with a sense of shared progress, so they can have realistic expectations of how quickly and how broad the impact can happen. Among others, this group often includes funders and influential, key donors.

- High interest, low power: Keep informed. These are stakeholders who are interested in what you do, so keep them involved through being informed on your progress and impact. This category can include community members and groups with an interest or stake in the work being done.
- Low interest, high power: Keep satisfied. Due to their power, these stakeholders have the ability to use their power to make your impact easier or more challenging. Keep them in the loop as needed because they do not have an active stake or interest in your impact and work. These folks may include those who issue permits, rent space, or play other roles that are important to the work you are trying to do, but who do not have a personal interest or stake in your organization's impact.
- Low interest, low power: Monitor (minimum effort). It is advisable not to spend too much energy engaging these stakeholders, as they will likely not help or hinder efforts. This group is the general public who is unaware, not affected, or not interested in the organization's efforts.

But Wait – That Sounds Like Work!

Indeed, it does. Just three simple tasks, but accomplishing those tasks can take months, and sometimes years. You see, there's an underlying element that must be established before the data you gather from these tools can make any real sense.

Before you begin any process of community-based program development, you must earn the trust of the community. I know that we just talked about this a few pages back, but it's too important to just leave there. In my opinion, earning the trust of the community, and being viewed as a partner, is probably the single most important key to the success of any social change initiative, regardless of how it's funded.

The folks who have spent their lives in this corner of the world refer to this work as "community organizing" or "community engagement." And by itself, it is work that can consume an entire career. Before anything else happens, you need to establish credibility with those you hope to help. I know of two community organizers in my hometown of Baltimore (both white, and both seeking to serve in predominantly African American neighborhoods) who moved into the neighborhood in order to build the necessary trust (working on the theory espoused by many that it's hard to hate up close). Michael Gecan, in his brilliant book on community organizing (*Going Public: An Organizer's Guide to Citizen Action*), declares that "all real living is meeting" (2004, p. 19). He says, "In a culture of quick encounters and multiple contacts, of instant access and empty photo-ops, there are fewer and fewer public relationships of depth and quality. The absence of these relationships creates great gaps in our society" (p. 32). Further, when working with underserved communities, there is also a level of accumulated trauma that can significantly increase the barriers to trusting relationships. Gecan observes that "you don't build relationships in a vacuum" but in a "tough and noisy world" (2004, p. 33).

BOX 6.6   COMMUNITY ORGANIZING OR COMMUNITY ENGAGEMENT

As you start to make progress on your social enterprise concept, it is important to acknowledge the power of the community you plan to serve:

> Community organizing is all about building grassroots support. It's about identifying with the people around you with whom you can create a common, passionate cause. And it's ignoring the conventional wisdom of company politics and instead playing the game by very different rules. (Tom Peters, author[2])

Make sure to make the best use of your community members' knowledge and energy by checking in with yourself throughout your enterprise-building journey to make sure you are including them. Community members who are empowered and encouraged to join you can be some of the most enthusiastic, informed, and dedicated supporters you can have!

While we're exploring this concept of developing a relationship with those you wish to help, we should probably spend some time getting you familiar with some basic concepts. The first is the matter of terminology. The two terms that are used the most are "community engagement" and "community organizing," as mentioned above. These two terms are similar, and there is debate as to the distinctions between them (Kselman, 2011; McDowell et al., 2005). Since I don't have room to air that debate here (and it's not the point of this chapter), I'll offer my take. Community engagement is more about helping folks who don't have a voice to develop leadership capabilities within communities, and helping individuals and groups interface more effectively with established systems (mostly government but also large anchor institutions like universities). Community organizing is more about rallying a group of people to work towards a specific objective, such as voters' rights or healthcare access.

In either case, it starts with developing a relationship. As a friend of mine likes to say, "Systems [and communities] are best unlocked from the inside." Said another way, you can't organize or engage a community effectively unless (and until) it accepts you. Felix Rivera and John Erlich put out a great little book on this topic, *Community Organizing in a Diverse Society* (1998). In it, they list several personal characteristics that can help or hurt an organizer. These characteristics include:

- Similar cultural and racial identification
- Familiarity with community customs, traditions, social networks, and social values
- Intimate knowledge of language and subgroup slang
- An understanding of the political and economic contexts and issues in the community
- An awareness of one's personal strengths and limitations

Rivera and Erlich (1998) also list a number of skills that are needed to be successful in executing the organizing of a community. These skills include:

- Knowledge of various organizing strategies and their strengths and limitations
- The ability to build consensus and empower individuals

- The ability to assess community dynamics and group psychology
- An understanding of organizational behavior
- Skills in evaluation and participatory research
- Skills in developing and planning a project and managing its execution

---

BOX 6.7   A SYSTEMS APPROACH TO SOCIAL CHANGE

In previous chapters, the challenges of relying on traditional charity models have been highlighted, including their tendency to favor the short term over the long term and address the surface-level problems rather than approaching the underlying issues. This charity approach, while it may do great work in the here and now, is likely not solving the problem for years down the line.

It would be a rare conclusion to state that a social challenge is a result of one thing. Homelessness and housing insecurity is not a problem solely due to there not being enough affordable housing. Gun violence does not only exist because there are too many guns. These two examples highlight only part of a greater picture of interconnected elements.

A systems approach aims to look for sustainable, longer-term solutions through examining the existing, interconnected elements that are helping the social challenge to stay in place. By looking at the broader system, we can better understand and organize the elements to make them support our desired outcome. A great book on this area is David Stroh's *Systems Thinking for Social Change* (2015), where he identifies four of the most common challenges of change and how systems thinking tackles each of them:

1. Systems thinking motivates people to change because they discover their role in exacerbating the problems they want to solve (p. 21);
2. Systems thinking catalyzes collaboration because people learn how they collectively create the unsatisfying results they experience (p. 21);
3. Systems thinking focuses people to work on a few key coordinated changes over time to achieve systemwide impacts that are significant and sustainable (p. 22); and
4. Systems thinking stimulates continuous learning, which is an essential characteristic of any meaningful change in complex systems (p. 22).

Again, targeted self-reflection, collaboration, collective action, and a learning mindset all help the systems approach to change to be more sustainable.

Models

Much like social entrepreneurship, there are many different approaches to the task of community engagement and organizing. And, much like a social enterprise, the right method to use depends a good bit on the context of the community and the goal of the organizing. Goals and objectives at the community level call for skills in organizing and implementation. Goals at the sector level (such as a specific social class or demographic) call for skills that are more technical in nature, while projects aimed at systemic issues call for sophisticated skills in organizational change (Hyman, 1990). It's also vitally important to be able to assess and evaluate the existing forms of capital in the community. In addition to physical assets such as roads, buildings, transportation, and the like, communities have economic capital (earnings and accumulated wealth), political capital (voice and influence), human capital (specific individuals with skills and abilities), information capital (accumulated knowledge and wisdom), and spiritual capital (beliefs and moral systems). Each of these assets needs to be assessed, evaluated, understood, and catalogued. If there are community assets that need to be strengthened, that work might need to occur before any social innovation models can be tested or implemented (Homan, 2016).

Community Capital

Let's talk for another minute about these assets, and why they are so important. It's easy to understand these assets in economic terms (the monetary value that they have). Physical assets can be assessed in order to determine their value (either for tax purposes or in preparation for a sale). Earnings and accumulated wealth can also be assessed in monetary terms. Even political capital can be converted into a dollar figure if you consider that voters are also taxpayers. Information assets can sometimes be defined in monetary terms as well (for example, in the legal concept of intellectual property). But the notion of spiritual capital takes us into another dimension, where we need to rethink the purpose of community development and community organizing (and perhaps social innovation as well).

In this context, what we mean by "spiritual capital" is the level of compassion, concern, and forgiveness that exists in a community. It is those elements of the community (and its individual members) that inspire folks to do what is right and good, both for ourselves and for others. While these characteristics are valued in most world religions, they are not the exclusive property of any one faith or belief system (Center for Community Health and Development, 2017). However, these core values are a critical component of the creation of a vibrant community (Chile and Simpson, 2004). Happily, these values can be developed and encouraged within individuals and communities (McKnight and Block, 2012).

While specific religions and religious practices can be a force for either unification or division (Dinham et al., 2006), the presence of strong faith leaders in a community is certainly an indicator that there are spiritual assets that can be developed. Further, in those cases where individual faith leaders can reach across the divisions of their belief systems and unite around common goals, "multi-faith" coalitions can be a significant force in helping a community move forward in a positive way (Dinham and Lowndes, 2008). These local faith leaders can also serve as centers of influence for community developers, making them a critical asset in this inventory and assessment process (Gordon and Perkins, 2013).

Specific moments in time within a community can also increase (or decrease) this level of spirituality. Disasters and clear injustices can be points in time where communities rally and build inner strength (Francis, 2015), or times when despair leads to pessimism and cynicism. Being sensitive to the history of a community and the specific highs and lows it has experienced can be very helpful in assessing its current spiritual health (Elfenbein, Hollowak, and Nix, 2011). Perhaps most importantly, this knowledge of spiritual health is a key indicator of the potential for social innovations to take root in a community and become a sustaining source of communal health.

SUSTAINABLE COMMUNITIES

One of the words that you hear often in social entrepreneurship circles is "sustainability." It's used in a lot of ways and has different shades of meaning in different contexts. In conversations about the environment, "sustainable" is often used as a synonym for "recyclable" or "renewable" (Mintzberg, 2015) – in the sense that reusable resources allow us to sustain this fragile little biodome that we all live under. In social enterprise circles, "sustainable" refers to an earned-income strategy that reduces an organization's dependence on donated revenue (from either individuals or foundations) (Bowman, 2011; Cohen and Winn, 2007). But in the community engagement and organizing world, "sustainable" refers to a level of independence and self-sufficiency, in that the community can chart its own path based on its needs and desires. A sustainable community is one where the concerns of all stakeholders are valued, considered, and held

Source: iStock.com/. Used with permission

in balance, where no one group or interest exploits or takes advantage of another, and where dependence on social services is not necessary in order to ensure basic survival (Green and Haines, 2016).

Now, let's dig out something that I slipped in a few paragraphs back. Maybe you didn't notice it (or maybe it made your heart stop). I said that community organizing and community engagement is work that can consume an entire career. Indeed, there are thousands of folks who spent many years as professional community organizers (one even made it to the Oval Office in the White House once). If you caught that, your mind probably went quickly to a moment of depression – with an internal dialogue that sounded something like this:

> I'm a social entrepreneur. I want to build something. But you're telling me that I need to engage with the community first, and that community engagement can become a life's work on its own. So how the heck am I supposed to ever start something if I spend my life in community engagement?

My answer is that entrepreneurship (social or not) is a continuous process of refinement (and that this is probably a good time to review the content on pivoting in Chapter 2). Also, the folks that spend their lives in this work are often working on multiple initiatives within a community, whereas you are (hopefully) trying to change one thing. So, the notion of rapid prototyping also comes into play here. The specific nature and make-up of the community is also a factor (as well as how much you personally differ from the community in your personal demographic). So, as with much of your entrepreneurial journey, this process of community engagement is one of enlightened trial and error, rather than one specific perfect process.

There's an adage that says that Perfect is the enemy of Done. To my mind, this is a reminder that we're never going to get things quite right, and that if we wait until everything is ideal (which never actually happens) we'll never get going. And while it doesn't excuse the need to do careful work to try to build relationships, understand the needs and desires of a community, and develop solutions that meet those needs in a manner that the community can embrace, it does give some comfort to the recognition that community engagement is hard work. So, take heart my friend – and start building relationships. Onward!

BOX 6.8   COMMUNITY ENGAGEMENT AND DEVELOPMENT

One of the most famous examples of social entrepreneurship (more specifically, social business) is Grameen Bank. Grameen Bank was started by an economics professor named Muhammad Yunus, who saw an issue within the village of Jobra, which neighbored his employer, Chittagong University Bangladesh. He noticed that the women involved in craft work were not getting a fair portion of funds for their work. They did not have the funds to buy supplies and equipment, so if wanting to work they had to owe money to someone else in the chain, who did not present the women with reasonable loan conditions.

Yunus thought that charitable giving helped do good but kept people in place. In contrast, if these women had access to loans, they could invest in their work and, in turn, themselves and their families. Thus, microcredit and microfinance were born. Yunus has been an avid proponent of social business as a model for community engagement and development, stating that "a charity dollar has only one life, [but] a social business dollar can be invested over and over again" (Yunus Social Business, 2019).

While Yunus was not someone living in Jobra, he spent a bit of his time there, talking to people and understanding the problems and needs of the community. The idea of microfinance was born from his time listening, rather than telling everyone what they needed. He built relationships with the community and invested his own money to show his trust and belief in the women. However, instead of keeping the power dynamic of himself as lender and community women as borrowers, he built the model of accountability for repaying the loan back to the members of the community, rather than outside of it.

While the stories of Grameen Bank, Yunus, and microlending have each been recognized through awards and told through many films, reports, books, and articles, his orientation on the importance of the community and its involvement shows how social entrepreneurs need to build relationships and be "in tune" with the community and its issues and needs. Furthermore, Yunus worked with the community to look at its assets and ecosystem in order to determine its existing benefits and needs. As a leader, he empowered others within the community to grow Grameen Bank along with him and to share in the benefits and responsibilities that came with it.

CHAPTER SUMMARY

This chapter centered around the importance of the community in the work that social entrepreneurs do. The community's commitment, interest, participation, and ownership are all essential to the success of any social venture that involves it. Within their partnership with the community, social entrepreneurs work with others to assess community assets and to organize them through helpful tools. Assets span the many different types of capital: economic, political, human, information, and spiritual capital. These measures – involving the community, assessing and organizing the community's assets, and identifying the various types of capital within the community – all reflect a sustainable, systems approach to change, which is the central mindset of social entrepreneurs.

QUESTIONS FOR DISCUSSION

The following exercises will utilize the common table below that covers both assets and ecosystems.

1. Think about yourself as a social entrepreneur, either the founder with a new idea or project or as the head of an existing organization. Using the Assets column, think of what you would be able to bring to a social enterprise by generating a list or visual map of your individual assets.

   A. What assets would you bring to a project or idea of interest?

   B. What are your weakest assets? What assets are you missing?

   C. Considering your previous responses, what are some ways you can account or compensate for your individual asset strengths and weaknesses? What would be your next steps?

2. To better understand your community of interest at a close or micro-level, conduct an empathy-mapping exercise. Using the chart shown in Box 6.2, interview a potential customer or beneficiary from within the community, and record their responses on the empathy-mapping table. If time permits, try this exercise with two to three different individuals.

   A. After filling in each part of the table, what did you learn from their responses?

   B. What information was noted within multiple areas?

   C. Did any of the responses seem to contradict one another? How might a social entrepreneur handle a perceived contradiction?

   D. How do you think this tool has helped you shape or reflect upon your idea?

3. Using the same idea or project of interest or existing social enterprise, try to conduct a participatory-asset-mapping exercise. Starting with the same Assets column, reflect on the assets available at different levels, including your team (co-founders, staff, volunteers), partners (other local organizations, donors), and community (neighborhood, town/city). Please note that ideally you would involve others from the community to help you in developing this collective asset map, but should that not be possible, you can work with fellow classmates or others within a group to work through your thoughts on what collective assets are available.

   A. What assets does your collective environment bring to your project or idea of interest?

B. What are your weakest collective assets? What collective assets are you missing?

C. Considering your previous responses, what are some ways you can account or compensate for your collective asset strengths and weaknesses? What would be your next steps? Are there any other partners or community assets that could be brought in?

4. As a final step, reflect on the broader ecosystem. Use the same new idea or project or existing social enterprise. Review each of the categories and subcategories of entities within the ecosystem. Please note, the distinction of "public" varies from country to country, and this is just a list to start the reflection and mapping process.

A. Rewrite a list or draw a map of the entities within the list that are relevant to your new idea or project or existing social enterprise. If having difficulty identifying which ones are relevant, revisit the collective asset list or visual you recreated. How might drafting out your ecosystem map encourage certain thoughts and realizations? To explore this question, try organizing your ecosystem list or map in different ways. If wanting some inspiration, do a search online for "entrepreneurial ecosystem" images to see how others have classified their visuals in different ways and with different categories. After trying this with your own list, what changes, additions, or edits did you make to your ecosystem list? Were you able to combine or show a different relationship than originally thought?

B. Based on this list and your asset-mapping work, what supports and strengths exist within your ecosystem? How do these individuals, institutions, groups, and public entities and agencies each play a role within the successes and progress of your organization?

C. In contrast, where did you identify gaps or weak points? Considering your conclusions, what would you recommend as next steps for action?

5. Now having done asset- and ecosystem-mapping exercises, what did you learn about using these as tools for starting, developing, and reflecting upon a social venture? What was meaningful for you in this activity, and why? What questions or thoughts still remain for you when reflecting on the assets and ecosystem of a community?

Assets		Ecosystem
Individual assets	**Collective assets (Levels: team, partners, community)**	**Entities**
Capital: • Economic capital (earnings, accumulated wealth) • Political capital (voice, influence) • Human capital (staff, talent, skills, abilities) • Information capital (accumulated knowledge and wisdom) • Spiritual capital (beliefs, values, moral systems)		Individuals: • Self • Co-founder(s) • Staff • Partners • Volunteers • Community beneficiaries • Customers • Other business owners and entrepreneurs

Assets		Ecosystem
Individual assets	**Collective assets (Levels: team, partners, community)**	**Entities**
Breakdown of specific assets:		Institutions:

Breakdown of specific assets:

- Time
- Vision
- Money
- Knowledge
- Experience
- Skills, talents, and abilities
- Creativity and entrepreneurial mindset
- Energy, passion, and enthusiasm
- Physical space (including commercial, residential, and public spaces)
- Material resources
- Natural resources and supplies
- Personal background and story
- Supports (family, friends, mentors)
- Connections and networks
- Donors
- Human resources (staff, volunteers)
- Values and faith
- Culture, traditions, and events
- Leadership

Institutions:

- Businesses
- Nonprofits (food banks, social service, environmental)
- Foundations
- Banks and financial institutions
- Educational institutions (schools, colleges/universities, training, and vocational schools)
- Research institutions
- Medical, health, and wellness organizations
- Religious institutions
- Service organizations (law, accounting)
- Media organizations (print, social media, websites, TV)
- Communications and technology (telecom, Internet)

Groups:

- Associations and clubs (interest, sport, cultural, arts, youth, senior, professional, sports/fitness)
- Unions (teacher, trade, craft, service)
- Community organizations (neighborhood, social, service, recreational, arts)
- Policy, political, and advocacy groups
- Advisory boards
- Promotional (competitions, awards, recognition)

Public entities and agencies:

- Governmental governance institutions and agencies (local, state/regional, national, international)
- Public safety and law enforcement (police, firefighters, courts)
- Educational institutions (schools, libraries, colleges/universities)
- Social and health agencies (human services, public housing, employment/unemployment, public health, disaster relief, substance abuse, nutrition)
- Transportation units
- Public infrastructure (sewage, trash, water, electricity)
- Environmental protection agencies (water, air, land, plants, agriculture)
- Economy, economic environment, and commercial activity (local, state/regional, national)

6. Select a social enterprise you are familiar with, and think about all of the stakeholders of the organization. Using the Stakeholder Power/Interest Grid below, categorize each stakeholder into where they might fall within the grid.
   A. In completing this exercise, what realizations or conclusions do you have?
   B. How might social entrepreneurs benefit from doing this type of reflective exercise?
   C. Under what conditions might a stakeholder move from one category to another?
   D. Compare your grid with that of a peer, and respond to the following:
      - Introduce your selected organization.

- Do your selected organizations share any stakeholders in common? If so, did you both place the stakeholder in the same box? Why, or why not?

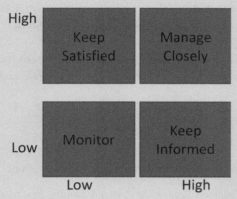

LEVEL OF POWER

High

Keep Satisfied

Manage Closely

Low

Monitor

Keep Informed

Low   High

LEVEL OF INTEREST

- What differences do you see in your stakeholders or their positions, and why?
- Are there any stakeholders missing?
- Are there any who you would have placed in another box instead? Why, or why not?

Source: Adapted from Mendelow, A. L. (1981). Environmental scanning: The impact of the stakeholder concept. *ICIS 1981 Proceedings*, Paper 20.

BUILD IT YOURSELF: STEP TWO

The next step in developing your own social enterprise is to use the knowledge you've gained in this chapter to start to identify specific areas where you can create effective and sustainable social change. Armed with the list of social concerns you identified in the last chapter, you now need to go out into the community. Step two in the "build it yourself" process requires you to do two things:

1. Interview members of the communities impacted by the social concerns you have identified.
2. Use that information to identify specific opportunities where the needs of these populations of concern are not being met.

RECOMMENDED RESOURCES

European Commission (2020). *Social Enterprises and Their Ecosystems in Europe: Comparative Synthesis Report*. Luxembourg: Publications Office of the European Union. Accessed 27 April 2021 at https://europa.eu/!Qq64ny.

Gecan, M. (2004). *Going Public: An Organizer's Guide to Citizen Action*. New York, NY: Anchor Books.

Global Entrepreneurship Monitor (n.d.). Accessed 27 April 2021 at http://gemconsortium.org.

Lupton, R. (2011). *Toxic Charity: How Churches and Charities Hurt Those They Help (And How to Reverse It)*. New York, NY: HarperCollins.

Social Enterprise Ecosystems Report (n.d.). Accessed 27 April 2021 at https://socentcity.org.

Stroh, D. P. (2015). *Systems Thinking for Social Change: A Practical Guide to Solving Complex Problems – Avoiding Unintended Consequences, and Achieving Lasting Results*. White River Junction, VT: Chelsea Green Publishing.

Yunus, M., and Jolis, A. (2007). *Banker to the Poor: Micro-Lending and the Battle against World Poverty*. New York, NY: Public Affairs.

NOTES

1. For more great insight on this topic, read Michael Gecan's *Going Public: An Organizer's Guide to Citizen Action* (2004) and Robert Lupton's brilliant *Toxic Charity: How Churches and Charities Hurt Those They Help (And How to Reverse It)* (2011).

2. Accessed 27 April 2021 at www.brainyquote.com/quotes/tom_peters_461711#:~:text=Tom%20Peters%20Quotes&text=Community%20organizing%20is%20all%20about%20building%20grassroots%20support.,game%20by%20very%20different%20rules.

REFERENCES

Ansoff, H. I. (1965). *Corporate Strategy: Business Policy for Growth and Expansion*. New York, NY: McGraw-Hill.

Berger, P. L., and Neuhaus, R. J. (1980). *To Empower People: The Role of Mediating Structures in Public Policy*. Washington, DC: American Enterprise Institute for Public Policy Research.

Bloom, P. N., and Dees, J. G. (2008). Cultivate your ecosystem. *Stanford Social Innovation Review*, Winter, 46–53.

Bowman, W. (2011). Financial capacity and sustainability of ordinary nonprofits. *Nonprofit Management and Leadership*, 22(1), 37–51.

Bryson, J. M. (2004). What to do when stakeholders matter: Stakeholder identification and analysis techniques. *Public Management Review*, 6 (1), 21–54.

Burns, J. C., Paul, D. P., and Paz, S. R. (2012). *Participatory Asset Mapping: A Community Research Lab Toolkit*. Los Angeles, CA: Advancement Project–Healthy City Community Research Lab.

Center for Community Health and Development (2017). Community Tool Box. Accessed 27 April 2021 at https://ctb.ku.edu/en.

Chile, L. M., and Simpson, G. (2004). Spirituality and community development: Exploring the link between the individual and the collective. *Community Development Journal*, 39(4), 318–331.

Cohen, B., and Winn, M. I. (2007). Market imperfections, opportunity and sustainable entrepreneurship. *Journal of Business Venturing*, 22(1), 29–49.

Craig, G., and Mayo, M. (eds) (1995). *Community Empowerment: A Reader in Participation and Development*. London: Zed Books.

Dinham, A., Farnell, R., Finneron, D., and Furbey, R. (2006). *Faith as Social Capital: Connecting or Dividing?* Bristol: Policy Press.

Dinham, A., and Lowndes, V. (2008). Religion, resources, and representation: Three narratives of faith engagement in British urban governance. *Urban Affairs Review*, 43(6), 817–845.

Elfenbein, J. I., Hollowak, T. L., and Nix, E. M. (2011). *Baltimore '68: Riots and Rebirth in an American City*. Philadelphia, PA: Temple University Press.

Francis, L. G. (2015). *Ferguson and Faith: Sparking Leadership and Awakening Community*. St. Louis, MO: Chalice Press.

Frohock, F. M. (1979). *Public Policy*. Englewood Cliffs, NJ: Prentice-Hall.

Gecan, M. (2004). *Going Public: An Organizer's Guide to Citizen Action*. New York, NY: Anchor Books.

Gordon, W., and Perkins, J. (2013). *Making Neighborhoods Whole: A Handbook for Christian Community Development*. Downers Grove, IL: InterVarsity Press.

Green, G. P., and Haines, A. (2016). *Asset Building & Community Development*. Los Angeles, CA: SAGE.

Homan, M. S. (2016). *Promoting Community Change: Making it Happen in the Real World*. Boston, MA: Cengage Learning.

Hyman, D. (1990). Six models of community intervention: A dialectical synthesis of social theory and social action. *Sociological Practice*, 8(1), 32–47.

Kretzmann, J. P., and MacKnight, J. L. (1993). *Building Communities from the Inside Out: A Path towards Finding and Mobilizing a Community's Assets*. Chicago, IL: ACTA.

Kselman, J. (2011). *Defining Our Terms: A Conversation on Community Organizing and Related Terms.* Accessed 27 April 2021 at www.bolderadvocacy.org/wp-content/uploads/2012/08/Defining_Our_Terms_A_Conversation_on_Community_Organizing_and_Related_Terms.pdf.

Lightfoot, E., Simmelink McCleary, J., and Lum, T. (2014). Asset mapping as a research tool for community-based participatory research in social work. *Social Work Research, 38*(1), 59–64.

Lupton, R. D. (2011). *Toxic Charity: How Churches and Charities Hurt Those They Help (And How to Reverse It).* New York, NY: HarperCollins.

McDowell, C., Nagel, A., Williams, S. M., and Canepa, C. (2005). Building knowledge from the practice of local communities. *Knowledge Management for Development Journal, 1*(3), 30–40.

McKnight, J., and Block, P. (2012). *The Abundant Community: Awakening the Power of Families and Neighborhoods.* San Francisco, CA: Berrett-Koehler.

Minkler, M. (1990). Improving health through community organization. In K. Glanz, F. M. Lewis, and B. K. Rimer (eds), *Health Behavior and Health Education* (pp. 257–287). San Francisco, CA: Jossey-Bass.

Minkler, M., Wallerstein, N. B., and Wilson, N. (2008). Improving health through community organization and community building. In K. Glanz, B. K. Rimer, and K. Viswanath (eds), *Health Behavior and Health Education: Theory, Research, and Practice,* 4th ed. (pp. 287–312). Hoboken, NJ: John Wiley & Sons.

Mintzberg, H. (2015). *Rebalancing Society: Radical Renewal beyond Left, Right, and Center.* Oakland, CA: Berrett-Koehler.

Rivera, F. G., and Erlich, J. (1998). *Community Organizing in a Diverse Society.* London: Allyn & Bacon.

Rothman, J. (2001). Approaches to community intervention. In J. Rothman, J. L. Erlich, and J. E. Tropman (eds), *Strategies of Community Intervention* (pp. 27–66). Itasca, IL: F. E. Peacock.

Yunus Social Business (2019, July 5). The social business revolution: Why is venture philanthropy the most effective form of giving? [Blog] Accessed 27 February 2021 at www.yunussb.com/blog/2019/5/23/why-is-venture-philanthropy-the-most-effective-form-of-charity.

7
Social Change Theory as product design

Learning objectives

After studying this chapter, you should be able to:
1. Utilize several practical tools for developing social change, including Theory of Change models, Logic models, and (Social) Business models.
2. Apply the following feasibility analyses: break-even analysis, social return on investment, and market opportunity analysis.
3. Understand the concepts of direct and indirect competition and critique the unique manifestation of direct and indirect competition for the social impact sector.

As we reach the halfway point in our journey, it's a good time to take a quick look back before we take our next steps. Hopefully, there are a few things we know now that we didn't know before we started this adventure. We know that the successful social entrepreneur needs to embrace all the basics of the craft of building a new venture (building and testing models, understanding that the process is iterative, recognizing the importance of being able to pivot, and so on). We know that the social enterprise will be more complex because we are dealing with people, not products. We know that we need to find some way to measure the social change that we seek to bring about, and to be able to determine if our intervention is what caused the change. We know that we need to draw expertise from multiple disciplines and combine them into something that makes a whole that is greater than the sum of its parts. We know that we need to establish a structured process for managing the development of the innovation and the enterprise that will deliver it. And last, but far from least, we know that we need to involve the community in the process, early and often. And while those are all great ideas (and important foundational concepts), none of them really answers the challenge of how to build an effective and sustainable social enterprise.

The good news is that this is the chapter where we really dive into the nitty-gritty of practical tools for developing social change. The bad news is that this is one of the more technically oriented chapters in the book. In this chapter, we're going to introduce you to some important tools that will allow you to start mapping out the ways and means of implementing the change you seek. We're going to talk about Social Change Theory, introduce you to the Logic model for social change, the social business model, the feasibility analysis, and the market opportunity analysis. At the end of this chapter, you'll have a much better sense of how to turn an idea into an actionable opportunity. Ready?

THEORY OF CHANGE

Let's start by talking about Social Change Theory. It's a fancy term, but a simple concept. At its most basic, it's nothing more than the reason(s) that you believe change will occur (Knowlton and Phillips, 2009). The most basic form for a Theory of Change is an "If/Then" statement – "If we do X, then Y should follow as a result." Let's take a simple personal goal as an example.

Source: iStock.com/SmShoot. Used with permission

I could stand to lose about 20 pounds. But unless I have a plan of action, that's just a wish (or a hope). But if I decide to watch my diet more carefully and exercise more, then I have a plan. So, in this case, my Theory of Change is that additional exercise and a more conscientious diet will result in weight loss. Or, said in If/Then format, if I eat right and exercise more, then I will lose weight. Pretty straightforward, right?

Well (as with most things) it's not quite that simple. First, my theory needs to be based on some sound thinking, and hopefully some sort of external validation. In other words, the theory can't be based just on our own ideas but needs to have some sort of proven logic behind it (Anderson, 2014). Happily, there is plenty of evidence that diet and exercise lead to weight loss (on the other hand, a Theory of Change that eating more ice cream will lead to weight loss might be hard to defend).

Second, you need to identify all the assumptions that are included in the theory (Anderson, 2014). One of the assumptions in my weight-loss theory is that I want to lose weight. Another is that I am physically capable of exercising. Other assumptions include my ability to acquire healthy food, monitor my caloric intake, and manage the various emotions that come with diet and exercise (quite a long list for such a simple theory).

Now, let's apply this concept to a more relevant (and complex) issue. Let's take juvenile literacy as an example. You've developed a relationship with a group of folks, and together you've determined that the youth in this community are not reading at the appropriate level. In response to this expressed need, you decide to develop an after-school program to improve students' reading skills. A simple Theory of Change in this situation might be that the introduction of an after-school tutoring program will help students improve their skills. Let's start to dissect that theory and see what happens.

First, this theory does not identify a specific population. So, perhaps a better theory would say that students in grades 3–8 in the Hollins Market neighborhood of West Baltimore would benefit from an after-school tutoring program. More critically, the reasons why this after-school program should work are not readily identified. So, finding some sort of independent research that shows that after-school reading programs are effective would help.

Further, some specifics on the activities that will take place might be useful, since it's not likely that an afternoon spent playing video games will help (unless it's a reading tutorial disguised as a video game – which might be your specific new idea!).

But just improving reading proficiency is probably not your ultimate goal – it's probably more like increasing graduation rates, or seeing more students being admitted to college. And here's where our old friend causality comes back to greet us. As mentioned previously, the further away you get from the actual activity, the harder it is to prove that your intervention brought about the desired result (Bronte-Tinkew and Redd, 2001). In order to improve the odds that your specific program will produce the desired result, you need to identify specific programs that have worked on the issue of reading proficiency, and find out what has worked and what hasn't worked. Since this issue is fairly common, it's likely that there is some fairly strong research that's been done in this area (and if you're unsure about how to find that research, your local reference librarian will be happy to help!).

So, what about the assumptions that go into this Theory of Change? Well, in order to read, one must be able to concentrate. But that gets hard if you are hungry. And we know that hunger is more prevalent in challenged neighborhoods. So, this particular Theory of Change assumes that the student can concentrate, which may not be the case. Other assumptions include the ability to access the appropriate materials and instructors as well as adequate facilities that are conducive to learning and easily accessible (sometimes referred to as "mobilization"; Blum, 1974). One of the trickiest assumptions is that the students will be open to the instruction provided in the program. Experts in the field refer to this as "impetus" or "motivation" (Blum, 1974). Just like I need to be motivated to lose weight, the student in the reading program needs to be motivated to learn. Assumptions may also exist in the various legal and social structures present in the community (Blum, 1974). Please also note that you should resist the temptation to develop solutions that resolve any issues you identify – there will be plenty of time for that soon. But right now, let's turn to a useful tool for mapping out these theories.

BOX 7.1   THEORY OF CHANGE MODEL

Compared to Logic models, Theory of Change (ToC) models are broader, "big picture" models that help strategically work through how an organization thinks about change and the rationale for why an organization operates as it does. ToC models can help serve as a roadmap for social entrepreneurs as early as the ideation phase to intentionally think through the complexity of social change. ToC models can help test assumptions, which can help social entrepreneurs think more at the organizational, community, or systems levels.

LOGIC MODEL

You'll recall from our earlier chapters that one of the hallmarks of an effective entrepreneur is that they build and test models. You'll also recall that testing models is a lot cheaper, faster, and easier than launching a project without having thought it through.

In building a social enterprise, the most important model is the Program Logic model (generally referred to as a Logic model). The reason this model is so important is that it is the tool for mapping out your Theory of Change in more detail. It's also the place where you uncover assumptions and identify gaps in the theory you have developed. When you're done, a good Logic model should clearly show the path from the current state to the desired state and define how we know when we've reached the desired state. The good news is that there are a number of guides, tools, and templates for developing these models.

But before we get to the practical, we need to talk in general terms about what this Logic model is. Perhaps the simplest way to think about it is that the Theory of Change is an idea (hence the use of the word "theory"), while the Logic model is a plan (albeit a high-level plan). Let's use a simple example to talk this through.

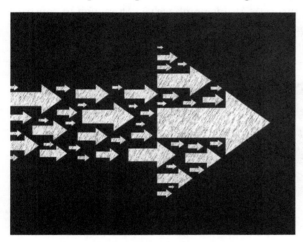

Source: iStock.com/Phototechno. Used with permission

Let's say that it's getting towards evening, and you've been studying all afternoon. You're probably starting to get hungry. A Theory of Change would say that getting something to eat will relieve your hunger. A Logic model would show that you are going to get a pizza, eat it in the student center, and then go back to studying while newly refreshed and no longer hungry.

To take this discussion to a deeper level, the Theory of Change outlines an intent, while the Logic model outlines a way to achieve the intent. The Logic model has been a fundamental tool in the development and management of effective social programs for over 40 years, and presents a credible and rational model of how the Social Change Theory will be carried out (McLaughlin and Jordan, 1999). At its simplest level, it is a basic flow chart that identifies the resources needed, the specific activities that will be used to bring about the change, and the expected results (Cooksy, Gill, and Kelly, 2001). More complex models can include distinctions about the various populations or constituencies being served, the strategic intent behind specific activities, and distinctions between short- and long-term outcomes (Funnell and Rogers, 2011).

Let's go back to the weight-loss example we used a minute ago and see if we can construct a Logic model around our theory. Remember that the theory is that diet and exercise will help me lose weight. You can probably see quickly that these are two separate initiatives, so you're going to need two Logic models (one for diet, one for exercise). Let's start with exercise.

First, the Theory of Change does not identify a specific type of exercise. Since I'm a runner, let's use running as the activity. The good news is that running does not require a lot of equipment – a good pair of running shoes, some shorts, a T-shirt, a decent pair of socks, and some underwear and you're out the door. But right away there are some basic assumptions.

The most fundamental is that you are ambulatory, but there are others, like having a safe place to run (the Logic-model experts sometimes refer to these as "conditions" or "requirements"; Knowlton and Phillips, 2009).

So, now we've got some resources and some requirements. The activity is simple – go run! But we do need to define how long and how often we expect folk to run in order to achieve the desired goal. So, we go back to our research and find a well-documented study that says that running 2.5 miles a week for a period of 17 weeks can bring about weight loss (and such a study does exist – see Lewis et al., 1976). In order to make the activity easier to implement, we decide that the plan should be to run 1 mile a day, three days a week. So, now the activity is defined; but what about the results? Our study suggests that this activity should result in a weight loss of about 6 percent (Lewis et al., 1976). This adds credence to our Theory of Change (and should be part of the research that builds the theory!). At this point, we've got enough to construct a basic Logic model that would look something like the figure below.

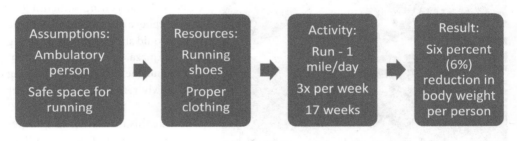

Source: Authors' design.

Keep in mind that this is an extremely simple example – your model is likely to be far more complex. The good news is that the Internet offers a number of great resources for building Logic models (my personal favorite is the one developed by the W. K. Kellogg Foundation, but there are many good ones, and a list of some recommended resources is provided for you at the end of this chapter).

There is one last critical point about Logic models that needs to be stressed here (and ties back into our earlier discussions). The Logic model is not something that should be developed in isolation. Remember that the voice of the constituent is a critical component in the development of a social enterprise. So, once you've developed a draft Logic model, you need to take it with you and meet with the various stakeholders that have an interest in your project, and make sure that the Logic model is accurate, that it makes sense, and that it has the necessary level of detail (McLaughlin and Jordan, 1999).

As with the other chapters in this book, the point here is not to make you an expert in constructing Logic models. The point is that you need to understand that they exist, that they are critical to the development of a sustainable social enterprise, and that you would be well advised to develop one before trying to implement your project.

BOX 7.2   LOGIC MODEL

Aiming to provide clarity when working through a new initiative or program – or an existing one that is being revised or revamped – Logic models can help social entrepreneurs to dissect, reflect, and reset. According to the W. K. Kellogg Foundation (1998), a program-based Logic model "is defined as a picture of how your organization does its work – the theory and assumptions underlying the program. A program logic model links outcomes (both short- and long-term) with program activities/processes and the theoretical assumptions/principles of the program" (p. iii).

Logic models provide social entrepreneurs with a helpful tool to create, evaluate, validate, modify, and report. Logic models look at the following components: inputs, activities, outputs, outcomes, and impact.

- *Inputs* are the resources (human, material, financial, and structural) contributing to or doing the work.
- *Activities* refer to what is done with these resources that yields certain results (the outputs, outcomes, and impact).
- *Outputs*, as introduced previously, refer to the created products and services of the activities and inputs.
- *Outcomes* are the specific, produced results or change. These can be changes to behaviors, skills, function, or growth.
- *Impact* is the change within institutions, communities, and systems that shows whether or not all of the inputs and activities resulted in a difference, intentional or otherwise.

When working on a new idea, you would fill in your planned work and results. With an existing initiative, it can be a tool to measure whether the inputs and activities yielded the intended results.

BUSINESS MODEL

Armed with a logical Theory of Change and a sound Logic model, we now move one level deeper in our planning process and begin to construct a business model. If a Theory of Change is a concept, and a Logic model is a plan, then perhaps a business model is a blueprint. In other words, this is the time when we start to think about details, about resources, and about specific steps to be taken to build an effective social enterprise. Another way to think about this is to see the Theory of Change as the "why," the Logic model as the "what," and the business model as the "how."[1]

One of the leading thinkers in this space is Alexander Osterwalder, who defines a business model as:

A conceptual tool that contains a set of elements and their relationships and allows [the] expressing [of] the business logic of a specific firm. It is a description of the value a company offers to one or several segments of customers and the architecture of the firm and its network of partners for creating, marketing, and delivering this value. (Osterwalder, Pigneur, and Tucci, 2005, pp. 17–18)

Osterwalder (the creator of the Business Model Canvas – one of the more popular tools for illustrating the model) talks about the business model as having four "pillars" (product, customer interface, infrastructure management, and financial aspects). Each pillar contains building blocks that describe specific aspects of the operation. Conceptually, these pillars shake out like Table 7.1.

Table 7.1   Business model pillars

Pillar	Business model building block	What the block describes
Product	Value proposition	The specific product or service the organization produces, and the benefit it provides
Customer interface	Target customer	The specific group of individuals or companies that want or need the product or service
	Distribution channel	The path that will be taken to deliver the product or service to the target customer
	Relationship	The various ways that the company will communicate with the target customer
Infrastructure management	Value configuration	The steps needed to assemble, produce, and deliver the product or service
	Core competency	The portion(s) of the value configuration produced by the organization
	Partner network	The collaborations needed to fully deliver the value to the target customer
Financial aspects	Cost structure	All the expenses necessary to deliver the value
	Revenue model	The ways that the organization is compensated for its efforts

Source: Adapted from Osterwalder, Pigneur, and Tucci (2005, p. 18). Used with permission

And while this is a great concept, the best part of Osterwalder's work came five years later, with the design of a process that uses sticky notes to map out each of these building blocks, allowing you to quickly see the relationships and dependencies that exist between the blocks (Osterwalder et al., 2010). Because this process uses sticky notes as its underlying mechanism, it also allows for easy changes in the model as the venture develops and evolves. Because of its simplicity, clarity, and flexibility, the business model has become a popular tool for entrepreneurs and educators (Trimi and Berbegal-Mirabent, 2012; Türko, 2016).

The business model has also developed several iterations that consider the additional complexities of a social enterprise. Most importantly, these social business models recognize that the value proposition for the constituent (the one receiving the service) is likely to be quite different from the value proposition that appeals to those who are paying for the service (Vial, 2016). One adaptation also takes into account the environmental issues that may face a venture that is socially conscious (Joyce and Paquin, 2016).

Once again, we need to stress that the point here is to introduce you to a tool. The ways in which you will use that tool are part of the application process that you will develop as you walk down the path of discovery that is entrepreneurship. And, as with the Logic model, there is a list of websites and other references at the end of the chapter that you can use to develop your skills in using these tools.

And while the business model is a great tool for seeing relationships and dependencies, it is easily changed as a venture evolves, and can be adapted to a number of different contexts; its greatest strength is that it can be an aid in the process of analyzing the feasibility of the proposed venture.

BOX 7.3   SOCIAL BUSINESS MODEL CANVAS

As mentioned, the Social Business Model Canvas was adapted from the Business Model Canvas to better serve social businesses. So, what are the differences between the Business Model Canvas and Social Business Model Canvas?

While the two are very similar, the Social Business Model Canvas helps social entrepreneurs to reflect specifically and intentionally on how the social value is delivered, how the interventions will be measured, how the segments are split into beneficiaries and customers, and how any excess funds or profit will be spent. The Social Business Model Canvas also breaks out the type of intervention, as that can be a great reflection point for social entrepreneurs, as social impact can come from different types of interventions (for example, products, workshops).

FEASIBILITY ANALYSIS

There are many good tools for performing a feasibility analysis. In a minute, we'll talk about a few that I like (you will likely find some of your own that work better for you). But before we do that, let's talk about purpose.

No matter what tool you use, the feasibility analysis is intended to answer a very simple, but critical question – will it work? In other words, will this grand idea of yours be able to produce the results you desire? If the answer is no, then you need to go back and re-examine your models to see if you can figure out what needs to be fixed. If the necessary changes are not possible, then you are faced with one of the saddest moments in any entrepreneurial journey – that time when you need to put the dream down and move on to some other idea. The good news is that you do this on paper, before you've invested significant time and money into building the enterprise. The bad news is that it still hurts like heck to have to see a dream die.

To explore this point further, let's talk about airplanes. Did you know that the modern jet airplane does not actually fly in the traditional sense? On paper, the aerodynamics are such that the wings do not create enough lift to support the weight of the plane. But if you strap a couple of large rockets onto the wings (which is essentially what a jet engine is), you create enough force to overcome the deficiencies in the aerodynamics, and you can now get across the Atlantic Ocean in just over seven hours (and we'll leave the carbon footprint issues of jet travel aside for now).

To stretch this metaphor even further, the typical design process for a modern jet airplane is very much like the entrepreneurial journey we've been describing throughout this book – moving from sketches to models to testing of prototypes before going into actual production. In that sense, the feasibility analysis is akin to the computer-aided design testing that is done by the engineers that design the modern jet plane (see, you're developing all kinds of new skills!).

If you're coming to this journey from a business perspective, then you can probably think of several rudimentary tools for analyzing the feasibility of an enterprise (such as the break-even analysis or a simple calculation of return on investment). And making sure that the internal operations can be sustained over time is the most critical thing to analyze (after all, you can't effect change if you can't keep the doors open!). But focusing only on internal operations does not allow you to see the whole picture (a view that is critical in any enterprise, but even more important in one that is hoping to create value in multiple contexts). One of the most important external measures of feasibility involves assessing both the market and the competition. The likelihood of being able to obtain the necessary funds is also important at this stage. Let's take a short walk through each of these concepts.

Source: iStock.com/alex mit. Used with permission

Break-Even Analysis

I like to think of break-even analysis as something similar to managing a household budget. The key question is, do you have any money left at the end of the month? In other words, is your income enough to cover all your regular obligations (rent, food, clothing, transportation, and so on)? If not, you have two choices. You can either try to make more money or reduce your expenses. In the same fashion, the aspiring social entrepreneur needs to develop a rudimentary budget for the operation that includes salaries, rent, advertising, office expenses, and the like. This budget will then give you an idea of how much money you need to have coming into the organization. If that amount seems high, then you can either trim your budget or go back and revise your models so that you operate in a more cost-efficient way (for example, is there some other organization doing part of your planned work that you could partner with rather than trying to do it all yourself?). Or, is the model so expensive that you need to go back to square one and revisit the entire concept? (This is a moment we all dread, but too many avoid, even though this is the right time to make this assessment.)

BOX 7.4 BREAK-EVEN ANALYSIS

The break-even analysis is a calculation tool for the point of profitability. A break-even analysis looks at how many units (products or services) need to be sold in order to cover all of the costs of operating. The equation to calculate the volume of units needing to be sold to break even is as shown below (Gallo, 2014):

$$\text{Breaking-Even Volume (BEV)} = \frac{\text{Fixed costs}}{\text{Revenue per unit} - \text{variable cost per unit}} = \frac{\text{Fixed costs}}{\text{Unit margin}}$$

This means that, for example, if all the fixed costs (discussed in Chapter 2) to deliver a social impact summer program is $10,000, your cost to your participants is $200, and the cost to deliver the program is $50 per participant, that would look like the following:

$$\text{BEV} = \frac{\$10,000}{(\$200 - \$50)} \rightarrow \frac{\$10,000}{\$150} \rightarrow 66.67 \text{ units (or 67 participants)}$$

Based on this calculation, you would need to sell 66.67 units to break even, or because it's a program and we're using participants as our unit, it would take 67 participants to pay for your program for your organization to break even.

Despite being a very useful tool, a break-even analysis is really only a bare-minimum threshold measurement. For a social entrepreneur to have a sustainable organization, you will want to aim to make a substantial enough profit to invest back into your work or to help cover unforeseen challenges, while balancing considerations of accessibility to your beneficiaries. However, doing a break-even analysis is a starting point that can be helpful when thinking about pricing and fixed costs.

BOX 7.5 SOCIAL RETURN ON INVESTMENT

The notion of return on investment (ROI) has helped investors to determine the value of their investments, based on the amount of revenue generated for the investment made. ROI focuses on monetary outcomes, which are generally straightforward.

A social return on investment (SROI) is a bit more challenging to quantify, as it involves looking at both the tangible and intangible benefits from an investment. Forti and Goldberg (2015) define SROI as "the ratio of impact generated per client, to net cost per client." As introduced in Chapter 1, double- (DBL) and triple-bottom-line (TBL) approaches are the foundation of social entrepreneurship because a social enterprise's value is profit and people and, in TBL, the planet too. Figuring out an SROI helps to articulate your broader value to your stakeholders. Outputs and outcomes were introduced in Chapter 3, and these concepts can also help social entrepreneurs to calculate and articulate their social value.

It is important to note that calculating SROI comes with many challenges. Social enterprises may realize that some aspects of their value are not quantifiable (or that the value is not easily linked back to the investment) and that the process to calculate and articulate SROI is time-consuming and likely costly as well. Furthermore, social enterprises can feel pressured to portray positive results rather than reflect on the value delivered. Also, SROI should not be the only criteria for investment, as there are other impact types that may also illustrate the outcomes better (Forti and Goldberg, 2015).

All considering, social entrepreneurs need to allocate the time and resources to calculate and articulate an honest SROI for their stakeholders and themselves, in order to determine the true social value delivered today to create an even better tomorrow.

Market Opportunity Analysis

Any business (regardless of its orientation towards profit) needs to be concerned about market opportunity. A social enterprise needs to look at the issue from two perspectives (we'll add a third in a few chapters when we talk more about marketing the firm).

Is There a Market?

The first notion of "market" that needs to be analyzed is the one most often used in building a profit-oriented enterprise. Using demographic information from census data and other surveys, the aspiring entrepreneur wants to make sure that there are enough potential customers in the area that have an interest in the product or service being sold, as well as the ability to pay the price that is needed for the

Source: iStock.com/sommart. Used with permission

new venture to operate profitably (and links to tools that can help you determine that question are included in the Recommended Resources section). While you may think that examining a potential customer base is a worthless exercise for a social service (since a simple physical observation of a community in need will confirm that there are plenty of folks who can use a hand), the concept of a critical customer base is very important if your strategy for earning income involves selling a product or service.

Who Else is Here?

But since we're using profit for a purpose, and since the core operation is a social service, the other part of market opportunity that needs to be looked at closely is what I call "service sector overlap." For reasons that I find somewhat baffling, it seems that it's easy to find more than one nonprofit or non-governmental organization doing work on a specific issue in a specific community. One recent study suggests that there are 10 times as many nonprofits doing work in an area as there are areas in which to do the work (Bose and Bruce, 2015). I have personally witnessed communities where two different nonprofits are doing the same work in offices across the street from one another. It doesn't take long to realize that the two firms would likely be much more efficient and effective if they joined forces, but this is (in my observation) rarely done.

So, another market analysis that needs to be done in building a social enterprise is to look at who else is serving the community you're planning to work with. Once specific organizations are identified, you next need to look at the work that they are doing and see if it's effective. If not, then you have an opportunity to build something that is more effective. But if they are good folk doing good (and effective) work, that might be a sign that you need to look elsewhere – either geographically (to another community) or strategically (to another area of need within the community) (Frumkin and Sosa, 2014).

Who are the Competitors?

One other area that needs to be looked at in analyzing a market is the matter of direct and indirect competition. So far, we've been talking about direct competition – other firms and organizations delivering the same services to the same market(s). Unfortunately, looking only at direct competition is a somewhat selfish and short-sided approach. To truly understand a market, you need to look at all the other options available to the consumer. The easiest way to think about this is to start with a pizza.

We all know of a local pizza shop that we love. We also know that there are companies that operate large chains of pizza delivery stores (in the U.S, Domino's Pizza is perhaps the largest). It's easy to see that these two firms (the small local shop and the large national chain) are competitors. It's also easy to see that the frozen pizza you can buy in the grocery is a competitor, as are the various pizza kits available to make your own pizza at home. But you might not think of Netflix or Budweiser as competitors – until you put yourself into the place of the consumer.

Imagine that it's Friday night, and you've got $10 in your pocket to spend. You could buy a pizza. You could buy beer. You could rent a movie. But you can't do all of them, because you only have $10. So, you must choose (by the way, you could also save the $10 and go to the library to read a book). So, the real competition is with all the direct and indirect choices available in your selected market.

Before we leave this specific point, we need to talk about a big problem in challenged communities. When incomes are low, folks are often faced with some very dramatic choices that reflect this issue of direct and indirect competition. Sometimes, it's a choice between medication and food, or a choice between rent and utilities. And (just like with the pizza example above) you need to look at life from the perspective of those you hope to help (and if need be, go back and re-read Chapter 6).

> ## BOX 7.6   DIRECT AND INDIRECT COMPETITION IN THE SOCIAL SECTOR
>
> As discussed within the chapter, the idea of direct competition tends to be simple for most social entrepreneurs to see. Direct competition might look like another organization that offers a similar product or service, serves the same community or beneficiary, and has the same customers or donors. In contrast, indirect competition might serve the same goals.
>
> Either way, in the social sector, the notion of competition is different, and the reason why ecosystems (discussed in Chapter 3) are even more critical within social entrepreneurship. Social entrepreneurs should be interested, first and foremost, in solving the challenges they aim to address and serving the needs of the community and their beneficiaries. Partnerships and collaborations should be part of a social entrepreneur's "playbook." So, whether another organization can be considered direct or indirect competition, a discussion should be in place on how both (or all) organizations can best collaborate to serve their common goals and interests.

Why Are You Making My Head Hurt?

Right about now, that's probably the question you're asking. And I admit that all this talk about theories and models can be complicated, and even frustrating. But think back to the conversation we had in Chapter 2 about skydiving (or re-read it if it's slipped your mind). The first thing you learn is the mechanics of how the operation will work. And you build those mechanics on paper, and you test them by getting feedback from your potential constituents. And you modify, re-test, and modify again.

The reality of this phase is that it can take months – sometimes even years. In some schools, entire semesters are devoted to just this one set of concepts. This chapter is really a superficial introduction to a way of thinking that folks have spent their entire careers working on. But the need to get it right on paper before you spend the time and effort to build the venture is time well spent – and it's a lot cheaper and easier than trying to fix something after it's built. That's true no matter what type of venture you are building.

But a social enterprise makes a broader promise – a promise to affect someone's life in a positive way. So, if you get it wrong, you stand a pretty good chance of leaving that person no better off, and a reasonable chance that you may make their life even worse. This direct human impact makes the stakes a lot higher and the need for careful thought in modeling even more critical. But if you take the time and get it right (or close to right), the payoff is substantial. When you go to launch the venture, you'll get it up and running faster and for less money. And you'll be able to track the effects of your efforts in both the short and long term (which is the topic we'll dive into next).

So, take some aspirin and get a good night's sleep, knowing that you are better equipped to build effective change than you were a short time ago.

CHAPTER SUMMARY

This chapter centers on the utilization and application of different models and analysis tools for successful social intervention. The Theory of Change helps to uncover assumptions about making change and helps with reflection, and Logic models help social entrepreneurs to align inputs and activities with the desired outputs, outcomes, and impact. To bring this all together, a (social) business model can help to further look at the more specific aspects of a social enterprise and help position alignments. Tools like a break-even analysis can help social entrepreneurs to create a baseline for how much they will need to charge for their product or service, in order to just cover costs. Figuring out an SROI can help social entrepreneurs to evaluate and demonstrate how their investment translates into impact. A market opportunity analysis helps to evaluate whether or not there is an adequate market for the idea through identifying who else is working in the space and by looking at the problem and existing options for solutions. To this end, the concepts of direct and indirect competition play out differently for the social impact sector due to the collaborative nature of tackling social challenges. Dealing with a social challenge requires individuals and organizations to work together to best serve their common goals and interests.

QUESTIONS FOR DISCUSSION

1. In this exercise, you will have the opportunity to use a ToC model. Visit https://diytoolkit.org/tools/theory-of-change/ to find a printable PDF model and user guide for a ToC model.
    A. The ToC model will ask you to start with a problem (left-hand side) and to think about your long-term vision or goal (right-hand side).
    B. Continue working through the different steps of the model, from left to right, and use the guide to help you through the process, as needed.
    C. Under each step, you are asked to unpack your assumptions. How does this portion of the exercise align well with the essence of the Theory of Change?
    D. Work through the entire model, and go back to revise your responses as needed.
    E. At the end of the process, you are asked to revisit your identified long-term goal. Does it align with the steps and assumptions made?
    F. After completing this model, reflect on the value of the exercise. In your opinion, how might completing a ToC model be helpful for a social entrepreneur?
2. Next, you will be able to try completing a Logic model, as presented below.
    A. Draw out the Logic model below.
    B. Start with Inputs, and move through each box from left to right. Feel free to go back and revise, add, or edit previous boxes as you feel it is appropriate.
    C. At the end of the process, reflect on your experience filling in the Logic model. In your opinion, how might a Logic model be helpful for social entrepreneurs?

INPUTS	ACTIVITIES	OUTPUTS	OUTCOMES	IMPACT

Source: Authors' design

Sample Logic model template

3. Now, having completed both a ToC model and Logic model, answer the following questions:
    A. How did the two differ?
    B. How were they similar?
    C. How do your responses compare to what you reviewed within the chapter?
    D. When, or at what points, do you feel each of these models would be helpful for social entrepreneurs to complete or return to review?
    E. What audiences or stakeholders might also find the Logic-model experience helpful?
4. A business model helps social entrepreneurs to organize and align their thoughts in one space. Select one specific social concern that you will use to develop your business model. Using one of the business models' links provided within the Recommended Resources section below, try to fill in the sections of the canvas, and reflect on the following questions:
    A. What type of canvas are you using (for example, Business Model Canvas, (Social) Business Model Canvas)?
    B. When filling out individual sections, take note of any adjustments between sections that have occurred. If none are happening, you might not be reflecting enough on alignment, so have the bravery to adjust.
    C. Once completed, what has this exercise using a (Social) Business model done for your concept's development?
5. Finally, you will do a simple break-even analysis for one of the activities from your Logic model.
    A. Reference the equation below from Box 7.4, and try to estimate the fixed costs, variable costs per unit, and the anticipated revenue per unit.

$$\text{Breaking-Even Volume (BEV)} = \frac{\text{Fixed costs}}{\text{Revenue per unit} - \text{variable cost per unit}} = \frac{\text{Fixed costs}}{\text{Unit margin}}$$

B. After figuring out the break-even point for the activity, does it seem as feasible as initially anticipated? Why, or why not?

C. If moving forward with this idea, what has the break-even analysis helped you realize about other elements of the concept? What might you adjust or change?

BUILD IT YOURSELF: STEP THREE

In the last step, you identified specific opportunities that existed within the community you are working with. You now need to take two more steps forward in developing your own solution.

First, you need to understand who else is already working in this field. So, you need to do some research on other organizations working in this space. When you gather this information, you may discover that some of the ideas you have are already being worked on. This means that you develop a process of elimination that leads you to narrow down your solution set. So, for this step in building your own social enterprise, you need to:

• Identify and describe what (if any) organizations are currently serving the populations of concern identified.

• Select one specific social concern that you will use to develop your business model.

RECOMMENDED RESOURCES

Theory of Change and Logic models:

Annie E. Casey Foundation (2004). *Theory of Change: A Practical Tool for Action, Results and Learning.* Accessed 11 April 2021 at www.aecf.org/m/resourcedoc/aecf-theoryofchange-2004.pdf.

Better Evaluation (n.d.). Creating program logic models. Accessed 11 April 2021 at www.betterevaluation.org/en/resources/guides/creating_program_logic_models.

Center for Evaluation Innovation (2013). Pathways for change: 10 theories to inform advocacy and policy change efforts. Accessed 11 April 2021 at www.evaluationinnovation.org/publications/pathways-change-10-theories-inform-advocacy-and-policy-change-efforts.

Center for Theory of Change (2021). What is Theory of Change? www.theoryofchange.org/what-is-theory-of-change/.

Innovation Network (n.d.). Logic Model Workbook. www.innonet.org/media/logic_model_workbook_0.pdf.

Leap of Reason (n.d.). https://leapofreason.org/get-the-books/.

W. K. Kellogg Foundation (2006). W. K. Kellogg Foundation Logic Model Development Guide. www.wkkf.org/resource-directory/resource/2006/02/wkkellogg-foundation-logic-model-development-guide.

SROI:

Sopact (n.d.). Social return on investments: Comprehensive guide. www.sopact.com/social-return-on-investments-sroi.

Business models:

hwww.alexandercowan.com/business-model-canvas-templates/.
Business Model Toolbox (n.d.). Tools and methods. https://bmtoolbox.net/tools/.
Strategyzer (n.d.). The Business Model Canvas. www.strategyzer.com/canvas/business-model
-canvas.
Tandemic (n.d.). (Social) Business Model Canvas. www.socialbusinessmodelcanvas.com/.

NOTE

1. It's important in this section to not take the use of the word "business" too literally. Of course, we're talking about a social enterprise, not a profit-oriented firm. On the other hand, it's important not to fully dismiss the notion of "doing business", as a well-functioning organization is critical to the success of a social change initiative.

REFERENCES

Anderson, A. (2014). *The Community Builder's Approach to Theory of Change*. Retrieved from Accessed 28 April 2021 at www.aspeninstitute.org/sites/default/files/content/docs/rcc/rcccommbuilde rsapproach.pdf.

Blum, H. L. (1974). *Planning for Health: Development and Application of Social Change Theory*. New York, NY: Behavioral Publications.

Bose, B., and Bruce, N. (2015). *Essays on Nonprofit Competition*. Dissertation, University of Washington.

Bronte-Tinkew, J., and Redd, Z. (2001). *Logic Models and Outcomes for Youth Entrepreneurship Programs*. Washington, DC: DC Children and Youth Investment Corporation.

Cooksy, L. J., Gill, P., and Kelly, P. A. (2001). The program logic model as an integrative framework for a multimethod evaluation. *Evaluation and Program Planning*, 24(2), 119–128.

Forti, M., and Goldberg, J. (2015, November 18). Measuring social return on investment before you invest. *Stanford Social Innovation Review*. Accessed 28 April 2021 at https://ssir.org/articles/entry/measuring_social_return_on_investment_before_you_invest.

Frumkin, P., and Sosa, S. (2014). Competitive positioning: Why knowing your competition is essential to social impact success. *Nonprofit Quarterly*, 21(3), 32–43.

Funnell, S. C., and Rogers, P. J. (2011). *Purposeful Program Theory: Effective Use of Theories of Change and Logic Models*. San Francisco, CA: Jossey-Bass.

Gallo, A. (2014, July 2). A quick guide to breakeven analysis. *Harvard Business Review*. Accessed 28 April 2021 at https://hbr.org/2014/07/a-quick-guide-to-breakeven-analysis.

Joyce, A., and Paquin, R. L. (2016). The triple layered Business Model Canvas: A tool to design more sustainable business models. *Journal of Cleaner Production*, 135, 1474–1486.

Knowlton, L. W., and Phillips, C. C. (2009). *The Logic Model Guidebook: Better Strategies for Great Results*. Los Angeles, CA: SAGE.

Lewis, S., Haskell, W. L., Wood, P. D., Manoogian, N., Bailey, J. E., and Pereira, M. B. (1976). Effects of physical activity on weight reduction in obese middle-aged women. *American Journal of Clinical Nutrition*, 29(2), 151–156.

McLaughlin, J. A., and Jordan, G. B. (1999). Logic models: A tool for telling your programs performance story. *Evaluation and Program Planning*, 22(1), 65–72.

Osterwalder, A., Pigneur, Y., Clark, T., and Smith, A. (2010). *Business Model Generation: a Handbook for Visionaries, Game Changers, and Challengers*. Hoboken, NJ: John Wiley & Sons.

Osterwalder, A., Pigneur, Y., and Tucci, C. L. (2005). Clarifying business models: Origins, present, and future of the concept. *Communications of the Association for Information Systems*, 16(1), 1–25.

Trimi, S., and Berbegal-Mirabent, J. (2012). Business model innovation in entrepreneurship. *International Entrepreneurship and Management Journal*, 8(4), 449–465.

Türko, E. S. (2016). Business plan vs Business Model Canvas in entrepreneurship trainings: A comparison of students' perceptions. *Asian Social Science, 12*(10), 55–62.

Vial, V. (2016). A Business Model Canvas for social enterprises. *Sains Humanika, 8,* 1– 8.

W. K. Kellogg Foundation (1998). *Using Logic Models to Bring Together Planning, Evaluation, and Action: Logic Model Development Guide.* Accessed 28 April 2021 at www.aacu.org/sites/default/files/LogicModel.pdf.

8
Outputs or outcomes

Learning objectives

After studying this chapter, you should be able to:
1. Discuss the role of cause and effect in social change work and recognize the difference between correlation and causation.
2. Understand the role of a clear social mission and examine the challenge of mission creep and mission drift.
3. Compare and contrast leadership and management within social impact work.
4. Define and value each of the following concepts: performance management, performance goal setting, performance measurement, outcomes-based budgeting, formative evaluation, and summative evaluation.

ORDER AND CHAOS

Believe it or not, there is something called Chaos Theory (of course, if you've ever tried to get a toddler fed and dressed in the morning, you know that chaos is a fact, not a theory). The essence of this theory is that little things can have a big effect. The example used by many folks is the notion that a butterfly flapping its wings somewhere in Europe could cause a tornado in South America. Far-fetched, maybe. Or maybe not.

This theory of chaotic effect has been applied to many fields. My personal favorite is its application to the field of economics in general and markets in particular. The idea here is that small activities made by individual actors can have substantial effects on the larger economy (for a great read on this topic, check out *Butterfly Economics* by Paul Ormerod, 2001).

This notion of a small effect having a large impact is also popular in the current world of social innovation. Over and over, you hear folks being encouraged to take action that can change the world. One of the most popular quotes in the social change world is one attributed to Margaret Meade,[1] a noted anthropologist: "Never doubt that a small group of thoughtful, committed citizens can change the world; indeed, it's the only thing that ever has."

Source: iStock.com/Siphotography. Used with permission

But if you really think about it, changing the entire world is a tall order. I'd like to suggest that the issue here is not the veracity of Chaos Theory or the supply of inspiration needed to bring about social change. I'd like to suggest that the issue is the definition of "world."

If we define it in the literal sense, then we certainly have our work cut out for us. But if we define it more in terms of that part of the globe in which a specific person lives and moves and has its being (your world, my world, their world), then things become a little bit more manageable. And that's the focus of this chapter.

For the next few pages, we're going to talk about how to build a social enterprise so that it's manageable. We're going to examine how to structure the venture so that you can clearly tell (and tell others) that you are having the desired effect on the community you wish to serve.

But before we begin, I need to make sure you properly prepare yourself for this part of our journey. If you enjoyed the systems nature of the last chapter, then you're going to enjoy this one as well. But if the last chapter gave you a headache, I'd suggest that you take another aspirin now. This chapter is full of systems and models, albeit focused on a different set of issues.[2]

As you read this chapter, you may also note a change in tone. In many places in the following pages, the language will sound very business-like. That's on purpose. The subjects touched on in this chapter have their roots in commercial enterprise and owe much to the work of folks like Frederick Taylor, Max Weber, Peter Drucker, and many others (Drucker's work alone would provide you with a perspective on administration equal to any MBA program). And (sad to say) these administrative matters are often left unattended (and not just in social benefit organizations) in favor of things that are more exciting or attractive. However, no effort can be successful without strict attention to dozens of small details. That's what this chapter is about.

Ready? Let's go!

BOX 8.1   FREDERICK WINSLOW TAYLOR, EFFICIENCY, AND SCIENTIFIC MANAGEMENT

When thinking of some of the foundational threads of management across industries, Frederick Winslow Taylor (1856–1915) is best remembered for his efforts to identify ways to be more efficient in the process of work. His book, *The Principles of Scientific Management*, is the source of Taylor's Principles, or "Taylorism," as many of us recognize it. Taylorism positions systematic management as the solution to inefficiencies. According to Taylor, efficiency "rest[s] upon clearly defined laws, rules, and principles, as a foundation" (1911, Kindle Locations 32–34). This foundation is supported by working with the talents and interests of the team and having well-defined positions. The role of managers should be to monitor performance, oversee the work, plan, and train their workers, while workers should focus on the required tasks.

Taylor's Principles are the groundwork of our modern approaches to management. They also serve as an important reminder for social entrepreneurs that the management of their impact should be strategic, informed by data, and centered on collective talent:

> Science, not rule of thumb.
> Harmony, not discord.
> Cooperation, not individualism.
> Maximum output, in place of restricted output.
> The development of each man to his greatest efficiency and prosperities.
> (Taylor, 2011, Kindle Location 1371)

UNDERSTANDING CAUSE AND EFFECT IN SOCIAL CHANGE

This may sound like an oxymoron, but the first thing you need to understand about managing social change is that you can't manage social change. At least, not completely. Because we are talking about humans (and usually more than one human), there are far too many intervening variables to be able to truly say that a specific social intervention is the direct and sole source of a specific social change. As I write this, I'm in training to run a marathon. Each week, there is a long run, and each week, the long runs get longer. Sometimes the long runs go well. Sometimes, not so well. What you learn from that is that the number of variables that you need to control is vast. Did I get enough sleep the night before? Did I eat the right things? Have I been stretching? (The list goes on, but you get the idea.) And that's just one person trying to make one small change.

This takes us back to the topic of causality (I know, we keep coming back to this – maybe because it's *that* important). The first thing that a true understanding of the variables involved in social change should give you is a sense of humility. None of us is ever truly all-powerful – at best, we can play a small part in making our corner of the world a little better. The second thing that you gain should be a sense of relief in knowing that bringing about the change that you seek is not fully on your shoulders. You should do the best you can with what you've got and leave the rest up to others (or whatever higher power you may choose to recognize). Armed with the recognition that you will never fully be able to control the process of social change, you can now do several specific things to help control some aspects of the change.

BOX 8.2   DISTINGUISHING BETWEEN CAUSATION AND CORRELATION

The common saying that "correlation does not imply causation" is important for determining how to approach a social problem. Correlation is when we notice a pattern in how two (or more) things relate to one another. For example, entrepreneurs have two times the incidence of depression than non-entrepreneurs (30 percent compared to 15 percent) (Freeman et al., 2015, p. 14). That's an example of correlation: seeing a relationship between entrepreneurship and depression. There is a distinct difference between acknowledging a connection, pattern, or trend and assuming that one causes another, which would be causation. For example, that could look like assuming that either (1) being an entrepreneur causes depression or (2) being depressed causes people to become entrepreneurs. Neither of these is true as stated because there is a bit more information that needs to be understood before coming to those types of conclusions.

Social entrepreneurs really need to understand this distinction. For instance, a social entrepreneur is working to help the housing-insecure to find affordable, long-term housing within a particular community, and she becomes aware that homelessness in her community is frequently coupled with higher incidences of mental health conditions. Understanding this connection as a possible correlation would allow the social entrepreneur to understand that her beneficiaries might need additional support for mental health needs. Nonetheless, if she were seeing this as a causal relationship, the social entrepreneur might think that either providing housing would help solve the higher incidence of mental health conditions or providing mental health support could help resolve the housing issues. The correlation acknowledges the complexity of need within the social challenges at hand, whereas the causation example oversimplifies the situation to provide support for only one of the two challenges.

Clear Mission

Perhaps the most important thing you can do in developing a social enterprise is to have a clear mission for the venture. And that clear vision needs to include not just the type of change, but the specific results you hope to produce (Hunter, 2013). Many times, I've seen mission statements that say things like "changing lives one day at a time." While that may be a useful slogan, that's not a mission statement that can allow you to make any sort of measurement. However, "reducing the rate of poverty in the Poppleton neighborhood of West Baltimore by 15 percent within five years" is a statement that can guide your efforts much more directly. It's also something that you can directly measure. A clear mission also allows you to begin to isolate those parts of the project that you can control and allow for the parts you can't control (because you've already identified them in your Logic model, right?).

BOX 8.3   TROUBLESHOOTING MISSIONS

The mission of a social enterprise plays a critical role in how it enacts the good it intends to deliver. As Peter Drucker stated so well, "a mission statement has to be operational, otherwise it's just good intentions" (Drucker, 2006, p. 4). An organization's mission frames the organization's purpose both internally and externally, and it keeps the organization centered on its primary aims and goals. Carefully managing activities to align with the organization's mission is a key process for social enterprises, as there is often a strong temptation to follow the funding.

While the missions of social enterprises can be changed over time as the community's needs change, the phenomenon of mission creep or mission drift happens when an organization strays from its primary mission by broadening or sidestepping its engagements to the point that it distracts from its original mission.

The challenging thing about mission creep and mission drift is that they are often unintentional. With social enterprises striving to be financially sustainable, it can be appealing to social entrepreneurs to take on an opportunity to bring in money and stability for their organization. Nonprofit social enterprises might be tempted to take on a grant project or donation that takes its energy and resources away from its primary mission. For-profit social enterprises can also lose sight of their mission through taking on a new investor or partner or chasing a trendy niche in the market. In either situation, it can also be a result of poor leadership or poor decision-making.

In any case, mission creep and mission drift can be avoided through performance management, as well as reflecting upon goals and mission as new opportunities and activities arise. Organizations need to consistently ask themselves, "Are we serving our primary mission in the best way possible through this new engagement?" If yes, then great! Go on, and move forward. If not or if unsure, it might be time to either consider a new opportunity or to look back to assess if the current mission is still serving the area of need well.

Performance-Oriented Leaders and Managers

To understand this point, we need to begin by making a distinction between leadership and management. While the two traits can exist within the same individual, the skills and abilities of each role are quite distinct.

Leaders provide a sense of purpose and direction and can inspire others to join in a shared mission. They encourage and challenge the team to hold true to the vision and mission of the organization. They are (to use an old British term) the keepers of the faith. Effective leaders are also the first to express dissatisfaction when the organization does not achieve its stated goals. Managers are the ones who work on the day-to-day details of how the mission and vision are carried out. They make sure that the team has the tools needed to carry out the mission (be they supplies, training, or information). The manager's role calls for a bit more flexibility, adapting both the mode and style of communication to meet the needs of each individual on the team (Yukl, 1990). The manager is also the one who is responsible for day-to-day control of quality, productivity, and the monitoring of results. Since the manager is more directly involved in the details of daily operations, they are often the first to know when the work at hand veers off course and are responsible for developing and implementing small corrective measures to improve performance. To summarize the distinction, "Leaders focus on driving strategic performance," while managers concentrate on tactical performance (Hunter, 2013, p. 27).

Two of the most often confused words in the world are "strategy" and "tactics." Close behind (and closely related) are "leadership" and "management." Since the overlaps are similar, and the concepts related, let's take a minute to unpack this conundrum. Said simply, "strategy" is direction, and "tactics" is directions. And the addition of that one letter makes all the difference in the world.

Source: iStock.com/Olivier Le Moal. Used with permission

Perhaps you're reading this as part of a course of study. Hopefully, that course of study will lead you to some sort of event where you obtain a designation (a degree of some sort). So, your direction is towards the completion of that degree. Along the way, you will take a few classes, and each of those classes will require you to perform certain tasks (such as reading a specific book or books, completing various assignments, and the like). Each of those steps along the way is a direction.

While working on my Master's, I encountered a particularly difficult instructor who was teaching a subject that was outside my comfort zone. Unfortunately, that instructor was unwilling to work with me to provide the additional help I needed, so I was forced to drop the class to protect my Grade Point Average. The following semester, I arranged for a tutor so that I could improve my skills and then take a second shot at the troublesome course. In addition to helping me sharpen my capabilities, the tutor informed me that a different instructor would be teaching the course the following semester. Happily, I was able to complete the course and graduate (albeit a year later than I had planned).

So, my plan (my direction, my strategy) was to complete an MBA. But my tactics (the steps I took to complete the plan) changed over time and were adjusted as needed (while never losing sight of the goal). To expand this into the notion of leadership, the leader's job is to define the strategy, and maintain a constant devotion to its achievement. The manager is responsible for tactics – defining the specific steps that need to be taken on a day-to-day basis.

While these two roles are distinct, they share an unflagging devotion to the mission of the organization and are equally committed to strong performance and accountability. The performance-oriented leader never stops asking questions about how well the mission is being delivered and is uncompromising in their devotion to superior results. Further, they work to instill this same level of dissatisfaction with "business as usual" down into every level of the operation. Performance-oriented managers drive the accountability process and take swift and sure action whenever results do not meet expectations (particularly in the matter of individual employee performance).

Jim Collins, one of the most popular authors in the performance management field, uses a great metaphor to illustrate this point when he says that you need to get the right people on the bus, and get them into the right seats on the bus (Collins, 2001). Implicit in this notion is also the concept that you need to get the wrong folks off the bus quickly. One of my first bosses taught me a great lesson about this when he advised me to "hire slow and fire fast." In other words, take your time making sure you have the right person in the role, and take swift and sure action when that person does not meet expectations.

It's also important to note that leadership and management need to be kept in balance with one another. Strong leadership without strong management will create chaos and frustration. Strong management without strong leadership will produce an organization that is very efficient but moves in circles (Hunter, 2013).

So, the leader sets the direction and the manager determines the specific steps to take to move towards that direction. But any good navigator will tell you that without a compass, you're only guessing. And if you've got a GPS system, that's even better. That leads us to our next critical element – management systems.

BOX 8.4　　LEADERSHIP IN THE SOCIAL SECTOR

One of the most challenging things about leading a social enterprise is that the ultimate goal is to tackle significant systemic challenges. To approach these aims, it can be a challenge to prioritize activities because those doing this type of work can "consider everything they do to be righteous and moral and to serve a cause, so they are not willing to say, if it doesn't produce results then maybe we should direct our resources elsewhere" (Drucker, 2006, pp. 10–11). Because social entrepreneurs are passionate about what they do, it can be hard to separate out their internal commitment and passions for solving the social problem at hand and the objective efficiency their interventions have in chipping away at that issue. Ego has no place in social entrepreneurship leadership, especially in contrast to commercial entrepreneurship.

So, what makes for a strong social enterprise leader? Drucker (2006) advises that these leaders must be disciplined listeners and good communicators, and possess patience, humility, honesty, and perfectionism. While many of these skills seem intuitive, the perfectionism piece needs a bit of explaining. For Drucker, "we either do things to perfection, or we don't do them" (2006, p. 20). The ethos of social enterprise leaders should be one of strong ethics, values, and responsibility to serve their missions and to serve them as well as possible.

Performance-Oriented Management Systems

It's a great thing to have direction, and it's good to know the path you want to take to reach your destination. But you also need to have the right tools in place to tell when you've gone off course. And those tools need to reach all the way down to each individual who is working to move the organization forward.

Accountability

The first step in setting up such a system is to develop a list of the important things that need to be measured to monitor the progress of the organization. This list would probably include things like operating efficiency, quality of the product or service being delivered, use of financial resources, worker and customer satisfaction, and many others. The list is going to be different for each organization, but each item being measured should be one that clearly supports the overall objective.

Once this list is generated, the performance-oriented manager needs to determine how each item will be measured. It's important here to make sure that the measurements are specific and clearly understood by everyone. The measurement process also needs to be transparent – meaning that the data and results need to be shared widely and openly. It's also important that measurements be taken regularly and at consistent intervals (for example, daily, weekly, monthly). The minute that any result falls short of the desired outcome, swift action must be taken.

Often, the shortfall is the result of human error. So, the performance-oriented manager must also have systems in place to support the worker that needs assistance and address the worker who is unable to adapt to the system. The manager needs to make sure that the right conditions are in place for the worker to achieve the desired results, and that the worker is properly trained to perform at the desired level. With that assurance in hand, both the manager and the employee need to be monitoring performance and jointly diagnosing any problems as soon as they occur. However, if the corrective action does not take hold, then additional actions need to be taken, up to and including the discharge of the staff member who is not able to meet the standard (and that goes for managers and leaders, too!).

Equally important is the need for transparency in the use of these systems and the information they provide. It does little good if the performance results are kept secret or only shared with a few key leaders (and yet you'd be surprised at how many firms do just that). Information on organizational performance needs to be shared widely and shared regularly. Information on the performance of specific individuals also needs to be shared regularly, although some aspects of the performance of a specific person may need to be shared only with that person for reasons of personal confidentiality.

The reason you want to set up these systems is so that every person in the organization has a standard set of metrics that are used to keep everyone accountable for the work they do, and to make sure that the work is aligned with the goals of the organization.

BOX 8.5   PERFORMANCE MANAGEMENT AND EFFECTIVE PERFORMANCE GOAL SETTING

Performance management centers on looking at the activities and outputs and comparing them to the organization's goals and its expectations for productivity, efficiency, and performance for those engagements. While these expectations can be adjusted for the organizational, unit/team, or individual level, in many organizations they are a top-down directive.

The rationale for performance management is to reflect on – and be accountable for – alignment and the standards set for productivity and efficiency.

According to Pulakos (2004), effective performance management can also help accomplish the following outcomes:

- Clarifying job responsibilities and expectations
- Enhancing individual and group productivity
- Developing employee capabilities to their fullest extent through effective feedback and coaching
- Driving behavior to align with the organization's values, goals, and strategies
- Providing a basis for making operational human capital decisions (for example, pay)
- Improving communication between employees and managers (p. 1)

To get started, it is important to create and frame goals that are centered on performance. Pulakos (2004) suggests the following guidelines for establishing effective performance goals:

- Goals must clearly define the end results to be accomplished
- To the extent possible, goals should have a direct and obvious link to organizational success factors and goals
- Goals should be different, but achievable, to motivate performance
- Goals should be set in no more than three areas – attempting to achieve too many different goals at once will impede success (p. 6)

Another popular tool for performance goals that are able to be measured and managed are SMART goals: (1) Specific, (2) Measurable, (3) Achievable, (4) Relevant, and (5) Time-bound.

Specific.   The goal is specific and clear in its aims.

Measurable. The goal is able to be measured.

Achievable. The goal is attainable, possible, and realistic within the given conditions (for example, time, available resources).

Relevant.   The goal is something that is necessary, timely, and/or exciting to the involved stakeholders.

Time-bound. The goal has a set of specific time indicators (for example, start and end times, or number of days, weeks, or months).

Once they have set solid performance goals, social entrepreneurs can hold themselves and their teams more accountable for performance through reflecting on them throughout the iterative cycle of inputs, activities/processes, outputs/outcomes/impact, evaluation, review, feedback, and planning.

Outcomes-Based Budgeting

Making sure that everyone is on the same page and is being held accountable to the same goals in the same way is critical. But there also needs to be a transparent process for making sure that the appropriate resources are available to move things forward. In this regard, it's helpful to think more like an entrepreneur and less like a nonprofit.

Far too often, the typical nonprofit focuses its budget on current operations, and does not set aside enough money for the important work of building the organization (Egger and Yoon, 2004; Pallotta, 2010). Building a process that supports accountability and encourages performance takes time, and that means that money needs to be set aside to support that effort. It also means training and professional development opportunities are supported and encouraged. It even includes making sure that all the more mundane things like desks and computers and supplies are readily available. The full complement of systems and facilities that are needed to make sure folks are performing reliably and sustainably must always be in place.

Results-oriented budgeting also means that funds are set aside for investing in the growth of the organization. In understanding this point, we can borrow a bit from basic accounting in relation to the concept of cash flow (which is a means to measure how money moves through an organization).

It's easy to understand that even a simple hot dog stand needs to invest some money upfront in order to operate. You need to buy supplies (hot dogs, buns, mustard, and so on) and equipment (a grill at the very least, as well as the stand itself), as well as many other things. So, money is spent in building the operation, but the cash (in terms of hot dogs sold) only flows once that happens.

In the same way, building an effective social enterprise requires investment up front (a process we will explore in detail in Chapter 11) before it can bring about its desired change. As it grows, it will also need additional seed funds to launch new initiatives and expand its reach.

Effective budgeting for outcomes and performance also includes the need to make sure that ineffective efforts are not supported. If something isn't working, it's important to try to diagnose the problem and implement the appropriate efforts to correct the situation (which is also something that requires time and money). But, just like the worker who is unable to perform and must be dismissed, the budgeting process needs to be able to take quick and effective action to reduce or eliminate funds for projects and programs that are not directly supporting the goals of the organization.

This program budgeting system has been known as outcomes-based budgeting (OBB) or effectiveness budgeting (Martin, 2002) (for the sake of simplicity, we will return to using OBB).

BOX 8.6   UNDERSTANDING THE ROLE OF OUTCOMES-BASED BUDGETING

When approaching the topic of outcomes-based budgeting (OBB), it can be helpful to start with the word "outcome." As introduced in Chapter 3, "outcomes" refer to how things end up, which encompasses perceptions of quality, value, impact, and success, whereas "outputs" are the end-of-process production or delivery amounts.

This distinction is important to rehash when introducing OBB as outcomes tend to be more challenging to measure because, according to Rajala, Laihonen, and Vakkuri (2018),

> Performance information often focuses on output levels because these are easy and less costly to define, measure, and analyze. By comparison, program

> outcomes tend to be much more difficult to identify, measure (for example, Robichau and Lynn, 2009), and analyze (for example, Mascarenhas, 1996). (p. 11)

Furthermore, there are cases when outcomes are very challenging, if not impossible to measure. So then, with outcomes being more costly and more difficult to measure and analyze, why would OBB be necessary?

Simply put, output and outcome focuses yield two different kinds of budgeting with two different levels of focus. According to Kettner, Moroney, and Martin (2017), budgets dealing with inputs and outputs yield a functional budgeting system, which is management focused (for example, productivity, efficiency), whereas budgets looking at inputs and outcomes are program budgeting systems (including OBB) that center on planning with a focus on effectiveness. With its planning orientation, OBB has the ability to prioritize cost-effectiveness (for example, cost per outcome) and focus on strategy and innovative practices and approaches to drive effective social change.

The relationship between functional budgeting and program budgeting mirrors that of management and leadership, respectively. You need to both focus on the day-to-day operations and performance of a social enterprise, as well as its longer-term planning, strategy, and vision.

Measuring What Matters

So, let's assume that you've done all of the things we've outlined in this chapter (and if you have, give yourself a hand because you're already ahead of most folks, regardless of the type of venture). You've got a clear mission, a leadership team that is committed to performance-based management, and budgeting that aligns with goals and objectives. But there is still one crucial element missing – and that is the actual information needed to make sure that activities and outcomes align with objectives and do so consistently.

Our friend David Hunter explains this quite well when he says that

> The issue for performance management is not whether to collect data, it is which data to collect – and then how to convert performance data into actionable information to support both tactical and strategic decision making. (Hunter, 2013, p. 31)

Source: iStock.com/Creative Touch. Used with permission

Well, that's simple enough (not!). So, where does the anxious and perplexed social innovator go to figure out what to measure? Happily, the answer is at hand (and was discussed in the last chapter).

The key to determining the specific things that need to be measured is the Theory of Change and Logic models that have been built to map the organization's mission. So, pull those models back up on your laptop and take a look at the goals you hope to achieve – then ask what specific things you might want to measure to make sure that those goals are being achieved.

To walk through this on a practical level, let's go back to the weight loss example I used in the last chapter. You'll recall that my Theory of Change was that diet and exercise would lead to weight loss. You'll also recall that my Logic model included running for 1 mile per day, three times per week, with an expected outcome of a 6 percent weight loss after 17 weeks.

So, it would seem like weekly logs of running activity would be a good thing to measure and report. That way, if I miss a run I can quickly make it up the next week. If I don't measure and report this activity regularly, I could easily fall behind, leaving me unable to achieve my goal. Regular weigh-ins would also seem to be called for – maybe not every week, but probably more than once a month. Occasional health checks would also be a good idea, just to make sure that I'm not injuring myself in the process.

To move this to a more relevant example, a high-performing social enterprise would probably want to measure the number of people served (per week or per month), the specific services used (as well as how many times each service was used, and by whom), the number of folks who successfully complete the program, the quality of the programs being delivered, and the progress made by current and former program participants toward the stated social objective.

It's also important to mention that measurements themselves need to be well crafted. They need to be expressed in concrete language that uses operational terms, and linked directly to the specific variables being measured. The data need to be collected efficiently and affordably, but also contain a level of detail appropriate to the area being measured. Last but not least, the data need to be within the abilities of the organization to collect and analyze (Kusek and Rist, 2010). But before we leave this issue of measuring what matters, we also need to talk about internal bias.

BOX 8.7   PERFORMANCE MEASUREMENT VS EVALUATION

Measuring what matters entails both performance measurement and evaluation. Performance measurement plays an important, ongoing role in the monitoring and reporting of the quality, efficiency (outputs), and effectiveness (outcomes) of performance (Kettner, Moroney, and Martin, 2017; Martin and Kettner, 2010). Performance measurement supports transparency to stakeholders, through reporting information pertinent to management and finances.

While performance measurement is an ongoing process, evaluation measures things at a particular point in time and comes in two broader types: formative and summative. Formative evaluations center on improving and shaping things as you go along. There are many different kinds of formative assessment, including needs assessments, process evaluations, and implementation evaluations (Giancola, 2020). Of these, needs assessments can be of particular use for social entrepreneurs, as they look at the various stakeholders and their needs in order to determine types of products, services, and programs that are needed or of possible interest to those stakeholders.

In contrast, summative evaluations are summarizing in nature at the end of a program, process, or delivery of a product or service. The results of a summative evaluation can help to make decisions on continuation, adjustments, and scaling. Summative assessments can include cost-benefit analyses, cost-effectiveness analyses, outcomes evaluations, and impact evaluations (Giancola, 2020). Social entrepreneurs utilize many of these summative evaluations in their practice.

At first glance, it can be tricky to separate the roles and natures of performance measurement and evaluation, especially within the area of impact evaluation. As a point of clarification, performance measurement is an ongoing activity that reports outputs, outcomes, and quality and deals with the performance effectiveness over time; in contrast, impact evaluation has an episodic frequency, marking a particular point in time, and asks questions of interest to stakeholders (McDavid, Huse, and Hawthorn, 2013).

No matter how hard we try, no human can be fully objective about their own work. The same goes for any organization. So, from time to time, anyone who is serious about performance measurement needs to also engage the services of an external evaluator. These "program audits" should include both operational analysis (is the program working the way it's supposed to work?) and an examination of the level to which the program is achieving its intended result. An external review of the measurement process, the tools and techniques being used to measure and monitor, and the basic assumptions underlying the operation should all be on the table for review. Finally, the external reviewers need to be competent to perform the review, and sufficiently far removed from the organization to make sure that the review is fully objective (Hunter, 2013; Kusek and Rist, 2010).

ARE WE HAVING FUN YET?

Sorry Not Sorry is a great title that came out of pop music a few years back. And it's quite fitting as the summation of this chapter on the management of social innovation.

Depending on your perspective, effective management of day-to-day operations can be either frighteningly dull or wonderfully comforting (personally, I always thought it was dry until I had to do it – and I've since come to embrace it). But no matter how it makes you feel, it can make or break an enterprise. And with everything that's at stake in a social venture, it not only makes the difference in the success of the organization, but also is often the determining factor in how well (or poorly) we are able to improve the lives of those we hope to help.

At the beginning of the chapter, I "apologized" for both the tone and the content of this section. In truth, I'm not really sorry at all, and I hope that you realize that it's because effective management of organizational performance – from clear mission all the way down through effective evaluation – is truly the key to making sure that the goals of the enterprise are met.

So, get out that measuring tape and start evaluating. Onward!

CHAPTER SUMMARY

This chapter sets a foundation for understanding managing a social enterprise and leading change by first framing the cause-and-effect nature of social change and the important distinction between correlation and causation. In order to have an impact, it is critical to first set a clear mission for your social enterprise; that way, you will be able to recognize what activities and opportunities take you away from the work that you should be doing. To enact the mission, social entrepreneurs need to acknowledge the distinct but complementary roles of managers and leaders and their responsibilities in the execution and vision for change, respectively. In order to avoid some of the common pitfalls of the nonprofit sector, social entrepreneurs need to consistently manage performance and set effective performance goals, and intentionally engage in OBB, which prioritizes the activities deemed to yield the best cost-effectiveness breakdown. The basic functions of, and differences between, performance measurement and evaluation were highlighted in order to understand how monitoring, assessing, and reporting on performance, quality, efficiency (outputs), and effectiveness (outcomes) help social entrepreneurs to be transparent and accountable to themselves and their stakeholders.

QUESTIONS FOR DISCUSSION

1. Take a social issue of interest to you, and outline some of the complexities of the issue and their possible cause-and-effect relationships.
   A. Create a visual chart, mind map, or web to help show your guesses and assumptions about the connections between the issues. The table below shows an example of a starting point.
   B. Once taking a guess as to these connections, do some research.
      - Are there data available that help to support your guesses?
      - Do the available data alter or add to the complexity to your original sketch or chart? For example, you could start off with something like the table below only to determine that the initial cause could actually start elsewhere. An individual could face a health challenge that results in a job loss or someone could experience bankruptcy, which can make it difficult for them to get access to housing and a new job.
   C. How might these issues be geographically and culturally bound? For instance, in many countries a job loss might not result in a lack of health coverage or an increased danger of getting into medical debt.
   D. Based on this exercise and the reading, what conclusions do you have about cause-and-effect relationships?

Potential cause Job loss	Potential effect 1 Housing	Potential effect 2 Health	Potential effect 3 Education	Potential effect 4 Finances
• Job loss • Inconsistent wages • Inconsistent work • Low wages	• Displacement of individuals and families • Temporary housing insecurity/ homelessness • Episodic housing insecurity/ homelessness • Chronic housing insecurity/ homelessness • Unplanned multi-generation housing increases	• Lack of adequate physical health support • Lack of adequate mental health support • Less available funding for healthy eating and exercise support • Risk of substance use and addiction • Lack of access to reproductive care and support • Risk of medical debt • Risk of poorer health outcomes • Risk of social isolation	• Inconsistent schooling environment • Absenteeism • Lack of an ability to support education of children (tutoring, disability supports) • Inability to pay for re-skilling and further education and training for adults • Inability to pay towards student fees, debt, or loans	• Bankruptcy • Difficulties with credit • Depletion of savings and retirement accounts

2. In this chapter, we connected how goals play a role in performance management. For this exercise, you will create 3-5 SMART performance goals for a social venture idea that you have or for an existing social enterprise. If possible, work with a partner or group to make sure these goals are effective performance goals.
    A. How would these goals support the mission of the social enterprise?
    B. How are these goals "performance goals," and how do these goals connect with performance management?
    C. How would you envision measuring these goals through ongoing performance measurement?
3. Based on your understandings of leadership and management from the chapter, outline the differences and similarities between the two within a Venn diagram. When generating this list, think intentionally about their roles for social change and their unique and common tasks and responsibilities.
    A. Once you have completed your Venn diagram, think about how leaders and managers can be held accountable for each item listed.
    B. In some social enterprises, especially new ones, a leader and manager might be the same person, while in others the roles might be split between multiple people. Discuss the considerations for each of these scenarios.
        •   What might the weaknesses, risks, and vulnerabilities be for each case?
        •   What might the strengths and opportunities be for each case?
4. Use the various tools discussed in the previous chapters (Logic models, Social Business Model Canvas, asset maps, and so on) to design an operating model for your social enterprise idea or the existing social enterprise you have been using. Be sure to develop an initial budget, and include the ways that you will measure

the performance of the enterprise. Once you have completed this, ask yourself the following questions:

A. How do goals play a role across all of your previous models and new operating model?
B. What is the role of goals with OBB?
C. How does your operating model and budget reflect and consider the concept of performance management?
D. How does your operating model and budget reflect and consider OBB?
E. What questions arise for you regarding performance measurement and evaluation? How might each of these look for your social enterprise?

BUILD IT YOURSELF: STEP FOUR

Now that you've determined the specific solution you intend to use to address the social issue you've identified, it's time to start drawing up some plans! So, for this step in building your own social enterprise, you need to use the tools and techniques we've laid out for you.

Design the operating model (business model) for your social enterprise, including an initial operating budget.

RECOMMENDED RESOURCES

Drucker, P. F. (2006). *Managing the Non-Profit Organization*. New York, NY: HarperCollins.
Kettner, P. M., Moroney, R. M., and Martin, L. L. (2017). *Designing and Managing Programs: An Effectiveness-Based Approach*. Washington, DC: SAGE.
Ormerod, P. (2001). *Butterfly Economics: A New General Theory of Social and Economic Behavior*. New York, NY: Basic Books.

NOTES

1. The actual author of this quote is disputed. Accessed 20 November 2021 at https://quoteinvestigator.com/2017/11/12/change-world/.
2. The bulk of this chapter owes a huge debt of gratitude to two great minds – Mario Morino and Dr. David E. K. Hunter, both of whose ideas are heavily referenced throughout the chapter. You can read the entirety of their two great books on these issues by downloading them for free at www.leapofreason.org.

REFERENCES

Collins, J. C. (2001). *Good to Great: Why Some Companies Make the Leap – And Others Don't*. New York, NY: HarperCollins.
Drucker, P. F. (2006). *Managing the Non-Profit Organization*. New York, NY: HarperCollins.
Egger, R., and Yoon, H. (2004). *Begging for Change: The Dollars and Sense of Making Nonprofits Responsive, Efficient, and Rewarding for All*. New York, NY: HarperBusiness.

Freeman, M. A., Johnson, S. L., Staudenmaier, P. J., and Zisser, M. R. (2015). Are entrepreneurs "touched with fire"? Accessed 28 April 2021 at https://michaelafreemanmd.com/Research_files/Are%20Entrepreneurs%20Touched%20with%20Fire%20(pre-pub%20n)%204–17–15.pdf.

Giancola, S. P. (2020). *Program Evaluation: Embedding Evaluation into Program Design and Development*. Thousand Oaks, CA: SAGE.

Hunter, D. E. K. (2013). *Working Hard & Working Well*. Hamden, CT: Hunter Consulting.

Kusek, J. Z., and Rist, R. C. (2010). *Ten Steps to a Results-Based Monitoring and Evaluation System: A Handbook for Development Practitioners*. Washington, DC: World Bank Publications.

Martin, L. (2002). Budgeting for outcomes. In A. Khan and W. Hildreth (eds), *Budget Theory in the Public Sector* (pp. 246–260). Westport, CT: Quorum Books.

Martin, L. L., and Kettner, P. M. (2010). *Measuring the Performance of Human Service Programs*, 2nd ed. Thousand Oaks, CA: SAGE.

Mascarenhas, R. C. (1996). Searching for efficiency in the public sector: Interim evaluation of performance budgeting in New Zealand. *Public Budgeting and Finance*, 16(3), 13–27.

McDavid, J., Huse, I., and Hawthorn, L. (2013). *Program Evaluation and Performance Measurement: An Introduction to Practice*, 2nd ed. Thousand Oaks, CA: SAGE.

Morino, M. (2011). *Leap of Reason: managing to outcomes in an era of scarcity*. Washington, DC: Venture Philanthropy Partners.

Pallotta, D. (2010). *Uncharitable: How Restraints on Nonprofits Undermine Their Potential*. Medford, MA, and Lebanon, NH: Tufts University Press and University Press of New England.

Pulakos, E. D. (2004). *Performance Management: A Roadmap for Developing, Implementing and Evaluating Performance Management Systems*. Alexandria, VA: SHRM Foundation and Society for Human Resource Management. Accessed 28 April 2021 at www.shrm.org/hr-today/trends-and-forecasting/special-reports-and-expert-views/Documents/Performance-Management.pdf.

Rajala, T., Laihonen, H., and Vakkuri, J. (2018). Shifting from output to outcome measurement in public administration: Arguments revisited. In E. Borgonovi, E. Anessi-Pessina, and C. Bianchi (eds), *Outcome-Based Performance Management in the Public Sector*, 2nd ed. (pp. 3–24). Cham, Switzerland: Springer.

Robichau, R. W., and Lynn, L. E., Jr. (2009). The implementation of public policy: Still the missing link. *Policy Studies Journal*, 37(1), 21–36.

Taylor, F. W. (1911). *The Principles of Scientific Management*. New York, NY: Harper & Brothers, and Kindle Locations.

Yukl, G. A. (1990). *Skills for Managers and Leaders*. Englewood, NJ: Prentice Hall.

The early days of the DC Central Kitchen (DCCK) were fast and furious, filled with hard work, 18-hour days, and little sleep. A gregarious and engaging individual, Robert Egger used his passion, his personality, and the skills he had gained promoting musicians to quickly gain fans and followers, picking up donors, supporters, and staff members along the way.

DCCK's first full-time employee came out of a casual conversation at a soccer game. The first operations manager was a former volunteer who became infected with Egger's zeal and saw the need for an "inside" manager to complement Egger's "outside" perspective. Its first formal location (a converted rowhouse) came rent free, by virtue of a barter arrangement with a local homeless shelter that owned the building and needed to feed its residents. The first head of culinary services (aka head chef) was hired away from his job as night manager at the shelter that was providing the building. The first head of volunteer services was a graduate of the culinary training program who was pressed into service when a larger than expected group of volunteers showed up one day.

The DCCK, like many startups, operated on a process of improvisation and experimentation. Nothing was bought that could be borrowed, nothing was purchased new that could be found used, and each day brought new lessons, new techniques, and new workers (both paid and unpaid). A chance encounter in 1992 brought DCCK a second location and its first true commercial kitchen, with a similar agreement, albeit with a much larger need. DCCK needed to produce 2,000 meals a day (a four-fold increase from its previous 400 or so meals per day).

Throughout this period of intensive growth, financial management continued to work on a make-do basis, and staff evaluations consisted mostly of making sure folks showed up every day and made it through the grueling pace of life in the rapidly expanding enterprise.

As with many charitable efforts, the increasing need for infrastructure became harder and harder to pay for with grants and donations (donors often prefer to pay for direct services), so Egger and his team decided to open a catering business that could earn a profit, and then use that money to help pay for some of the things that were not attractive to traditional fundraising sources. This model also offered an opportunity to expand the culinary training program and put program participants to work (with the hope that this work would help them to rebuild a résumé). They called the new company Fresh Start.

From the beginning, Fresh Start had two constraints that its competitors didn't have.

First, the DCCK leadership team was committed to paying a living wage, while other catering companies were paying only the legal minimum wage. Second, the complex relationships that DCCK had built with many of its suppliers meant that aggressive competition in the catering business might alienate key partners.

The addition of the Fresh Start program meant that the small DCCK leadership team was managing

Source: Courtesy of Robert Egger. Used with permission

four distinct programs – the original feeding program that launched the organization, the food recycling efforts that served as a key supply line, the job training efforts that had grown out of the kitchen operations, and this new for-profit social enterprise. After 10 years of operations, the organization continued to struggle with erratic funding, high staff turnover, and weak infrastructure.

QUESTIONS FOR DISCUSSION

1. Discuss the ways in which DCCK managed innovation.
2. Summarize the stakeholder engagement techniques deployed by DCCK.
3. Describe DCCK's strategic planning process.
4. Analyze the performance-management tools deployed by the DCCK team.
5. Explain the competitive analysis issues faced by DCCK.

PART III
WHAT DIFFERENCE DOES IT MAKE?

9
Metrics matter

Learning objectives

After studying this chapter, you should be able to:
1. Understand that value can be both objective and subjective, having both worth and merit, and being able to be viewed from a variety of directions.
2. Identify the individual roles and supports needed in your corner.
3. Define the commonly used financial terms.
4. Conduct basic financial calculations and use standard financial tracking measures and evaluations: Income Statement/Profit and Loss statement, Balance Sheet, Cash-flow statements, Cost–Benefit Analysis, Cost–Effectiveness Analyses.
5. Value the role of monitoring and reflecting upon the financial pieces of a social venture as a mechanism to sustain and grow the organization's impact.
6. Contextualize the important role of legitimacy for social enterprises, from basic levels of following laws, to being true to their mission, to helping to validate the ability for social entrepreneurship to strike the balance between social value and financial sustainability.

METRICS MATTER

The previous chapter talked a lot about the reasons why you need to measure the various activities of your social enterprise. This chapter will talk about specific things that need to be measured and give you a basic understanding of how those measurements work. We'll start with some simple financial measurements, then move into some larger economic matters, before turning our attention to measures of social impact and community engagement. In a later chapter, we'll talk about how to turn these measurements into sustainable revenue that can support your efforts.

Before we begin, we need to understand that many of these topics are quite complex, and the effective leader will know when they need to bring in experts in a specific matter to help with the technical issues. My goal here is not to make you an expert in any of these matters, but to give you enough basic knowledge that you can talk intelligently to the folks who have deep expertise in these areas.

FINANCIAL PERFORMANCE

We start with basic finance for several reasons – but the most important one is that without a sound financial footing, no venture (regardless of its purpose) will survive for very long.

Source: iStock.com/nd3000. Used with permission

To put it even more simply, you've got to keep the lights on if you want to make a difference. And since the electric company (and many others) expects to get paid regularly and will turn off your power if you don't pay your bill, it's important to understand the basic finances of an organization.

As an added benefit, much of this applies to your personal finances as well (hey, two for one!). As a reminder, the point of this section is not to make you an accountant. You can (and should) hire one of those (and sooner rather than later). The point is to give you enough basic knowledge to be able to speak intelligently with your accountant and understand the key issues that you need to manage.

BOX 9.1   THE MEANINGS OF "VALUE"

In this chapter, there is mention of the term "value" throughout. Social entrepreneurs, and those who support them, all have opinions on what they perceive as valuable. How valuable is social impact? Is profitability valuable? What about sustainability?

Worth is a measurement of value relative to something else. Compared to other meanings of "value," the notion of worth is more quantifiable. This can be something that we can compare to competitive market rates; for example, an assessment of worth could be weighing money relative to time (for example, is this three-week task worth the compensation offered?). Assessing worth can also be utilized to compare like with like (for example, net costs in currency compared with money saved in the same currency). We will discuss this more later in the chapter when we introduce cost–benefit analysis.

Merit, on the other hand, is more subjective than worth, as it is in the "eye of the beholder." Merit can signify the personal importance and desirability of a particular program or intervention. Other areas, like uniqueness and novelty, can fall on the merit side of value, as paving a new, innovative path may be important (or valuable) to some stakeholders and less so with others.

Unpacking the multiple meanings of "value" can help social entrepreneurs to represent their value in a fuller perspective. Social entrepreneurs should not only think about the variety of stakeholders, but also how each stakeholder group may have different perceptions of value, based on both worth and merit.

As one final note about social value, Social Value UK (2015) provides a helpful lens for thinking about the aspect of social value through proposing seven principles of social value:

1. Involve stakeholders – Inform what gets measured and how this is measured and valued in an account of social value by involving stakeholders.
2. Understand what changes – Articulate how change is created and evaluate this through evidence gathered, recognizing positive and negative changes as well as those that are intended and unintended.
3. Value the things that matter – Making decisions about allocating resources between different options needs to recognise the values of stakeholders.

Value refers to the relative importance of different outcomes. It is informed by stakeholders' preferences.

4. Only include what is material – Determine what information and evidence must be included in the accounts to give a true and fair picture, such that stakeholders can draw reasonable conclusions about impact.

5. Do not over-claim – Only claim the value that activities are responsible for creating.

6. Be transparent – Demonstrate the basis on which the analysis may be considered accurate and honest, and show that it will be reported to and discussed with stakeholders.

7. Verify the result – Ensure appropriate independent assurance.

The above seven principles show guidelines and best practices to determine what is valued and measured, to articulate and report value, and to prioritize providing stakeholders with honest and verified claims from the measurements.

Basic Accounting

The first thing to understand about accounting is that it's not about math. Accounting is a system of rules for tracking money and other financial assets. And it's managed using basic arithmetic. Even better, the most basic accounting procedures are limited to addition and subtraction (with multiplication and division thrown in when things get more complex).

The second thing that you need to know is that there is a difference between accounting and bookkeeping. Bookkeeping is the process of recording financial activities. It should be a daily task, and requires substantial discipline. Happily, there are dozens of commercial software programs that make it fairly easy. Accounting is the process of analyzing the financial activities to make sure that the objectives of the firm are achieved. They both use the same raw data, just in different ways. So, now that your anxiety level is a bit lower, let's tackle some basic financial management issues.

BOX 9.2   CHART OF BOOKKEEPING AND ACCOUNTING

The following table further details the roles and responsibilities of bookkeepers and accountants, to help highlight the differences between the two. While the two work together closely to help an organization with its financial health, the two roles have different contributions.

Table 9.1 Bookkeepers and accountants

Bookkeeping	Accounting
Support with organized, detailed, accurate financial record-keeping	Provide insights, analysis, recommendations, and advisement
More consistent, regular, or daily activity	Check-ins (for example, quarterly, twice a year, annually, as things arise)

Bookkeeping	Accounting
Can be trained on the job or can hold a training certificate	Tend to require formal education and training credentials
Help with present transactions and payroll	Help prepare annual tax returns, perform audits, review financial records, do financial problem-solving, and make financial forecasts and projections

So, as a social entrepreneur, which one will you need? The answer is both! Social enterprises can have an internal or external bookkeeper, with the internal one working directly with the social enterprise or the external one hired to independently review incoming and outgoing money on a regular basis. Unless you have experience doing so yourself, you will likely need an accountant to help with annual tax filing, but accountants are a handy partner to have as opportunities and challenges come your way. Although accounting services can be an expense for new social entrepreneurs, having a specialist's perspective can help in financial decision-making and can save money and time.

Cash Flow

The single most important part of managing your finances is what the finance folks call "cash flow." What this means in layperson's terms is "cash on hand." It's no more complex than managing the balance in your bank account from day to day. It seems simple to say it, but it's important to make sure that you have enough money to cover your bills. It becomes a little more complicated when you understand that the timing of incoming money (receiving a grant or donation or getting paid for a service) does not always match the timing of when a bill is due.

Using my own personal finances to give an example, I have one utility bill that has a very short window to be paid – within 10 days of when I get it. The problem is I only get paid every two weeks (every 14 days). So, if I don't manage my personal cash flow well, I may not have the money on hand to pay the bill when it's due. That means the utility may impose a late payment penalty, or (in severe cases) shut off my service.

Taking this back up to a business level, there are certain regular payments that must be made – rent, utilities, and so on. And in most enterprises, the employees expect to be paid

regularly as well. Unfortunately, the folks paying you do not operate on the same time frame as those who expect payment from you. In the case of a major grant, it could be several months after the grant is approved before you get the money. So, managing the balance in the bank account becomes a vital (and daily) function. In fact, poor cash-flow management is one of the biggest reasons an organization fails.

It's also important to note here that cash and profit are not the same thing. Profit is the difference between the organization's total income and total expenses (a matter we will turn to in just a moment).

Source: iStock.com/Olivier Le Moal. Used with permission

Cash is the money that is on hand and readily available to pay bills as they come due. The successful manager should be able to plan for the cash needs of the enterprise, know when actions need to be taken to conserve cash when possible, and be aggressive in locating and securing the cash needed to keep the enterprise afloat.

Profit

A word that is loosely thrown around in many contexts, the accounting definition of "profit" is quite simple – it's the difference between your total income and all your expenses. If that difference is negative (meaning you spent more than you made), the accountants call that a "loss." But like many other matters, this simple concept can get complicated quickly.

The simplest form of accounting is known as "cash-based." In this context, profit and cash flow look quite similar – if I still have cash in my bank account, then I'm profitable (at least for the moment). The more sophisticated version of accounting is called "accrual." The difference is that a cash basis records revenue and expenses when money changes hands, while accrual records them when the agreement is made to pay, even if the actual payment is not received for some time (in some cases, 90 days or more). As an organization grows, most accounting professionals will recommend using the accrual basis, and that is where cash flow and profit can become conflicting matters.

Consider the case where a large grant has been received. As I mentioned a minute ago, it can often take time before the grant check is issued. Since the grant has been earned but not received, the accrual process records it as revenue. But since the check has not been deposited, the cash flow of the enterprise is quite weak. So, the enterprise is profitable but cash-poor.

Staying with that same big grant, the entrepreneur agrees to purchase some much-needed equipment that the grant money will fund. Once the agreement to purchase is made, the expense is recorded. So now the venture may be less profitable, even though its cash flow has not changed (no actual money has come in or gone out at this point).

Once the long-awaited check arrives and is deposited, the firm's cash position is now sound. But since it may be some time before more income is received, the firm needs to understand another concept related to cash and profit, something the investing world calls "burn rate."

This somewhat indelicate term is used to describe how much cash the firm has on hand, and how quickly it expects to use up that money (how quickly it will "burn" through the funds). This requires making some solid projections on regular expenses (rent, payroll, taxes, insurance, and the like) and then determining how

Source: iStock.com/valiantsin suprunovich. Used with permission

many months the venture can survive with the current funds on hand (sadly, this is never as long as one would hope). More important to the current discussion, this can mean that a firm is cash-rich but unprofitable (because it's losing money in the long run).

Before we leave the conversation on profit, we need to reinforce that the popular label of "nonprofit" is a major misnomer. It simply reflects a tax-status election and indicates how a firm can and cannot distribute its earnings. Regardless of the tax structure of the entity (for profit or nonprofit), you cannot continue to operate unless your income exceeds your expenses.

BOX 9.3   GROSS AND OPERATING PROFITS

Throughout the chapter, "Gross Profit" (or "Gross Income") refers to the total revenue minus the direct costs of goods sold (COGS), meaning that this includes the inputs and processes needed to deliver the good or service to the customer or beneficiary.

Total Revenue – Total COGS = Gross Profit

For example, a service-based social enterprise runs programming that supports 500 people a month. The programming receives a $50,000 annual grant from a local foundation, $230,000 in other donor and small-grant supports, and $120,000 in program-related sales.

$50,000 + $230,000 + $120,000 = $400,000 total annual program-related revenue

How can you think about calculating the costs, and what does this include? Social entrepreneurs need to think about all of their direct costs, which include inputs (materials, labor, equipment) and activities (programming, manufacturing/assembling, sales/credit card fees, shipping). To deliver the program, the social enterprise calculates that all the direct program costs (input and activities) total $20,000 per month.

$400,000 total annual revenue – ($20,000 monthly direct program costs x 12 months)
= $400,000 total annual revenue – $240,000 annual direct program costs
= $160,000 annual Gross Profit

To calculate the Gross Profit margin, the social enterprise would need to divide Gross Profit by Total Revenue.
While the annual Gross Profit ($160,000) and the Gross Profit Margin (40 percent) both look strong and encouraging, calculating Operating Profit (or Operating

$$\frac{\text{(Total Revenue – Total cost of goods sold or services delivered)}}{\text{Total Revenue}} = \frac{\text{Gross Profit}}{\text{Total Revenue}} = \text{Gross Profit Margin}$$

$$\frac{\$160,000}{\$400,000} = 0.4 = 40\% \text{ Gross Profit Margin}$$

Income) helps to create a more detailed and accurate picture, as it includes a picture of the fixed costs (rent, other salaries, insurance, accounting, and legal services), as you can assign a portion of these expenses towards the total costs.

For example, if your rent is $3,000 per month, your other salaries are $8,000 per month, and your insurance and legal and accounting services all total $2,000:

$3,000 + $8,000 + $2,000 = $13,000 estimated indirect, fixed costs per month
$13,000 indirect, fixed costs per month x 12 months = $156,000 indirect, fixed costs per year

These total annual indirect, fixed costs ($156,000) can be added to the total annual direct programming costs ($240,000) to calculate the annual Gross Profit of the social enterprise.

$400,000 total program revenue – ($240,000 direct costs + $156,000 indirect costs) =
$400,000 total program revenue – $396,000 total costs of services delivered = $4,000 annual operating profit

This is all assuming that programming is all that the social enterprise does, but that initial $160,000 profit figure and the actual $4,000 annual Gross Profit figure give two very different pictures, but this is exactly why social enterprises need to keep on top of their actual financial picture. By doing accurate calculations, social enterprises can make informed decisions and adjustments moving forward.

Basic Financial Statements

In order to manage the financial health of an enterprise, you need to generate regular reports that show both the short- and long-term status of the organization. There are three key reports that need to be understood – the Income Statement, the Balance Sheet, and the cash-flow Statement.

Income Statement

The Income Statement is often also referred to as the "Profit and Loss statement," and that may be a more useful name as the purpose of this report is to show all of the money that has come into the organization (income) and all the money that has gone out (expenses). The somewhat obvious goal is that the report shows more income than it does expenses. If not, the quickest way to remedy the imbalance is to reduce expenses (quick, yes – but not always easy). In most organizations (particularly ones with a social purpose), payroll is the single biggest expense. So, if an organization needs to quickly cut expenses, it may mean that staff must be reduced – either by cutting back someone's hours or eliminating a specific position within the firm (which is never an easy or fun thing to do). Depending on the size of the organization and its complexity, an Income Statement should be produced and reviewed at least monthly, if not every other week. It's also important to watch for trends in the Income Statement so that problems can be addressed before they become critical. To understand how to do that we need to talk about what's known as a "Profit Margin."

Simply stated, the Profit Margin is the difference between income and expenses, shown as a percentage. So, if an enterprise has income of $100,000 and expenses of $90,000, it has a Profit Margin of 10 percent. Now, suppose that the next month's report shows a Profit

Margin of 7 percent. This means that either income has gone down or expenses have gone up. And it should be the impetus for a management inquiry into the source of the difference so that the problem can be corrected before that magic margin number turns negative (meaning that you are losing money).

BOX 9.4   NET PROFIT MARGINS

While many social entrepreneurs want to think first and foremost about their social impact, the profitability of the social enterprise helps to sustain and scale that important social impact. Calculating Profit Margins is a simple way to assess how financially sustainable an activity or product is for a social enterprise to do.

For example, if a social enterprise has three products, each of which has different expenses and profit, it is helpful to see the financial comparison of the different products. It is important to note that social entrepreneurs are typically more interested in the social impact and the effectiveness of their work in creating the change they want to see, but they also need to be able to articulate the value of what they do to all of their stakeholders, including those who donate to and invest in their enterprise.

For Product 1, it costs the social enterprise $3 to produce it, with all expenses considered (including operating expenses and taxes). For products 2 and 3, the total costs are $9 and $7, respectively. With all of the products 1–3, the sales figures per item were $14, $20, and $10, respectively. So, what does this mean for a Profit Margin? While there are different types of Profit Margins, we will focus on one of the most common, "Net Profit Margin." That would mean that the Net Profit Margin calculations of the three products are the following:

Net Profit Margin of product 1: ($14-$3) / $14 = 0.786 x 100 = 78.6%
Net Profit Margin of product 2 ($20-$9) / $20 = 0.55 x 100 = 55.0%
Net Profit Margin of product 3: ($10-$7) / $10 = 0.30 x 100 = 30.0%

When calculating Net Profit Margin, it is much easier for social entrepreneurs to use

$$\left(\frac{\text{Net Profits}}{\text{Net Sales or Revenue}} \right) \text{ X } 100 = \text{Net Profit Margin}$$

this information for internal and external needs. Internally, they can weigh decisions on what activities, products, and services are needing additional review (for example, problem-solving to lower production costs or increase net sales). For external purposes, social entrepreneurs can use this information within grant applications or when speaking with prospective donors or investors. Looking at Net Profit Margin over time can also show how social entrepreneurs have been mindful of their profitability, which allows them to lead more sustainable organizations.

Balance Sheet

The second common financial statement is the Balance Sheet, which presents a higher-level perspective on the overall financial health of the enterprise. The name comes from the relationship between the three main components – assets, liabilities, and equity.

The two main sections of this document are the assets (things of value that you control) and the liabilities (items that you owe to others). Both assets and liabilities are then further divided into "current" and "long term." Let's take a minute to pull each of those apart.

Current assets are things that can be converted into cash in a short amount of time (usually less than 30 days). This would include actual cash on hand, bills or invoices that you have issued but are not yet paid (known as "accounts receivable"), and any materials that you may have on hand that are used to produce a product or service (known as "inventory"). Long-term assets (also known as "fixed assets") are things of value that would take more time to turn into cash (like a building you might own, or the furniture and equipment that you use to run the enterprise).

In the same way, current liabilities are items that you are going to have to pay very soon (also usually within 30 days). This would include bills (like rent, utilities, and supplies) as well as wages and taxes. Long-term liabilities would include things like the total amount due on a mortgage or long-term loan. The difference between the Total Assets and the Total Liabilities is referred to as Owner's Equity (although you may or may not have actual equity in the firm depending on your legal structure, a matter we will address further in Chapter 12). The accounting principle underneath all of this is that Assets equal Liabilities plus Equity (and if they don't, you've got a bookkeeping problem).

When it comes to managing the enterprise, the most immediate areas of concern in the Balance Sheet are the Current Assets and the Current Liabilities (the short-term financial obligations that are owed and the liquid assets on hand to pay for them). Financial managers use two tools to measure the health of the firm's Balance Sheet that they call the Current Ratio and the Quick Ratio. The difference between the two is that the Current Ratio is a bit broader and the Quick Ratio is a bit more conservative. The important point for this conversation is that these ratios should always be higher than 1:1 (most financial managers recommend a Current Ratio of at least 2:1 and a Quick Ratio of at least 1:1).

BOX 9.5   CURRENT AND QUICK RATIOS

Current Ratios compare an organization's Current Assets to its Current Liabilities. The word "current" in this context frames things with the context of a year. So, this means Current Assets are both current cash and other types of assets that can become cash within the context of the year (for example, accounts receivable, inventory, assets that can be liquidated). In turn, Current Liabilities hold to the same framework of a year, with things like wages, taxes, loan and rental payments, and accounts payable.

  Current Ratio = Current Assets / Current Liabilities

More conservatively, Quick Ratios look at an organization's assets that are quicker and easier to liquidate (for example, cash, marketable securities, accounts receivable), rather than also including things that can take longer (for example, inventory). The equation below is very similar to that of Current Ratios, apart from limiting what is considered an easily liquidated asset.

Quick Ratio = Quick Assets / Current Liabilities

Now that all of this has been explained, why are these ratios helpful for social entrepreneurs? Like Profit Margins, Current and Quick Ratios can show potential donors and investors how financially healthy your organization is. Particularly with those providing loans and investments, they want to be sure that their funds are able to be paid back in a timely manner. Ratios around 2:1 (assets to liabilities) are considered to hit the ideal balance of organizations that are financially healthy and sustainable, yet moving their funds in a way that is not too conservative (for example, there is a calculated risk, the funds are being reinvested in scaling).

Return on Investment

There is one more basic concept that we need to discuss before we move on to other types of measurements, and that is the notion of "return on investment" (ROI), as introduced in Chapter 7. A concept that gets tossed around a lot, the simple definition of ROI is that assets invested in an effort should produce an outcome greater than the value of the assets when they are invested. The simplest example of this is a small loan from a bank.

When the bank lends you money, it charges an interest rate that is added to the amount borrowed. Let's say that you borrow $10,000 to buy a used car. The bank charges 5 percent annual interest and you agree to a three-year loan (36 months). The monthly payment on that loan would be $299.71 (trust me on the math here – or check it yourself if you wish). But the total of those 36 payments is $10,789.52, which means that the bank is making $789.52 in profit from your loan (an 8 percent return on its investment[1]). The critical concept here is that any asset used in any work should produce some sort of value that is greater than the value that it had before it was deployed. Which leads us to a much larger discussion about the nature of value.

BOX 9.6   COMPARING STATEMENTS

As mentioned within the chapter, these three statements – an Income Statement, a Balance Sheet, and a cash-flow statement – are frequently paired together to provide a fuller picture of the enterprise's financial picture. What does each of these do, and how do they compare to one another? According to Investopedia.com, here is a comparative summary of the various types of statements:

Table 9.2 Comparative summary of statements

	Income Statement/Profit & Loss (P&L) statement	Balance Sheet	Cash-flow statement
Function	• Overviews revenue, expenses, and costs over a year or quarter	• Shows an organization's snapshot of assets, liabilities, and shareholder equity (if applicable)	• Reports the cash inflows and outflows over a particular period of time

How is this helpful?	• Shows enterprise's ability to increase revenue and/or reduce costs
	• Can indicate efficiencies/inefficiencies, and performance
	• Helpful for year-by-year or quarter-by-quarter comparisons
		• Breaks down (1) assets (for example, cash, inventory, accounts receivable, marketable securities, long-term securities, prepaid expenses, equipment, property, copyrights/patents); (2) liabilities (reoccurring expenses – like rent, utilities, payments, payroll – loans, debt); and (3) shareholder equity
		• Allows for a review and reflection on liquidity, efficiency, and leverage
			• Follows three cash flows coming from the following:
			  • Operations ("CFO," operational business activities)
			  • Investments ("CFI," investment gains and losses, including the buying and selling of property and equipment)
			  • Financing ("CFF," debt and equity)

Equation(s)	(Revenue + Gains) – (Expenses + Losses) = Net Income	Total Assets – Total Liabilities = Stakeholder Equity Liabilities + Shareholder Equity = Assets	Operations Cash Flow + Investment Cash Flow + Financing Cash Flow = Net Cash Flow

FINANCIAL SYSTEMS

Up to this point, we've talked about value within the context of a single entity. But no organization operates in a vacuum, and no person is an island unto themselves. We all live in communities; we all interact with each other in many ways. In the same way, organizations exist within environments. These environments go by many names but the two that are the

Source: iStock.com/anyaberkut. Used with permission

most common are "markets" and "economies." We need to take a minute to understand each of these frameworks so that our conversation on value makes more sense.

Markets

At its simplest, a market is a mechanism that provides for an exchange to take place between two parties. I'm sure you can quickly picture a basic market in your mind – perhaps your local grocery store, where you exchange your hard-earned money for bread, milk, eggs, and cereal.

Using our just-completed discussion on profit and loss, you understand that the grocery store needs to sell the food for more than it costs it to buy it, display it, pay for the rent and electricity (as well as its workers), and so on.

The notion of value enters this exchange when you think about what the food you buy is worth. While you may think that the food is of equal value to the money that you give up to pay for it, the truth is that what you receive in any exchange of value has to be worth more to you than what you give up – otherwise you wouldn't make the exchange. For a market to work, that must be true for both parties. Without even thinking about it, we use this measurement all the time when we say that something was "worth it." It might be that it was worth our time, or that it was worth the effort, or that it was worth the money. No matter what the means of exchange, what we receive has to be more valuable to us than what we give up (and it isn't always money that we exchange).

Economies

Continuing to oversimplify (and probably annoy economics professors everywhere), when you put a bunch of markets together you get an economy. So, if markets are a collection of individual exchanges, then an economy is a collection of markets (and economics is the study of how these collective markets behave). In both cases, the underlying notion is the exchange of value. And the concept of value is how we build the bridge to our next level of measurement.

ECONOMIC VALUE

You probably hear conversations about how business contributes to the economy. Just like a business needs to have basic financial measurements to make sure it is healthy, there are also some basic measurements that are used to tell if a business (or a market) is creating value for the economy. The two most important measures of economic value are "buying power" and "tax contribution."

Source: iStock.com/Fizkes. Used with permission

Buying Power

In our conversation about financial health a few pages back, we talked about needing to track expenses. While payroll is almost always the largest expense, there is also a lot of money spent securing all the things that an organization needs in order to do its work. From basic office supplies to computers and phones to office space and electricity, there are many things that any business regularly pays for (and for the purposes of this discussion, we're going to say that all those things are "bought"). When an organization buys these things, it is also producing revenue for other firms. The total that an enterprise (or a group of enterprises) spends on these expenses can be thought of as its buying power (and you can quickly see that more expenses means more power).

This notion of total expenses can also be thought of as direct buying power, since it is all under the control of the organization. The firm also has indirect buying power through the wages it pays to its workers, who most likely take their paychecks and use them to buy food, clothing, shelter, transportation, and other personal needs. If you add up the total direct and indirect buying power of an enterprise (or a market), you start to understand what folks mean when they talk about "economic contributions." But buying power isn't the only contribution that an organization makes.

Tax Contributions

Depending on how the venture is organized, the Net Profit it generates may be subject to income tax (this may even be true for some "non"-profits). Any owned property (such as a building) may also be subject to taxes. In some cases, the employer may also be required to pay taxes on various employee-related expenses such as contributions to unemployment funds. And no matter how the firm is set up, the salaries and wages paid to the workers are subject to income taxes. Each of these tax payments goes to various government entities and is used to provide a wide range of public benefits (such as public safety, aid to the less fortunate, public transit, water and sewer services, roads and maintenance, and many others). Added together, these payments into various government systems are referred to as the tax contribution of the enterprise. And just like buying power, you can separate them into direct and indirect, with direct tax contributions being those tax payments made by the firm, and indirect tax contributions being those made by the employees.

While keeping track of these economic contributions is not necessary for the direct management of the firm, they are important when it comes to attracting investors (which is made more difficult due to the multiple objectives of a social enterprise). We'll get into more detail about how that works in Chapter 11, so right now the important thing to know is that there are ways that an enterprise contributes directly to an economy, and that knowing your firm's economic impact will be helpful going forward. This journey into the larger questions of economics also leads us to the next notion of value that we need to talk about – the concept of "social value."

SOCIAL VALUE AND SOCIAL EFFECTIVENESS

In order to understand how social value enters an economic discussion we need to take a step back in order to take a few steps forward. So, let's zoom out to the big-picture level and talk about how we make the world a better place.

The human desire to care for those less fortunate is as old as humankind itself. For most of recorded civilization, that care has been delivered through informal networks within the community (such as family, friends, faith communities, and the like). What we know today as organized charity is a relatively modern invention (Critchlow and Parker, 1998). In the same way, the value of that care has been measured mostly in emotional terms (Emerson, 2003). You regularly hear about how good it makes you feel to volunteer at the local soup kitchen, or to be a tutor for a disadvantaged student. When it comes to fundraising for these social programs, the emotional appeal is often the leading argument used to attract donors (Saul, 2011).

When you start to dig into the financial structures of the nonprofit economy, you find that a large portion of the revenue for the typical social program comes from government sources (either as a direct subsidy or as a fee for services provided) (Young, 2006). But what's interesting (and relevant to this conversation) is not where the money comes from, but how we measure what it does.

Social Outputs as Economic Outputs

Source: iStock.com/Romolo Tavani. Used with permission

You've heard mention before in this book that there is a distinct difference between what's known as a social output and a social outcome. To review, outputs are activity-based measurements (number of people served, number of houses built, and so on). Outcomes are ways that the social condition being addressed is reduced or eliminated (improved scholastic test scores, lower disease rates, and so on) (Bryson, 2004). Happily, the measurement of social program effectiveness is moving towards outcome-based measurements (Morino et al., 2011). But what really matters to the social entrepreneur is not just how effective a program is, but how that effectiveness impacts the economy. To dig a little deeper into this topic, let's look at an example that recently hit my inbox.

The other day, I got a copy of an annual report from a local nonprofit that works with military veterans who are dealing with substance abuse. This organization reported that in the past year, it served 277 residents (folks who were living in the facility during their recovery). It also reported that 131 of these residents were funded by the government (through the U.S. Veterans Administration). The organization had 1,141 volunteers that showed up to help provide services, and 107 business donations.[2] It received $213,243 in individual donations (in addition to grants from the government and several foundations), and obtained 60 percent of the food it served from donated sources, which saved it $78,000 in expenses. All of that is wonderful, but it's simply a report of the organization's activities. They are outputs, just like you would measure the output of an engine in horsepower or the output of a lightbulb in watts. And none of those measures talk about how (or even if) any of the people it cares for are better once they've received the services of the organization. Happily, this program does also report some statistics about the outcomes it produces.

This same annual report states that 93 percent of the folks who entered the program successfully completed it. It also says that 75 percent of those who completed the program obtained permanent housing after being discharged, and that 88 percent of the program graduates either obtained or retained employment. Those are all very good things that show that the organization is producing results. But if you are thinking about this from an economic standpoint, there are probably a few other numbers you might want to see.

For example, what was the economic contribution (the buying power and tax contribution) of those folks who are now clean, sober, and regularly employed? Since the program graduates are now contributing to the economy, having that information might help to make a case for increased governmental support. It might also be used to increase the support from area businesses that benefit from the purchasing power of these folks (after all, the success of the program means that these businesses are getting more customers). Taking this to an even deeper level, it might be helpful to think about how the success of this program is saving money for society.

The annual report showed total income of just under $3.4 million. This means that the program spends just over $12,000 per program participant to receive its reported outcomes. One source[3] estimates that the cost of addiction in the United States is $578 billion per year, and another estimates that there are 21 million folks who are currently dealing with addiction in one form or another. This means that each person dealing with addiction is costing the U.S. economy roughly $27,500 per year. And for about $12,000, this program can help that person recover.

Just to take the math one small step further, the 93 percent success rate means that the cost per successful outcome is just over $13,000 – which is still a saving of over $14,000. Multiply that by the number of folks helped, and you find out that this program is saving society almost $3.7 million per year. That's quite an economic contribution! Stated in financial terms, this program is producing an 8 percent return in its invested dollars – not bad for a small nonprofit! In the next chapter, we're going to talk about how a social entrepreneur can turn this economic profit into a source of sustainable revenue. For now, it's enough to know that a social purpose organization can produce economic value in the same terms as a profit-oriented venture.

BOX 9.7   COST-BENEFIT AND COST-EFFECTIVENESS ANALYSES

In the eyes of financial contributors, the outcomes of a social enterprise's efforts – via a program or intervention – are only as good as it can measure and articulate. Social entrepreneurs need to know how they can measure and show their value to their stakeholders. Two ways to do this are through a "Cost–Benefit analysis" (CBA) and a "Cost–Effectiveness Analysis" (CEA).

A CBA, or a "Benefit–Cost analysis" as it is sometimes called, compares the net costs of a program to the benefits of the program, with both costs and benefits being positioned in the same unit of measurement: a currency (for example, USD, GBP, euros, and so on). A CBA allows social enterprises to show, in currency, how beneficial an investment in a program or intervention is. For instance, a social enterprise that employs and trains returning citizens who were formerly incarcerated may want to show the costs of delivering this program, relative to how much money it may be saving the community (for example, lower incidences of recidivism, less dependence on unemployment or other public benefits). By framing the benefits in the same unit of currency, funding bodies, investors, and donors can see the direct monetary value of their contributions. This also allows the social enterprise to continue to use its funds for the interventions that most cost-efficiently yield the desired outcomes.

Like the cost–benefit analysis, a CEA also weighs costs relative to outcomes. However, a CEA expresses outcomes in units that align with the program or intervention's aims, rather than looking at currency. This also allows programs, organizations, and efforts to be compared to one another. For example, a social enterprise is piloting two different youth health and wellness programs aimed at reducing incidences of adolescent obesity. The first program supports the goal through providing young people with yoga training and conscious-eating guidance, and the second program offers a walking club with nutrition education. Both programs are aiming to reduce and prevent adolescent obesity in the community over the school year, but for future years it might be interesting to monitor which of the two yielded the best results. In this scenario, the social enterprise can review the net costs of each program compared to the number of adolescents who moved out of an obesity-range body mass index.

As noted in the previous chapter, it is important to remember that program effectiveness can be challenging to measure, especially in the short term. Oftentimes, the impact of a program or invention can be seen years later. Because of this, social entrepreneurs need to be able to find ways to measure both immediate and longer-term outcomes whenever possible in order to show the fuller value of their efforts and work.

Measuring social effectiveness also has many benefits that are more qualitative. Starting at the most basic level, it is no small thing to help a fellow human overcome an obstacle and move on to a better life. In the case of our current example, recovering from the disease of addiction most certainly helps the addict; but the act of helping also helps the one who is doing the helping. We all know that wonderful feeling we get when we do a good deed. So, when one person is helped, two people can benefit. And if 277 are helped, then it's likely that several hundred more benefit.

Society is also made better in many non-economic ways. Because the folks suffering from addictions also often have other problems, it's fair to say that helping folks recover might also reduce the number of individuals experiencing homelessness (and the presence of homeless folk on the streets is generally viewed as a negative thing by most civic boosters). Since possession of a controlled dangerous substance is a crime in many places, fewer drug users could reduce the crime rate in a specific area – and there are many that argue that reducing the "demand" for drugs would go a long way in reducing the higher-level crimes that go along with drug trafficking (French et al., 2000).

I'm sure you can think of many more ways that the world is made a better place when folks are able to overcome the challenges they face. The thing to remember here is that an effective social purpose organization can produce direct benefits for society – both in actual economic terms and the "softer" context of a better world.

Taking a second to review, in this chapter we've talked about how to measure financial performance in day-to-day operations and for the long term. We've talked about how to measure the direct economic contributions of a firm, as well as the quantitative and qualitative contributions a social purpose organization makes to the community and the world. But before we move on to talk about how to build sustainable funding streams, we need to look at one more aspect of measurement that is unique to the social enterprise – the notion of "legitimacy."

Organizational Legitimacy

To unpack this complex phrase, we need to start by going back to the dictionary, where we find that "legitimate" means "conforming to the law or to rules" (Lexico, n.d.). So the first level of legitimacy that we need to track is to make sure that our social venture is in compliance with all applicable laws and regulations (Bagnoli, 2011). This includes things like paying the appropriate taxes, complying with all the various health and safety laws, maintaining the appropriate levels of employee and client confidentially, and many more (the services of a good attorney and a good accountant are strongly advised).

Source: iStock.com/MichaelUtech. Used with permission

The second level of legitimacy has to do with being true to your mission (Bagnoli, 2011) – another way to think of this is that the enterprise is seen as credible (that is, it is taken seriously). While tracking your social effectiveness goes a long way to making sure that the organization stays on course, there are other, more subtle things that can also indicate how well the venture is keeping to its mission. For example, a nonprofit that is seeking to reduce social inequities might want to make sure that there is diversity in its leadership team that mirrors the diversity of the folks it hopes to help. On a more basic level, things like buying locally, participating in fair trade programs, paying a living wage to even the lowest paid workers, and being careful to make sure that high-level executives are not receiving exorbitant salaries and benefits can go a long way towards making sure that the organization is seen as legitimate. It's important to note here that maintaining your credibility is hard, and losing it is quite easy (just think for a second about your own personal reputation, then multiply it by the total number of stakeholders that your venture might touch).

The higher levels of legitimacy have to do with the very nature of social enterprise. Since the expressed goal is to blend profit and purpose, there are many who will not take the venture seriously (Dart, 2004). One place that this may manifest itself is in relationships with vendors, suppliers, and other partners in the business world, who may not see the social enterprise as an equal partner (Spear, Huybrechts, and Nicholls, 2013). This lack of legitimacy may become particularly challenging when trying to secure funding. Banks may see the firm as too risky (after all, you are diverting profits to pay for needed services when you could be using them to pay back the loan). Traditional charitable and governmental funding sources may think that you have less need for their funding since you have some sort of earned income (Brooks, 2000; Carroll and Stater, 2009).

At the highest levels, this notion of legitimacy has to do with being seen as a valid organizational concept, rather than a jumbled pile of conflicting and contrasting goals and objectives (Nicholls, 2010). Since the field is new, there are not as many standard practices as there are in more established industries. In addition, the blended objectives can be seen as a lack of focus rather than a clear vision (Dart, 2004; Nicholls, 2010).

While none of these concepts of legitimacy are as important to the day-to-day operations as things like cash flow and profit margin, they can be equally important to the long-term health and success of the venture.

PULLING IT ALL TOGETHER

By this point in this chapter (and by this point in our journey), you are probably thinking seriously about getting a regular job with a regular paycheck where you don't have so many different things to worry about and keep track of. Or maybe you're so exhausted that you just want to go sit on a beach somewhere and stare at the ocean. But you probably also know in your heart that this is work worth doing, and you're going to press on. So let's take a minute to restore, reset, and re-energize.

The first thing to remember is that nobody expects you to be an expert in all things. One of the strongest traits of a leader is understanding their strengths and weaknesses (Yukl, 2010). One of the mistakes we make is in thinking that we need to work to strengthen our weaknesses. The smart entrepreneur understands that hiring folks who are strong in areas where they are weak is one of the smartest things you can do.

The second thing to remember is that many of the topics we've covered are areas to which subject-matter experts devote their entire careers (and we've covered them in just a few pages). So, take solace in the knowledge that you are now aware of things that will help you and better understand the places where you will need help. Since you now have this awareness, you are better equipped to have intelligent conversations with those who have specific expertise.

Finally, recall from our earlier discussions that social entrepreneurship is a messy blend of many disciplines. There is no one perfect balance that applies to all organizations. And there are so many things to keep track of that it is not humanly possible to have everything working perfectly all the time. Managing any enterprise (social or otherwise) is a constant juggling act, so it only stands to reason that we're going to drop a ball now and then. The point is to know which balls to watch, and what to do when you do drop one, so that you can pick it up and keep moving.

Avanti!

CHAPTER SUMMARY

Chapter 9 centers on the premise that the financial aspects of a social enterprise are what helps to sustain and grow the organization's impact. Social enterprises are responsible for the delivery of value, which means a breadth of different things, including economic value, buying power, tax contribution, social value, and social effectiveness. Social entrepreneurs need to prioritize the financial health of their organizations by getting the right supports needed in their corner and by knowing the basics of common financial terminology, equations, and evaluations. Good financial knowledge and habits help to establish the legitimacy of the social enterprise, which in turn helps to sustain and scale the social value delivered.

QUESTIONS FOR DISCUSSION

For each of these questions below, you will need to first select a social enterprise of interest (this can be an existing organization or, if you have been working on your own organization, use that). Using the selected social enterprise, answer the following questions:

1. Reflect on the ways in which "value" was defined throughout the chapter. What is the breadth of ways that the selected organization has value? Describe the variety of values of the enterprise has, and connect this to what was learned in the chapter.

2. Think about the elements of cash flow, profit, and ROI, which were defined in the chapter. How do these elements relate to the selected social enterprise? What do you think knowing these figures enables the selected enterprise to do or to accomplish?

3. How might the selected social enterprise think about the different levels of legitimacy? Are these unique to social entrepreneurship, or are these common with other types of organizations?

4. Now you will have a chance to think about some of the basic financial calculations introduced within the chapter. Think of a very simplified service or program that your social enterprise will offer. Looking back to your Logic model from Chapter 7 might be a great starting point. To start, think about the inputs and try putting together a basic budget that projects the basic costs involved. After making these estimates, try doing a rough calculation of the Gross Profit and a Current Ratio.

    A. What are you seeing?
    B. What did you learn?
    C. What would you need to do to make all of this work?
    D. What is the value and the role of monitoring and reflecting upon the financial pieces of your social venture?

BUILD IT YOURSELF: STEP FIVE

Using the tools provided in Chapters 7, 8, and 9, develop specific, measurable outcomes for your social enterprise. Be sure to include economic, civic, and social outcomes in your suite of metrics.

RECOMMENDED RESOURCE

Investopedia. www.investopedia.com.

NOTES

1. The reason the return is 8 percent and not 5 percent has to do with compound interest, which is a technical point that is beyond the scope of our current discussion.

2. Accessed 28 April 2021 at https://baltimorestation.org/.

3. Accessed 28 April 2021 at https://recoverycentersofamerica.com/economic-cost-substance-abuse/ and www.addictioncenter.com/addiction/addiction-statistics/.

REFERENCES

Bagnoli, L. (2011). Measuring performance in social enterprises. *Nonprofit and Voluntary Sector Quarterly*, *40*(1), 149–165.

Brooks, A. C. (2000). Is there a dark side to government support for nonprofits? *Public Administration Review*, *60*(3), 211–218.

Bryson, J. M. (2004). *Strategic Planning for Public and Nonprofit Organizations: A Guide to Strengthening and Sustaining Organizational Achievement*. San Francisco, CA: Jossey-Bass.

Carroll, D. A., and Stater, K. J. (2009). Revenue diversification in nonprofit organizations: Does it lead to financial stability? *Journal of Public Administration Research and Theory*, *19*(4), 947–966.

Critchlow, D. T., and Parker, C. H. (1998). *With Us Always: A History of Private Charity and Public Welfare*. Lanham, MD: Rowman & Littlefield.

Dart, R. (2004). The legitimacy of social enterprise. *Nonprofit Management & Leadership*, *14*(4), 411–424.

Emerson, J. (2003). The blended value proposition: Integrating social and financial returns. *California Management Review*, *45*(4), 35–51.

French, M. T., McGeary, K. A., Chitwood, D. D., McCoy, C. B., Inciardi, J. A., and McBride, D. (2000). Chronic drug use and crime. *Substance Abuse*, *21*(2), 95–109.

Lexico (n.d.). "Legitimate." Accessed 28 April 2021 at www.lexico.com/definition/legitimate.

Morino, M., Thompson, C. C., Lowell, W., and Cheryl, C. (2011). *Leap of Reason: Managing to Outcomes in an Era of Scarcity*. Washington, DC: Venture Philanthropy Partners.

Nicholls, A. (2010). The legitimacy of social entrepreneurship: Reflexive isomorphism in a pre-paradigmatic field. *Entrepreneurship Theory and Practice*, *34*(4), 611–633.

Saul, J. (2011). *The End of Fundraising: Raise More Money by Selling Your Impact*. San Francisco, CA: Jossey-Bass.

Social Value UK (2015, May 19). What are the principles of social value? Accessed 28 April 2021 at https://socialvalueuk.org/what-is-social-value/the-principles-of-social-value/.

Spear, R., Huybrechts, B., and Nicholls, A. (2013). The role of legitimacy in social enterprise–corporate collaboration. *Social Enterprise Journal*, *9*(2), 130–146.

Young, D. R. (2006). Complementary, supplementary or adversarial? Nonprofit-government relations. In E. T. Boris and C. E. Steuerle (eds), *Nonprofits and Government: Collaboration and Conflict* (pp. 37–79). Washington, DC: Urban Institute Press.

Yukl, G. (2010). *Leadership in Organizations* (7th ed.). Upper Saddle River, NJ: Prentice Hall.

10
Marketing has three faces

Learning objectives

After studying this chapter, you should be able to:
1. Understand the unique requirements for marketing a social enterprise.
2. Define the "4 Ps" of marketing and the three social enterprise marketing interests, identifying their relevance and parts within the marketing landscape.
3. Combine the 4 Ps and three interests to form the "12 Ps."
4. Apply the 12 Ps to a real social enterprise case or example.
5. Reflect on how you might create a marketing plan or strategy that balances the 12 Ps.

AND NOW FOR SOMETHING COMPLETELY DIFFERENT...

In the last few chapters, we've worked really hard on metrics and measurements – lots of technical stuff that is complex and geeky. In the next chapter, we're going to get deep into some financial structures, which will also be complex and geeky (but contain a huge payoff, so stay tuned!). So, in order to shift gears and use a slightly different part of our brains, this next chapter is going to focus on marketing – equally geeky, but in a different way. But before we dive into the nuts and bolts of this topic, I want to set out a few thoughts on why this is so important to the development of an effective social enterprise.

If you think back to our conversations in Chapter 2, you'll recall that a successful social venture must pay attention to the basics of entrepreneurship. So, just like a for-profit venture, a sound marketing plan is critical. But the thing about marketing a social enterprise is that you have several different audiences, each with their own interests, motivations, and perspectives. While there are as many different interests as there are stakeholders, the three that matter the most to the marketing effort are the market (the folks buying the product or service you're selling), the money (the folks paying for all this), and the community (those you hope to serve). So, the fun-

Source: Glen Carrie, Unsplash. Used with permission

damental premise of this chapter is summed up in its title – the successful marketing of a social enterprise needs to have three distinct "faces" in order to attract the interest of each of these unique groups (Padanyi and Gainer, 2004). In the next chapter, we'll talk about how each of these audiences can be a source of revenue (and we'll add another source in addition to these), but for now we'll stick to the ways that we can attract the attention of these groups.

In order to try to make some sense of this, we're going to spend a little time talking about marketing in general, with a focus on the basic elements of the marketing mix. Once again, it's worth a reminder that this section takes an entire discipline and summarizes it in a few short paragraphs, merely scratching the surface of a fascinating and complex subject.

With that brief background in hand, we're then going to walk through how each of the elements of the mix needs to be adjusted so that you achieve maximum impact with each of the distinct audiences you will encounter.

WHAT IS MARKETING?

As someone whose primary field is marketing, I've always found it fascinating to talk with folks about common perceptions of what marketing is and is not. Most often, people think of the act of promotion as the primary marketing activity, with advertising being the main function. The reality is that there is a lot of work that must be done ahead of time for a promotional campaign to be effective.

BOX 10.1 DEFINING MARKETING

According to the American Marketing Association (AMA) website (2017), "marketing is the activity, set of institutions, and processes for creating, communicating, delivering, and exchanging offerings that have value for customers, clients, partners, and society at large" (definition updated in 2017).

The 4 Ps (And the Best P)

If you've already taken a basic marketing course, you've probably run across the popular concept of the Marketing Mix, also known as the 4 Ps. Originally designed by Eugene MacCarthy in 1960, this framework has become the standard lens for evaluating and discussing the development of a marketing strategy (MacCarthy and Perreault, 1960). By way of a quick review, the 4 Ps are product, price, place, and promotion. Of these four, there are many (me included) who think that product is the most important.

Product

One of the great gurus of new product development is Dr. Robert Cooper (who you met briefly in Chapter 2, and in more detail in Chapter 5). Cooper has done a number of very sophisticated studies of the factors that make a new product successful, and the number one factor – by far – is the ability to demonstrate sound value to the potential customer (Cooper, 2011). But to do that, you need to know who your customer is, and what needs they have.

So, the first step in product development is a needs analysis (which should sound familiar from Chapter 5), followed by the development of a viable solution that meets those needs. Dr. Cooper's research supports the belief that doing those two things well will have a greater impact on your success than anything else (Cooper, 2011). The critical factor is that the customer must perceive the benefit the product or service provides as valuable (which takes us back to Chapter 2 and the need to build and test models).

Price

In Dr. MacCarthy's model, the next P is price, which has several components to it. The first and most important component is cost recovery. Recalling the economics of one unit from Chapter 2, the price of the product or service needs to be set so that all the costs of producing the product are recouped. Recall also that both direct cost (costs of material, labor, and the like) and indirect cost (rent, utilities, and other fixed expenses) need to be accounted for in calculating the total cost of producing the product or service.

Once you've made sure that you are recovering your costs, there are several pricing strategies that a firm can pursue. The most basic of these is what's known as "cost-plus," which means that a predetermined percentage is added to the total cost and serves as the profit margin for that product. There are many ways to determine the appropriate amount to add in using this tool, but the rule of thumb in for-profit ventures is to use the level of demand as a barometer. In practice, this means that you raise your total price until the demand for your services starts to fall off (we'll talk about a different way to determine this in a minute when we get to price in a social venture).

Competitive pressures also influence price, so sometimes the market will determine how much or how far you can raise your price. There are also pricing strategies that can be used to gain market share or establish a brand as a leader in either premium or low-cost markets.

Place

The third P in the marketing mix is place, which most folks think of as the physical or virtual location where the transaction occurs (such as a store, a showroom, or a website). But in technical marketing terms, place also includes all the steps that are needed to support the completion of a purchase, and things like the supply chain, distribution channels, and modes of delivery.

So, if the product is a can of beans, the place is not just the grocery store shelf, but also the set of steps that the can follows from the manufacturer to the wholesaler and eventually to the store. It also includes the environment in the store (the way the store looks and feels), the means for paying for the purchase, and the way you take the product home (so things like self-check-out kiosks and discounts for bringing your own shopping bags can and do make a difference).

Promotion

Finally, we have promotion, the fourth (and perhaps most well-known) P. Promotion certainly includes advertising in its many forms, but also includes all the other forms and methods of communications used to "get the word out" about your product. This includes things like branding, public relations, special events, signage, and packaging, as well as direct selling. Perhaps the trickiest part of a good promotional campaign is making sure that the message is consistent across all the communication channels.

THE TWELVE Ps

Since there are three distinct marketing audiences that a social enterprise needs to address, and there are four Ps in the marketing mix, we now have a matrix of 12 total items to discuss, which we'll do in the following section. We'll use each of the distinct primary audiences (market, money, and community) and

Source: Tom Crew, Unsplash. Used with permission

discuss how the "face" of the marketing effort needs to change to meet the unique interests of each audience.

The Market

To start off on this particular journey, we need to go all the way back to our first few chapters and remember that one of the main definitions of a social enterprise is that it "address[es] a basic unmet need or solve[s] a social or environmental problem through a market-driven approach" (Social Enterprise Alliance, 2014). What this means to the marketing effort is that the path we described earlier in this chapter is the right way to market the product or service that the social enterprise produces.

Product

This means that above all else, the product the social venture produces creates superior value in the eyes of the customer (which is also the number one reason why a new product succeeds; Cooper, 2011). The notion of receiving good value for the money spent is often referred to in marketing circles as an "exchange" – meaning that I exchange something of value (my money) for something that I see as having more value (the product I'm buying). But the real meaning of a valuable exchange is that each party views what they are receiving as being worth more than what they are giving up (most of us understand this as the idea that we "got a good deal").

Price

The same goes for price – the market wants to know that the price of the product is on par with other alternatives that may be available to meet these same needs. One of the more fascinating aspects of this concept of being "price competitive" is that the enterprise needs to think beyond its immediate competitors and consider every alternative that the potential customer has for spending the money that you're asking them to give to you (up to and including not spending it at all).

One of the mistakes that I've seen many aspiring social entrepreneurs make is to think that they can be priced higher than the competition and then justify that price because the customer knows that the money is going to a good cause. While it is true that generous individuals will donate to a good cause, the logic of pricing a product this way turns the organization into a charity offering a fundraising premium (think of the Public Radio fundraisers where you get a tote bag or a T-shirt as a "thank you gift") rather than an enterprise that is seeking to create value and be compensated for it.

Place

In appealing to a market, the main concern about place for a social enterprise is that you want to make it as easy as possible for your potential customer to find you and make the purchasing process as easy as possible. One of the ways that this arises is in retail businesses, where the location of the store can be a critical factor in its success. With restaurants and thrift shops being two popular concepts, this issue is critical to the practice of social enterprise.

Promotion

Promoting a social venture to a market audience takes an approach very much like the place strategy – the promotional campaign needs to meet the potential customer where they already are. Much like the pricing error I just mentioned, many aspiring social entrepreneurs also think that word will somehow spread on its own because of the good work being done. Sadly, this is almost never the case.

So, the market wants to know that it is getting a good product for a competitive price that can be easily acquired without a lot of searching – and if you can do that, you are likely to be able to build a business. And the market will care that you are a social enterprise, but not enough of them will care enough to consistently pay a higher price, accept an inferior product, or endure poor customer service. Pretty straightforward when you think about it.

Marketing to money gets a bit more complex, because the sources of money involved in a social enterprise are a bit more complex.

The Expectations of Money

Before we dive into this topic, let's go back to the much simpler world of the commercial entrepreneur. In that environment, money comes into a firm from two sources. The first is from the market, when a customer or client buys a product or service and pays the firm. The second comes from an investor, who expects to be paid back when the venture produces a profit. The only real variable in the expectation of a commercial investor is how much they want to receive and how often they want to receive it. A bank wants a specified interest rate (a relatively small percentage of the total investment) and expects to get paid every month for the life of a loan. A venture capitalist typically expects to receive eight to 10 times as much money as they put in but is willing to wait several years to receive payment (Sherman, 2005). Other investments fall somewhere along the spectrum between these two, but the expectation of financial return is invariable – with the only variable being the terms under which the return is provided.

The money that comes into a social enterprise also has the same expectation of return. The main difference is that the terms under which the return is provided vary more widely than they do in a commercial enterprise. To understand this variation better, we need to look at three separate categories of funding for social ventures – gifts, grants, and investments.

Gifts: Pass the Hat, Please

Source: iStock.com/Stas_V. Used with permission

In nonprofit fundraising, you hear the word "gift" used a lot. It can be used to describe both individual donations as well as more structured grants provided by professionally managed foundations. In order to provide the needed clarity, we're going to use "gift" exclusively to describe money given by individuals to causes they wish to support. While global statistics on charitable giving are hard to come by, the best information I've seen suggests that charitable donations around the world total just under $340 billion in U.S. dollars per year, with the United States providing over three-quarters of that amount (Charities Aid Foundation, 2016).

Much of this money is solicited through fundraising, an art and science that is sophisticated enough to have developed its own trade organization, training programs, and professional designations (perhaps the most well-known being the Association of Fundraising Professionals; see https://afpglobal.org). The best practices in fundraising talk about building relationships, finding the donor's areas of passion and empathy, and aligning the request for a donation with the donor's interest (Phillips, 2016). In other words, the fundraiser needs to create conditions where the donor identifies with the cause on an emotional level. In fact, most charitable donations are made from some sort of personal, emotional connection (and sometimes, more from the personal gratification received by the donor – the oft-cited "warm glow") (Saul, 2011).

A marketing effort designed to appeal to charitable money needs to focus on a truly compelling story that clearly demonstrates a dire need for financial support, drawing out the empathetic nature of the individual donor. It will use powerful images of the individuals that the donation will support and makes a clear call to action by directly requesting a donation be made on that day (Mixer, 1993; Phillips, 2016).

Using our lens of the 4 Ps, the product in the charitable fundraising scenario is the person who the program hopes to help. This individual (or group of folks) can be portrayed either in the state of need or in the state of triumph over the condition that the nonprofit supports. In either case, the "value" that the "product" represents is purely emotional, and the "exchange" in this scenario is that the donor receives the satisfaction of knowing that they have helped.

The price in this charitable scenario is highly variable and is determined mostly by the donor's ability to give (in fact, many large fundraising operations have entire departments that do nothing but research a donor's giving capacity).

BOX 10.3 "CHARITY PORN"

The notion of "charity porn" or "poverty porn" is one that is a challenge within the social impact marketing space. Marketing of social challenges should raise money and awareness and not trivialize the social issue at hand. Some charity porn marketing campaigns, instead, have raised funds through superficial storytelling that does not educate on the complexity of the social challenge and how it came to exist or what reinforces it. While those in the social impact sector may know to look out for this, the public may not be able to recognize the problem of charity porn, so social entrepreneurs need to commit to helping to educate the public on the social challenge they hope to tackle through providing them with data and nuance. The issue – along with the communities impacted – needs to be treated with care and respect, and this orientation needs to be at the forefront of social entrepreneurs' minds.

Place and promotion in charitable fundraising go hand in hand and are also highly variable. Large-scale campaigns appealing to many donors can be delivered by direct mail, through social media, in televised advertisements, by text message or phone call, and even via traditional advertising media like newspapers, magazines, and billboards. These broad-ranging efforts are usually designed to solicit a high number of relatively small donations. Larger donations are usually solicited in face-to-face encounters held over time, with relationship development and the exploration of the donor's desires and interests being explored by a team of professionals who eventually ask the donor for the gift.

To sum this up, the individual charitable donor is most often motivated by an emotional message, appealing either to empathy or ego. So, marketing to that audience needs to reflect that strong emotional appeal. But when we move to the more ordered world of grantmaking, the tone of the message shifts.

Apply for a Grant

Even though it is often referred to as a "gift", obtaining a grant from a charitable foundation or governmental entity is a much more structured process. While the details vary greatly, the process itself is fairly consistent. The individual or organization seeking the funding completes an application that is reviewed by the funder and accepted or rejected.

Source: iStock.com/Vadzim Kushniarou. Used with permission

There are different levels of complexity in this process (that is, the length of the application, the amount of time it takes to review, the number of applicants accepted, and the amounts received) based on the size of the organization, the amount being funded, the activities being funded, and the relationship between the grantor and the grantee. Safe to say, if you've seen one grantmaker, you've seen one grantmaker.

BOX 10.4 GRANTMAKING

"Grantmaking" refers to the process of a foundation, entity, organization, or individual offering a sum of money to a nonprofit or social entrepreneur to deliver a particular social impact within a particular time frame. Responsive grantmaking is an open, grantee-driven process, with most grantmakers specifying a broad area or two of interest. This type of grantmaking allows for creative, untraditional, and community-centered ideas that might not be on the minds of funders and can approach the more immediate needs of the community. Proactive or strategic grantmaking has more directed, focused goals driven by the funder, which can help produce meaningful and deep learning and impact on their target social issue or issues. Both types of grantmaking have their benefits and challenges and play an important role in the grantmaking landscape. Some more progressive grantmakers are shifting the power dynamics to be more inclusive of community members in the decision-making process, which is referred to as "participatory" grantmaking.

In addition to a more formal application and review process, structured philanthropy usually expects the money to produce some specific result. Sometimes it's a simple output measurement (for example, the number of people served), but there is an increasing focus on the need for outcomes (long-term effects like increased literacy or reduced hunger) (Morino et al., 2011). Most funders also expect some sort of report that indicates how well the stated objective was achieved, as well as a financial statement showing how the money was spent (again, the amount of detail and complexity varies greatly). Sometimes, the money may not all come at once, but in a series of payments tied to specific milestones or objectives. If the organization does not achieve the desired objectives, it can impact the ability to receive future funding. The grantee is also responsible for ensuring that any applicable tax and legal issues are taken care of, and is usually expected to confirm these with the grantor.

Thinking back to our earlier discussion on the notion of return, it's worth noting that the grantmaker, like the individual donor, does not expect any sort of financial return (in other words, they don't want the money back). But unlike the individual donor, the grantmaker does expect to see specific social changes occur.

In the context of applying for a grant, the product is the output or outcome that the social venture produces. Unlike the individual donor, this product must be carefully measured. In most cases, it must also align with the mission of the funder, which can be quite specific – many funders restrict their grantmaking to specific geographic areas, defined social causes, and even sometimes the size and scope of the organization requesting the funding. To demonstrate that the desired product can be produced, the applicant is often asked to provide a detailed Social Change Theory and Logic model (remember those from Chapter 7?). Some sort of demonstration that the team doing the work can produce the desired result is also often needed.

Price also becomes a more technical matter, requiring a planned budget showing how the money will be spent. Care must be exercised in developing this budget, as it may be scrutinized for excesses in various categories, such as rent, payroll, and other supporting expenses (although it's changing now, for many years a proposed grant budget would be required to meet a standard of 85 percent of funds going directly to the front lines of service delivery).

Most grant funding comes from an organization's response to a request for proposals issued by a funder, so the concepts of place and promotion really don't apply in this context. After all, the purpose of those two Ps is to attract the attention of the potential customer and facilitate the transaction, which is just not the way structured grantmaking works. However, place and promotion are important when seeking funding from an investor, which is the next source of money we need to look at.

BOX 10.5   REQUESTS FOR PROPOSALS (RFPs)

Requests for proposals, or "RFPs," are announcements that serve to make organizations aware of opportunities to submit a proposal responding to a particular call. RFPs provide project or program specifications that inform organizations on what would be expected of the awardees in terms of outputs, outcomes, and impact, as well as project scopes, timelines, and budget guidelines. RFPs can range from supplementary services for the existing programming of the funding entity (that is, contract support) to the full responsibility of a project's conceptualization, delivery, and evaluation.

Attracting Investors

No matter what the purpose of the venture might be, every organization needs money to establish its operations, build its infrastructure, and expand its reach. And a social enterprise is no different. But before we look at the specific marketing efforts needed to attract investors, we need to lay to rest some confusion about some basic terminology.

In some nonprofit circles, the word "investment" is used to describe a particularly large donation. To be clear, that's not what we're talking about here. We're talking about money that expects a financial return. Also, we're including commercial financing vehicles such as banks and other lenders as part of this group, mostly because the expectation of return doesn't change (just the terms and the rates, as discussed a few pages back).

When you're marketing to an investor audience, the product is the return on investment (ROI). All of the other stuff that makes it a good product in the eyes of the market (solving a need, creating value, and the like) are important, but they are seen as a means to an end, namely that the investor will get their money back in the manner they expect. In the same way that a grantmaker expects a sound Logic model that shows how specific outcomes can be achieved, an investor expects solid financial projections that clearly account for all expenses and demonstrate the organization's ability to produce enough revenue to pay the investor back. You could go so far as to say that these financial exhibits are the product, which underscores the need for them to be professionally rendered.[1]

BOX 10.6 NOTE: THE ART OF PARTNERSHIP, COLLABORATION, AND HIRING

While the various hats worn through launching and running a social enterprise are diverse and many, it does not mean that social entrepreneurs themselves need to bear the burden of responsibility for all of these roles. There is no reason for them to try to fake their way through or to delay progress in order to learn each of these areas. In fact, that is counterproductive to the responsibility and urgency social entrepreneurs feel for their work. Instead, social entrepreneurs commonly consider different types of partnerships, collaborations, and hiring options.

For example, if detailed financial projections are not in their wheelhouse, social entrepreneurs can find someone through hiring a qualified ad hoc contractor or part-time staff member, or someone willing to provide that support pro bono or without a charge. The latter is especially common with new social startups that might not have the funds to hire staff with the depth of skill level needed to approach the breadth of roles and responsibilities needed. Point being, do not feel you have to go it alone; through including others, you are giving more people a piece of ownership in the great work you do.

For the investor, price is the return itself (often referred to as the "rate of return"). In discussing the rate of return, you will often come across the concept of the "time value of money," which refers to the relationship between the amount of time the investor is willing to wait to get paid and the amount of additional return expected. Stated simply, the longer the wait, the higher the return (which is one of the reasons why venture capitalists expect returns that are eight to 10 times their original investment) (Sherman, 2005). It's also important to note that price is usually negotiated on an individual basis for each transaction, and that the main variable in setting the price is the amount of risk the investor believes they are taking on. As the amount of perceived risk goes up, so will the expected rate of return.

Place and promotion are a bit tricky when marketing to an investor, as there are as many pathways to these funds as there are folks who make these investments, and they range from the simple to the convoluted. If the investment is coming from a bank, there is little need for place and promotion as you can simply apply for a loan (although you do need to have solid financials and some sort of collateral to pledge against the loan). If it's venture capital funding, the journey to a successful deal can involve several meetings and presentations and a complex series of negotiations (it's also important to note that this type of funding only happens about 5 percent of the time) (Stangler, Tareque, and Morelix, 2016). It's safe to say that there is no one way to present an investment opportunity to a potential funder; nor is there any single best way to promote the existence of the opportunity to a prospective audience of funders.

While there are several variations in the area of marketing to money, the one constant is that money expects a return, and that the terms and conditions by which that return is made are unique to each type of investment. In the next chapter, we'll talk more about specific ways to attract financing across the spectrum of funding opportunities. But for now, we've got one more key audience to discuss, and that's the folks who receive the social services that are our reason for being.

The Needs of the Community

If you think back to the conversation we had in Chapter 3, you'll recall that one of the unique aspects of social entrepreneurship is that we are dealing with people, not products. It's easy to lose sight of that when we get deep into conversations about marketing and pricing and promotion, so it's good to take time to regularly remind ourselves that it's care and concern for humans that brings us to this work.

When it comes to the delivery of a social service, it's very easy to become convinced that we know what's best for a specific community. Armed with this knowledge and a well-thought-out Logic model (and maybe even some initial grant funding), we then proudly introduce ourselves to the neighborhood and set up shop. We may even have some initial success in bringing about positive change. But far too often that change is short-lived. The program runs out of money, and life in that neighborhood never really changes. I'm convinced that the reason this happens is because we don't take the time to build relationships in the community and develop the trust that is needed to effect lasting change.

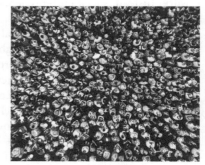

Source: iStock.com/Dmytro Varavin. Used with permission

If this is sounding familiar, it may be because we've talked about community organizing and community engagement in Chapter 6, and again in Chapter 9. In those conversations, we talked about how important it is to engage the community in the process of developing your intervention and the ways that change can be measured. But an engaged community is also a vital part of the strategy for gaining acceptance and participation in the program that you . develop (and if that's not marketing, then I don't know what is!).

Product

When it comes to marketing to the community, the product is the program that you hope will bring about the desired change. To be successful, the program needs to be presented in such a way that the community can understand and accept it. Perhaps more importantly, the community needs to believe that you have its best interests at heart, and that you are in it for the long haul. Finally, the program needs to be presented in a way that makes folks want to participate.

A good way to think about this is to remember that specific vegetable that you hated when you were a kid. For me, it was broccoli – I just couldn't stand those wooden stalks. But put some cheese sauce on it, and all of the sudden I'm a member of the clean-plate club.

A more direct example comes from a friend of mine who is a pastor in a church in a challenged neighborhood in East Baltimore.

With the best of intentions, the good folks in this church saw a need for fresh produce in the neighborhood, so they set up a food pantry with an array of vegetables available for free. Much to their disappointment, there were not many takers. They asked a few folks in the area why they weren't coming, and found out that most of the neighbors had never seen vegetables in their raw state, so they didn't know what to do with this "stuff." Realizing that they weren't meeting people at the point of their need, they started labeling the produce and providing recipe cards with instructions on how to prepare and cook the produce. In no time, the traffic in the food pantry went way up (to the point where they had to limit access until they could get a more abundant supply!).

It turns out that marketing to the community is a lot like appealing to the market – you need to demonstrate value, but you also must demonstrate that you understand your "customer" and can relate to their needs and their world view. Said simply, you need to be part of the community in some way, because you're not going to get cooperation without some level of trust (Chilenski et al., 2016; Homan, 2016; McKnight and Block, 2012).

Price

On the other hand, price takes on a very different face when considering the community. The main reason for this is that the recipient of a social service is often not the one paying for it (Padanyi and Gainer, 2004). Since there is often no direct exchange of funds for a given service, it's easy to think that price is irrelevant in this context. But if you take a step back, you see that price is more than just a monetary concept. Price can also mean the things that you need to contribute or give up in order to obtain something. And in our social benefit world, the biggest one of those is time. If a social services program has long wait times, a complicated application process, or significant requirements that must be met to obtain benefits, it is likely that many potential recipients are going to give up and forfeit a much-needed benefit. In this context, time really is money. To combat this, the aspiring social entrepreneur needs to make sure that ease of use for the constituent is a core element of the design of the program.

Place

In working with a community, ease of access is also the key to place, since this P represents the means and methods used to deliver the product or service to the "consumer." In a digital age, it's important to note that access does not just mean physical location, but also a website that is easy to navigate, online forms that are clean and simple to use, and multiple electronic contact points such as text, online chat, email, and phone lines, all staffed with competent customer service staff who are available, responsive, and on duty during the hours that the community needs them (there are few things more useless than a social service program that is only available during the hours when most of its constituents are working). On the other hand, the social entrepreneur must realize that the "digital divide" is real, and that the distribution strategy for the program needs to align with the capabilities of the community. This may mean that multiple points of contact need to be deployed, with robust physical and digital "locations" being maintained. Consistency of service is also a key point here as word of mouth is a huge factor in a community. The old adage that a happy customer may tell one or two folks but an unhappy customer will tell four or five applies well here. In fact, the need for consistent service may be even more important in this context as you are likely not the first person to try to help this community.

BOX 10.7   THE DIGITAL DIVIDE AND MARKETING

The COVID-19 pandemic has led to more public attention on the concept of the digital divide, but this has been a longer-standing issue. Since technology has become more and more essential for our daily lives, there has been a growing divide of who can afford to participate and access technology. This includes computers, smartphones, and affordable plans and coverage to support them (for example, Internet access, Wi-Fi, telecom networks). This divide, both internationally and locally, presents barriers to accessing information, education, and employment resources, and creates technological skill gaps in those who are less frequently able to access technology.

The digital divide is an important factor to consider as it cuts across many of the populations that social entrepreneurship aims to serve (for example, those living in poverty, the housing-insecure, vulnerable populations, those residing in remote or under-resourced locations). This means that the beneficiaries of your product (idea, good, or service) might not have the same training or access to different forms of technology and technology platforms. For example, social media might not be as meaningful as a marketing platform for those working with the elderly, or virtual video sessions might not be accessible to those with limited or no access to reliable Internet or Wi-Fi connections. It is important that social entrepreneurs consider the digital divide when thinking through their marketing strategy and plans.

Promotion

Promoting a social service to a community is also a process of building relationships. While generating awareness (that is, traditional advertising and promotion) is important, long-term participation is likely to lag unless the community believes that you truly have its best interests at heart. Consistency of message is also crucial, as your carefully earned reputation can be quickly tarnished with one simple misstatement or casual comment. In this regard, monitoring all the various communication channels is also critical, as the misstatement may not come from inside your organization. Knowing what the community thinks about your program is vital to the maintenance of your credibility (Durham, 2010).

BOX 10.8 SUMMARIZING THE 12 PS

This table summarizes the 12 Ps, which cross the "4 Ps" of marketing (product, price, place, and promotion) with the three primary interests of social enterprise marketing (market, money, community), as defined throughout the chapter.

Table 10.1   The 12 Ps of marketing for social enterprise

	Market	Money			Community
		Gifts	Grants	Investors	
Product	Exchange; produces superior value for customer	Value of helping the beneficiaries	Ability to deliver a particular outcome	ROI (with investment being related to desired impact)	Program
Price	Competitive price	Donors' ability to give	Awarded based on a planned budget	Rate of return (for example, time)	Time and resources to deliver the program
Place	Easy for customers to find and purchase the product	Ways in which the donor can contribute	N/A. Grant is a result of an RFP	May or may not be applicable, depending on the type of investor (applications, meetings, presentations, negotiations)	Distribution strategy for the program, as informed by the community itself
Promotion	Meets customers where they are	How the donor learns of the opportunity to donate	N/A. Grant is a result of an RFP	May or may not be applicable, depending on the type of investor (applications, meetings, presentations, negotiations)	Building relationships and awareness that drive participation

THREE FACES IN REVIEW

Once again, we've covered some very complex subjects in a very short period. It's important to keep in mind that the main purpose of these chapters is to make you aware of things you will need to address in building your social enterprise.

I started this chapter with the idea that marketing a social enterprise has three distinct "faces" or audiences, and that each one has its own needs. In appealing to a market-based audience, the value of the product is the primary objective, and everything needs to tie back to that single point. When marketing to money, it's all about the return (even though the definition of "return" will vary based on the type of money that you're trying to attract). But the community you want to serve must know that you care, that you're in it for the long haul, and that you have its best interests at heart. Three very distinct messages for three very distinct audiences.

Once again, a social enterprise is a different animal. A for-profit venture only has to worry about the market, and a single aspect of money. A traditional nonprofit can ignore the market, and the only return it needs to show is a social outcome. But effectively marketing a social venture means that all these audiences must be expertly addressed in a coordinated and consistent manner, all the time.

Daunting, yes. But critical as well. And full of subtle nuances that must be constantly tended. Almost makes you want to jump back into something more quantitative, right? Well, that's where we're going next.

CHAPTER SUMMARY

This chapter focuses on building an understanding of the unique requirements for marketing a social enterprise. The "4 Ps" of marketing, which include product, price, place, and promotion, serve as the foundation of marketing, as the three interests of market, community, and money help to frame the 4 Ps towards the social enterprise area. Building an understanding of each of these cross-sections shows the need for social entrepreneurs to try to balance them all.

QUESTIONS FOR DISCUSSION

Through these questions, you will develop a "12 P"-informed marketing plan for your social enterprise for each audience identified in this chapter.
1. Create a "12 Ps" matrix for your selected social venture. Use the table as shown in Box 10.8, and start filling in the chart based on the case or example of a social enterprise you have been using in prior chapters.

	Market	Money			Community
		Gifts	Grants	Investors	
Product					
Price					
Place					
Promotion					

2. Once you have filled in as many of the boxes as applicable to your case or example, think about each of them. Are there one or two that stand out as being dominant or more important to a particular stakeholder group?
3. How does each P interact with other Ps (that is, are they complementary or in conflict)? Are they balanced with one another, or is there a potential or present imbalance?
    A. If there is an imbalance (or a potential for one), why, and how might you balance these things?

B. If there seems to be a good balance or potential for balance, why, and how do you maintain it?
4. After reflecting on each of these questions, what are your takeaways, thoughts, or impressions from doing this activity? How might your conclusions from this activity have implications for one or more of the following, and why?
    A. The establishment of marketing goals
    B. Planning your marketing budget
    C. Determining the impact metrics of your marketing and measuring them
    D. Strategizing or planning your relationship-building plan with particular stakeholders

BUILD IT YOURSELF: STEP SIX

Develop marketing plans for your social enterprise for each audience identified in this chapter.

NOTE

1. Pro tip: This is not a time to try to fake your way through a skill. If detailed financial projections are not your thing, find someone who can do them for you.

REFERENCES

American Marketing Association (2017). Definitions of marketing. Accessed 12 April 2021 at www.ama.org/the-definition-of-marketing-what-is-marketing/.

Charities Aid Foundation (2016). *Gross Domestic Philanthropy: An International Analysis of GDP, Tax and Giving*. Accessed 12 April 2021 at www.cafonline.org/docs/default-source/about-us-policy-and-campaigns/gross-domestic-philanthropy-feb-2016.pdf.

Chilenski, S. M., Perkins, D. F., Olson, J., Hoffman, L., Feinberg, M. E., Greenberg, M., …, Spoth, R. (2016). The power of a collaborative relationship between technical assistance providers and community prevention teams: A correlational and longitudinal study. *Evaluation and Program Planning, 54,* 19–29.

Cooper, R. G. (2011). *Winning at New Products: Creating Value through Innovation*. New York, NY: Basic Books.

Durham, S. (2010). *Brandraising: How Nonprofits Raise Visibility and Money through Smart Communications*. San Francisco, CA: Jossey-Bass.

Homan, M. S. (2016). *Promoting Community Change: Making it Happen in the Real World*. Boston, MA: Cengage Learning.

MacCarthy, E. J., and Perreault, W. D. (1960). *Basic Marketing: A Managerial Approach*. Homewood, IL: Irwin.

McKnight, J., and Block, P. (2012). *The Abundant Community: Awakening the Power of Families and Neighborhoods*. San Francisco, CA: Berrett-Koehler.

Mixer, J. R. (1993). *Principles of Professional Fundraising: Useful Foundations for Successful Practice*. San Francisco, CA: Jossey-Bass.

Morino, M., Thompson, C. C., Lowell, W., and Cheryl, C. (2011). *Leap of Reason: Managing to Outcomes in an Era of Scarcity*. Washington, DC: Venture Philanthropy Partners.

Padanyi, P., and Gainer, B. (2004). Market orientation in the nonprofit sector: Taking multiple constituencies into consideration. *Journal of Marketing Theory and Practice, 12*(2), 43–58.

Phillips, G. (2016). *The Art of Fundraising: The Appeal, the People, the Strategies.* North Charleston, SC: CreateSpace.

Saul, J. (2011). *The End of Fundraising: Raise More Money by Selling Your Impact.* San Francisco, CA: Jossey-Bass.

Sherman, A. J. (2005). *Raising Capital: Get the Money You Need to Grow Your Business.* New York, NY: AMACOM.

Social Enterprise Alliance (2014). About Social Enterprise Alliance. Retrieved from https://se-alliance.org/about.

Stangler, D., Tareque, I. S., and Morelix, A. (2016). Trends in venture capital, angel investments, and crowdfunding across the fifty largest U.S. metropolitan areas. Accessed 12 April 2021 at www.kauffman.org/what-we-do/research/2016/trends-in-venture-capital-angel-investments-and-crowdfunding.

One of the natural outcomes of success is that other folks want to copy what you are doing and see if they can make it work for them. True to form, Robert Egger had a unique take on the many requests he received for his "recipe."

Egger adopted an "open source" philosophy, meaning that anyone who wanted to replicate the DC Central Kitchen (DCCK) model was free to do so. Over time, this philosophy led to the founding of over 60 similar operations across the U.S., often consuming substantial amounts of time for Robert and his team. It also led to an interesting experiment to indoctrinate the next generation of Food Fighters.

In 2001, Egger launched an initiative known as Campus Kitchens. Using the core assumption that had driven the DCCK (namely, that lots of uneaten prepared food goes to waste), the Campus Kitchen project looked to the college cafeteria system as a source of food that could be recycled and repurposed to reduce hunger in college towns across the country. The core processes were also quite like those of the DCCK.

Source: Courtesy of Robert Egger. Used with permission

A specific college or university would sponsor a team of students who would go to the kitchen of the campus dining hall in off-hours, pick up the unserved but usable food, prepare meals using that food (along with food donated from local food banks, grocery stores, and the like), and deliver those meals to organizations in the area that supported the underserved.

Founded in part by a recent college graduate who came to work at DCCK, the project took off when a major vendor of college food services stepped up with a substantial supporting grant. At its height, there were over 60 Campus Kitchen projects working to reduce hunger throughout the nation. In 2019, the Campus Kitchen project merged with the Food Recovery Network. Together, these efforts are now supporting over 230 chapters, have recovered over 3.9 million pounds of food, donated 3.2 million meals, and reduced carbon dioxide (CO_2) emissions by 7.4 million pounds.[1]

While the immediate effects of the Campus Kitchen project were undeniable (folk were being fed who otherwise might go hungry, and food waste was significantly reduced), the long-term effects of the program were also intriguing. Stories abound of students who worked in the program going on to serve significant roles in government and academia, as well as leading nonprofit and social enterprises.

QUESTIONS FOR DISCUSSION

1. Do you agree with Egger's "open source" philosophy?
    A.   Why, or why not?
2. What other approaches might Egger have taken to spreading the DCCK model?
3. Do you think the Campus Kitchen project supported the mission of the DCCK?
    A.   Why, or why not?
4. What other approaches might have been taken to enlisting student support for the DCCK mission?
5. What other factors might have led Egger to drive the Campus Kitchen initiative?
6. Was the merger with the Food Recovery Network a wise decision?
    A.   Why, or why not?

NOTE

1.   Accessed 28 April 2021 at www.foodrecoverynetwork.org.

PART IV
HOW DOES THIS WORK?

11
Finance follows function

After studying this chapter, you should be able to:
1. Identify the three different subgroups of financing available to social entrepreneurs: charitable contributions, structured grantmaking, and investor funding.
2. Compare and contrast financing approaches and their benefits and limitations.
3. Define important finance-related terms (for example, emotional return on investment, crowdfunding, restricted and unrestricted grants, earned income, and so on).
4. Strategize how to attract capital to a social enterprise.

SHOW ME THE MONEY

I have a theory. It's completely untested and may even be unprovable. But I feel it to the depths of my bones (actually, maybe it's more of a belief, but that's a debate for another day). No matter what you call it, I know it to be as true as the fact that you're reading this right now. My theory (my belief, my knowledge) is that social purpose organizations produce more value than any other sector of the economy.

By "value," I mean actual dollars and cents (pounds, euros, rupees, yen – you get the drift); not the emotional, mental, or spiritual value that we're used to talking about when we set out to make the world better. Real, measurable economic value. But for various reasons that we'll go into shortly, the folks doing all this good work are not trained in how to quantify that value, nor are they skilled at making the case for being paid for the value they create. Well, that changes right here, right now.

Your reward for all the headaches I gave you a few chapters back is that all of this measurement stuff is how you develop the case to get paid for the value you create. But before we get to that (soon, I promise), we need to understand the traditional ways that good work for social change has been paid for.

> ### BOX 11.1 EMOTIONAL RETURN ON INVESTMENT
>
> Following up on the previous chapter on marketing, the emotional return on investment (ROI) of an organization's customers, donors, and investors is something to consider along with looking at the financial and social ROIs. Particularly in the social sector, many of these stakeholders are passionate about the potential for change and being a part of it. Understanding these emotions and motivations can not only help you to craft a better marketing message, but it also helps you to know how some of your stakeholders are moved to purchase, donate, or invest, which allows you to better speak to them when raising and securing capital. Emotionally connecting with customers has been found to be even more valuable than customer satisfaction (Zorfas and Leemon, 2016), which speaks to the importance of getting to know your customers, donors, and investors to see how they are emotionally connecting to the work you do.

THREE TYPES OF MONEY

In the last chapter, we talked about three different audiences that need to be addressed in marketing a social enterprise. But if you paid careful attention, you noticed that the "money" audience was further divided into three separate subgroups – charitable contributions, structured grantmaking, and investor funding, each with its own expectations of how the money produces a return. In this chapter, we'll discuss the specific steps needed to attract funding from each of those sources. We'll also discuss how to get paid for delivering a product or service, and add in a new source of long-term funding that many think holds the key to the future success of social innovation (Bugg-Levine and Emerson, 2011).

Charitable Donations

Source: iStock.com/pinkomelet. Used with permission

Since we've already covered the fact that empathy and ego are the two main ways to appeal to a charitable donor, let's turn to the practical aspects of this type of funding, which does have some significant benefits. First, it is relatively easy to quickly raise small amounts (and the cornucopia of crowdsourcing platforms makes this even easier). Constructing an effective appeal is also not complicated, as most folks are sympathetic and want to help others. It's also easy to manage from an administrative perspective as the reporting requirements are minimal (although there are certain tax laws that you may need to comply with).

The drawbacks of charitable funding are also substantial. Perhaps most critical is that it is harder to raise large sums of money on a consistent basis (which is why many large nonprofits have entire teams of trained fundraising professionals). There is also a lot of competition for these dollars, and not a lot to separate one cause from another – in fact, the reason many donors give is because they have a personal connection to the cause (for example, if you lost a loved one to cancer, you might be more likely to donate to an organization supporting folks with that type of cancer). Charitable funding is also highly susceptible to market forces and the whims of society, so a once-dependable source of donations can dry up very quickly (Barman, 2008; Khodakarami, Petersen, and Venkatesan, 2015).

Appealing to empathy also creates some concerns for someone who is seeking to increase human dignity. First, it creates an us/them situation, where the recipient of the donation is seen as "less fortunate," which may also classify them as "not like us," creating a barrier to authentic relationship building. Second, as the recipient of the charity is often held out as an example when fundraising appeals are made, it means that we may unintentionally be taking advantage of the folks we're trying to help by exploiting their weakness in order to build empathy. Nonetheless, private charitable support amounts to roughly 13 percent of the total revenue for nonprofits in the U.S. (McKeever and Pettijohn, 2014), so it must be recognized as a significant source of funding. It is up to the leader of the social enterprise to make sure that any effort to obtain charitable funding also supports and maintains the dignity of those we are trying to help.

BOX 11.2   CROWDFUNDING

Compared to other types of funding that are coming from a solitary source or small number of sources, crowdfunding is as it sounds – drawing from a larger number of individuals, typically in smaller monetary increments. Crowdfunding is a popular option among micro, small, and medium-sized enterprises. A crowdfunding campaign works through a website that supports online transactions and helps to market the opportunity to others who might be interested in contributing.

While crowdfunding is an easily understandable concept, there are many types of crowdfunding, and there are even hybrid concepts that combine one or more of the following types:

- Donation-based crowdfunding: Those supporting the organization are giving donations, and the crowdfunding platform serves to help incentivize donations through putting a time frame and/or goal amount to encourage donations.
- Rewards-based crowdfunding: Supporters are offered a tangible reward, item, or offer conditioned on the monetary support or level of support they give. This reward can also be a prototype item.
- Equity crowdfunding: Backers receive equity in the for-profit organization, essentially becoming an investor with an ownership stake in the business.
- Debt crowdfunding: This type of crowdfunding is less common, but supporters are essentially lending the company money to be paid back, likely with interest.

Grantmaking

The means and methods for appealing to a formal grantmaking program were covered in the last chapter, so this section will look more at the pros and cons of this type of funding.

Source: iStock.com/Olivier Le Moal.
Used with permission

One of the main benefits is that you can often secure larger dollar amounts from a single source. The funding is usually provided for a longer period (typically one to three years) and can be applied to support significant new strategic initiatives. On the other hand, the reporting requirements are more substantial, the amount of time that elapses between the application and the funding can be significant, and the restrictions on the use of the funds can be a challenge for well-established programs that need to support ongoing services (Reich, 2005; Saul, 2011).

Another challenge in seeking funding from structured philanthropy is that the funding may be restricted to a specific use. Many funders prefer to fund new projects and programs, but may be less interested in providing general operating support (although this is happily becoming less of an issue) (Emerson, 2018; Reich, 2005; Saul, 2011). These restrictions on income are one of the factors that drove the current interest in social enterprise (Dees, 1998a).

One other important note here is that the term "grant" is also often used to refer to funding from governmental agencies. But the practical reality of that type of grant is that it's more often a fee paid to an organization for providing a service, which is where we go next.

BOX 11.3   RESTRICTED AND UNRESTRICTED GRANTS

To follow up on the grant information covered in Chapter 10, there are some important considerations when mulling grants as a way to finance a social enterprise. Grants can come from governments, foundations (private and public), corporations, and intermediaries, and they fall within two categories: "restricted" or "unrestricted."

Restricted grants are program-specific grants that provide funds that directly relate to programming activities that serve a particular set of objectives. Restricted funds are the most commonly available and accessible funds for social enterprises.

In contrast, unrestricted grants are flexible funds that are able to be used as the organization needs or sees fit. These are more desirable funds because they can help support the day-to-day needs and sustained growth of the organization as needed, but these types of grants are significantly less common.

Earnings

Fee for Service

Many social purpose organizations receive funding from various government sources to support their activities. One reputable source suggests that this represents roughly one-third of the revenue for nonprofits in the U.S. (McKeever, 2015). Typically, this money represents a sort of "sub-contracting," where the government chooses to pay a local entity to provide a public service rather than trying to provide it directly (such as a government health department paying a local nonprofit to provide healthcare services to those experiencing homelessness).

The political and social reasons for this are complex (Light, 2008) and beyond the scope of our conversation, but it is a substantial source of funding that can provide long-term support for direct operations (an advantage over philanthropic dollars). However, the application process is quite complex and the time lapses between approval of the funding and receipt of the actual monies can be maddeningly long.

Fees for delivering direct services also come from so-called "private" sources (depending on the specific sub-sector, as much as 50 percent of total revenue; McKeever, 2015). But much of this funding stream comes from reports by hospitals and universities (which are very often nonprofits). In fact, these two "industries" are some of the oldest examples of social enterprise. Universities collect tuition from students and provide an education. Hospitals provide medical care and are paid accordingly – although the use of the term "private" in the case of a hospital is a bit of a misnomer as the money usually comes from some sort of insurance fund (and outside the U.S., often from governmental health insurance programs; Preker, Zweifel, and Schellekens, 2009).

While not well quantified, there is also a growing trend in social enterprise for providing services to the public for a fee. I recently had a conversation with a local nonprofit that has been part of the maintenance support for our local city parks as a government subcontractor. It is now exploring the idea of providing landscaping services to private homes. Other local social enterprises are providing catering for events, home maintenance services, and many other types of direct service.

No matter the source, "fee for service" means that the social purpose organization is a direct provider of a specific set of services. To manage such a program, the enterprise needs to make sure that the full cost of delivering the service is accounted for in the fee. This full cost includes not just salaries, materials, rent, and other operating expenses, but cash reserves and all the other sound practices of running a business.

Product Sales

One of the most popular forms of earned income in the early years of the growth of social enterprise (and still a significant revenue stream today) is the sale of a product. Perhaps the most well-known of these is a firm located in the Bronx in New York, called Greyston Bakery. Greyston makes brownies that are a central ingredient in the world-famous Ben & Jerry's ice cream. Greyston runs the bakery just like any other production bakery and competes for the Ben & Jerry's contract in an open market. Another example on a smaller scale is Local Color Flowers. Just like fee for service, obtaining revenue from product sales requires skilled management, proper accounting for expenses, and allocation for contingencies and cash reserves.

BOX 11.4   GREYSTON BAKERY

Greyston is a nonprofit organization that aims to create an ecosystem to promote self-sufficiency, centering on work, development, and wellness. What makes Greyston so notable in the field of social entrepreneurship is how its model has withstood the test of time. In 1982 Greyston was a pioneer in establishing a for-profit social enterprise bakery that countered the logic of other employers by not asking for references or an employment history. Through this approach, they are able to support many people who experience limitations when seeking traditional employment, such as having a criminal background, lacking professional experience or having inconsistent experience, and experiencing housing insecurity. Greyston Bakery gives those disadvantaged in seeking employment the opportunity to work for a consistent income and build their skills and employment history. Furthermore, Greyston has built up an ecosystem of partnerships and programming to support those making these transitions to have reliable housing and access to services to help stabilize their lives and support their ability to work (for example, child care, health services).

While Greyston has iterated and grown over time, it continues to serve as an influential proof of concept for so many social enterprises. In fact, according to its website, Greyston Bakery was rated within the top 10 percent of B Corps in the world in 2015. For more information about the initiatives of Greyston and Greyston Bakery, read more on their website, www.greyston.org.

UNRESTRICTED INCOME

The early popularity of social enterprise, which was a movement toward earned income as a means to reduce dependency on charity and philanthropy, was driven by many factors – not the least of which was that earned income allowed the enterprise to spend the revenue in any manner it saw fit. This freedom from the administrative burdens of grant reporting and the constant efforts to raise charitable dollars became a significant factor in the growth of this movement (Center for the Advancement of Social Entrepreneurship, 2008; Dees, 1998b; Dees and Anderson, 2006).

A Business or a Mission?

While earned income is extremely attractive, it also presents a very real challenge to a social purpose organization, because it means that folks who have been trained to serve others in a mission-oriented context must now enter the competitive world of commercial business. Strategically, this means that the leaders of the enterprise need to be able to quickly shift mindsets and perspectives, jumping back and forth between generous empathy and pragmatic commercialism (Weisbrod, 2000). Operationally, it requires substantial skills in several disciplines that are not normally combined (Santos, Pache, and Birkholz, 2015).

One way that this can be solved is by hiring individuals from each of these perspectives, so that businesspeople run the business and social services people run the social service. But this solution doesn't integrate the two processes, and can cause substantial division. Let's take the example of

Source: iStock.com/mirzamlk. Used with permission

a local nonprofit I worked with a few years ago whose mission is housing for low-income seniors.

They were part of a program I ran at a local university that paired MBA students with area nonprofits to develop earned-income models. When the day came for the team to present their concepts, we were all a bit surprised to hear that it wanted to sell greeting cards. Its reasoning was that it had a member of its board who was skilled at making hand-painted greeting cards. Its market research had indicated that this was a highly profitable niche market, and it felt that it could earn a substantial profit by mass-producing these high-end greeting cards. What it failed to realize was that this meant that it would be in the printing business, which has market dynamics that are unique, and not at all like the housing services that it provided at the time. (Sad to say, it fell in love with the idea, and is still operating this sideline, which has never produced a profit, and has often required funding support from the parent organization.)

An earned-income strategy can also become a challenge to the core principles of the organization. The folks who study these sorts of things refer to this issue as "mission drift" (Copestake, 2007; Mittelman and Osland, 2014). The concern is that the pursuit of profit (even when that profit is intended for use to support the social program) can cause an enterprise to lose its focus and misplace the reason it exists in the first place. For example, the firm might need to increase its marketing budget to support the sales of its product. The intrinsic risks of running a business mean that such an investment could produce less than the desired return, forcing leadership to make reductions in operating budgets, resulting in possible reductions in services to those in need.

Finally, the inherent risks of running a business may mean that the profitmaking venture fails entirely, or that the mission drift is so severe that the organization becomes unrecognizable. This concern is known as "reputation risk" (Austin, 2000; Austin and Seitanidi, 2012). While embarrassment and public humiliation are definitely concerns in losing one's reputation, the critical issue here is that loss of reputation can have a direct impact on the organization's ability to raise funds from charitable and philanthropic sources (Schloderer, Sarstedt, and Ringle, 2014). Any one of these factors (lack of business skills, mission drift, or reputation risk) can turn a hoped-for source of additional income into an unanticipated expense.

BOX 11.5 REPUTATION IN SOCIAL ENTREPRENEURSHIP

Reputation plays a special role in the social entrepreneurship landscape. With the rise of social media, there is more marketing and socializing of a brand outside of the company's control and in the hands of the public. What this shift in control means is that an organization's reputation is no longer curated in the image it wants to see, as it is more transformed by what the customers and public make it.

According to Eccles, Newquist, and Schatz (2007), there are three determinants of an organization's exposure to reputational risk: reputation–reality gap, changing beliefs and expectations, and weak internal coordination. The first determinant, reputation–reality gap, is a particularly challenging one for social enterprises because they are expected to be the exemplars of ethical practices and fighting for social justice. The second determinant, changing beliefs and expectations, is a risk with mission drift, and the third determinant, weak internal coordination, happens when there are miscommunications, poor coordination, or different expectations within the organization.

> When a social impact organization's reputation goes into question, it can be detrimental, or it can be a pivotal moment for improved impact. This was the case with TOMS (www.toms.com), an American retailer best known for its shoes, when it experienced reputation–reality gap reputational risk, as its one-for-one shoe model was receiving critiques that the reality was not meeting the narratives of transforming the impoverished communities that it was portraying to its customers. It either had to lower customer expectations or better its practices, and it chose to change its practices and increase transparency.

The use of product sales to support a social mission can be very effective, particularly if it is aligned with the mission of the firm (for a great example, skip back to our profile of Local Color Flowers in Chapter 1). It can also be a great way to ruin an effective nonprofit. Happily, there is a new way of thinking about earned income that looks at the direct value created by the social program, and that's the next topic we're going to analyze.

EARNED VALUE

A few years back, I spent some time as a consultant working with local nonprofits to help them figure out how to develop earned-income strategies like the ones we've just reviewed. I met a lot of great people during those years and helped a number of them think through what it might mean to implement a product or service strategy. One of the biggest lessons I learned was that most social purpose organizations are leaving money on the table because they don't know how to measure the value they produce, nor do they know how to build a case to claim the appropriate compensation for that value.

This realization came to me after working with several workforce-development programs (a service that is quite common in the nonprofit sector). As a program, the Logic model for workforce development is straightforward. You start with an individual who is returning from a difficult situation (often addiction or incarceration). You then train that individual in a skilled trade (carpentry, plumbing, electrical work, and food service are popular examples). Once that person is trained, you place them with an employer. If the placement is successful, you use the person you trained as a success story for future fundraising. You might even ask the employer to donate to your efforts. But nobody ever asks to get paid for making the placement.

However, if you ask the employer, you will find out that they have a line item in their budget for talent acquisition, and are ready, willing, and able to pay for good employees. In the U.S. alone, the staffing and recruiting industry represents over $167 billion in revenue (American Staffing Association, 2018) – so this is clearly big business. And yet, time after time, every nonprofit workforce development program I spoke to had never even thought about asking for a placement fee from the employers they worked with.

The reasons for this reluctance are many and varied, the subject of much debate, and far beyond the scope of this book. But it seems clear that, as first discussed in Chapter 3, there is money to be made here, that employers are comfortable with paying for such a service, and that the only thing holding these programs back is their own reluctance (and maybe a lack of some basic pricing tools to figure out how much to ask for).

BOX 11.6   DAN PALLOTTA

Dan Pallotta is a lecturer, writer, and thought leader who has given many talks – including two TED talks – on philanthropy and innovation. He is also known as the original creator of the multiple-day charity event.

One of his most notable points comes from his 2010 book *Uncharitable: How Restraints on Nonprofits Undermine Their Potential*, which argues that some of the assumptions of the philanthropic world actually disadvantage its ability to attract the best talent and pilot new and innovative ideas. Among the undermining assumptions are the notions that those working in the nonprofit sector should make meager salaries and that charitable organizations need to only invest in the immediate needs of the population in need, rather than the sustainability of the organization and the longer-term vision of creating change. This message has been helping to change the dialogue within the nonprofit sector, but these undermining assumptions still persist.

Pallotta's other books, *The Everyday Philanthropist: A Better Way to Make a Better World* (2020) and *Charity Case: How the Nonprofit Community Can Stand Up for Itself and Really Change the World* (2012), also provide messages of how to improve philanthropy and the nonprofit sector. The guidance within Pallotta's works connects to the message within this chapter that the traditional notion that social impact organizations should "fundraise, fundraise, fundraise" pushes the energy of its staff into an immediate-term type of survival mode, rather than coming up with a funding model that will help sustain the organization and its mission for years to come.

With this understanding in mind, let's jump back to the theory that I opened this chapter with (the one that says that social purpose organizations are leaving money on the table). A quick web search tells me that in the U.S. there are almost 21,000 nonprofits with the words "workforce development" as part of their name. Let's say that they were able to access 5 percent of the staffing and recruiting market – that would mean an additional $8.3 billion dollars in revenue, without having to add a new product or service but just by claiming the value in what they already do.

Right now, I want you to do me a huge favor. I want you to re-read the last paragraph, and then put the book down and let this notion sink in. I'll wait.

OK, now that this concept of earned value is starting to sink in, we're ready to take this to the next level.

Pay for Success

Compensating a social purpose organization for the positive outcomes it produces is a small but growing idea, which currently is referred to as "pay for success." Rather than spend a lot of time on the theory behind this concept, let's walk through an example I developed for my students.

In this example, the social problem we're working on is recidivism (which is the tendency for folks who have been incarcerated to eventually end up back in prison). There are many reasons why this happens, but a short list includes inadequate support systems and a lack of legitimate employment opportunities (Maltz, 1984). Like many topics we touch on, this work is complex, and many great minds have devoted entire careers to addressing it.

In my home state of Maryland, we spend just over $37,000 to keep one person in jail for a year (Petteruti et al., 2015). When we release them, there is a 41 percent chance that they will not successfully re-enter society (Petteruti et al., 2015). This means that out of every 100 people released from prison, 41 are eventually going back. What this means in financial terms is that the taxpayers of Maryland assume a future cost of over $15,000 (see Table 11.1) each time a person is released from jail.

Now, let's suppose that you have developed an awesome social intervention that reduces the recidivism rate by 50 percent. So, the rate for folks who go through your program is 21 percent – half of the rate for those who don't receive the suite of services that you provide. What this means is that your program saves over $7,500 in future costs for each person you work with. Now, let's say that you can help 200 people per year. That means that you have saved the taxpayer over $1.5 million per year. Not bad for a small local social program. (The arithmetic for these calculations is shown in Table 11.2.)

If you are running a typical non-profit, you report the 50 percent reduction, but probably don't track the total savings. If you're a bit more sophisticated, but still working in a nonprofit mindset, you may even calculate the savings. If you're really advanced, you might even use the savings to justify your next round of grant applications. But you don't think of this as earned value (not

Table 11.1   Current financial impact

Current Financial Impact			
Cost of Incarceration (PP/PY)			
$37,200			
Recidivisim Rate			
41%			
Future Cost of Current Release (PP/PY)			
$15,252			

Table 11.2   Savings from effective intervention

Savings from Effective Intervention			
Intervention		Program Capacity/year	
50% Reduction		200	
2%			
Savings (PP/PY)		Total Savings	
$ 7,626		$ 1,525,200	

because you're not smart, but because no one ever trained you to look at it this way). While this is sinking in (and it does take a while to settle in one's brain), let's take a brief trip back to some basic business principles.

One of the simplest business models to understand is a small restaurant. A talented chef takes some basic ingredients and turns them into a delicious meal. The restaurant owner pays the chef and pays the various folks who supply the ingredients. The patron pays for the meal, and the price paid is more than the sum of all the costs needed to provide the food. By combining the ingredients and serving the meal, the restaurant has increased the value of the raw ingredients. To say it simply, the process of preparing the meal has added value – an increase we recognize and accept when we pay for the meal.

Yet for any number of reasons, the traditional nonprofit does not think of value in the same way – we don't think that by reducing the rate of recidivism (or homelessness or hunger or any one of the many good things we do) we are creating direct economic value. And that (more than any philosophical perspective) is what separates the social entrepreneur from the rest of the pack. So now that you know that you are different, let's get back to calculating how this pay-for-success concept might work.

Income for Results

Hopefully, this discussion has made it clear that an effective social intervention produces direct economic value by reducing the cost of an existing social service. Once you've crossed that intellectual bridge, you need to dip into the well of bravery that all entrepreneurs eventually find and summon the courage to demand payment for the value you've created. But before you go marching into the governor's office looking for your $1.5 million, you need to understand that any politician will want to be able to show their voters that they've saved them money (after all, the original source of these funds is tax payments, which are made by the same people who vote the governor into or out of office).

The practical reality is that no elected official is going to just hand you the full amount that you so cleverly saved. Recognizing this, the more prudent path is to ask for a portion of the savings, leaving a reasonable percentage in the hands of the government so that it can demonstrate its effectiveness too. But how much is the right amount? Well, in part, the answer to that question is "How much can you get?" But there's a better way that adds some logic to the process and inserts several sustainable funding streams into the picture as well.

IMPACT INVESTING

Going back to the program you've developed to reduce recidivism, let's say that you've done enough homework to estimate that you need $250,000 to launch this program and $500,000 per year to keep it running. In the world of commercial entrepreneurship, it's generally recognized that early investments should cover several years of anticipated expenses to allow the venture to get on its feet, so let's give this nascent social enterprise five years of upfront capital (a total of $2.5 million). Add in the startup costs of $250,000 and you've got a total capital need of $2.75 million. In the traditional nonprofit world, you'd need to find enough grants and gifts to cover this expense (no easy trick for a new program – particularly when multi-year grants are hard to find). But since we know we can produce economic value, we go to the investment market instead!

Table 11.3   Potential impact investing structure

Potential Impact Investing Structure			
Impact Investing			
Startup			
	$250,000		
Operating Expenses			
	$500,000		
Upfront Investment (Private)			
	$2,750,000	(5 yrs OpEx + Startup)	

Table 11.4 Potential return on investment

Potential Return on Investment	
Annual Cash Flow	
Program	$500,000
Government	$ 512,600
Investor	$ 512,600
Years to repay Investor	
	5.4

An investor puts up the entire $2.75 million. You run the program and save the taxpayer $1.5 million per year. You take $500,000 of that money to keep your program running for another year (leaving the balance of the invested capital in reserve just like any smart businessperson would do). The balance of the savings is split 50/50 between the government and the investor. And in five and a half years, the investor is fully repaid on their initial investment.

At this point, the investor begins to realize a profit on their investment, so maybe they hang around for another year or two of payment to reach whatever level of financial return they sought (which you negotiated up front before entering into this agreement). And the governor can still show that they are saving the taxpayer over $500,000 dollars per year (and supporting an effective social program in an innovative fashion). But most important of all, you're getting paid for the successful outcomes you're producing.

The full set of calculations is here:

Table 11.5 Complete impact investing scenario

Cost of Incarceration (PP/PY)			Intervention			Program Capacity/year
$37,200						
Recidivisim Rate			50% Reduction			200
41%			21%			
Future Cost of Current Release (PP/PY)			Savings (PP/PY)			Total Savings
$15,252			$ 7,626		$	1,525,200
Impact Investing			Annual Cash Flow			
Startup			Program	$500,000		
$250,000			Government	$ 512,600		
			Investor	$ 512,600		
Operating Expenses						
$500,000						
Upfront Investment (Private)			Years to repay			
$2,750,000	(5 yrs OpEx + Startup)				5.4	

THE REAL DEAL

Just in case you're thinking that this is some sort of fantasy world, or some mathematics exercise made up by some crazy professor, I want to take a few minutes to offer you some facts about impact investing. There is a wonderful organization in the U.K. called Social Finance (www.socialfinance.org.uk) that tracks these types of deals around the globe. As of April 2020, it reported that there were almost 140 of these agreements in place, with $441 million in capital invested and over 1.7 million lives impacted.

Another organization that is active in this space is the Global Impact Investing Network, known as the GIIN (www.thegiin.org). It estimates that there is over $500 billion (yes, billion) in capital interested in pursuing deals that can demonstrate both social and economic returns (Mudaliar and Dithrich, 2019). So, this is clearly an active market that represents real opportunity.

BOX 11.7   SOCIAL IMPACT BONDS

Driven by the desire to reduce initial social program costs, social impact bonds (SIBs) are a relationship between three primary parties: governments, investors, and social enterprises. SIBs, which can also be known as social, social benefit, pay-for-benefits, and pay-for-success bonds or pay-for-success financing, are not really bonds but are "future contracts on social outcome" and are complex, with the involvement of many stakeholders (Galitopoulou and Noya, 2016, p. 4). While SIBs can vary in their structure or model, investors, often through the support of an intermediary, provide working capital to service providers who are responsible for providing intervention services. In turn and based on the social impact performance of the program delivered, the government will pay the investor, potentially with interest.

According to the OECD (Galitopoulou and Noya, 2016), SIBs can (1) incentivize scaling based on performance and, if successful, programs can serve as a proof of concept for further and sustained governmental investment; (2) spark social innovation to try new and untested methods for achieving new rates of impact; and (3) create financial returns for the government in the forms of savings through more efficient outcomes and preventive and sustained impact over time.

While many are excited about this newer form of social impact financing, others feel there is room for concern (Roy, McHugh, and Sinclair, 2018). SIB documentary filmmaker Nadine Pequeneza notes that of the "151 SIBs in 29 countries, [...] there is little evidence that they are delivering on their promises" (2019). There is an argument that SIBs are favoring tried-and-tested models, rather than innovative, novel, and experimental ones that may produce the new model programs of the future (Pequeneza, 2019; Roy, McHugh, and Sinclair, 2018). Furthermore, there may exist limitations of current SIBs to tackle complex systems and root causes, which are even more complicated to organize, administer, and evaluate; the evaluation of SIBs is a particularly problematic area, as everything needs to be quantifiable even beyond notions of quality (Pequeneza, 2019).

Barriers to Adoption

If you're smart (and I know you are), you probably have a question in your mind right now (OK, probably several). The question sounds something like "If this is so great, why isn't it common practice?" And a good question deserves a good answer.

First, while the basic math for these deals is straightforward, the technical complexities of making them work can be quite daunting. For example, making sure that the right outcomes are being measured in the right way can take a lot of time. The need for collecting detailed data on each constituent in the program can also be quite burdensome. There can also be substantial expense incurred in managing the multiple accounts needed to properly track the flow of funds between the parties. There are also genuine moral concerns that using such an approach reduces individual lives into a set of statistics, essentially removing the "human" from the art of "human services." Finally, there is the political reality that the governmental entity (for any number of reasons) may not want to share the savings (Roy, McHugh, and Sinclair, 2018).

BOX 11.8   BALANCING STAKEHOLDER PRIORITIES

One of the most challenging challenges for social entrepreneurs to handle with regard to the financing of their enterprise – apart from bringing in the funds to create a sustainable organization – is balancing the various funding stakeholder priorities.

As shown throughout the chapter, different stakeholders and stakeholder groups have different expectations for contributing funds and what they expect in return. An individual contributing to a rewards-based crowdfunding campaign expects whatever token gift they select for their donation; another person donating may not expect an item in return but may care about seeing a thank-you card and an annual report. A high-net-worth donor might expect more stewardship and connection to the work and delivered impact. A grantmaker might expect a higher level of program evaluation, or even an external evaluator to assess the program's outcomes and impact. An impact investor might want to see a notable social or financial return on their investment. A government might want figures comparing alternative scenarios of delivering a program versus the status quo.

For a social entrepreneur, especially a new one, managing all of these needs can feel overwhelming, if not impossible. The social entrepreneur can be drawn in by the appeal of the funds, but when applying for and soliciting funding from others, it is important for them to also consider the work that comes along with each of those funds. By considering all of the needs of the full cycle – from attracting the funds through the end-of-cycle measurement, communications, reporting, and relationship management – social entrepreneurs will be able to think carefully about what funds and funding combinations are worth the time and effort.

YOU CAN DO THIS!

Throughout this book, I've been repeatedly making the point that effective and sustainable social innovation is not easy. This concept of being paid for success is probably the hardest part of it all – and building a venture that can pull off this trick is certainly the biggest challenge in the entire set of challenges that an aspiring social entrepreneur will face. It requires a sound Social Change model, deep community engagement, an effective team that is focused on measuring performance and continuous improvement, and the mastery of a broad range of skills that come from many different disciplines. But it is happening, and that means it can be done. It also means that with the right amount of support and a great deal of tenacity, you can do it too.

BOX 11.9 MICROFINANCING

While microfinancing might not be in the picture for many social entrepreneurs reading this book, its roots are such a significant part of social entrepreneurship that it deserves a mention. Unlike other loans, microloans (which are just smaller-monetary-amount loans) can be given out via a variety of different platforms, and not just from commercial banks. That variety means there is significant variation in the conditions and terms and even populations served with microloans. The concept of microfinancing has been especially associated with impoverished communities and developing-country contexts, particularly because small amounts of capital have the ability to have great impact in those areas.

As noted in Box 6.8 in Chapter 6, Muhammad Yunus is attributed as the founder of microfinancing; more specifically, microcredit. Microcredit was crafted to provide small loans to those in need who are unable to access financing or fair financing otherwise, on the premise that a small loan can help the individual to become independent and autonomous as a small business owner. For many, microfinancing has been transformative and liberating as a way out of cyclical poverty patterns for them and their families, which represents a large part of the lure of microcredit.

While the successes of microfinance led to Yunus's 2006 Nobel Peace Prize, there are many critiques of microfinancing as well. While the repayment rates of Yunus's microfinancing were very strong, and higher than in commercial lending, some argue that microfinancing is holding those who were already vulnerable in longer-term debt, as they might be able to repay in small amounts but may struggle to ever pay off the full amount.

CHAPTER SUMMARY

Chapter 11 centers on the ways in which social enterprises attract capital. There are three main subgroups of financing available to social entrepreneurs: charitable contributions, structured grantmaking, and investor funding. Each of these subgroups has its own benefits and drawbacks, including the necessary staff management and attention, frequency of stakeholder engagement, and conditions set. For each type, there are notable stakeholder perspectives (for example, emotional ROI) and priorities (for example, outcomes and impact measurement). Earned-value models aim to bring in funds through their ability to provide direct value for a particular stakeholder. Newer investment models that base their funding on the "success" of the program are also becoming more popular, as they are helping to fund interventions that show both promise and results to scale; however, they are not without critique. An ideal strategy would be to eschew total dependency on one of these areas of financing with a diverse array of funding sources, a concept we will continue to explore in the next chapter.

QUESTIONS FOR DISCUSSION

1. First, we will consider what you need to work through when weighing your approach to soliciting for charitable contributions.
   A. What are the positive aspects of asking for charitable donations?
   B. What are the potential limitations of asking for charitable donations?
   C. What are some of the possible expectations of these stakeholders?
   D. Based on these possible benefits and drawbacks, would you consider running a donation campaign? If so, why, and how would you do this? If not, what are your reservations?
2. The next subgroup for consideration is grants.
   A. What are the positive aspects of applying for grants?
   B. What are the potential limitations of applying for grants?
   C. What are some of the possible expectations of these stakeholders?
   D. Based on these possible benefits and drawbacks, would you consider applying for grants? If so, why, and how would you do this? If not, what are your reservations?
3. The final subgroup is investor funding.
   A. What are the positive aspects of seeking out investor funding?
   B. What are the potential limitations of seeking out investor funding?
   C. What are some of the possible expectations of these stakeholders?
   D. Based on these possible benefits and drawbacks, would you consider applying for grants? If so, why, and how would you do this? If not, what are your reservations?

4. Based on your responses to questions 1–3, fill in the following table.

	Charitable donations	Grants	Investor funding
Benefits/positive aspects			
Limitations/negative aspects			
Stakeholder expectations			
Decision (for example, pursue or do not pursue?)			

5. What would be the benefits of diversifying your funding? What are the potential challenges?
6. What are your reflections after doing this exercise?

BUILD IT YOURSELF: STEP SEVEN

Develop and explain the various funding sources you will use to build your social enterprise. (Hint: You will likely need both tables and text to properly illustrate this.)

RECOMMENDED RESOURCES

Simon, M. (2017). *Real Impact: The New Economics of Social Change*. New York, NY: PublicAffairs.
Social Finance. Accessed 28 April 2021 at www.socialfinance.org.uk.

REFERENCES

American Staffing Association (2018). *ASA Fact Sheet*. Alexandria, VA: American Staffing Association.
Austin, J. E. (2000). Strategic collaboration between nonprofits and businesses. *Nonprofit and Voluntary Sector Quarterly*, *29*(1_suppl), 69–97.
Austin, J. E., and Seitanidi, M. M. (2012). Collaborative value creation: A review of partnering between nonprofits and businesses – Part I: Value creation spectrum and collaboration stages. *Nonprofit and Voluntary Sector Quarterly*, *41*(5), 726–758.
Barman, E. (2008). With strings attached: Nonprofits and the adoption of donor choice. *Nonprofit and Voluntary Sector Quarterly*, *37*(1), 39–56.
Bugg-Levine, A., and Emerson, J. (2011). *Impact Investing: Transforming How We Make Money While Making a Difference*. San Francisco, CA: John Wiley & Sons.
Center for the Advancement of Social Entrepreneurship (2008). *Developing the Field of Social Entrepreneurship*. Accessed 28 April 2021 at https://community-wealth.org/sites/clone.community -wealth.org/files/downloads/paper-case.pdf.
Copestake, J. (2007). Mainstreaming microfinance: Social performance management or mission drift? *World Development*, *35*(10), 1721–1738.
Dees, J. G. (1998a). Enterprising nonprofits. *Harvard Business Review*, Jan–Feb. Accessed 28 April 2021 at https://hbr.org/1998/01/enterprising-nonprofits.
Dees, J. G. (1998b). *The Meaning of Social Entrepreneurship*. Durham, NC: Duke University.
Dees, J. G., and Anderson, B. B. (2006). Framing a theory of social entrepreneurship: Building on two schools of practice and thought. *Research on Social Entrepreneurship: Understanding and Contributing to an Emerging Field*, *1*(3), 39–66.

Eccles, R. G., Newquist, S. C., and Schatz, R. (2007, February). Reputation and its risks. *Harvard Business Review*. Accessed 28 April 2021 at https://hbr.org/2007/02/reputation-and-its-risks.

Emerson, J. (2018). *The Purpose of Capital: Elements of Impact, Financial Flows, and Natural Being*. San Franciso, CA: Blended Value Group.

Galitopoulou, S., and Noya, A. (2016). *Understanding Social Impact Bonds*. OECD Report. Accessed 28 April 2021 at www.oecd.org/cfe/leed/UnderstandingSIBsLux-WorkingPaper.pdf.

Khodakarami, F., Petersen, J. A., and Venkatesan, R. (2015). Developing donor relationships: The role of the breadth of giving. *Journal of Marketing*, *79*(4), 77–93.

Light, P. C. (2008). *A Government Ill Executed: The Decline of the Federal Service and How to Reverse It*. Cambridge, MA: Harvard University Press.

Maltz, M. D. (1984). *Recidivism*. Orlando, FL: Academic Press.

McKeever, B. S. (2015). *The Nonprofit Sector in Brief 2015*. Accessed 28 April 2021 at www.urban.org/research/publication/nonprofit-sector-brief-2015-public-charities-giving-and-volunteering.

McKeever, B. S., and Pettijohn, S. L. (2014). *The Nonprofit Sector in Brief 2014*. Washington, DC: Urban Institute.

Mittelman, R., and Osland, A. (2014). The controversial launch of Kiva in the United States: Mission drift or market extension? *Journal of Critical Incidents*, *7*, 59–62.

Mudaliar, A., and Dithrich, H. (2019). *Sizing the Impact Investing Market*. Accessed 28 April 2021 at https://thegiin.org/assets/Sizing%20the%20Impact%20Investing%20Market_webfile.pdf.

Pallotta, D. (2010). *Uncharitable: How Restraints on Nonprofits Undermine Their Potential*. Medford, MA, and Lebanon, NH: Tufts University Press and University Press of New England.

Pallotta, D. (2012). *Charity Case: How the Nonprofit Community Can Stand Up for Itself and Really Change the World*. San Francisco, CA: Jossey-Bass.

Pallotta, D. (2020). *The Everyday Philanthropist: A Better Way to Make a Better World*. Manhattan Beach, CA: CThings.

Pequeneza, N. (2019, May 31). The downside of social impact bonds. *Stanford Social Innovation Review*. Accessed 28 April 2021 at https://ssir.org/articles/entry/the_downside_of_social_impact_bonds.

Petteruti, A., Kajstura, A., Schindler, M., Wagner, P., and Ziedenberg, J. (2015). *The Right Investment? Corrections Spending in Baltimore City*. Accessed 28 April 2021 at www.prisonpolicy.org/origin/md/.

Preker, A. S., Zweifel, P., and Schellekens, O. (2009). *Global Marketplace for Private Health Insurance: Strength in Numbers*. Washington, DC: World Bank.

Reich, R. (2005). A failure of philanthropy: American charity shortchanges the poor, and public policy is partly to blame. *Stanford Social Innovation Review*, Winter. Accessed 28 April 2021 at https://ssir.org/articles/entry/a_failure_of_philanthropy#.

Roy, M. J., McHugh, N., and Sinclair, S. (2018). A critical reflection on social impact bonds. *Standford Social Innovation Review*. Accessed 28 April 2021 at https://ssir.org/articles/entry/a_critical_reflection_on_social_impact_bonds.

Santos, F., Pache, A.-C., and Birkholz, C. (2015). Making hybrids work: Aligning business models and organizational design for social enterprises. *California Management Review*, *57*(3), 36–58.

Saul, J. (2011). *The End of Fundraising: Raise More Money by Selling Your Impact*. San Francisco, CA: Jossey-Bass.

Schloderer, M. P., Sarstedt, M., and Ringle, C. M. (2014). The relevance of reputation in the nonprofit sector: The moderating effect of socio-demographic characteristics. *International Journal of Nonprofit and Voluntary Sector Marketing*, *19*(2), 110–126.

Weisbrod, B. A. (2000). *To Profit or Not to Profit: The Commercial Transformation of the Nonprofit Sector*. Cambridge: Cambridge University Press.

Zorfas, A., and Leemon, D. (2016, August 29). An emotional connection matters more than customer satisfaction. *Harvard Business Review*. Accessed 28 April 2021 at https://hbr.org/2016/08/an-emotional-connection-matters-more-than-customer-satisfaction.

12
Form follows function: operating models first, legal structures second

Learning objectives

After studying this chapter, you should be able to:

1. Understand the reason why "form follows function," meaning that operational models need to come first, followed by the legal structure.
2. Rationalize and select an organizational structure for a selected organization: for-profit or nonprofit.
3. Appreciate and determine the distinctions between nonprofits and for-profits, including the roles and influence of shareholders and stakeholders, in addition to the financial opportunities and limitations of each structure.
4. Develop and explain the capital-stack strategy for a social enterprise.
5. Reflect upon and determine if starting a new social venture is really the best route to achieving the optimal social impact.

By now, you've probably noticed a certain rhythm to our conversations. In each topic that we've discussed, there has been a consistent theme – that the world of the social entrepreneur is more complex and complicated than that of the for-profit venture. In this chapter, I'm happy to say that the reverse is true. In this chapter, we're going to take a concept that has become far more complex than it needs to be and give you some blessed relief in simplifying the matter.

FORM FOLLOWS FUNCTION

In working with hundreds of aspiring social entrepreneurs, there is one question that comes up every time – "What organizational structure should I use?" The truth is that it depends. The deeper truth is that it matters far less than you think.

The reality is that the selection of an organizational structure is not a once-in-a-lifetime decision. Organizations restructure all the time, and no one thinks them any the worse for doing

Source: Steven Wie, Unsplash. Used with permission

so (in fact, it is viewed as a wise management decision). It's also important to note that specific legal structures vary by jurisdiction – so talking about things like limited liability companies (LLCs) and benefit corporations doesn't make a lot of sense for our purposes, because the rules where you live are probably different (and engaging the services of a competent attorney to sort through your options is money well spent). To avoid going down that particular rabbit hole, we're going to talk about types of organizations and the strategic choices that each one represents, and leave the legal details to you and your lawyer. We're also going to assume that you will form some sort of legal entity, because running any venture (social or otherwise) without some sort of legal protection is just plain foolish. So, with this framework in mind, let's start to consider the options.

BOX 12.1   BASICS OF ORGANIZATIONAL STRUCTURE DIFFERENCES

While for-profits and nonprofits are behaving more like one another than ever, with for-profits being more socially conscious and nonprofits being more enterprising, there are some important distinctions. Although both can have social missions, for-profit businesses distribute profits to their shareholders, with the premise that it needs to make more money than it spends. The for-profit company's leader, shareholders, and, if it has one, its board focus on the financial metrics and growth of the business as the entity's top priority.

Because nonprofit or nonprofit organizations (NPOs) have tax benefits, stakeholders have expectations for the delivery of their social mission. To that end, NPOs are not able to distribute profit to the organization's owners like for-profits do. Excess revenue is reinvested back into the organization to continue to serve its mission. To this end, the term "nonprofit" can be misleading, as NPOs need to be generating healthy profits in order to sustain and scale their impact. NPOs' boards, a requirement of their structure, play an important role for the organization's decision-making, strategic planning, and impact; in fact, nonprofits' boards play an important role in ascertaining the ethical use of funds and can be held legally accountable for the misuse of funds.

The term "non-governmental organization" (NGO) may also come up when discussing social purpose organizations. Depending on country classifications, NGOs are mostly nonprofits that work in areas that complement governmental efforts without direct oversight from the government (for example, public health, education, economic development, poverty, and women's and minorities' rights). Some notable examples of NGOs include Partners in Health and Doctors Without Borders (Médecins Sans Frontières).

Strategic Screening for New Organizations

Rather than jumping into a specific structure, perhaps you should consider a series of strategic questions, and then use those answers to select the appropriate structure. The first question you need to ask is what the purpose of the organization is – not in some vague mission-statement language but in the highly specific terms of the Social Change Theory and Logic model. Be sure that you are crystal clear on the work that you are doing, and why it's being done. Next, think long and hard about how you will know that your goal has been accomplished – in other words, what are the key metrics that will tell you what is happening in your enterprise? Third, be sure you clearly understand every step along the way from the current state to the desired outcomes – know exactly how you will get from start to finish. Fourth, be clear on how your activities will be paid for, and who or what will be the source of that cash flow. With those four answers in hand, the final question is to look at who might find this package of activities and outcomes most appealing.

BOX 12.2   CRITICAL SELF-REFLECTION QUESTIONS

Here is a recap of the critical self-reflection questions when thinking about what organizational type might best fit your project:

1. Purpose: What is the purpose of the organization?
2. Measurement: How will you know that your goal has been accomplished/what are the key metrics that will tell you what is happening in your enterprise?
3. Process: What are the steps from the current state to the desired outcomes?
4. Funding: How will your activities be paid for/who or what will be the source of that cash flow?

THE MENU, PLEASE

The two main categories of organizational structures are for-profit and nonprofit. Let's take some time to consider how each of these might work in practice.

For-Profit

Let's say that you've decided that your social enterprise will produce a product or service that will generate income (and of course, serve as a means toward achieving your social change objective). Any enterprise that produces goods and services is going to need infrastructure – tools and equipment, machines, furniture and fixtures, transportation and delivery systems, and the like. Acquiring those things takes money, and the money needs to come into the organization well before the revenue from the sale of the product can be realized. This means that someone, somewhere, will need to make an investment in the organization – with the

Source: Guillaume Gryn_DVS, Unsplash. Used with permission

expectation of return. To minimize risk, the investor will usually want some sort of guarantee – known in the trade as "collateral." The reason for this is that the investor wants to know that they have some other means to get their money back if the planned project doesn't pan out. So, the entrepreneur may pledge other assets, or make a personal guarantee (meaning that their own assets can be tapped if the venture fails). For various legal reasons, this sort of arrangement is best done in a for-profit structure. So, if a product or service is central to your plan, it might make sense to set up as a for-profit venture.

Nonprofit

Now let's assume you've decided to take a place-based strategy – working in a tightly defined area and trying to do everything you can to help those folks. Programs like this provide a wide array of services in health care, job readiness and job training, parenting and childcare, and many other areas. There is no doubt that this type of program is doing great work, and such efforts are often the cornerstone of a challenged neighborhood. But the broad array of services makes it very hard to track down any one specific outcome and tie it back to the work of the organization. This makes it unlikely that the enterprise will be able to attract funding that is looking for any sort of financial return, even if the return is framed in an impact investing context. Such a venture is probably going to be dependent on charitable income (grants and donations) for most of its support, so a nonprofit structure makes the most sense.

No Need to Rush

The important point here is that the social entrepreneur first determines how the venture is going to work, and then designs the organizational structure that is most appropriate. And since we know that the way the venture will work only comes after substantial modeling and experimenting, the longer you can wait to decide, the better. Fortunately, there is a way to remain flexible while still receiving funding for the design stage of the enterprise.

BOX 12.3 HARLEM CHILDREN'S ZONE AND ITS PLACE-BASED STRATEGY

Harlem Children's Zone (HCZ) is a strong example of an organization that has turned an ambitious goal into change within several cities. HCZ has a mission "to end intergenerational poverty in Central Harlem and lead the way for other long-distressed communities nationwide and around the world to do the same" (https://hcz.org). HCZ centers its values around six principles: children first, excellence, respect, strategic relentlessness, army of love, and best selves to best serve. Each of its values reinforces one another, together comprising its overarching approach, a place-based strategy.

A place-based strategy approaches the variety and breadth of active issues faced by the community due to the interconnected nature of social challenges. It also strives, through strong partnerships between sectors and actors, including both public and private institutions, to come up with comprehensive solutions and for the opportunity to have sustainable, longer-term transformation and broader impact on communities.

A Bridge over Troubled Water

If you ask any entrepreneur (social or not) what they need more than anything else, the answer is almost always money. And in the context of a profit-oriented venture, most folks have a pretty good sense of how that works. They know that the firm goes from bootstrapping (relying on the personal assets of the founders and its own revenue for the funding to build and grow) and the 3 Fs (friends, family, and fools), to angel investors, to venture capitalists and commercial lending. Most folks know how to evaluate and price the risk and return scenarios at each level, they know how each level of investor receives their return, and they have a relatively well-established structure of intermediaries and a settled market that provides signals and pathways to all the participants (Emerson, 2000; Kaplan and Grossman, 2010; Stangler, Tareque, and Morelix, 2016).

BOX 12.4   FINANCING SOCIAL ENTERPRISES

As highlighted throughout the chapter, one of the determining factors that will shape social entrepreneurs' decision on what type of organizational structure they choose is how they anticipate that they will be able to best finance and sustain the impact they seek to have over time.

There are many different types of financing, and Table 12.1 highlights some of the differences and common spaces.

Table 12.1   Sources of funding for social enterprises

Source of financing	Nonprofit	For-profit
Self	Yes	
Friends and family	Yes	
Donations	Yes	Traditionally not
Grants	Yes	Traditionally not
Competitions	Yes	
Crowdfunding	Yes	
Loans	Yes	
Angel investors	Yes; investors use their own funds (usually in the early stage)	
Venture capital	Yes; investors use their firm's funds. Expectations for returns are high	

The traditional means of funding a social mission (usually through a nonprofit or NGO) are also well established. Return is measured (albeit in usually qualitative terms), the process of soliciting funds is generally accepted, and the terms and conditions of the "investment" are fairly straightforward (ranging from a tax donation for smaller investments to your name on the side of the building if the donation is big enough) (Bowman, 2002; Khodakarami, Petersen, and Vekatesan, 2015).

But when you blend together the desire to make the world better and the need to produce market income, these well-worn pathways turn into thickets and brambles (Emerson et al., 2007). And while there is a lot of good work being done to clear the brush away, most of that is focused on specific tools that only fit at certain stages of development (Kickul and Lyons, 2012). For example, the emerging field of impact investing is only available to a firm that has developed and tested a Theory of Change and built an operating model that demonstrates economic and social impact (Scarlata, Alemany Gil, and Zacharakis, 2012). It also requires an entrepreneur that is sophisticated enough to be able to produce the level of detailed projections and analysis that will support the proposed investment. In other words, both the venture and the entrepreneur need to be pretty sophisticated (Martin, 2011).

Early-stage social enterprises seem to be more dependent on funding sources that look more like those of traditional nonprofits (that is, grants and gifts). But in order to receive that money, the organization needs to have a legal status that allows the donor to receive verification of a charitable contribution (Emerson, 1998). On the other hand, the firm seeking market-based funding will often need to offer equity or collateral, both of which are problematic in a nonprofit structure (Kickul and Lyons, 2012).

Source: iStock.com/Erich Karnberger. Used with permission

From a practical standpoint, this leaves the aspiring social entrepreneur with a difficult decision – namely, what legal structure to use to build the enterprise (Raz, 2012). The problem is that the firm may not yet know which path is best – and making the wrong guess will result in additional energy and expense being used up to file a change of legal status just when the venture needs all the cash and vitality it can muster to build programs and processes (Kawasaki, 2015). Happily, there is an existing process that can smooth this over. And as with many great solutions, it's right in front of us.

Fiscal Sponsor

In the world of social innovation, an underutilized tool exists in the process of fiscal sponsorship – a contractual agreement where an existing nonprofit entity can assume various financial or legal responsibilities on behalf of another entity (Spack, 2005). The sponsored organization can take whatever legal form works best for the founder. The fiscal sponsor can serve a wide variety of roles, from simply managing grant funds to handling payroll and benefits and any number of other "back-office" obligations. There is typically a fee involved for the service, although it is not unheard of for a fiscal sponsor to perform services for the sponsee at no charge if the sponsored project is particularly well aligned with the mission of the sponsor. The process has been well tested for legal and financial sufficiency, and there is even a small trade association for fiscal sponsors: the National Network of Fiscal Sponsors (www.fiscalsponsors.org) (Spack, 2005).

For the aspiring social entrepreneur, use of this process can accelerate funding as there is no need to file for nonprofit status – grants and gifts can be received immediately (literally on the day the sponsorship agreement is executed). Further, it allows for the messy work of proof of concept and organizational models to be developed thoughtfully rather than being rushed to completion to meet funding needs (Emerson et al., 2007; Kelly et al., 2016).

Using this tool more frequently has been a hope of the nonprofit community for some time. Using it to solve a critical challenge for developing effective social enterprises could unleash its true power.

A HIGHER PURPOSE

Now that we've identified a viable path for funding early-stage social enterprises without getting tied up (or tied down) by a specific organizational structure, there's a deeper issue that we need to explore – namely, the power dynamics that exist in any organization.

Organizations and Power

Human societies create organizations to achieve objectives that cannot be achieved by the actions of a sole individual. In so doing, organizations assume structures that produce various power dynamics and relationships. At their simplest, these structures create hierarchical relationships where a specific individual is charged with defining the organization's goals and the strategies used to achieve those goals, and assigns specific roles to other individuals who then carry out the various tasks needed to produce the desired result (Perrow, 1970). The fundamental purpose of these organizational structures is to define ownership and control. In economic terms, these issues of ownership and control can relate to the raw materials needed to produce goods and services, the means of production (that is, the tools and techniques used to produce the goods), the finished product, or the economic benefit created. Whether intentional or circumstantial, rules and structures are developed that address these matters in order to facilitate decision-making and the implementation of decisions such as the terms and conditions that determine ownership, the means by which ownership issues are resolved and adjudicated, and the way economic output is distributed (Gregory and Stuart, 2014). These rules then determine who is in charge, the means and methods for managing changes in leadership, the person(s) or group(s) that makes key decisions, the process for distributing any economic gain, and the identification of how any risk is managed (Klein et al., 2019).

Source: iStock.com/WestLight. Used with permission

Organizational structures also define authority, control, and the distribution of the fruits of the organization's labor. In almost all its forms, power within an organization exists in a vertical hierarchy, with the majority of control centralized in the upper layers (Daft, 2016), where the supply of resources and information are controlled (Kanter, 1979). At the top of this pyramid are the owners of the firm, followed by its customers and suppliers, with employees and the public coming further down the ladder (Kanter, 1979). This concentration of power (within organizations or economic systems) has led to calls for greater balance in these structures (Emerson, 2018; Mintzberg, 2015).

Each evolution of organizational structures has been an attempt to resolve issues in prior systems (Clark, 2016). Widely credited as the strongest system for encouraging economic growth and increased efficiencies (Novak, 1982), the capitalist system has deeply moral underpinnings (Barnes, 2018). However, its current practices have raised significant concerns about equity in both economic and social terms (Mintzberg, 2015; Porter, 2015). In seeking to develop more equitable systems, some voices are calling for a more "evolved understanding of value itself" that expands the notion of capital beyond financial return (Emerson, 2018). However, these voices are working with a context of existing corporate structures, seeking to change organizational behaviors without examining the underlying issues in the organizational structure.

Analysis of Organizational Structures

Hierarchical organizational structures have been with us as long as there have been communities and social structures. Kings, pharaohs, emperors, and tribal chiefs have ruled for millennia (Clark, 2007). The Hebrew Scriptures refer to the appointment of middle managers to resolve low-level disputes, with the more complex cases being referred up the chain of authority (Exodus 18:13–27).

Legal Entities

From a legal perspective, formal organizations typically are structured as corporations, with a designated board of directors who are legally responsible for the actions of the corporation. These boards also serve as the central source of power and authority, with a central chairperson as the leader (Hambrick, v. Werder, and Zajac, 2008). A corporation formed to pursue profit maximization may also have a legally distributed pool of owners who hold shares of stock in the corporation. Regardless of strategic objective, a larger group of interested parties exists in the form of customers, employees, various business partners, and the general public. Each of these stakeholders can exert influence on the organization to varying degrees based on the level of power each group holds (Hambrick, v. Werder, and Zajac, 2008; Klein et al., 2019; Pfeffer, 1986).

In a corporation seeking to pursue profit maximization, the primary stakeholder group is the shareholder, whose interests are represented by the board of directors (often shareholders themselves). Within this context, the board members are stewards of the financial interests of the shareholders (Low, 2006), and act as agents for the shareholder (Mason, Kirkbride, and Bryde, 2007). In the nonprofit corporate structure, limitations on the distribution of assets shift the dominant stakeholder to a larger group that includes the recipients of the organization's services, the funders of the effort (who are usually not the recipients), and the general public (Hansmann, 1981, 1986). In this setting, the board members seek a more democratic set of objectives, and take the varied interests of this larger set of stakeholders into consideration (Low, 2006).

BOX 12.5 SHAREHOLDER VS STAKEHOLDER ORIENTATION

Organizations tend to have one of two orientations: a shareholder orientation or a stakeholder orientation. Shareholders own a portion of the company, and through having a financial interest in the company, the shareholder is both shareholder and a stakeholder. In contrast, stakeholders are not necessarily shareholders, but they may have invested other resources (for example, time, hope, in-kind donations, and volunteered services) into the entity and its success. Stakeholders can be community members, customers, beneficiaries, employees, or anyone who cares about the decisions made by an organization. Shareholders may come and go as they buy and sell their shares of the business, but stakeholders typically have a longer-term connection to the organization and its efforts.

Typically, for-profit businesses, due to their need to pursue profit maximization, have held a shareholder orientation through which their primary decision-making filter has been around whether a strategic plan of action increases shareholders' return on investment. That is not to say that other stakeholders in the picture are not important to the business's decision-making process, but typically the choices made would need to align with what is in the best interest of the company's bottom line and competitive position in the market.

In contrast, nonprofits have typically held a strong stakeholder orientation, which aligns strategic decision-making and actions with what is of interest to the various stakeholder groups. This orientation regards the stances of stakeholders as being valued and legitimate, giving weight and power to the perspectives of some that might not have held much otherwise.

The distinctions between shareholder and stakeholder orientations are gradually becoming less strict, particularly within for-profit entities, as there are emerging legal structures and models that are increasingly prioritizing the social responsibility the company holds within the ecosystem.

Challenges to Power

Stakeholder pressures are an increasingly important issue for every organization, but the levels of influence and the complexity of the relationships vary significantly between for-profit and nonprofit firms. With a common orientation to improving the financial bottom line, the for-profit firm has a less complex web of interests (Donahue and Nye, 2002). The broader interests represented by the nonprofit context create a more diverse set of interests and concerns that must be managed by both the board and senior leaders of the organization (Cornforth, 2012).

The source of funding is a particularly influential stakeholder in both the for-profit and nonprofit contexts. In the nonprofit sector, the funder's expectations can influence governance structures and behaviors regarding both operational efficiency and democratic representation of community needs (Cornforth, 2012). The nonprofit also faces tensions between the legal governance process (the things it must do by law or regulation) and the broader concerns of its community, constituents, volunteers, and donors in a manner that more closely resembles a public political process (Stone and Ostrower, 2007).

Power and Governance in Social Enterprises

Increased interest in social enterprise has brought with it a growing body of research into the governance of these organizations (Low, 2006). The for-profit social enterprise, beholden only to shareholders, lacks external oversight, while the nonprofit social enterprise, in its quest for democratic governance, lacks internal oversight due to the dilution of direct reporting and control by the organization's board of directors (Ball, 2015).

Hybrid Organizations

In examining these organizations, the concept of hybridity has become quite popular as a framework for describing those firms that seek to develop value across multiple metrics (Battilana and Lee, 2014; Lumpkin and Bacq, 2019; Pache and Santos, 2013; Santos, Pache, and Birkholz, 2015). However, two critical issues are left unaddressed in the current conversations. The first is that the underlying legal structures still fall into one of two buckets – for-profit and nonprofit – each of which forces the organization to operate within specific constraints that may not serve the needs of a venture seeking a broader set of values. The second is that central to each of these studies is the notion that the management of the firm (that is, the board of directors and the senior leaders) are the ones implementing the prescribed strategy, and that the lower-level worker carries it out, leaving a hierarchical management structure in place.

Cooperative Organizations as an Alternative Solution

In seeking to develop a more socially conscious organization, issues of equity and inclusion should be just as important within the organization as they are in the delivery of products and services to the organization's constituents. Unfortunately, the current array of organizational structures fails to fully address this tension. Therefore, exploration of an additional form of governance is called for. It may be that the cooperative is a more effective model to resolve this tension.

The concept of cooperative trade is not new. The roots of the modern-day cooperative can be traced back to the craft guilds and mercantile trade associations of the Middle Ages (Battilani and Schröter, 2012; Clark, 2007). The popularity of the cooperative model has grown significantly in the past 50 years, in large part as an effort to combat some of the observed flaws in industrial capitalism (Battilani and

Source: iStock.com/ALotOfPeople. Used with permission

Schröter, 2012). The cooperative sector is estimated to generate over $1 trillion in annual revenue worldwide (Battilani and Schröter, 2012).

While there are many variations in the nature of the cooperative organization, they can generally be broken down into three categories: producer cooperatives, consumer cooperatives, and worker cooperatives (Battilani and Schröter, 2012). Cooperatives can and do serve multiple purposes (Battilani and Schröter, 2012), but each variation is deployed to provide some level of power or equity not otherwise available to the individual members. In so doing, the cooperative organization has always been seen as a socially conscious undertaking (Sommer, 1991). Consumer cooperatives and other forms of purchasing cooperatives are organized to give the members increased buying power, usually to negotiate lower prices or protect consumers from exploitive efforts being imposed by other actors in a particular market (Hall and Hall, 1982). Producer cooperatives are generally formed to give market and bargaining power to smaller players in a market, such as a farmers' cooperative or fisheries cooperative (Birchall, 2014; Ostrom et al., 1999). Worker-owned cooperatives are developed to provide a more stable and equitable employment platform where the fruits of the organization's labor are distributed more broadly than in an investor-owned firm (Battilani and Schröter, 2012; Birchall, 2014). Although the issues of democratic governance are common to all three categories, the focus of this section is on the worker cooperative.

Dual Nature of Co-Ops

In seeking to generate an economic profit, cooperatives are like investor-owned businesses. They diverge in how they devise the means and methods for the distribution of those profits. In an investor-owned business, profit is distributed based on the number of shares the investor holds (as well as the relative hierarchy of those shares). In cooperative enterprises, profits are more often distributed based on the performance of the worker, or in some other more equitable means (for example, by even distribution to all members). This notion of shareholders and shareholder classes also influences voting rights. In an investor-owned company, the number of votes controlled by a particular investor is directly proportional to the number of shares that investor holds. The voting rights in most cooperatives are tied to membership status and are not affected by relative changes in the amount of capital invested in the firm (Battilani and Schröter, 2012).

Cooperatives also share traits with nonprofits and NGOs. In both instances, there is a significant amount of concern for the health of society, and the elevation of the less fortunate to a more equitable place in society. In many cases, worker-owned cooperatives are organized specifically to obtain bargaining power and operational scale that are not possible for individual enterprises to obtain – thus making the co-op a tool for economic empowerment (Battilani and Schröter, 2012).

Success and Failure of Cooperatives

While the common perception of a cooperative business is that it is harder to manage (and often less profitable), numerous studies have shown that cooperative businesses are more stable, particularly in times of market turmoil (Birchall and Ketilson, 2009; Corcoran and Wilson, 2010; Murray, 2011). In worker-owned cooperatives, productivity is generally higher, as is job satisfaction (Battilani and Schröter, 2012; Corcoran and Wilson, 2010). While not without its flaws (Chaddad and Cook, 2004), increased use of this form of organization in the pursuit of social good may strengthen the legitimacy and validity of the effort to create a more just and sustainable economy.

BOX 12.6   CO-OPS IN PRACTICE

Earlier in the chapter, we unpacked the distinction between shareholders and stakeholders. When looking to the co-op model, there can be an interesting intersection between the two depending on how they are structured. Employees, within nonprofits and for-profits, tend to be stakeholders but not shareholders (unless they work in a for-profit that offers employees stock options). In co-op models, many of the employees who are members are not only stakeholders, but also shareholders. Member status can vary based on the equity model of the co-op and it can be an immediate buy-in or something earned over time. What this means is that the employees who are members have a stake in the success and decision-making process of the co-op, which is a drastic shift in the governance and power dynamics of an organization.

Mondragon is one of the most famous examples of a large, established co-op model, having been founded in 1956 and become the largest co-op in the Basque country and one of the 10 largest organizations in Spain. As of early 2021, it has over 81,000 members (who serve as the organization's owners and operators), 98 self-governing cooperatives spanning 44 countries (with sales in over 150 countries), and 14 research and development centers (www.mondragon-corporation.com/en/about-us/). Within Mondragon, there are some employees who are not members, but this can shift with more time at the organization.

While the Mondragon example is an impressive one, it might not be the one that we have personally encountered before. One of the more common examples of co-op models are co-op food stores, markets, and clubs. Within these models, a customer has the opportunity to buy membership and/or volunteer with the organization in order to be in good standing as a member. Membership entails being able to weigh in on decision-making processes (for example, on buying, marketing, and membership rules).

CAPITAL STACK IN SOCIAL VENTURES

A few pages back, we talked about how the path to funding in a profit-seeking venture is well known. The technical phrase for the process of injecting capital into an organization in a structured, strategic fashion is known as a "capital stack" (Sherman, 2005). The notion here is that different types of investments are appropriate at different stages of growth. Often, the enterprise will rely on bootstrapping. If outside funding is needed or wanted, there is a series of steps that are often taken to build the business.

In the very early stages, the investor needs to have a very high tolerance for risk and be willing to wait a very long time to see a return. This type of money usually comes from the founder's own local sources (the 3 Fs). As the concept begins to gel, the firm may be able to attract revenue from more sophisticated investors that work professionally with early-stage firms (such as angel investors or venture capitalists). These professional investors still take a long-term view but are more focused on moving the enterprise forward. Once the firm is up and running, commercial bankers may be a source of funding for growth and expansion.

In building a social enterprise, the capital stack becomes much more complex, and can cross back and forth between charitable and profit-seeking investors. If the firm is looking to deploy the sort of value-capture strategy described in the last chapter, it will probably need a few years to develop a track record and data set that is mature-end sophisticated enough to make a solid case for support from an impact investor.

So, another way to think about how to structure the organization is to map out the capital needs of the venture over time, and then set the operation up in a way that

Source: iStock.com/Nastco. Used with permission

meets the needs of each layer of the capital stack (or is able to adjust its structure to adapt to the changing needs of the various funders).

BOX 12.7   CAPITAL STACKS

While the concept of a capital stack is utilized with greater frequency in real estate investment, it can be helpful for new entrepreneurs as well because (1) it helps to think about the overall picture of financing of the social enterprise and (2) different funding sources are appropriate at different stages of the organization's growth. Capital stacks not only encompass the portfolio of financing of the organization, but also the nature of the financing and conditions around the equity and repayment (for example, risk and return of the investment).

Table 12.2   Sample capital stack

Common equity
Referred equity
Mezzanine debt
Senior debt

The capital stack is organized based on who has legal rights to particular assets and income. From top to bottom, the stack goes from the highest risk and highest expected return, to the lowest risk and lowest expected return. You may notice other depictions that are in reverse order, with lowest risk and lowest expected return at the top. For our purposes, the specifics of these terms do not matter, but the idea is that entrepreneurs need to be aware of the conditions of all of their financing and their proportions to one another.

As mentioned, different types of funding are more accessible than others, depending on where the social enterprise is in its growth process. Social startups in the initial phases may find that their own funds, along with their immediate network's funds, may be the only starting option, as loans, grants, and investors might want to see more in terms of a history, reputation, and trajectory. With a more detailed model and business plan in place, some financiers, like a bank or other commercial lender or perhaps a local foundation or economic development funder, might become interested. The more established the organization, the more opportunity there is to diversify its financing.

Who is my Angel?

While we're on the subject of capital stacks and angel investors, there is another point that needs to be brought forth in this discussion, regarding the early-stage funding of a social enterprise.

At several places in this book, we've made the point that developing the data needed to build a case for long-term social impact takes time. We hope that it's also become clear that the main objective of any social enterprise should be to do just that – have a lasting positive effect on a community. But since you are a smart person, you've probably realized that there's a bit of a problem in this goal, namely that you need to fund the operation in the short term while you build the venture for the long term. Happily, there is a solution for this, and it's right in front of us. So, I'd like to introduce the notion of angel philanthropy.

To explore this a bit, we need to take a step back and recall our conversation from Chapters 10 and 11 about the expectations of philanthropic funding (which is to show some sort of social impact has been produced). While this may seem daunting, the good news is that developing and testing new models of social change is an attractive proposition for many philanthropic funders (Frumkin, 2003; Scarlata, Alemany Gil, and Zacharakis, 2012; Slyke and Newman, 2006). Better yet, since they don't expect a financial return, these funders can become quite useful as a source of seed capital, playing a role very much like that of an angel investor in a profit-seeking venture.

The practice of funding new models and experiments in effective social change is not new to the philanthropic world. What is new is the notion of using this funding in a strategic capital stack that builds toward an impact investing model. This also means that the philanthropic funder is not going to be asked to provide long-term operating funds (a matter of significant contention in the traditional nonprofit world; Reich, 2005).

The Do-Nothing Option

There are many cases where forming an entirely new entity may do more harm than good. In truth, there are many ways that lasting social change can be produced within an existing organization.

While the nonprofit industry has many flaws, there are also many folks doing great work in this field. In this chapter, we've reviewed how maintaining a nonprofit structure may be the best way to go. So, if you already have that structure set up, your best path may be to leave it alone and work for more effective outcomes in your existing organization. In the same way, a for-profit organization with a strong social conscience can be a very effective vehicle for social innovation. If you find yourself in that framework, you might want to devote your efforts to improving the civic and social performance of the enterprise and spend less time worrying about how it's structured.

BOX 12.8   TO START-UP OR TO SUPPORT?

When outlining the opportunities and constraints of nonprofit and for-profit structures, it is important to also note that having a social impact in the world does not necessarily require an organizational structure. First of all, throughout the exercises and reflections of each chapter, you may already have come across an organization (or five) that is already doing what you want to do, and perhaps already doing it well in your area.

In cases like this, a great starting point may be to work with or for the organization. There is a lot that can be learned from doing so, and you will be helping it to grow and improve its impact as you better inform yourself, your knowledge, and your skillsets. Another option might be to see if you can expand an existing model to a new community or location. Similar to the example highlighted of the HCZ, there may be an existing entity that has a well-established model that can be adapted to a new context, at which point you will have guidance on if and when to form a legal structure.

Otherwise, there are other social enterprises that have spread their impact through an open-source approach to their work, including Go Baby Go (https://sites.udel.edu/gobabygo), an international movement to create accessible mobility options for immobile infants and adults in order to help them meet their social, linguistic, and physical developmental needs. Thousands have benefited from the work of Go Baby Go's efforts, which does not, in itself, have an organizational structure; rather, it partners with existing structures of nonprofits, universities, and schools to bring in and manage funds.

Again, this further emphasizes that structure needs to follow the clarity that comes with reflection, experience, exposures, and workshopping over time.

CHAPTER SUMMARY

This chapter opens with the notion that organizational structures matter far less than most people think. It should be operating models first, legal structures second. The reason for this is that the goal is not a specific type of organization, as effective social change can come from any sort of entity (and even no entity at all). Remembering the adage that says that "form follows function," this chapter has shown how the aspiring social entrepreneur needs to think first about how the organization will operate (function) and then choose the appropriate structure (form). To determine this, social entrepreneurs need to be clear on the following things: (1) the purpose of the organization, (2) the work that you are doing and why it is being done, (3) the desired outcomes and their key metrics that will help you determine the success of your efforts, and (4) how you will financially sustain this impact. Again, there is no one right format; there is only the format that is right for what you want to accomplish.

QUESTIONS FOR DISCUSSION

1. Before reviewing this chapter, did you have an organizational structure – nonprofit or for-profit – in mind for your social enterprise? If so, which one was it, and why? If not, why not?

2. Now to use the proper ordering of "form follows function." Using your same social enterprise concept, ask yourself the following questions:
   A. Purpose: What is the purpose of the organization? What change do you want to see? What are the outcomes you hope to achieve?
   B. Measurement: How you will know that your goal has been accomplished? What are the key metrics that will tell you what is happening in your enterprise?
   C. Process: What are the steps from the current state to the desired outcomes? What are your inputs and activities?
   D. Funding: How will your activities be funded? Who or what will be the source of that cash flow? What types of funding might be less feasible?
3. Based on your assessments on the purpose, measurement, process, and funding, what reflections or conclusions do you have about what organizational structure, if any, that you might select? What led you to this conclusion? What would the argument be for the opposite choice?
4. Having thought through some of the funding possibilities for your concept, develop and explain the capital-stack strategy for your social enterprise. If you are working with a simple concept, consider the funding that you will need to scale and grow.
5. Now that you have been working on a social enterprise concept for several chapters, consider what other pathways you could take to have a similar impact. What other organizations out in the world already have an impressive impact? How could you help contribute to growing their impact?

BUILD IT YOURSELF: TAKE A BREAK AND REVIEW YOUR WORK

For this chapter, rather than continuing to move ahead on building your social venture, take a few minutes to catch your breath. This is also a good time to go back over the work you've done so far and see if there are any changes or updates that might be needed before you press on.

REFERENCES

Ball, A. S. (2015). Social enterprise governance. *University of Pennsylvania Journal of Business Law*, 18, 919.

Barnes, K. J. (2018). *Redeeming Capitalism*. Grand Rapids, MI: William B. Eerdmans.

Battilana, J., and Lee, M. (2014). Advancing research on hybrid organizing: Insights from the study of social enterprises. *Academy of Management Annals*, 8(1), 397–441.

Battilani, P., and Schröter, H. G. (2012). *The Cooperative Business Movement, 1950 to the Present*. New York, NY: Cambridge University Press.

Birchall, J. (2014). *The Governance of Large Co-Operative Businesses*. Manchester: Co-Operatives UK.

Birchall, J., and Ketilson, L. H. (2009). *Resilience of the Cooperative Business Model in Times of Crisis*. Geneva: International Labour Organization.

Bowman, W. (2002). The uniqueness of nonprofit finance and the decision to borrow. *Nonprofit Management and Leadership*, 12(3), 293–311.

Chaddad, F. R., and Cook, M. L. (2004). Understanding new cooperative models: An ownership–control rights typology. *Applied Economic Perspectives and Policy*, 26(3), 348–360.

Clark, B. S. (2016). *The Evolution of Economic Systems: Varieties of Capitalism in the Global Economy*. New York, NY: Oxford University Press.

Clark, G. (2007). *A Farewell to Alms: A Brief Economic History of the World*. Princeton, NJ: Princeton University Press.

Corcoran, H., and Wilson, D. (2010). *The Worker Co-Operative Movements in Italy, Mondragon and France: Context, Sucess Factors and Lessons*. Kentville: Canadian Worker Cooperative Foundation.

Cornforth, C. (2012). Nonprofit governance research: Limitations of the focus on boards and suggestions for new directions. *Nonprofit and Voluntary Sector Quarterly, 41*(6), 1116–1135.

Daft, R. L. (2016). *Organization Theory & Design*. Boston, MA: Cengage Learning.

Donahue, J. D., and Nye, J. S. (2002). Market-based governance: Supply side, demand side, upside, and downside. Washington, DC: Brookings Institution Press.

Emerson, J. (1998). The US nonprofit capital market: An introductory overview of developmental stages, investors and funding instruments. *American Philanthropy Review*, Fall, 1–46.

Emerson, J. (2000). *The Nature of Returns: A Social Capital Markets Inquiry into Elements of Investment and the Blended Value Proposition*. Boston, MA: Division of Research, Harvard Business School.

Emerson, J. (2018). *The Purpose of Capital: Elements of Impact, Financial Flows, and Natural Being*. San Francisco, CA: Blended Value Group.

Emerson, J., Freundlich, T., Fruchterman, J., Berlin, L., and Stevenson, K. (2007). *Nothing Ventured, Nothing Gained: Addressing the Critical Gaps in Risk-Taking Capital for Social Enterprise*. Oxford: Skoll Centre for Social Entrepreneurship.

Frumkin, P. (2003). Inside venture philanthropy. *Society, 40*(4), 7–15.

Gregory, P. R. and Stuart, R. C. (2014). *The Global Economy and Its Economic Systems*. Mason, OH: South-Western Cengage Learning.

Hall, B. F., and Hall, L. L. (1982). The potential for growth of consumer cooperatives: A comparison with producer cooperatives. *Journal of Consumer Affairs, 16*(1), 23–45.

Hambrick, D. C., v. Werder, A., and Zajac, E. J. (2008). New directions in corporate governance research. *Organization Science, 19*(3), 381–385.

Hansmann, H. B. (1981). The rationale for exempting nonprofit organizations from corporate income taxation. *Yale Law Journal, 91*(1), 54–100.

Hansmann, H. B. (1986). The role of the nonprofit enterprise. In S. Rose-Ackerman (ed.), *The Economics of Nonprofit Institutions* (pp. 57–84). New York, NY: Oxford University Press.

Kanter, R. M. (1979). *Power Failure in Management Circuits*. Boston, MA: Harvard Business Review Press.

Kaplan, R. S., and Grossman, A. S. (2010). The emerging capital market for nonprofits. *Harvard Business Review, 88*(10), 110–118.

Kawasaki, G. (2015). *The Art of the Start 2.0: The Time-Tested, Battle-Hardened Guide for Anyone Starting Anything*. New York, NY: Portfolio/Penguin.

Kelly, M., Duncan, V., and Dubb, S., with Perry Abello, O., and Rosen, C. (2016). *Strategies for Financing the Inclusive Economy*. Washington, DC: Democracy Collaborative.

Khodakarami, F., Petersen, J. A., and Vekatesan, R. (2015). Developing donor relationships: The role of the breadth of giving. *Journal of Marketing, 79*(4), 77–93.

Kickul, J. R., and Lyons, T. S. (2012). *Understanding Social Entrepreneurship: The Relentless Pursuit of Mission in an Ever Changing World*. New York, NY: Routledge.

Klein, P. G., Mahoney, J. T., McGahan, A. M., and Pitelis, C. N. (2019). Organizational governance adaptation: Who is in, who is out, and who gets what. *Academy of Management Review, 44*(1), 6–27.

Low, C. (2006). A framework for the governance of social enterprise. *International Journal of Social Economics, 33*(5/6), 376–385.

Lumpkin, G. T., & Bacq, S. (2019). Civic wealth creation: A new view of stakeholder engagement and societal impact. Academy of Management Perspectives, *33*(4), 383–404.Martin, M. (2011). Understanding the true potential of hybrid financing strategies for social entrepreneurs. Impact Economy Working Papers, Vol. 2. Accessed 28 April 2021 at www.impacteconomy.com/papers/IE_WP2_EN.pdf.

Mason, C., Kirkbride, J., and Bryde, D. (2007). From stakeholders to institutions: the changing face of social enterprise governance theory. *Management Decision, 45*(2), 284–301.

Mintzberg, H. (2015). *Rebalancing Society: Radical Renewal Beyond Left, Right, and Center*. Oakland, CA: Berrett-Koehler.

Murray, C. (2011). *Co-Op Survival Rates in British Columbia*. Port Alberni: B.C.–Alberta Social Economy Research Alliance.

Novak, M. (1982). *The Spirit of Democratic Capitalism*. New York, NY: Simon & Schuster.

Ostrom, E., Burger, J., Field, C. B., Norgaard, R. B., and Policansky, D. (1999). Revisiting the commons: Local lessons, global challenges. *Science, 284*(5412), 278–282.

Pache, A.-C., and Santos, F. (2013). Inside the hybrid organization: Selective coupling as a response to competing institutional logics. *Academy of Management Journal, 56*(4), 972–1001.

Perrow, C. (1970). *Organizational Analysis: A Sociological View*. London: Tavistock.

Pfeffer, J. (1986). *Power in Organizations*. London: HarperCollins.

Porter, E. (2015, April 29). Income inequality is costing the U.S. on social issues. *New York Times*.

Raz, K. G. (2012). Toward an improved legal form for social enterprise. *NYU Review of Law & Social Change, 36*(283), 42–48.

Reich, R. (2005). A failure of philanthropy: American charity shortchanges the poor, and public policy is partly to blame. *Stanford Social Innovation Review*. Accessed 28 April 2021 at https://ssir.org/articles/entry/a_failure_of_philanthropy#.

Santos, F., Pache, A.-C., and Birkholz, C. (2015). Making hybrids work: Aligning business models and organizational design for social enterprises. *California Management Review, 57*(3), 36–58.

Scarlata, M., Alemany Gil, L., and Zacharakis, A. (2012). Philanthropic venture capital: Venture capital for social entrepreneurs? *Foundations and Trends in Entrepreneurship, 8*(4), 279–342.

Sherman, A. J. (2005). *Raising Capital: Get the Money You Need to Grow Your Business*. New York, NY: AMACOM.

Slyke, D. M. V., and Newman, H. K. (2006). Venture philanthropy and social entrepreneurship in community redevelopment. *Nonprofit Management and Leadership, 16*(3), 345–368.

Sommer, R. (1991). Consciences in the marketplace: The role of cooperatives in consumer protection. *Journal of Social Issues, 47*(1), 135–148.

Spack, J. (2005). How fiscal sponsorship nurtures nonprofits. *Communities and Banking*, Fall, 22–24.

Stangler, D., Tareque, I. S., and Morelix, A. (2016). *Trends in Venture Capital, Angel Investments, and Crowdfunding across the Fifty Largest U.S. Metropolitan Areas*. Kansas City, MO: Ewing Marion Kauffman Foundation.

Stone, M. M., and Ostrower, F. (2007). Acting in the public interest? Another look at research on nonprofit governance. *Nonprofit and Voluntary Sector Quarterly, 36*(3), 416–438.

13
Global perspectives on legal and operating structures

Learning objectives

After studying this chapter, you should be able to:
1. Understand the concept and role of the "third sector" of non-governmental organizations and its long-standing historical origins.
2. Explain the social enterprise structures of 10 different country contexts (the U.S., China, Japan, Germany, the U.K., France, Italy, India, Brazil, and Canada).
3. Compare and contrast the third-sector entities of different countries.

In the last chapter, we talked a good bit about the factors that can affect a decision about how to structure your social enterprise. The most important point in that chapter is the idea that form follows function. The wise individual thinks first about what the needs of the organization are, and what model might best suit those needs. The other, equally important point is that decisions about organizational structures are not lifetime commitments. They can (and do) change as the needs of the enterprise change. So, you are now armed with some tools for helping to make that decision. But the discussion of the different types was more philosophical than practical. This chapter will fill in the practical details by taking a deeper look at some specific types of organizations and discussing the situations that they are best suited for. To do that, we need to take a step back in time. Pretty far back, in fact. Back to the beginnings of organized charitable behavior.

PEOPLE JUST WANT TO HELP

Humans have been joining in voluntary assembly and organization for thousands of years; be it for purposes of religious worship (churches, synagogues, and mosques), education (universities), or the enhancement of trade (trade guilds and merchant associations) (Clark, 2007; Hall, 2010). In most developed countries, providing financial support for charitable activities is considered to be part of the normal behavior of a responsible citizen (Robbins, 2006). The roots of this behavior reach back to early recorded history.

Source: iStock .com/ sycther5. Used with permission

The obligation to perform charitable behaviors (giving money to the poor, providing hospitality to those less fortunate, or caring for the orphan, widow, or refugee) is expressed consistently in sacred Hebrew texts (Robbins, 2006). The specific notion of philanthropy has its roots in ancient Greece, where the term was used to describe an act of extraordinary generosity (Robbins, 2006). Wealth that was created by a specific individual was viewed as essentially a community asset. Consequently, Greek citizens who had obtained significant wealth were expected to provide financial support for civic projects such as the construction and maintenance of public buildings. Support for the arts, intellectual inquiry, and philosophical analysis was also expected (Robbins, 2006). Greek society also developed a series of rules and protocols that outlined how these duties were to be discharged (Robbins, 2006). While these rules were not codified into law, a citizen who did not live up to his obligations could expect to face significant public derision and disgrace. This failure to perform one's civic duty might also have a negative impact on business affairs as the individual would be viewed as less trustworthy (Robbins, 2006).

As the Roman culture began to develop just to the west, it not only adopted many of these concepts but enhanced and expanded them (Cameron, 1993; Gombrich, 2005; Robbins, 2006). Roman society also provides the earliest known examples of philanthropic behavior being codified into law, with the creation of a civic trust that would receive and hold individual donations and then disburse them for charitable purposes (Robbins, 2006). As this body of law developed, it also expanded into regulations regarding posthumous bequests as well as the development of mutual benefit societies, commercial guilds, and intellectual societies (Robbins, 2006). Drawing directly on the Jewish tradition of care for humankind, the Christian notions of charity, hospitality, and generosity moved the Greek and Roman concepts from an obligation of those with wealth to a duty for all peoples regardless of social or economic standing (Robbins, 2006). As the Christian church grew and became established, it also came to play a central role in the collection and distribution of charitable funds, as well as becoming the conduit for the delivery of social services to those in need (Robbins, 2006). Some historians point to the 3rd century CE as the time when the first notions of what we now know as a hospital began to take shape in society, enabled and supported by the Catholic Church (Robbins, 2006).

Around that time, philanthropic organizations with identities and legal status separate and distinct from the Church began to develop (Cameron, 1993; Gombrich, 2005; Robbins, 2006). This period also provides the first evidence of exemption from tax being granted to a charitable organization (Robbins, 2006). By roughly 1100 CE, the world began to see something resembling an organized and structured philanthropic sector in society (Robbins, 2006).

A landmark development in the history of philanthropy occurred in 1601 when the British parliament, during the reign of Queen Elizabeth I, ratified the Statute of Charitable Uses (Robbins, 2006). This Act specified what sort of charitable cause could be supported by philanthropic trusts – including assistance to the poor, care for orphans, the promotion of higher learning, and the advancement of religion (Robbins, 2006). The Elizabethan period also saw a change in the philosophical approach to the application of philanthropic activity, towards the notion of making investments in projects that would raise the social standing of those receiving support through training and education, and away from only meeting the direct needs of the recipient (Robbins, 2006). As the merchant economy began to produce a middle class that had some level of wealth and stability, it also fostered the role of a charitable organization as a conduit for individual donors to contribute to a cause that they might not be able to support without a collective process for gathering and distributing funds (Robbins, 2006). As Europeans began to colonize the North American continent, they brought these ideas with them.

These ideas form the groundwork for our modern notions of care and concern for others. With this background in mind, we now fast-forward to the current day to take a deeper look at how that care is organized in modern society.

THE THIRD SECTOR

The modern concepts of nonprofits and non-governmental organizations (NGOs) reflect a broader notion of a "third sector," used to identify organizations that are neither fully public (that is, operated by government) nor fully private (owned and operated by specific individuals for their own benefit) (Meghan and Terry, 2016). In most of the developed world, this third sector is comprised of nongovernmental organizations. A very useful definition (regardless of the unique characteristics that exist in different contexts), is that these organizations are

> self-governing, do not distribute profit, are primarily private and nongovernmental in basic structure, and are meaningfully voluntary, thus likely to engage constituents on the basis of shared interest. (Meghan and Terry, 2016, p. 3)

Source: Possessed Photography, Unsplash. Used with permission

Globally, these organizations fall into a few distinct groups, namely unincorporated and/or voluntary association; trusts, charities, or foundations; and not-for-profit companies or organizations formed or registered under specific NGO or nonprofit laws. In the late 1980s, a group of 45 European countries agreed to a consistent standard for NGOs and set out the rights, privileges, and responsibilities for these organizations (Stillman, 2007). Worldwide, there are more than 10 million of these organizations (Public Interest Registry, 2017), operating in multiple countries, each with its own set of rules and regulations. And that's where we're going now.

AROUND THE WORLD WITH A BUNCH OF LAWYERS

The laws governing the activities and practices of nonprofits and NGOs vary from country to country, and often differ within jurisdictions within the same country. So, the usual caveats apply to the next few pages. First, the services of a competent attorney are invaluable and highly advised. Second, what follows is a relatively brief overview of a topic that many can (and do) spend entire careers on. Finally, what follows does not consist of legal advice in any way (my lawyer made me add that one!). In order to be fair, we will discuss the laws around nonprofits and NGOs for a few of the largest global economies only, and do so in descending order of size (Accessed 4 February 2021 at https://worldpopulationreview.com/countries/countries-by-gdp).

SOCIAL ENTERPRISE AND NONPROFITS IN THE U.S.

In the U.S., organizations in this third sector are generally referred to as nonprofits – a label that comes from the type of organization that is most often used to serve this third-sector role (and a concept that is unique to the U.S. for various legal reasons) (Lee, 2007).

To quote from a noted authority in the field:

Source: iStock.com/Roman Bykhalets. Used with permission

In current practice, the charitable organization in the United States is protected from various tax implications by virtue of section 501(c) 3 of the Internal Revenue code, which provides an exemption from federal income tax for entities that are organized to support certain purposes (Colombo and Hall, 1995). It is also important to note that this relief from the tax burden is not done for altruistic purposes. In fact, there is a direct exchange expected from the nonprofit enterprise, namely that they are prohibited from distributing the profits of the venture to the investors and owners (Hansmann, 1981). Quoting from the tax code,The exempt purposes set forth in section 501(c)(3) are charitable, religious, educational, scientific, literary, testing for public safety, fostering national or international amateur sports competition, and preventing cruelty to children or animals. The term charitable is used in its generally accepted legal sense and includes relief of the poor, the distressed, or the underprivileged; advancement of religion; advancement of education or science; erecting or maintaining public buildings, monuments, or works; lessening the burdens of government; lessening neighborhood tensions; eliminating prejudice and discrimination; defending human and civil rights secured by law; and combating community deterioration and juvenile delinquency. (Internal Revenue Service, 2009)

This federal exemption is carried through to the state level, with the majority of states maintaining parallel statues [*sic*] that support and mimic the provisions of the IRS [U.S.

Internal Revenue Service] code and its accompanying restriction on distribution of profits (Colombo and Hall, 1995). (Kucher, 2012, pp. 149–150)

In order to obtain this status, an organization must file an application with the IRS, a process can take upwards of 180 days and involve substantial legal fees (Hammerschmidt, 2013). Despite these obstacles, there are over 1.5 million registered nonprofits in the U.S., contributing over $1 trillion to the U.S. economy (roughly 5.6 percent of the country's Gross Domestic Product, or GDP). While there are over 30 separate forms of tax-exempt entities in the U.S., 501(c)(3) public charities made up more than 75 percent of the income ($2 trillion) and expenses ($1.9 trillion) of the total for the sector (McKeever, 2020).

There are two benefits to obtaining this tax exemption. The first is that (with some exceptions) any revenue that is received by the organization is exempt from income tax. With some of the larger nonprofits bringing in hundreds of millions of dollars (McKeever, 2020), this is no small benefit. The other benefit is that individuals who donate to these nonprofits can deduct those donations from their personal income for tax purposes. With total private donations to nonprofits totaling over $425 billion a year (McKeever, 2020), you can easily see that this is quite a benefit. However, this benefit also has a substantial drawback.

Revenue and Investment in a Nonprofit Structure

Because the tax regulations specifically prohibit any profits being distributed to the shareholders, many of the typical venture capital investments are not feasible in a 501(c)3 organization (Baker and Nofsinger, 2012; Bugg-Levine and Emerson, 2011). This leaves the nonprofit with two basic options for raising growth-related capital. The first is to raise the money through a major donor effort (often referred to as a capital campaign) (Phillips, 2016). The second is to take on debt by obtaining a loan (Emerson, 1998).

Under some circumstances, a nonprofit can also earn revenue, which may or may not be taxable (depending on how closely the revenue-generating is related to the mission of the enterprise) (Emerson, 1998). This earned revenue can also become a source of growth capital if properly managed.

Like much of what we've discussed throughout this book, the nuances of nonprofit financial management are a specialty unto themselves, with this discussion once again just scratching the surface. But the basic truth is that choosing a nonprofit structure will most often force the venture into a donor-driven strategy, with all the pluses and minuses that entails.

For-Profit Social Enterprises

It's easy to see that the opposite of "nonprofit" is "for-profit" (or what I often refer to as "commercial enterprise"). In this section, we'll talk about how that looks in the U.S. (After that, we'll get to how things work in other parts of the world.)

While there are many forms of commercial enterprise available (some of which require virtually no legal structure whatsoever), most folks looking to build a profit-seeking venture will form some sort of separate legal entity, which is typically known as a corporation (and there are many types of corporations available, so the advice of a good attorney is always money well spent) (O'Keefe et al., 2014). Since the discussion of corporate forms could become its own book, we'll limit this discussion to the issues that may affect how you build your social enterprise.

Revenue and Investment in a For-Profit Structure

Unlike the nonprofit organization, the income earned by a for-profit enterprise is taxable. This income may or may not be taxable at various stages (for example, gross income from sales and/or net income from profits) depending on how the enterprise is structured and the type of industry it operates in (once again, a good accountant and good attorney are priceless advisors in making these decisions) (O'Keefe et al., 2014).

A for-profit venture is also able to distribute profit to shareholders. Most often, this profit distribution is done through the allocation of shares of stock, which represent a percentage of ownership in a company. This issuance of stock is true for both publicly traded and privately held companies (Baker, 2011).

BOX 13.1 PRIVATELY HELD COMPANIES VS PUBLICLY TRADED COMPANIES

Firms can vary significantly when it comes to key aspects of how they are governed and how they raise capital to fund strategic business activities. Privately held companies are funded, owned, and governed through private equity stock and bond issuance, among other financial instruments, such as loans. Private companies possess a great deal of latitude over a variety of key business decisions and typically do not need to consult non-owners or issue public reports about their financial performance to stakeholders who are not investors. One prominent example of a privately held social enterprise is Patagonia, Inc., registered in the U.S. as a benefit corporation.

In contrast, equity in publicly traded companies is fully or partially available for purchase in stocks or bonds through a public offering in stock exchanges, such as the NYSE in the U.S. or Tokyo Stock Exchange in Japan. Publicly traded companies can raise a great deal of capital through issuing stocks and bonds to remain competitive and accomplish strategic business objectives. Nevertheless, public companies also lose a significant degree of control in comparison to private firms given the stringent financial reporting and compliance transparency mandated by legislation such as the Sarbanes–Oxley Act (2002), among other notable examples. You can visit any major public corporation's website and look for its investor relations page to see examples of the various kinds of reports that it must periodically issue, from involuntary financial and accounting aspects of the business, to voluntary environmental, social, and governance (ESG) data.

In terms of governance, publicly traded companies are run by boards, who are appointed via shareholder voting procedures. In turn, these corporate boards hire teams of executives, who are tasked with steering the firm towards its financial and social performance goals for the benefit of the firms' shareholders and stakeholders. In this way, publicly traded firms are required to separate ownership and control, and to carefully manage relations with stockholders and pertinent stakeholders. Danone is a prominent example of a major multinational social enterprise that is publicly traded on the Euronext stock exchange.

When a for-profit company wants to raise money, it may do so by selling shares of stock to interested investors (those of you who might be fans of the *Shark Tank* television show will recognize this as the moment when the "sharks" offer money in exchange for a percentage of ownership in the company). While this may seem to be an attractive way to obtain capital, it does have a major drawback in that the investor now has a say in how the company is run (Baker, 2011). This loss of control can be frustrating to the founders and is particularly concerning to the aspiring social entrepreneur as an investor may be more concerned about generating profit and less concerned about effective social change. While there are some ways to contractually manage this issue, it is a major area of concern that needs to be watched carefully if one chooses the for-profit path. Nonetheless, the for-profit structure is becoming increasingly popular with social entrepreneurs (Dees and Anderson, 2003).

A Critical Decision or a False Choice?

Since you're clearly a smart person (you made it this far, right?), you can see that the decision about organizing as a for-profit or a nonprofit has some very real consequences. And I'm sure you'll remember from the last chapter that you can use the services of a fiscal sponsor in the early stages of developing your venture so that you don't have to make this choice before you're ready. But it's also worth noting that there have been several attempts to try to resolve the conflicts between these two primary organizational structures (each with its own pluses and minuses).

Other Options

The more popular of the for-profit and nonprofit is the benefit corporation (not to be confused with the B Corp, which we'll talk about in a minute). Introduced in 2010 and currently available in 36 states (with details that vary by state), the basic concept of the benefit corporation is that the corporate charter explicitly states that the organization is established with the specific intent of producing a social benefit. This structure was developed to both empower and obligate corporate leadership to consider ESG concerns along with the financial obligations that are the primary focus of a for-profit enterprise. Like many of the topics in the world of the social entrepreneur, there is debate about the effectiveness of the benefit corporation, and it certainly is not the right structure in every case (Blount and Offei-Danso, 2012; Cooney et al., 2014; Rawhouser, Cummings, and Crane, 2015). However, it is an interesting and often useful tool.

While often confused with the benefit corporation, B Corp is not a legal status at all, but a private certification process run by an organization called B Lab (www.bcorporation.net). To be certified as a B Corp, the organization must complete a series of internal assessments that are then validated by an external evaluation process. The folks at B Lab claim that there are over 3,500 certified B Corps in over 70 countries (obviously, the legal issues vary significantly). And, just like the benefit corporation, certification as a B Corp has its fans and its detractors (Cao, Gehman, and Grimes, 2017; Gehman and Grimes, 2017; Kim et al., 2016).

Less popular, but still active, is the L3C (also known as a low-profit limited liability company – a variation of a limited liability company, or LLC), designed as a firm that intentionally sets profit maximization aside in pursuit of broader social objectives. Introduced in 2008, it was quite popular when it was first rolled out but has been the subject of substantial legal criticism and fell out of favor when the benefit corporation laws started to appear (Bishop, 2010; Callison and Vestal, 2010; Cooney et al., 2014).

Both organizational structures (the benefit corporation and the L3C) are what's known as "hybrid" entities, a label that's becoming increasingly popular as a general term for firms that seek to produce social, civic, and economic value. And (as you know by now), the choice of which form to use depends on where you want to go (Santos, Pache, and Birkholz, 2015).

Clearly, the range of choices for organizing a social venture in the U.S. are varied and complex. But (despite how some Americans think), the U.S. is not the only major economy in the world.

SOCIAL ENTERPRISE IN EASTERN ASIA (CHINA AND JAPAN)[1]

It may surprise you to know that China is the second largest economy in the world. It may surprise you even more to know that there are over 800,000 registered nonprofit organizations in China. There are four basic organizational forms for these entities (social associations, social service organizations, foundations, and public institutions). Chinese nonprofit law is similar to U.S. law in several ways.

Nonprofits in China

Source: iStock.com/Dzyuba. Used with permission

Chinese nonprofits are exempt from income tax and are generally prohibited from passing operating profits along to owners or shareholders. Individuals who make donations to these organizations can deduct those donations from their personal income for tax purposes. The nonprofit must declare a charitable purpose and is not allowed to participate directly in the political process. There are also restrictions on earned income and other commercial activities (Council on Foundations, 2018a).

Although it is not the emerging phenomenon that exists in other countries, there is a growing interest in social enterprise in China (Zhao, 2012). Although they are loosening, the regulatory restrictions in China have kept the social enterprise movement on the fringes of Chinese civil society (Wang, Alon, and Kimble, 2015).

Nonprofits in Japan

China's close neighbor, Japan (the world's third largest economy), has several legal concepts in common with China. Japanese law allows for four forms of nonprofit organizations (associations and foundations, public interest associations, special nonprofit corporations, and other public interest organizations). However, income tax exemptions must be applied for and granted individually, and obtaining tax-exempt status is far from guaranteed (Council on Foundations, 2018c). Because of the many barriers to entry faced by Japanese NGOs, it is estimated that fewer than 21,000 NGOs exist in a country of 126 million people (Yamakoshi, 2020). In a similar fashion, the specific notion of social enterprise as a distinct endeavor is just beginning to enter the Japanese discourse (Kawamoto, 2020).

Source: iStock.com/ElenVD. Used with permission

NGOS IN EUROPE AND THE U.K.

The fourth largest global economy is Germany (the fifth is India, which we'll get to in a minute). The U.K. is sixth, France is seventh, and Italy is eighth. So, in the interest of geographic consistency, we'll spend the next few pages talking about these European models before heading to South Asia.

German NGOs

German NGOs can be formed using one of three legal entities (associations, foundations, and LLCs). Tax exemption is granted if the organization is serving a direct public or benevolent purpose (which includes religious organizations). However, there is no distinct legal form that is exclusive to the NGO in German law. Much like the American system, German NGOs are not allowed to use the proceeds of the organization to reward the owners. Unlike the American system, German law also prohibits excessive salaries. The German laws on earned income or other "economic activity" are also much like the American system, in that profits from activity directly related to the social

Source: iStock.com/esancai. Used with permission

mission are not taxed, but unrelated business income is taxed. German NGOs are also restricted in their ability to engage in political activities (as are U.S. nonprofits) (Council on Foundations, 2018b).

Since European economies are far older than those in North America, there are many forms of social benefit organizations that pre-date the current conversations about social enterprise as a unique hybrid entity. Perhaps the oldest of these (and quite common in Germany and other countries) is the cooperative, which has its roots in the trade guilds of the medieval period discussed earlier in this chapter. Germany also has a rich history of "welfare organizations," which began as private undertakings designed to help those less fortunate. Many of these have since been subsumed into the German public welfare system. Germany also has organizations that are a form of charitable foundation, where the entity exists primarily to gather financial capital and redistribute it to those in need, in a structured fashion. Germany also supports social organizations that exist to further the "idealistic" interests of a specific group (such as musical or historical societies) (Birkhölzer, 2015).

Hybrids in Germany

Faced with the common concerns of reduced public and private support, Germany saw a rise in the notion of hybrid organizations in the late 1960s and early 1970s. There are a wide range of potential models, and the legal implications of each would require their own book. Because the legal and organizational structures vary so widely, estimating the number of social enterprises in Germany is also difficult, but most sources suggest that there are well over 100,000 in Germany (a country with a population of just over 83 million) (Vincze et al., 2014).

NGOs and Social Enterprise in the U.K.

Source: iStock.com/29mokara. Used with permission

Moving west across the English Channel, we next peek at how NGOs and social enterprises look in the U.K. (England, Scotland, Northern Ireland, and Wales). Of these four confederated countries (with a total population of 66.5 million people), the English economy is the largest by far, representing over 85 percent of the GDP for the Union (Fenton, 2018). Due to some small, nuanced differences in the legal climate in Scotland and Northern Ireland, we will focus our attention on England when possible (and use general U.K. data when necessary). As British law forms the backbone of many of the precepts of common law around the globe, many volumes exist on its application (Apple and Deyling, 1995). Since our intent is to give a brief overview of the issues that relate to NGOs and social enterprises, we will make our apologies to legal scholars around the globe and move on.

Nonprofits in Britain

British law allows for several organizational structures to function as a nonprofit (including community interest companies, unincorporated associations, trusts, registered societies, and incorporated charitable organizations). Exemption from income and sales taxes is available to these entities with prior approval from the Charity Commission (which serves as the regulatory body), and NGOs must demonstrate that they serve one of 12 specific charitable purposes (or one other more general purpose). These charities are not allowed to distribute any operating profits to the owners of the organization, and there are also limits on salaries and other forms of executive compensation. Earning income from the sale of goods or services is allowed under limited circumstances, but for-profit subsidiaries can be formed to produce income that is then transferred to the charitable entity (Council on Foundations, 2019c). There are roughly 175,000 NGOs in the U.K. (Benard and Davies, 2018).

Social Enterprise in the U.K.

Arguably one of the leading economies to support social entrepreneurship (Nicholls, 2010), the U.K. has over 70,000 social enterprises (Richardson, 2018). The U.K. is also one of the leading economies supporting various forms of impact investing and social impact bonds (Hutchison and Eccles, 2020), and is home to several very successful impact bond projects (Disley et al., 2019).

This growth was driven in part by an intentional government strategy to enhance the third sector in general and social enterprise in particular. This strategy included a specific legal definition of a social enterprise, expansion of the use of cooperative forms of governance, and reduced tax burdens on charitably focused endeavors (aka social enterprises). It also includes an intriguing device known as an "asset lock," which specifically directs that profits from earned-income activities must be redirected towards the specified community purposes that the organization seeks to uphold (Snaith, 2007). With these clearly defined regulations and direct governmental support, the social enterprise landscape in the U.K. (although still emerging) is much easier to navigate than the convoluted structures currently existing in the U.S. Due in part to this positive environment, there are over 500,000 social enterprises currently operating in the U.K. (Stephan et al., 2017). This effort to grow the social enterprise sector has also spawned a relatively substantial ecosystem with several strong support organizations that are helping this sector to grow (Richardson, 2018).

BOX 13.2 SOCIAL ENTERPRISE GROWTH IN THE U.K.

In order to understand the value of social entrepreneurship in the U.K., this box will highlight some facts and figures from Social Enterprise UK (as of 2021; www.socialenterprise.org.uk).

Compared to traditional businesses, UK social enterprises:

- are "outperforming mainstream businesses in growth and innovation" with 25 percent of social enterprises being established less than three years ago
- enjoy more representative leadership, with 41 percent being led by women, 34 percent being led by a person from a minority group, and 36 percent being led by someone with a disability
- employ and support disadvantaged populations, at 69 percent and 40 percent respectively
- report that they are aiming to minimize their environmental impact (88 percent)

NGOs in France

France has a very strong history of concern for those less fortunate, a tradition which was solidified as part of French culture in the post-revolutionary period of the 19th century. As democracy took hold in French society, the notion of a "social economy" (a specific economic structure intended to reduce economic inequality) also became part of French culture. This movement led to the establishment of several distinct legal forms (cooperatives, mutual societies, and associations), each of which was designed to serve a specific purpose in support of the social economy (Fraisse et al., 2016). These legal structures, and the broader notion of solidarity and social equality, have been embedded in French society ever since, and there are now over 250,000 such entities in France (Petrella and Richez-Battesti, 2020).

Source: iStock.com/esancai. Used with permission

Social enterprise in France

Unlike many other European countries, the topic of social enterprise is not a matter of great interest in France, in part due to the establishment of a unique legal category known as the "Solidarity Enterprise of Social Utility" (*entreprise solidaire d'utilité sociale*), which became law in 2014 and includes various forms of socially oriented ventures, such as cooperatives, associations, and foundations.

This law places several constraints on the venture. First, it must have a primary purpose other than the pursuit of profits. Further, it must commit to reinvesting any profit back into the social concern the organization seeks to serve (an asset lock much like the law in the U.K.). The law also requires a democratic governance structure, and places limits on executive compensation.

Interestingly, the French law allows for the enterprise to take any one of a number of legal structures within this context, including what would otherwise be considered a commercial venture (Petrella and Richez-Battesti, 2020). This flexibility allows for the social entrepreneur to access a much broader suite of financial solutions to support the growth and expansion of the enterprise (Fraisse et al., 2016). The broad approach to social ventures has allowed almost 100,000 of these firms to flourish in France, and spawned the development of an expansive ecosystem of private and public support (Petrella and Richez-Battesti, 2020).

NGOs and Social Enterprise in Italy

Moving directly south from our exploration of the scene in France, we now peek at the world of social innovation in Italy, a country of just over 60 million people. Much like its northern neighbor, Italian culture has a long history of civil society that is embedded in the laws regulating commerce and enterprise in general. This concept is so deeply embedded that Italian law does not have a unique category for what would otherwise be known as a "charity" (Borzaga, 2020).

Italian law allows for the formation of an association, which is broadly defined as an entity that can serve just about any altruistic purpose. Once such an association registers with the government, it can receive government funding and raise financial support through philanthropic grants and charitable donations. These revenues are taxed at the same rate as for-profit entities. A 50 percent reduction in tax liability is available if the entity can demonstrate that it is performing a specific activity that has a benefit to society (usually the care of the less fortunate, but also other cultural or educational purposes) (Borzaga, 2020).

The social cooperative

Italy also has a strong history of cooperative organizations, which sprung up in large part during the reconstruction efforts after World War II (Corcoran and Wilson, 2010). Various reports suggest that there may be over 50,000 commercial cooperatives in Italy,

Source: iStock.com/ElenVD. Used with permission

employing upwards of 800,000 people (Borzaga, 2020; Borzaga et al., 2015). These factors have produced a broad concept of a "social economy" that includes over 200,000 non-recognized associations (informal charities), almost 70,000 registered associations (formal charities), and over 17,000 social cooperatives (Borzaga, 2020).

This social cooperative is a unique organization that looks very much like what is known as a social enterprise in other countries, yet provides some distinctive features not found in other contexts. Much like the commercially oriented cooperative, the Italian social cooperative is governed by the members of the co-op, rather than the owners of the corporation. In the Italian model, members of the social cooperative are divided into three groups – individuals who receive economic benefit (either in the form of a paycheck or in return on invested capital), individuals who benefit from the social mission of the cooperative, and members who volunteer their services to advance the mission of the cooperative. Unlike their commercial counterparts, the social cooperative's main mission is to pursue some sort of collective or public good, with economic profit being subservient to that goal. These collective goods include things like care for the elderly or infirm, job retraining and placement, and various fair-trade commercial pursuits. Much like the social enterprise model, these social cooperatives are funded from a mix of charitable and philanthropic dollars, and some sort of earned income. Much like the asset lock seen in other countries, the members of the social cooperative must agree to waive their rights to certain operating profits, and accept limits on the returns that they can receive from investment activities (Thomas, 2004).

Because the social cooperative has been so effective (and because Italian law allows for a broader use of the association and foundation forms of governance), Italy has not seen substantial growth of social enterprise as a separate structural form. However, if you measure these organizations by how they behave instead of what they are called, there could be over 100,000 social enterprises in Italy (Borzaga, 2020).

While the Italian social cooperative holds a unique place in the global landscape of social entrepreneurship, it most certainly takes a back seat to the level of activity that occurs in India, the largest democracy on the planet.

NONPROFITS, NGOS, AND SOCIAL ENTERPRISE IN INDIA

As a former British colony, the laws regarding nonprofits and NGOs in India look quite similar to those in the U.K. Organizations seeking to perform charitable services can be organized as public charitable trusts or societies (generally, membership organizations). The Indian Companies Act of 2013 also allows for the formation of LLCs that intend to advance

a social cause and agree to use profits to advance the benevolent mission and restrict the distribution of dividends to shareholders. Within certain constraints, these three types of organizations are exempt from corporate income taxes but not sales taxes. Individuals making donations to support these entities can deduct 50 percent of the donation from their personal income taxes (Council on Foundations, 2019d).

Social Enterprise in India

Various reports indicate that there may be well over 3.3 million NGOs in India (one for every 400 Indian citizens) (International Center for Nonprofit Law, 2020).

Source: iStock.com/Smart. Used with permission

However, many of these are not registered, and exist in rural contexts that operate more like mutual aid societies (Srivastava and Tandon, 2005). Roughly 70,000 organizations are formally registered as NGOs in India (International Center for Nonprofit Law, 2020). In a similar fashion, some reports suggest that there are well over 2 million social enterprises in India (British Council, 2016). Much like the reported number of NGOs, many of these social enterprises are quite small. It is also likely that there is substantial double-counting (meaning that the same organization is counted as both an NGO and a social enterprise). Nonetheless, these figures are quite large compared to the other countries we've reviewed. So, it's only right that we spend a few extra pages understanding why the NGO and social enterprise landscape is so different in India.

The prevalence of both NGOs and social enterprises in India is due to several factors. India has a unique combination of a very large population (over 1.3 billion people) and a very high rate of poverty (somewhere between 20 and 30 percent of the population) (British Council, 2016; Reserve Bank of India, 2014). In addition, over 70 percent of the population lives in remote rural areas that often lack access to basic services such as electricity, sanitation, and health care (Ganesh et al., 2018). These factors have combined to create a unique entrepreneurial culture in India, which is driven by the need for survival by whatever means are available (a phenomenon often referred to as "subsistence entrepreneurship") (Sridharan et al., 2014).

Responding in part to this vast need, the Indian government has developed a number of laws and polices that are designed to support these micro-enterprises (to the point of having a dedicated Ministry of Micro, Small & Medium Enterprises). One study suggests that over 40 different government policies and programs have been developed to support entrepreneurship in general and social enterprise in particular. There is also a broad network of incubators and accelerators that have sprung up to assist in the growth of these ventures (British Council, 2016). In addition to these favorable conditions, India was one of the first markets to develop expertise in microfinance.

NGOS AND SOCIAL ENTERPRISE IN BRAZIL

Crossing back over the Atlantic Ocean but staying in the Southern Hemisphere, we now take a look at Brazil, the ninth largest economy on the planet.

Historically, the idea of a separate social sector would have been a foreign concept in Brazilian society. With origins as a Portuguese colony with strong influence from the Roman Catholic Church, the notion of care for others was seen as a basic requirement of each citizen rather than the unique efforts of a specific type of organization (Landim and Hwang, 1993). However, these roots in a plantation economy under various forms of limited democracy and various forms of authoritarian governments limited these activities to loosely organized local efforts rooted in individual communities. With the establishment of a more broadly democratic government in the mid-1980s, that mindset began to change (Wampler and Touchton, 2015). In the mid-1990s, a small group of radicals began to push back against increasing authoritarianism in both the Church and the state, resulting in the passage of the first of many laws defining specific activities as private charitable undertakings and defining these new entities as "public interest civil society organizations" (Alves and Koga,

Source: iStock.com/ElenVD. Used with permission

2006). These laws were expanded several times (most recently in 2014), and now include nonprofits, cooperatives, and religious organizations within their scope. These organizations are exempt from taxes on their revenue and their assets, as long as they can demonstrate that they are fulfilling their charitable purpose (much like the 501(c)3 in the U.S.) (Council on Foundations, 2019a). The fluid political culture in Brazil makes counting the number of these organizations quite challenging, but one report suggests that there are over 300,000 civil society organizations in Brazil (Igarape Institute, 2018).

The extensive social instability in Brazil also makes it hard to assess the state of social enterprise as a unique organizational structure (Lewis, 2016). Even if we use the broader notion of social entrepreneurship, coming up with a reasonable estimate of activity levels in Brazil is challenging. Rather than try to pull a number out of my hat, we'll leave more detailed research on this to you and move on.

NGOS AND SOCIAL ENTERPRISE IN CANADA

Leaving sunny Brazil behind, we now move a good bit north to the parliamentary democracy of Canada, the last but not least part of our 10-country study.

Much like the U.S., the Canadian government uses a federal central structure that oversees and coordinates a series of regional governments, with 10 distinct provinces and three additional territories. There are no laws (either federal or provincial) that require an NGO to use a specific legal structure. Most often, the NGO is organized as a "non-share" corporation, a trust, or an unincorporated association (Council on Foundations, 2019b).

Source: iStock.com/Denys. Used with permission

Tax law in Canada requires an organization to declare as either a "charity" or a "nonprofit organization." In either case, these designations allow the entity to claim an exemption from income tax (although they are not exempt from the Canadian version of a sales or VAT, known as the Goods and Services Tax). Charities must also demonstrate a public benefit, while nonprofit organizations (NPOs; most often formed for the benefit of their members) do not. In both cases, there are legal restrictions on the distribution of income to shareholders and officers (Council on Foundations, 2019b). Credible sources indicate that there are over 86,000 registered charities in Canada, and rough estimates suggest that there are at least that many NPOs (Blumberg, Sawyer, and Blumberg, 2017). It is important to note that Canadian regulations do allow for charities and nonprofits to earn income under certain conditions, so many Canadian social enterprises exist within these contexts. Experts on the social enterprise environment in Canada also include a number of cooperative organizations (and some for-profit entities) among their ranks (LePage, 2017).

Provincial Distinctions

While the world of the NGO (or NPO) is regulated at the federal level, there is substantial innovation in the development of social enterprise at the provincial level. In 2012, British Columbia enacted a law that created a form of hybrid entity known as a community contribution corporation (or C3). Similar in some ways to the LC3 structure in the U.S., the Canadian C3 must have a social purpose as its primary objective, with profit motives being secondary. Much like the community interest company in the U.K., there is also an asset lock that allows for limited profit distribution to specific classes of shareholders (which also allows the C3 to attract equity investments) (Henderson, 2016). Much like the L3C in the U.S., this model has struggled to gain traction, with fewer than 50 C3s registered with the provincial government (Horel, 2016). In 2016, Nova Scotia adopted legislation allowing the formation of community interest companies. The rules governing these entities are a blend of the C3 regulations used in British Columbia and the U.K. model of the community interest company (Smith, 2016).

A LAWYER AND A PASSPORT

As I write this (in the fall of 2020), the notion of world travel seems like a strange concept. So, it just might be that this little journey in exploring the cultures and perspectives on NGOs and social enterprise around the world was just my way of escaping from the confines of a global public health crisis for a few pages. And it should be clear by now that sound legal advice from an attorney that has a strong understanding of these complicated matters, as well as the specific twists and turns of the regulations that apply in the place you hope to practice, is vital to your success. Hopefully, this overview has also given you a new perspective on one of the main points of this book – namely that the art of building an effective social enterprise is messy, complicated, and highly dependent on local circumstances.

Said differently, the answer to "how" is "it depends." But the answer to "why" is always the same. In the words of one of the founders of this movement, the late Greg Dees:

> The idea of 'social entrepreneurship' has struck a responsive chord. It is a phrase well suited to our times. It combines the passion of a social mission with an image of business-like discipline, innovation, and determination commonly associated with, for instance, the high-tech pioneers of Silicon Valley. The time is certainly ripe for entrepreneurial approaches to social problems. Many governmental and philanthropic efforts have fallen far short of our expectations. Major social sector institutions are often viewed as inefficient, ineffective, and unresponsive. Social entrepreneurs are needed to develop new models for a new century. (Dees, 1998, p. 1)

In the aftershock of these perilous times, the only thing that seems certain is that we will need each other more than ever. But reduced government funding, lower levels of individual charitable donations, and constrained grant funding mean that the usual paths to provide care for our human siblings will be more narrow and difficult than ever; and enterprises that can improve the human condition while reducing societal costs over time will be in high demand.

So, we need to build. We need to build effective, sustainable organizations that can improve the human condition. And while that work is hard and messy and highly dependent on local conditions, we must build nonetheless.

But we also need to build the community of practice by developing partnerships, alliances, and collaborative networks. In the next chapter, we'll look at few things that we can do (and a few things we need to stop doing) so that this community can grow.

CHAPTER SUMMARY

This chapter serves to give an overview of the concept of the third sector and its role across the world. There are many similarities across the third sector internationally, but the chapter helps to detail some nuances in 10 different country contexts as well: the U.S., China, Japan, Germany, the U.K., France, Italy, India, Brazil, and Canada. For example, in the U.S., social enterprises can be registered under a variety of different structures under the umbrella of either nonprofit or for-profit designations. While organizational structures were detailed in the previous chapter, this chapter helps to unpack the structures of social enterprise from across 10 of the world's largest economies.

BOX 13.3   EXPLORING ENTREPRENEURSHIP ACROSS THE WORLD

Searching for an authoritative source for learning more about the entrepreneurship ecosystems of the world? Look no further than the Global Entrepreneurship Monitor (GEM). In addition to other existing national- or continent-level reports of entrepreneurship and social entrepreneurship ecosystems, GEM provides country, global, and specialty reports funded through the generous support of Babson College as well as a network of national sponsors. The reports are used internationally by academics, students, entrepreneurs, policymakers, and other key stakeholders within the entrepreneurship ecosystem. When conducting your own research of entrepreneurship in other countries, make sure to check out the various GEM reports, which are available for free from www.gemconsortium.org.

QUESTIONS FOR DISCUSSION

1. Review the possible social enterprise structures within your home country or where you would plan to locate your social enterprise. What are some considerations you need to keep in mind? Does your research inform your previous leanings for an organizational structure, or would you possibly want to change your structure? Why, or why not?

2. Choose two international country contexts that were featured in the chapter (or challenge yourself with one not featured), and complete a triple Venn diagram to think about the similarities and differences you see between your social enterprise's home context and the selected international one. Please note, you will likely need to do some additional research to do this exercise well.

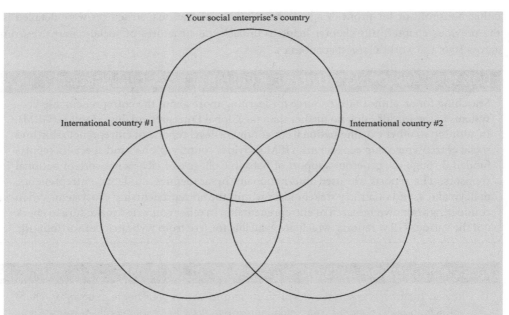

3. Based on your compare-and-contrast exercise above, imagine you had a friend or professional contact who wants to help you scale your impact internationally. Beyond the information highlighted within your triple Venn diagram, what would you tell them about these two other countries and their social entrepreneurship ecosystems? To aid in your research, be sure to reference Box 13.3 for a useful resource.

NOTE

1. Please note that China and Japan are grouped together due to geographic proximity and similar legal structures. The authors recognize and affirm that they are different and distinct cultures, each with their own proud heritage.

REFERENCES

Alves, M. A., and Koga, N. M. (2006). Brazilian nonprofit organizations and the new legal framework: An institutional perspective. *Revista de Administração Contemporânea, 10*(SPE), 213–234.

Apple, J. G., and Deyling, R. P. (1995). *A Primer on the Civil-Law System*. Washington, DC: Federal Judicial Center.

Baker, H. K. (2011). *Capital Structure and Corporate Financing Decisions: Theory, Evidence, and Practice*. Hoboken, NJ: John Wiley & Sons.

Baker, H. K., and Nofsinger, J. R. (2012). *Socially Responsible Finance and Investing: Financial Institutions, Corporations, Investors, and Activists*. Hoboken, NJ: John Wiley & Sons.

Benard, C., and Davies, J. (2018). *The UK Civil Society Almanac 2018 Summary*. London: NCVO.

Birkhölzer, K. (2015). *Social Enterprise in Germany: A Typology of Models*. ICSEM Working Papers, No. 15. International Comparative Social Enterprise Models (ICSEM) Project.

Bishop, C. G. (2010). The low-profit LLC (L3C): Progam related investment by proxy or perversion? *Arkansas Law Review, 63*, 243–257.

Blount, J., and Offei-Danso, K. (2012). The benefit corporation: A questionable solution to a non-existent problem. *St. Mary's Law Journal, 44*, 617.

Blumberg, M., Sawyer, M., and Blumberg, T. (2017). *Blumbergs' Snapshot of the Canadian Charity Sector 2017*. Accessed 12 April 2021 at www.canadiancharitylaw.ca/uploads/Blumbergs_Canadian_Charity _Sector_Snapshot_2017.pdf.

Borzaga, C. (2020). Social enterprises and their ecosystems in Europe: Updated country report – Italy. Accessed 12 April 2021 at https://europa.eu/!Qq64ny.

Borzaga, C., Carini, C., Carpita, M., and Lori, M. (2015). *The Relevance and Economic Sustainability of Social Economy in Italy*. Euricse Working Papers, 81.

British Council (2016). *Social Value Economy. A Survey of the Social Enterprise Landscape in India*. Accessed 12 April 2021 at www.britishcouncil.org/sites/default/files/bc-report-ch4-india-digital_0 .pdf.

Bugg-Levine, A., and Emerson, J. (2011). *Impact Investing: Transforming How We Make Money While Making a Difference*. San Francisco, CA: John Wiley & Sons.

Callison, J. W., and Vestal, A. W. (2010). The L3C illusion: Why low-profit limited liability companies will not stimulate socially optimal private foundation investment in entrepreneurial ventures. *Vermont Law Revuew*, 35, 273.

Cameron, R. E. (1993). *A Concise Economic History of the World: From Paleolithic Times to the Present*. New York, NY: Oxford University Press.

Cao, K., Gehman, J., and Grimes, M. G. (2017). Standing out and fitting in: Charting the emergence of certified B corporations by industry and region. In A. C. Corbett and J. A. Katz (eds), *Hybrid Ventures (Advances in Entrepreneurship, Firm Emergence and Growth, Vol. 19)* (pp. 1–38). Bingley: Emerald Publishing.

Clark, G. (2007). *A Farewell to Alms: A Brief Economic History of the World*. Princeton, NJ: Princeton University Press.

Colombo, J. D. and M. A. Hall (1995). The charitable tax exemption. Boulder, Westview Press.

Cooney, K., Koushyar, J., Lee, M., & Murray, H. (2014). Benefit corporation and L3C adoption: A survey. Stanford Social Innovation Review. Accessed 12 April 2021 at https://ssir.org/articles/entry/benefit _corporation_and_l3c_adoption_a_survey.

Corcoran, H., and Wilson, D. (2010). *The Worker Co-Operative Movements in Italy, Mondragon and France: Context, Sucess Factors and Lessons*. Accessed 12 April 2021 at www.socioeco.org/bdf_fiche -document-5780_en.html.

Council on Foundations (2018a). Nonprofit law in China. Accessed 12 April 2021 at www.cof.org/ content/nonprofit-law-china.

Council on Foundations (2018b). Nonprofit law in Germany. Accessed 12 April 2021 at www.cof.org/ content/nonprofit-law-germany.

Council on Foundations (2018c). Nonprofit law in Japan. Accessed 12 April 2021 at www.cof.org/ content/nonprofit-law-japan.

Council on Foundations (2019a). Nonprofit law in Brazil. Accessed 12 April 2021 at www.cof.org/ content/nonprofit-law-brazil.

Council on Foundations (2019b). Nonprofit law in Canada. Accessed 12 April 2021 at www.cof.org/ content/nonprofit-law-canada.

Council on Foundations (2019c). Nonprofit law in England and Wales. Accessed 12 April 2021 at www .cof.org/content/nonprofit-law-england-wales.

Council on Foundations (2019d). Nonprofit law in India. Accessed 12 April 2021 at www.cof.org/ country-notes/nonprofit-law-india#_ftn2.

Dees, J. G. (1998). *The Meaning of Social Entrepreneurship*. Durham, NC: Duke University.

Dees, J. G., and Anderson, B. B. (2003). For-profit social ventures. *International Journal of Entrepreneurship Education, 2*(1), 1–26.

Disley, E., Giacomantonio, C., Kruithof, K., and Sim, M. (2019). The payment by results Social Impact Bond pilot at HMP Peterborough: Final process evaluation report. *Annual Review of Policy Design, 7*(1), 1–20.

Emerson, J. (1998). The US nonprofit capital market: An introductory overview of developmental stages, investors and funding instruments. *American Philanthropy Review*, Fall.

Fenton, T. (2018). *Regional Economic Activity by Gross Domestic Product, UK: 1998 to 2018.* Accessed 12 April 2021 at www.ons.gov.uk/economy/grossdomesticproductgdp/bulletins/regionaleconomicact ivitybygrossdomesticproductuk/1998to2018/pdf.

Fraisse, L., Gardin, L., Laville, J.-L., Petrella, F., and Richez-Battesti, N. (2016). *Social Enterprise in France: At the Crossroads of the Social Economy, Solidarity Economy and Social Entrepreneurship?* ICSEM Working Papers, No. 34. International Comparative Social Enterprise Models (ICSEM) Project.

Ganesh, U., Menon, V., Kaushal, A., and Kumar, K. (2018). The Indian social enterprise landscape: Innovation for an inclusive future. Accessed 12 April 2021 at www.bertelsmann-stiftung.de/en/our -projects/germany-and-asia/news/the-indian-social-enterprise-landscape.

Gehman, J., and Grimes, M. (2017). Hidden badge of honor: How contextual distinctiveness affects cate-gory promotion among certified B corporations. *Academy of Management Journal, 60*(6), 2294–2320.

Girard, S. L., O'Keefe, M. F., Price, M. A., & Moon, M. R. (2014). *Business law basics: Learn what you need in two hours.* (self-published)

Gombrich, E. H. (2005). *A Little History of the World.* New Haven, CT: Yale University Press.

Hall, P. D. (2010). Historical perspectives on nonprofit organizations in the United States. In D. O. Renz (ed.), *The Jossey-Bass Handbook of Nonprofit Leadership and Management* (pp. 3–42). San Francisco, CA: Jossey-Bass.

Hammerschmidt, P. (2013, October 25). My application for tax exemption was submitted to the IRS. Why is it taking so long? *NonProfit Quarterly.*

Hansmann, H. B. (1981). "The Rationale for Exempting Nonprofit Organizations from Corporate Income Taxation." The Yale Law Journal 91(1): 54-100.

Henderson, G. E. (2016). Could community contribution companies improve access to justice. *Canadian Bar Review, 94,* 209.

Horel, B. (2016). *Community Contribution Companies in British Columbia.* Accessed 12 April 2021 at www.centreforsocialenterprise.com/wp-content/uploads/2019/04/C3_Research_Summary_2016-by -Bridget-Horel.pdf.

Hutchison, D., and Eccles, T. (2020). Impact Bond Global Database. Accessed 12 April 2021 at https:// sibdatabase.socialfinance.org.uk/.

Igarape Institute (2018). Listed as one of Brazil's top NGOs. Accessed 12 April 2021 at https://igarape.org .br/en/listed-as-one-of-brazils-top-ngos/#:~:text=There%20are%20more%20than%20300%2C000 ,which%20were%20competing%20for%20consideration.

Internal Revenue Service. Accessed 28th April 2021 at https://www.irs.gov/charities-non-profits/ charitable-purposes.

International Center for Nonprofit Law (2020). Civic Freedom Monitor, India. Accessed 12 April 2021 at www.icnl.org/resources/civic-freedom-monitor/india#resources.

Kawamoto, K. (2020). Lineage of Western social enterprise theory and Japan's state of introduction. *Rissho International Journal of Academic Research in Culture and Society, 3,* 135–152.

Kim, S., Karlesky, M. J., Myers, C. G., and Schifeling, T. (2016). Why companies are becoming B cor-porations. *Harvard Business Review, 17,* 2–5. Accessed 12 April 2021 at https://hbr.org/2016/06/why -companies-are-becoming-b-corporations.

Kucher, J. H. (2012). Social enterprise as a means to reduce public sector deficits. *Journal of Entrepreneurship and Public Policy, 1*(2), 147–158.

Landim, L., and Hwang, C. (1993). *Defining the Nonprofit Sector: Brazil.* Accessed 12 April 2021 at http:// citeseerx.ist.psu.edu/viewdoc/download?doi=10.1.1.202.5859&rep=rep1&type=pdf.

Lee, M. (2007). Revisiting the Dartmouth court decision: Why the US has private nonprofit agen-cies instead of public non-governmental organizations (NGOs). *Public Organization Review, 7*(2), 113–142. LePage, D. (2017). *The Canadian Social Enterprise Guide.* Accessed 12 April 2021 http:// secouncil.ca/wp-content/uploads/2017/10/the-Canadian-Social-Enterprise-Guide.pdf.

Lewis, D. (2016). Social entrepreneurship in Brazil: Surviving a crisis. *Stanford Social Innovation Review.* Accessed 12 April 2021 at https://ssir.org/articles/entry/social_entrepreneurship_in_brazil_surviving _a_crisis.

McKeever, B. S. (2020). The nonprofit sector in brief 2019. Accessed 12 April 2021 at https://nccs.urban .org/publication/nonprofit-sector-brief-2019.

Meghan, K., and Terry, C. (2016). *The Third Sector: Community Organizations, NGOs, and Nonprofits.* Urbana, IL: University of Illinois Press.

Nicholls, A. (2010). Institutionalizing social entrepreneurship in regulatory space: Reporting and disclosure by community interest companies. *Accounting, Organizations and Society*, 35(4), 394–415.

O'Keefe, M. F., Girard, S. L., Price, M. A., and Moon, M. R. (2014). *Business Law Basics: Learn What You Need in 2 Hours*. Herentals: Nova Vista.

Petrella, F., and Richez-Battesti, N. (2020). Social enterprises and their ecosystems in Europe: Updated country report – France. Accessed 12 April 2021 at https://europa.eu/!Qq64ny.

Phillips, G. (2016). *The Art of Fundraising: The Appeal, the People, the Strategies*. North Charleston, SC: CreateSpace.

Public Interest Registry (2017). 25 Facts and Stats about NGOs Worldwide. Accessed 12 April 2021 at http://techreport.ngo/previous/2017/facts-and-stats-about-ngos-worldwide.html.

Rawhouser, H., Cummings, M., and Crane, A. (2015). Benefit corporation legislation and the emergence of a social hybrid category. *California Management Review*, 57(3), 13–35.

Reserve Bank of India (2014). *Number and Percentage of Population Below Poverty Line*. Accessed 12 April 2021 at https://web.archive.org/web/20140407102043/http://www.rbi.org.in/scripts/PublicationsView.aspx?id=15283.

Richardson, M. (2018). *Social Enterprise in the UK*. Accessed 12 April 2021 www.britishcouncil.org/society/social-enterprise/reports.

Robbins, K. C. (2006). The nonprofit sector in historical perspective: Traditions of philanthropy in the West. In W. W. Powell and R. Steinberg (eds), *The Nonprofit Sector: A Research Handbook*, 2nd ed. (pp. 13–31). New Haven, CT: Yale University Press.

Santos, F., Pache, A.-C., and Birkholz, C. (2015). Making hybrids work: Aligning business models and organizational design for social enterprises. *California Management Review*, 57(3), 36–58.

Smith, N. (2016). An in-depth look at Nova Scotia's new community interest companies. Accessed 12 April 2021 at www.millerthomson.com/en/publications/communiques-and-updates/social-impact-newsletter/july-6-2016/an-in-depth-look-at-nova-scotias-new/.

Snaith, I. (2007). Recent reforms to corporate legal structures for social enterprise in the UK: Opportunity or confusion? *Social Enterprise Journal*, 3(1), 20–30.

Sridharan, S., Maltz, E., Viswanathan, M., and Gupta, S. (2014). Transformative subsistence entrepreneurship: a study in India. *Journal of Macromarketing*, 34(4), 486–504.

Srivastava, S., and Tandon, R. (2005). How large is India's non-profit sector? *Economic and Political Weekly*, 40(19), 1948–1952.

Stephan, U., Braidford, P., Folmer, E., Lomax, S., and Hart, M. (2017). *Social Enterprise: Market Trends 2017*. Accessed 12 April 2021 at https://assets.publishing.service.gov.uk/government/uploads/system/uploads/attachment_data/file/644266/MarketTrends2017report_final_sept2017.pdf.

Stillman, G. B. (2007). *Global Standard NGOs: The Essential Elements of Good Practice*. Durham, NC: Lulu Books.

Thomas, A. (2004). The rise of social cooperatives in Italy. *Voluntas: International Journal of Voluntary and Nonprofit Organizations*, 15(3), 243–263.

Vincze, M., Birkhölzer, K., Kaepplinger, S., Gollan, A. K., and Richter, A. (2014). *A Map of Social Enterprises and their Ecosystems in Europe. Country Report for Germany*. Accessed 12 April 2021 at https://evpa.eu.com/uploads/documents/2016_09_13-KEY-REPORTS_DE-Nexus-final-draft_EU-logo.pdf.

Wampler, B., and Touchton, M. (2015). Contracting, contesting, and co-optation: Civil society organizations' strategies under new institutional arangements in Brazil. *Journal of Politics in Latin America*, 7(1), 3–44.

Wang, H., Alon, I., and Kimble, C. (2015). Dialogue in the dark: Shedding light on the development of social enterprises in China. *Global Business and Organizational Excellence*, 34(4), 60–69.

Yamakoshi, A. (2020). The Changing Face of NGOs in Japan. Accessed 12 April 2021 at www.gdrc.org/ngo/jpngo-face.html.

Zhao, M. (2012). The social enterprise emerges in China. *Stanford Social Innovation Review*. Accessed 12 April 2021 at https://ssir.org/articles/entry/the_social_enterprise_emerges_in_china#.

One of the hardest things for a founder to do is step away from the project they founded. Yet that's exactly what Robert Egger did. In the wake of a financial scandal that Egger helped to uncover, he found himself as the newly appointed executive vice president of the National Capital chapter of the United Way (arguably the largest and most influential nonprofit in the District of Columbia). While he always has been (and remains) a vocal critic of much of the standard practices of the "nonprofit industrial complex," Egger knew that long-term substantive social change in Washington, DC didn't stand a chance unless the United Way remained healthy. Leaving the DC Central Kitchen (DCCK) in the hands of a trusted lieutenant, Egger implemented an aggressive reform campaign (including reducing the salary for the position he held by two-thirds). He then went on to begin a period of public organizing to enhance the stature of nonprofits in the public discourse.

Egger's departure left a huge hole in the public face of DCCK. Every organization has its own dynamics, and DCCK had been a very leader-centric entity from the day it was founded. While Robert's successor as executive director was highly competent, she was much more comfortable behind the scenes. Fortunately, she was smart enough to realize this, and called on the DCCK Board of Directors to step in and step up. After 11 months working to right the wrongs at the United Way, Robert returned to the DCCK in the newly created role of president, leaving the executive director's post intact and in the hands of his trusted colleague. But after four years of sprinting alongside the indefatigable Egger, she was exhausted, and decided to step down.

Source: Courtesy of Robert Egger. Used with permission

The new executive director brought with him a methodical nature that was the perfect complement to Egger's visionary style. As DCCK continued to grow and expand, new levels of professional organization and structure were added, including the first-ever dedicated director of development and fundraising, as well as a full-time senior level finance officer. The additional levels of organization were a substantial help in stabilizing DCCK, but they also brought to light several inherent flaws in the operation that had been ignored in the early break-neck days. Among other things, it became clear that many of the attempts to expand DCCK's programs did not always line up operationally and required the development of new skills that sometimes ran counter to the core competencies of the team.

One example of this disconnect between vision and operations was the development of a program known as Capital Carts. The idea was that DCCK would support a series of micro-entrepreneurs who would own and operate their own food carts, with supplies and support coming from DCCK. Robert had seen such a program work on the streets of India's cities, and he believed that it could provide economic liberation to some of the folks who had graduated from DCCK's culinary program. Unfortunately, the regulatory environment in the District of Columbia was quite complicated, and obtaining and maintaining the necessary licenses and permits to operate a food cart was a difficult task.

The logistics of supporting the carts out of DCCK's central location also proved challenging, as the cart operator needed to store the equipment in a separate location mandated by DC regulations. The Capital Carts program never got beyond its initial pilot project and was sold off to a friendly local restauranteur.

QUESTIONS FOR DISCUSSION

1. Describe the challenges that DCCK faced during these changes in structure.
2. Discuss the specific entrepreneurial traits that Egger displayed during this time.
3. What tools might DCCK have used to better manage this transition period?
4. What specific steps might DCCK have taken before implementing the Capital Carts program?

PART V
YOU KNOW IT WHEN YOU SEE IT

14
Don't worry, be happy

Learning objectives

After studying this chapter, you should be able to:
1. Understand that the definition of "social enterprise" – like "social entrepreneur-ship" – is not universally accepted and some may have stricter perceptions on their framing of social enterprise.
2. Explain the concept of scaling and a few different scaling options, and plan for the selected scaling approach.
3. Recognize failure as a natural part of the entrepreneurial process.

WELCOME BACK!

Now that you're rested from our virtual trip around the world (and all those exhausting legal issues), it's time to get back to the main purpose of our time together, which is to develop practical tools for building effective and sustainable social enterprises. If you look back at the subjects we've covered so far, you can see that there are a lot of factors to consider in making this idea of social entrepreneurship work. It's messy, complicated, and just plain tough going. Perhaps you've found all of that discouraging (although I suspect that many of you have found it inspiring). You now hold in your hands and head a wonderful set of tools that can help you build the change you want to see, and that's a beautiful thing.

Source: Hatham, Unsplash. Used with permission

The main reason I decided to write this book was that I believe in the power of social enterprise, not just to improve the condition of individual humans, but also as the answer to many of the problems facing society today. So, while I sincerely hope that you are inspired to try to build your own social enterprise, I also hope that you are starting to see that you are part of a growing movement that has the power to truly change the world.

Like any other movement, this one needs help to become the force that many of us think it can be. And there are many folks working to make that happen. Towards the end of the chapter, we're going to talk about some of the things that we can do to build this movement. But before we do that, we need to look at some of the lingering debates that are getting in the way.

WHAT'S A SOCIAL ENTERPRISE, ANYWAY?

Just about every serious discussion of social entrepreneurship begins with some sort of definitional statement (heck, we've devoted an entire section of this book to trying to define it). There are literally dozens of articles debating what defines a social enterprise and who qualifies as a social entrepreneur, and the field (unfortunately) is still debating this issue almost 50 years after Bill Drayton first described it. And while I'm not trying to disparage the important work of defining a field (and I confess that I have expressed strong opinions on the issue), we do need to point out that sometimes that debate is counterproductive. We've also pointed out that there are many variants involved in determining how best to build a social venture (for-profit or nonprofit, for example), and that legal structures can vary greatly from one jurisdiction to another. So, perhaps we need to focus more on what the enterprise does, and less on how it does it.

To Scale or Not to Scale

One of the most constant challenges that comes up in the discussion of how to build the social entrepreneurship movement is the concept of "scale." Before we talk about the pluses and minuses of scale, let's make sure we all have the same understanding of what "scale" means to an entrepreneur.

Way back in Chapter 1, we talked about the legendary Adam Smith. (No, we really did. Go ahead and take a look at the index and see for yourself.) In that chapter, we talked about how Smith's most famous work may not have been his most important, particularly when it comes to the motivation for building a social enterprise. However, Smith has made huge contributions in many other ways. The one that matters to this discussion is the notion of economies of scale.

Smith was the first to popularize the idea that specialization (also known as the division of labor) could make the process of production more efficient. This concept then led to the understanding that production could be even more efficient if we had more folks doing the same thing at the same time (and you'll be happy to know that we're *not* going down the rabbit hole of an economic discussion of reductions in marginal cost). Suffice it to say that more workers doing the same job at the same time reduces the overall expense per worker, and hence the overall expense of each component part of a product. And from that one idea comes almost all of our concepts about modern manufacturing (so if you weren't already convinced that Adam Smith was a rock star, you should be by now).

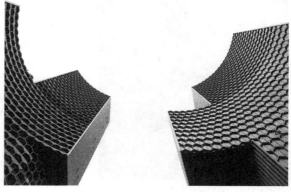

Source: T. H. Chia, Unsplash. Used with permission

This notion of economies of scale has become such a central part of how we think about growing an enterprise that just about every business plan has a section on how the business is going to expand – and the common term used for that expansion is "scale." Part of the concern about scaling the enterprise comes from the modern concepts of venture investing, where the funders want to see a substantial return on their investment in a very short period. The most effective way to do that is to "scale" the enterprise – meaning that the venture needs to grow from a small seed to a large tree quite quickly (even though rapid expansion can create any number of management issues).

You'll recall from our conversations in Chapter 2 that the basics of entrepreneurship as practiced in the commercial sector need to be applied in the practice of social enterprise. But this notion of scale as a necessary component of a social venture is one place where the rules of for-profit entrepreneurship need to be put aside (or at least dialed down a good bit). Despite many articles and speeches examining how to "scale" social enterprise, there are many cases where a small, local solution is best. And there are others where scaling is simply not possible.

Community First, Scale Second

I'm sure that you recall the many pages we've spent on the concept of community engagement. By now, you should fully understand the need to develop solutions that engage members of the community and address their needs as they see them. Holding that understanding in the front of your mind, it becomes clear that communities are often unique, which means that the solution is also unique (and therefore not able to be applied in other communities – which means that it can't "scale").

By way of example, there is a fabulous program that began in my hometown of Baltimore called Vehicles for Change. The underlying social problem that this organization identified is that the mass transit system in Baltimore is structured in a way that it does not serve the general public. So, by default, the only folks who use the system are those who are economically unable to afford other options (like owning their own car). Vehicles for Change developed a truly elegant solution for getting quality used cars into the hands of those in need in a way that increases both the dignity and independence of its constituents (and produces some impressive long-term results as well; see www.vehiclesforchange.org). The program has worked so well that there have been innumerable calls to scale the program. But the "secret sauce" of Vehicles for Change is such that it only works in urban areas where the mass transit is ineffective. So, a city like New York, or Chicago, or London, where mass transit is ubiquitous, does not have the same underlying conditions that allow the Vehicles for Change model to work.

In addition to solutions being specific to certain locations, attempting to scale an enterprise creates numerous management challenges and can turn someone who is really effective on the front lines into someone who is far less effective in a management role (if you need a refresher on this matter, take a minute and look back at our discussion of the E-Myth in Chapter 2). While this problem can be solved by making changes in management, the level of empathy and care needed to be effective in social innovation adds a layer of complexity to this decision. In a profit-seeking context, bringing in a new boss who is a more effective manager is an easy decision – not so in the more complex world of social enterprise.

It's About the Relationship

Perhaps more important is that much of the success of a social enterprise is the relationship that is built between the organization and its constituents. This vital and somewhat fragile bond of trust takes time to build and is easily broken. When an organization grows, it is often hard for the leadership team to stay in touch with its constituents. This means that the growth that we almost reflexively seek may do far more harm than good. Personally, I'd rather have a small, effective organization than a large, ineffective one.

Source: iStock.com/Prostock Studio. Used with permission

There are certainly things that any aspiring social entrepreneur can learn from the success (and failure) of the efforts of another. But the "copy, paste, repeat" method that scaling implies means that the specific operating model used in one neighborhood can be easily replicated in another community. With all that we know about the nuances of community engagement, it's not hard to see that this is often simply not practical.

None of this should be taken to imply that economies of scale should not be explored. There are certainly times where combining efforts can produce a more effective and efficient operation – and (for many reasons) the nonprofit world often has several organizations doing the same work in the same community. It's just that we need to make sure that the efforts to scale an entity are done for the right reasons, and after careful consideration of all the consequences (good and bad).

Said simply, in social entrepreneurship bigger is not always better. If our goal is to build the community of social innovation, then perhaps we need to worry less about bringing programs to scale, and more about making sure programs are effectively meeting the needs of their constituents. One way to do this is to form communities of practice (see below) where knowledge and expertise can be shared.

FINAL THOUGHTS

At this point in our journey, I hope that there are a few things that are now firmly stuck in your mind. Things like how important this work is, how complex it is, and how vital it is to involve the community in the development and delivery of the solution to the problem. In this section, I want to look at community in a different way and talk more about what's often known as "community of practice." To do that, I want to tell you two stories, both of which come from the time I was first exposed to this thing called "social entrepreneurship" in 2006.

BOX 14.1 PARTNERSHIPS AND REPLICATION

As noted in this chapter, scaling may not be possible or favorable for a social enterprise due to a variety of reasons, but there are other ways to broaden your impact without stretching yourself, your team, and your venture too thin. The first way to manage scaling impact without scaling your organization is through existing and new partnerships. With most social and environmental causes, there are typically many entities and organizations that are already working on chipping away at an issue. While this approach may not yield your unique stamp on the world, through forming coalitions for collective action partnerships can aid in creating more seamless coverage and may help to secure more funding (in fact, many grants are earmarked for such partnerships).

Another option to scale impact is through replication. Replication can exist in paid and unpaid forms where you are providing a model, product, or service for others to use in their local context. This can look like a social franchising model, where your venture would supply its model, brand, product/service blueprints or specifications, and any other intellectual property, so that someone can launch your branded venture in another geographic area. Alternatively, some social entrepreneurs give their intellectual property (and sometimes brand) away in order to spread their impact through an open-source, dissemination model. While doing an open-source model might not help your bottom line, it is a great way to help others create impact along with you!

In late 2005, I took a job as the founding executive director of a brand-new program designed to support student entrepreneurs at the University of Baltimore. Shortly after I started, I was handed a file that contained a brand-new grant agreement made between a consortium of local funders and the university to support a program that would team up area nonprofit leaders with MBA students to explore the possibility of developing earned-income strategies for their organizations. Working on that project led me to meet and learn from many of the early pioneers that you've heard me mention throughout this book (folks like Robert Egger, Jed Emerson, Greg Dees, Jerr Bosche, and many more), as well as some early efforts to organize folks through projects like the Social Enterprise Alliance. I remember begging several of these folks to meet with me to help understand this "thing" that I somehow knew had the power to truly change the world. And each time I gained some new information, I became more intrigued, and more convinced that these folks were really on to something.

As an eager graduate student, I was also looking for ways to develop my research stream, and I somehow came across a small conference being held at New York University. In 2010, I was accepted into that conference, and was exposed to several hundred researchers and practitioners all actively working to develop the field of social entrepreneurship and help folks build effective social enterprises. As I sat in that lecture hall in New York City, I began to realize that this somewhat unusual concept that business could be a force for good and not just a way to make folks wealthy was not something I was imagining, but rather a young and growing movement – a movement which has grown exponentially since then.

As I write this at the beginning of 2021, there are networks of social enterprise incubators and accelerators around the globe. Affinity groups and trade organizations exist in most of the major countries, and there are dozens of conferences and convenings happening almost every week. What was once a glimmer in the eye of Bill Drayton is now seen as a legitimate category of enterprise with a distinct methodology and focus. And that is a *very* good thing.

Despite all of the debates on what is, or what is not, a social enterprise, what's important now is that we focus our efforts on building each other up, not drawing narrow lines of division that decide who is or is not in the club. In my book (and this is my book), it's far more important to do the work of doing good than it is to worry about how that work is being done.

One of the best examples of how this field has done just that is in the way that earned income is viewed. In the early days of this movement, there were some who felt that one could not qualify as a social enterprise unless all the revenue for the organization was generated by the sale of a product or service. Happily, we've now come to understand that there are many ways to fund social innovation, and the right mix of founding sources is what makes sense for that venture at that stage in its development.

None of this is meant to say that we should settle for less than the absolute best as we develop these new ventures. Verifiable outcomes, sustainable revenue, direct and ongoing engagement with the community, sound operating practices, and a strong commitment to ethics and justice are absolutely critical. But there are many paths that lead to these goals, and we shouldn't discredit well-intentioned efforts simply because they don't follow the same path we've chosen.

This may be a bad analogy, but in some ways decisions about operating models are a bit like choosing a condiment. You may like mustard and I may like ketchup (heck, I knew a guy in college who put grape jelly on scrambled eggs!). What's important is that nourishment is being delivered. And in a world hungry for justice and righteousness, where deep social divides continue to fester and inequities abound, we need creative and sustainable solutions now more than ever.

As I write this, the support networks for building effective social innovation are far more developed than when we all first began this work. But there is still much work to be done if we are to achieve the potential that I'm convinced exists in this field. We still have a long way to go in building the financial networks that can support an enterprise that is focused on purpose over profit. Legal structures are still inconsistent and hard to navigate. And old habits of "begging for change" are hard to break.

While the dawn of this new age has come, we are still in early morning when it comes to building a better world. I hope that this journey has helped you see that this world is possible, and that you can play a part in making it so. But before we leave, I need to make sure that your head is in the right place.

A FEW THOUGHTS ON SUCCESS AND FAILURE

As we come to the end of our time together, we need to talk for a few minutes about where all this leads. If you're good, and you're lucky, the social enterprise you've set out to build will truly change the world (or at least a small part of the world). But if you're not, that does not mean that you have failed.

Throughout this book, you've been given multiple examples of how the successful entrepreneur tries and tries and tries again. We've talked at length about the pivot, about iteration, and how the idea that you start out with may look very different by the time you get to the finish line. We've talked about the value of discovering all the ways that something won't work as part of the process

Source: iStock.com/Sergei Chuyko. Used with permission

of discovering the way that it will work. We've even talked about that cold shower of a day when you realize that your idea doesn't work, and you need to pack your bags and move on. But until now, we haven't really talked about what happens after that. After you've exhausted all your resources and come to the inescapable conclusion that your project just won't work.

One of my attempts to build a new venture ended after a capital market collapsed just when we needed it most. We'd done everything right. The product concept was strong, the early testing was going well, we had several strong advisors that all agreed that we should move forward, and we had some early investors. It was time to take the next step and start to look for some angel investors. But the very day that we were scheduled to make our first venture presentation was the day that the U.S. suffered the terrorist attack that has become known as 9/11. Because Lower Manhattan (the seat of the U.S. financial system) was one of the places attacked, most of the speculative capital dried up overnight, and we realized that our own little entrepreneurial dream was dead. It took a few months to wind the thing down, and we were able to escape without too much financial damage, but it was heartbreaking nonetheless.

Shortly after it was all over, I received a note from one of the folks who had been advising the project. After expressing his condolences on how things had turned out, he wrote something that I will never forget. He said that "one of two things has happened here. Either you've been cured forever of a horrible disease, or you've caught hold of something that will drive you for the rest of your life. And I think I know which one it is."

The Serial Entrepreneur

Since receiving that note, I've gone on to build a few other things. Some of them have worked, some of them have not. But I've also come to realize that how a project turns out is not really the point. I've met tons of really great people, had incredible experiences, and come to see that each adventure leads to the next.

The notion of a serial entrepreneur is quite popular in the general public. Usually, it refers to someone who has successfully built a venture, had a strong financial exit, and is now moving

Source: Ahmed Hasan, Unsplash. Used with permission

on to another project, perpetuating the popular notion that "success breeds success." And while that may be true, I think it's also sometimes true that success is a lousy teacher. Sometimes, success (or failure) is as much a result of external factors as it is anything that you or your team has done. Sometimes the wind is at your back, and sometimes it's in your face. But because we too often see the entrepreneur as the lone genius (another notion that we've hopefully dislodged over the course of our time together), we think that the success of the venture is due to the efforts of the entrepreneur alone. And friends, that's just not true.

So, the very last radical thought I want to leave you with is that we need to redefine the meaning of the serial entrepreneur to include those brave souls who get back up off the floor after a crushing defeat, dust themselves off, and try again with a new project. Because I'm here to tell you that in entrepreneurship, as in life, it's not what happens to you that matters; it's what you do about it.

Thanks for coming along on the ride.

CHAPTER SUMMARY

This chapter recognizes that there is still a debate around the term "social enterprise"; however, requiring a social enterprise to fit into a narrow and highly specific definition is counterproductive and antithetical to serving the communities that need to be served in the best way we know how. Second, scaling the enterprise may be useful, but can also harm the social mission (which is, after all, the central point). There are other ways to think about scaling that may be more effective in spreading the impact that the world needs. Finally, we recognize that failure is a normal part of the entrepreneurial process that even the best people and ideas face. For those who "catch the entrepreneurial bug," the closing out of one project can be viewed as meaning that you're one step closer to finding the next opportunity to use your skills and talents for good in another form or fashion.

QUESTIONS FOR DISCUSSION

1. What is the value in broadly defining "social enterprise"? On the other hand, how might being inclusive be challenging?
2. Think about the core impact you have been looking to have with your venture. Apart from scaling your own venture, what are some other ways in which you might scale your impact? Be detailed and specific with your plans.
3. Do you think you will continue on with your venture? If so, what are your next steps? If not, why not, and would you still consider contributing to that social or environmental cause in another way?

Robert Egger is many things. Stationary is not one of them. With the DC Central Kitchen (DCCK) operations well in the hands of other competent folks, Egger began to explore several other issues around food and social justice. One of those ideas was to expand the DCCK model to other cities around the country. Despite being able to launch projects in several dozen cities, the nonprofit mindset was very hard to dislodge, and none of the early-stage ventures was able to develop to the level of social enterprise that Robert had built in DC. Another failed effort involved an alliance with regional food banks to support these community kitchens, but that partnership turned out to be unequal, and the food banks eventually subsumed the kitchens.

Another effort, which sought to reuse the food left behind in college cafeterias (much like the original reuse model that started DCCK), was more successful, in part due to a partnership with the largest college food service contractor in the country. Robert dabbled in political organizing, wrote a book, and spent several years on the speaking circuit trying to raise awareness about the perils of the traditional nonprofit mindset. But one itch had yet to be scratched. Having grown up in California, the needs of the hungry on the West Coast had always been in the back of his mind. With the largest homeless population in America, as well as higher than average rates of unemployment and poverty, Los Angeles was the perfect place to climb his next mountain.

Egger's success in DC, his book, and his growing fame as a speaker who wasn't afraid to call out the flaws in the "nonprofit industrial complex" (liberally sprinkled with a wide array of expletives) made his entrance into the LA scene almost as big an event as a major movie premiere. Deploying the same model of earned income mixed with charitable and philanthropic support that had worked so well for the DCCK, Robert set about to build the LA Kitchen.

One of the charitable aspects of LAK (note the clever word play of the acronym) was to reuse "imperfect" produce, much like the reuse model that had been deployed back east. Using the food preparation function to teach culinary skills to citizens returning from incarceration was another part of the program imported from Washington. And an early philanthropic win was the support of a national nonprofit funder that provided a $2 million loan to build a 20,000 square foot kitchen and processing center.

The fee-for-service portion of the LA project was premised on a local law that any city agency that purchased more than $10,000 of food annually was required to "buy local." Having done his homework, Robert knew

Source: Courtesy of Robert Egger. Used with permission

that all of the major food service contracts in town were handled by large national firms, and that there were very few local operators that could provide at his level. Add in the facts that LAK was reusing food that would otherwise go to waste and providing job training for returning citizens, and the value proposition became a "no-brainer." Egger presented a proposal to the LA Department of Aging to become the meal service provider for the department. But after three years of making his case to anyone who would listen (and a number of folks who didn't), Robert realized that the political winds were just not in his favor, and he needed to look elsewhere for the earned-income support that LAK needed to survive.

After several small efforts failed to get gain traction, LAK was able to secure a contract to be a food service provider for the Los Angeles International Airport. But ramping that effort up would require at least $1 million of new capital, in a town where private charitable donations were not nearly as plentiful as they were in DC. Robert's luck with structured philanthropy was also running out, and the "No thank yous" from the larger grantmakers were piling up. After much soul-searching and several late-night board meetings, Robert made the tough call and closed LAK.

He is now living in New Mexico and continues to be an advocate for food security and social justice.

QUESTIONS FOR DISCUSSION

1. Identify three things that were different about the entrepreneurial opportunity that existed in Los Angeles as compared to the environment that existed for DCCK.
2. Examine at least two issues that led to the demise of LAK.
3. What specific steps might Egger have taken that would have altered the outcome of the LAK effort, if any?
4. Where do you think Robert might go next?

APPENDIX: SAMPLE BUSINESS PLAN

APPENDIX DISCLAIMER

The following sample business plan was compiled using LivePlan, a service of Palo Alto Software – used with the gracious permission of the good folks at Palo Alto. Additional information on LivePlan can be found at liveplan.com. The plan involves a fictional business and fictional people.

Jim's Jobs LLc

Executive Summary

Opportunity

Problem

Forty-Five percent of the citizens returning from incarceration will end up reverting to old habits at some point in their lives, primarily due to lack of access to stable employment.

Solution

Jim's Jobs provides job training, job placement, life skills coaching, and record expungement services. This unique combination of services creates the strongest possible opportunity for long-term gainful employment for the returning citizen.

Market

Jim's Jobs bridges the divide between the for-profit staffing industry and the non-profit job training agency, using a combination of donor and grant funding as seed capital to develop a fee-based service revenue stream that sustains the effort over time. Jim's Jobs fills the gap in this market by providing free training to the client but charging a fee to the employer for the successful placement.

Competition

There are over 22,000 nonprofit organizations with the phrase "workforce development in their name (and likely twice that many that do this type of work). These organizations work with individuals recovering from difficult challenges such as addiction or a return from incarceration. The services are provided free of charge to the client, who is placed in permanent employment on completion of the training (typically in a service trade such as construction or the culinary arts). No fee is charged to the employer, although a compensating donation may be requested. These entities rely on grants and gifts for their funding.

The for-profit staffing industry in the United States is a $167 Billion industry. These firms place individuals in jobs at many levels, from skilled trades to senior executives. Upon successful placement, a fee is collected from the employer that ranges from Ten to Thirty percent of the employee's annual compensation. These firms tend to shy away from individuals who are recovering from challenges due to misplaced perceptions that these individuals are somehow less dependable.

Jim's Jobs LLc

Why Us?

Using a unique combination training in both job and life skills, Jim's Jobs is able to prepare the client to return to the world of work while providing the employer with the assurance that the individual will be the dependable and productive worker that the employer desires. The addition of record expungement services furthers the ability of the client to present a "clean slate" to the employer, increasing the chances for a successful, long-term placement.

Expectations

Forecast

Jim's Jobs will launch 1/1/22 with an initial seed grant of $500,000 and a projection of placing its first client on or about 6/1/22. Over the next five years, growth of fee revenue will reduce the organization's dependance on grant funding to the point where the entity will be fully self-sustaining in year 6.

Financial Highlights by Year

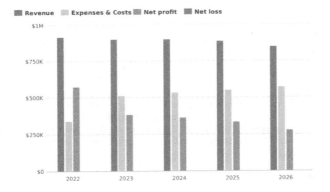

Financing Needed

Jim's Jobs will secure an initial seed grant of $500,000 to launch its operations. Over the next five years, growth will be funded through additional grant funding as well as through operating profits.

Jim's Jobs LLc

Opportunity

Problem & Solution

Problem Worth Solving

Citizens returning from difficult circumstances face substantial challenges in obtaining meaningful employment. These challenges include a lack of marketable skills, difficulties in managing the daily challenges of life and various civil records that may not be palatable to certain employers.

Our solution

Jim's Jobs provides job training, job placement, life skills coaching, and record expungement services. This unique combination of services creates the strongest possible opportunity for long-term gainful employment for the returning citizen.

Target Market

As a Social Enterprise, Jim's Jobs has two markets it needs to address. The first market is the client needing our services. Each year, approximately 4,000 citizens in the state of Maryland are released from incarceration[i]. At any given time, roughly 6,500 individuals in Maryland are experiencing Homelessness, and over 30,000 individuals are receiving support from Homelessness support agencies[ii].

The second market is the employer in need of skilled labor. The for-profit staffing industry in the United States is a $167 Billion industry, placing over 16 million workers every year. In the state of Maryland, this industry produces over $3.8B in sales and places almost 300,000 workers [iii]
Jim's jobs estimates that it will be able to place 150 workers in its first year, growing to approximately 300 workers in year five.

Competition

Current alternatives

Nonprofit workforce development agencies are currently the primary source for individuals in challenging circumstances to receive job training and life skills. Many of these agencies also offer job placement services. However, they rely on grants and gifts for their funding, which presents a challenge to their long-term viability.

The for-profit staffing industry is substantially more sustainable but tends to avoid servicing individuals with challenges due to perceived concerns from employers, often related to the existence of various negative civil or criminal records.

Our advantages

Jim's Jobs provides job training, job placement, life skills coaching, and record expungement services. This unique combination of services creates the strongest possible opportunity for long-term gainful employment for the returning citizen. Jim's Jobs bridges the divide between the for-profit staffing industry and the non-profit job training agency, using a combination of donor and grant funding as seed capital to develop a fee-based service revenue stream that sustains the effort over time. Jim's Jobs fills the gap in this market by providing free training to the client but charging a fee to the employer for the successful placement.

Marketing & Sales

Marketing Plan

A successful social enterprise requires a three-phased marketing approach. For early-stage philanthropic funders, Jim's Jobs will promote the social benefits of reduced recidivism and relapse that are the well-documented result of successful job-training programs.[iv] Marketing to attract potential constituents will be done through a combination of neighborhood outreach and collaboration with existing re-entry programs held in governmental and private facilities. Marketing to potential employers will be done through targeted social media outreach and direct selling efforts.

Sales Plan

As indicated above, a direct selling plan will be used to attract potential employers. Using existing trade specific directories, potential employers will be contacted by email and telephone. Jim's Jobs representatives will then engage in a structured needs analysis process and use relational selling techniques to secure employer commitments.

Operations

Locations & Facilities

Jim's Jobs will operate out of a dedicated training facility located in a industrial park in southwest Baltimore City. This location was chosen in part due to its proximity to a number of

Jim's Jobs LLc

mass transit resources, which will increase the ability of the constituent to access the training center. Utilizing an open design, the training center will be able to adapt to the needs of the various classes taught over time.

Technology

The technology needs of Jim's Jobs are quite basic, and the operation can be managed using standard office equipment.

Key metrics

Following the adage of "No Margin, No Mission", financial Solvency is the primary metric for Jim's Jobs. By obtaining a seed grant to launch the program and annual smaller grants, Jim's Jobs secures at least five years of financial solvency, which is projected to be sufficient to secure long-term viability.

Placement rates and long-term employment are also critical metrics, and will be monitored through monthly assessments and worker check-ins.

Employer satisfaction will be assessed quarterly. Employers will also be provided with a "hot-line" facility so that any observed issues with placed employees can be addressed immediately.

Company

Management team

Jim's Jobs is founded by Jim Johnson, who is a recovering addict with an extensive background in the construction trades. He is also a graduate of the University of Maryland School of Social Work and is a Certified Addiction and Drug Counselor. Jim is joined by Stephanie Smith, who has worked in Prison re-entry programs across the state for over 15 years. She is a Certified Life Skills trainer and a member of the Association of Fund-Raising Professionals. Additional staff will be added as the enterprise grows.

Advisors

Jim's Jobs benefits from an outstanding advisory team, including experts in addiction recovery, prison reentry, as well as members of the boards of the Maryland Associated Builders and Contractors and the Maryland Restaurant Association. A full contact list of the advisory board is available on request.

Jim's Jobs LLc

Financial Plan

Forecast

Revenue by Month

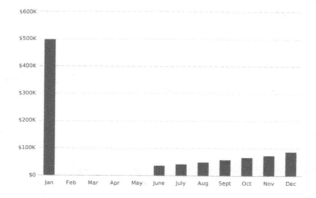

Expenses by Month

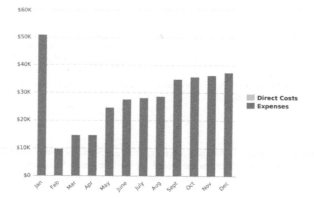

Jim's Jobs LLc

Net Profit (or Loss) by Year

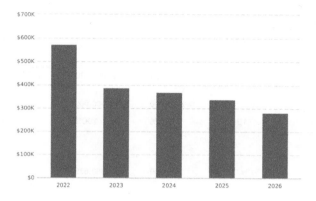

Financing

Use of funds

Funds will be used primarily for staff payroll and accompanying staff expenses. Additional expenses are those usual and customary to any business, and include Insurance, Rent, Taxes and Professional fees.

Sources of Funds

Initial seed funding will come from a grant from the Jones and Jones foundation, who have graciously agreed to support the launch of this effort. Additional philanthropic support will be obtained through area grant makers as well as individual donors. Earned revenue will increase over time and eventually supplant donors and grants as the primary funding source.

Jim's Jobs LLc

Statements

Projected Profit and Loss	2022	2023	2024	2025	2026
Revenue	**$917,500**	**$900,000**	**$900,000**	**$887,500**	**$850,000**
Gross Margin	$917,500	$900,000	$900,000	$887,500	$850,000
Gross Margin %	**100%**	**100%**	**100%**	**100%**	**100%**
Operating Expenses					
Salaries & Wages	$209,000	$362,700	$380,835	$399,878	$419,869
Employee Related Expenses	$41,800	$72,540	$76,167	$79,976	$83,973
Rent	$26,400	$26,400	$26,400	$26,400	$26,400
Heating & Electrical	$3,600	$3,600	$3,600	$3,600	$3,600
Insurance	$4,800	$4,800	$4,800	$4,800	$4,800
Website, Social Media, Blog	$3,000	$3,000	$3,000	$3,000	$3,000
Total Operating Expenses	**$288,600**	**$473,040**	**$494,802**	**$517,654**	**$541,642**
Operating Income	**$628,900**	**$426,960**	**$405,198**	**$369,846**	**$308,358**
Depreciation and Amortization	$4,000	$4,000	$4,000	$1,500	$1,500
Income Taxes	$51,554	$34,894	$33,099	$30,389	$25,316
Total Expenses	**$344,154**	**$511,934**	**$531,901**	**$549,543**	**$568,458**
Net Profit	**$573,346**	**$388,066**	**$368,099**	**$337,957**	**$281,542**
Net Profit / Sales	**62%**	**43%**	**41%**	**38%**	**33%**

Jim's Jobs LLc

Projected Balance Sheet	2022	2023	2024	2025	2026
Cash	$589,282	$971,885	$1,345,285	$1,685,691	$1,968,464
Accounts Receivable	$0	$0	$0	$0	$0
Inventory					
Other Current Assets					
Total Current Assets	**$589,282**	**$971,885**	**$1,345,285**	**$1,685,691**	**$1,968,464**
Long-Term Assets	$15,000	$15,000	$15,000	$15,000	$15,000
Accumulated Depreciation	($4,000)	($8,000)	($12,000)	($13,500)	($15,000)
Total Long-Term Assets	**$11,000**	**$7,000**	**$3,000**	**$1,500**	**$0**
Total Assets	**$600,282**	**$978,885**	**$1,348,285**	**$1,687,191**	**$1,968,464**
Accounts Payable	$0	$0	$0	$0	$0
Income Taxes Payable	$10,836	$8,723	$8,274	$7,648	$6,329
Sales Taxes Payable	$16,100	$8,750	$10,500	$12,075	$13,125
Total Current Liabilities	**$26,936**	**$17,473**	**$18,774**	**$19,723**	**$19,454**
Long-Term Liabilities					
Total Liabilities	**$26,936**	**$17,473**	**$18,774**	**$19,723**	**$19,454**
Retained Earnings		$573,346	$961,412	$1,329,511	$1,667,468
Earnings	$573,346	$388,066	$368,099	$337,957	$281,541
Total Owner's Equity	**$573,346**	**$961,412**	**$1,329,511**	**$1,667,468**	**$1,949,010**
Total Liabilities & Equity	**$600,282**	**$978,885**	**$1,348,285**	**$1,687,191**	**$1,968,464**

9

Jim's Jobs LLc

Projected Cash Flow Statement	2022	2023	2024	2025	2026
Net Cash Flow from Operations					
Net Profit	$573,346	$388,066	$368,099	$337,957	$281,542
Depreciation & Amortization	$4,000	$4,000	$4,000	$1,500	$1,500
Change in Income Tax Payable	$10,836	($2,113)	($449)	($626)	($1,319)
Change in Sales Tax Payable	$16,100	($7,350)	$1,750	$1,575	$1,050
Net Cash Flow from Operations	**$604,282**	**$382,603**	**$373,400**	**$340,406**	**$282,772**
Investing & Financing					
Assets Purchased or Sold	($15,000)				
Net Cash from Investing	**($15,000)**				
Net Cash from Financing					
Cash at Beginning of Period	$0	$589,282	$971,885	$1,345,285	$1,685,691
Net Change in Cash	$589,282	$382,603	$373,400	$340,406	$282,772
Cash at End of Period	**$589,282**	**$971,885**	**$1,345,285**	**$1,685,691**	**$1,968,464**

Jim's Jobs LLc

Notes

[i] Maryland Alliance for Justice Reform - https://www.ma4jr.org/wp-content/uploads/2020/01/2019-Reentry-Roundtable-Booklet.pdf
[ii] Maryland Interagency Council on Homelessness - https://dhcd.maryland.gov/HomelessServices/Documents/2018AnnualReport.pdf
[iii] American Staffing Association - https://americanstaffing.net/
[iv] Mohammed, H., & Mohamed, W. A. W. (2015). Reducing recidivism rates through vocational education and training. Procedia-Social and Behavioral Sciences, 204, 272-276.

INDEX